CREATING A NATIONAL COLLECTION

The Partnership between Southampton City Art Gallery and The National Gallery

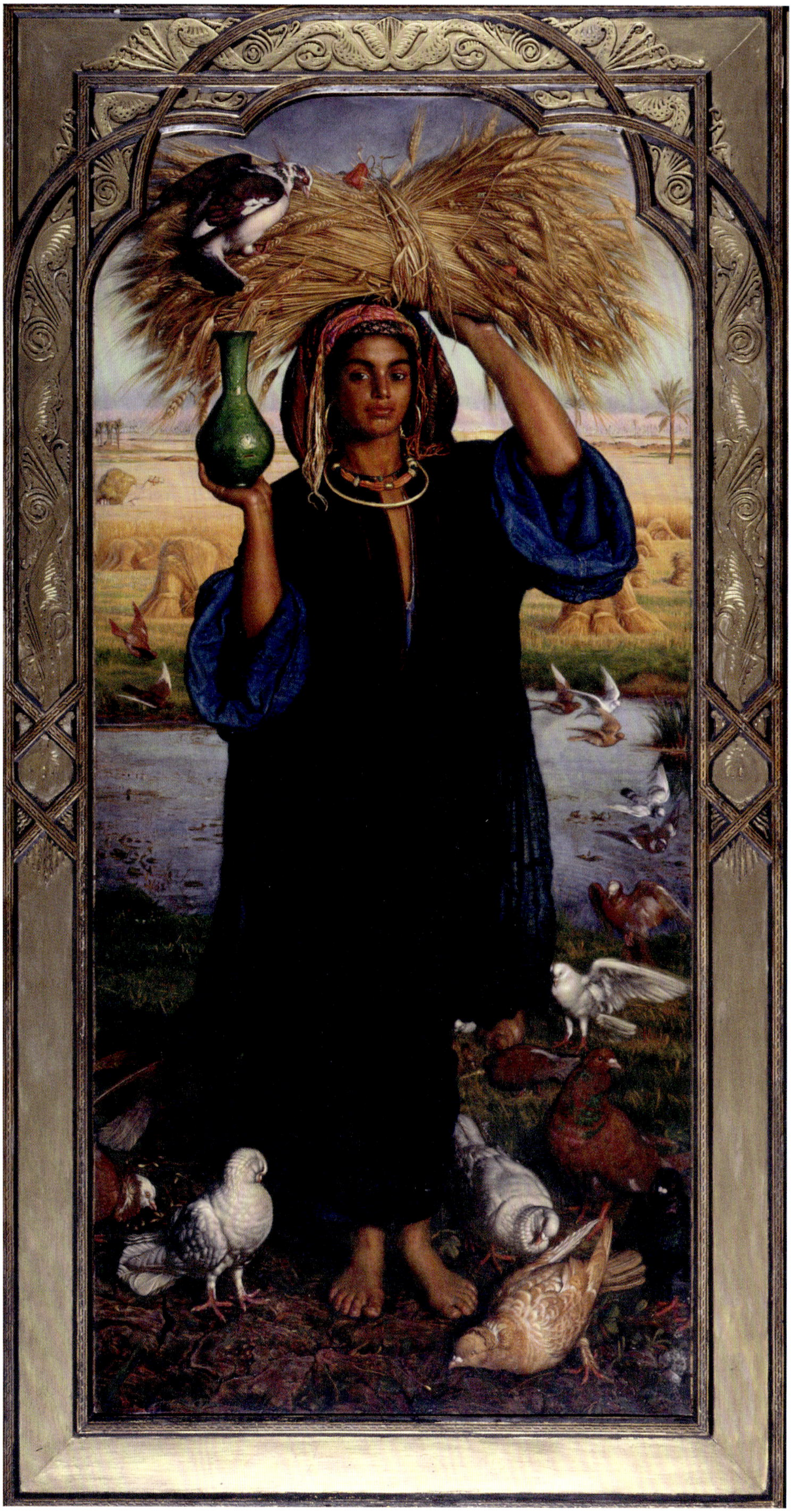

CREATING A NATIONAL COLLECTION

The Partnership between Southampton City Art Gallery and The National Gallery

Susanna Avery-Quash
Jemma Craig

Published to accompany the exhibition
Creating a National Collection: The Partnership between Southampton City Art Gallery and The National Gallery
28 May–4 September 2021

The exhibition and publication have been organised by Southampton City Art Gallery in partnership with the National Gallery.

The National Gallery Curatorial Trainee has been supported by Art Fund with the assistance of the Vivmar Foundation

Southampton City Art Gallery would like to thank the following:

Friends of Southampton's Museums, Archives and Galleries for their generous contribution and continued support of the City Art Gallery and Southampton's Cultural Services

The Audley Group for their support of this publication

Southampton City Art Gallery
Civic Centre
Commercial Road
Southampton SO14 7LP
www.southamptoncityartgallery.com

ISBN: 978-1-8384699-0-0

MIX
Paper from responsible sources
FSC® C114687

This exhibition has been made possible by the provision of insurance through the Government Indemnity Scheme. Southampton City Art Gallery would like to thank H.M. Government for providing Government Indemnity and the Department for Culture, Media and Sport and Arts Council England for arranging the indemnity.

British Library Cataloguing-in-Publication Data. A catalogue record is available from the British Library.

Edited by Rachel Giles
Designed by Adrian Hunt
Printed in Wales by Gomer Press

All measurements give height before width.

FRONT COVER:
Sofonisba Anguissola (about 1532–1625)
The Artist's Sister in the Garb of a Nun, 1551; detail, cat. 13

BACK COVER/PAGES 10–11:
Claude Monet (1840–1926)
The Church at Vétheuil, 1880; detail, cat. 41

J.M.W. Turner (1775–1851)
Fishermen Upon a Lee-Shore in Squally Weather, 1802; detail, cat. 31

INSIDE FRONT/BACK COVER:
Southampton Art Gallery, interior view, 1939.
W.R. Kay. Southampton Cultural Services.

FRONTISPIECE:
William Holman Hunt (1827–1910)
The Afterglow in Egypt, 1854; fig. 45

PAGE 173:
Cesare da Sesto (about 1477–1523)
Saint Jerome as a Hermit in the Desert of Chalcis, 1520; detail, cat. 24

CONTENTS

FOREWORDS

SOUTHAMPTON

COUNCILLOR SATVIR KAUR, Cabinet Member for Culture and Homes and CAROLYN ABEL, Head of Culture and Tourism, Southampton City Council

> *"My fervent desire is, and my Executors' aim shall be, the furtherance and encouragement of Art in the town of my adoption – Southampton... I authorise my Executors to build an art gallery which shall be free to the public..."*
>
> Councillor Robert Chipperfield, Last Will and Testament, 1911

Southampton City Art Gallery is the jewel in our city's crown and we are proud and delighted that the historic relationship between Southampton and the National Gallery will be recognised through the current exhibition and publication. The Chipperfield Trustees will continue to honour Councillor Chipperfield's civic-minded legacy and desire to build pride in Southampton through Culture.

Southampton has long been indebted to Chipperfield's generosity, whose 1911 bequest laid the foundation for the City's Art Gallery and collection. Crucially, he stipulated that any purchases of art using his bequest funds should be overseen by the director of the National Gallery. This bold and insightful idea, made without any consultation with London, was nevertheless adopted after discussions between the two institutions. As a result, Southampton holds a collection of such national significance that it was awarded Designated Status by Arts Council England in 1998.

The unique story of how this important collection developed under the guidance of the National Gallery is little known even in Southampton. Initially, a clear vision had to be laid before a committee of strong-willed councillors about the merits of purchasing paintings beyond what was immediately popular. However, the relationship quickly evolved into one of collaboration and respect. Southampton was fortunate to have the young, dynamic Kenneth Clark act as Southampton's art adviser in the 1930s. He was responsible for writing the first formal collecting policy in 1936, appointing the Gallery's first curator as well as overseeing seminal acquisitions such as Burne-Jones's *Perseus Series*, which is now on permanent display in the City Art Gallery's panelled Baring Room.

Successive National Gallery directors have worked closely with gifted colleagues in Southampton to build up the collection and its public profile. This led to the accumulation of important clusters of pre-1900 Western European paintings. Significantly, early support from the National Gallery also led to Southampton's acquisition of works by acclaimed early twentieth-century British figurative painters, including Camden Town Group members. This was a vital first step to building what is now considered one of the finest collections of modern and contemporary British art in the UK outside of London, which now includes work by 13 Turner Prize winners and over 20 nominees.

By the mid-1970s, the rise in prices for historical paintings meant that Southampton could no longer afford to purchase works by old masters, but the Gallery continued to make a mark, acquiring comparatively affordable works by up-and-coming modern British artists. Southampton's interest in modern and contemporary British art enabled it to be a pioneer in the field, as well as build a collection which narrates a broader history of art in the Western European tradition than is possible at the National

Gallery – whose collecting remit ends with the death of Monet in 1926. This change in focus meant that the National Gallery was no longer able to provide specialist advice to Southampton on its modern and contemporary acquisitions so the advisory role passed to the Tate Gallery; Tate remains the 'national adviser' to this day.

Southampton has, however, continued to maintain strong links with the National Gallery, developing its historic partnership in new directions, not least through ongoing loans and conservation projects. The current curatorial traineeship, supported by Art Fund with the assistance of the Vivmar Foundation, is the latest expression of this longstanding alliance and has provided an opportunity for the first time to explore and discuss the relationship in detail.

Our greatest thanks go to Art Fund and Vivmar Foundation for making this project possible, and our partners at the National Gallery who have worked with us to develop the exhibition and publication, in particular co-author and co-curator Susanna Avery-Quash who has mentored our trainee, Jemma Craig, and to the head of the curatorial department, Christine Riding. We must also thank the Friends of Southampton's Museums, Archives and Galleries, and the Audley Group, for their generous financial contributions towards this publication.

Thanks also to the generations of artists, staff and volunteers who continue to shape this striking national collection on behalf of Southampton's communities and audiences far and wide. In a similar spirit, we thank those who constantly champion, support and cherish this wonderful collection and the Art Gallery, particularly through tough times.

This culturally diverse city is absolutely committed to working together to realise our cultural ambitions, standing on the shoulders of all who have come before us while looking to a vibrant future where Culture can benefit everyone.

THE NATIONAL GALLERY

GABRIELE FINALDI
Director of the National Gallery

When the Second World War broke out, (George) Loraine Conran, the curator of Southampton Art Gallery, put on a series of lunchtime concerts which he said were inspired by those organised at the National Gallery by its director Kenneth Clark and the pianist Myra Hess. She generously agreed to open the Southampton series – and without charging any fee. This is just one of countless episodes of fruitful exchange between our two galleries.

The special relationship goes back to the foundation of Southampton Art Gallery, set up through the generosity of Councillor Robert Chipperfield in 1911 when he bequeathed his own art collection (of popular Victorian art) and left money to pay for an art gallery and for new acquisitions. Chipperfield stipulated that the director of the National Gallery should act as its adviser on a range of matters including acquisitions, loans and displays.

With the National Gallery as part of its original DNA, Southampton set its sights on building up a different kind of collection from those amassed in many regional art galleries, which, according to Giles Waterfield, the historian of museums (and my sixth-form history of art teacher), 'did not strive for eternity and [were] happy simply to provide a popular resource based on what was wanted and what was readily available'. Southampton's acquisition policy, devised by Clark, was predicated on a different model: intrinsic significance and aesthetic merit were the primary considerations and not whether a picture had a worthy moral to tell.

Galvanised by the National Gallery's vision – that it could become the most important art gallery in the south of England – various gifted and ambitious curators at Southampton worked first alongside Clark and later Philip Hendy and other directors to transform Southampton's collection into one of the most comprehensive in the UK. While Clark was keen to build up what he called 'a nucleus' of works by the old masters and early twentieth-century British figurative painters (including the Camden Town Group and St Ives School), Hendy also encouraged the purchase of abstract art and work by British Surrealists. Later, Southampton spread its wings with help from David Brown of the Tate Gallery and made bold forays into contemporary art, continuing a tradition of confronting the public with unfamiliar or challenging work.

As research for this book has revealed, the relationship between Southampton and the National Gallery has encompassed far more than purchasing works for the collection, and it also continued well beyond 1975 when, after the purchase of a very expensive painting by Monet, Southampton determined that its focus should be on acquiring contemporary British art. For instance, Clark offered advice on lending pictures (the first loan was the striking *Perseus Series* by Edward Burne-Jones); on the lighting system to be employed for the new, purpose-built gallery opened in 1939; and on the appointment of Southampton's first curator. In more recent times the relationship, which has become ever more one of equals, has encompassed negotiations over numerous long-term loans and travelling exhibitions. In 1997, when I was the National Gallery's Curator of Later Spanish and Italian Painting and on the Advisory Council of the Bilbao Museum of Fine Arts, I strongly encouraged Southampton's first (and most ambitious) international collaboration with the Bilbao Museum which involved Southampton sending over the exhibition *Modern British Painting from Reynolds to Nicholson* and receiving a collection of Basque art in return. Exciting conversations and collaborations have also taken place in other areas of museum life, notably from the 1970s between the then newly established learning teams at Southampton and the National Gallery; and especially since the 2000s, with colleagues in scientific and conservation departments. X-radiographs and infrared reflectograms have been produced of some of Southampton's key old master paintings, including Goswijn van der Weyden's *Saint Catherine and the Philosophers* triptych, a new frame for which was also made by a member of our framing department.

Kenneth Clark's work with Southampton has recently been acknowledged by James Stourton in his biography of Clark. The latter's visits to the regions are described as being hugely influential, not only 'for [Clark's] wartime thinking about the arts and who they were for, but also, crucially, in his approach to the foundation of Independent Television in the 1950s, which was regionally based.' Clark's successors have remained faithful to his commitment to the regions. In fact, during Neil McGregor's directorship in the 1980s, the National Gallery opened itself up to working with galleries across the UK, through systematic loans and special travelling exhibitions, jointly acquired paintings, academic partnerships and the establishment of the 'Subject Special Network for Paintings pre-1900' – all of which are initiatives that continue to flourish.

It is, nonetheless, fitting that a specific partnership has arisen again very recently with Southampton as part of an extended celebration to mark its 80th anniversary in 2019 – the year when the current Art Fund Traineeship started. This 22-month project has aimed to investigate the untold story of the historical relationship between our two institutions, and to share the findings through this publication and an exhibition at Southampton in 2021. The story that emerges of close collaboration over almost a century is unique in the National Gallery's annals in terms of its duration and breadth of outputs. It is certainly a tale worth telling and a story that deserves celebration.

ART FUND

JENNY WALDMAN
Director of Art Fund

In 2011, Art Fund and the National Gallery jointly established the Curatorial Traineeship Programme. Designed to address the need for object- and collections-based expertise, this programme has enabled young museum professionals the chance to develop their knowledge and curatorial practice over the course of nearly two years. Trainees first spend six months in London at the National Gallery, before joining a regional museum to curate their first exhibition or project under the expert guidance of their regional and national mentors and colleagues. *Creating a National Collection* is the result of this process. Co-curated by Jemma Craig, Curatorial Trainee, the exhibition explores the partnership between the National Gallery and Southampton City Art Gallery and is a testament to the transformative power of collaboration for museums and galleries.

The National Gallery is a place of formative artistic education for so many: its collection and its approach to partnerships are rooted in the tradition of great national museums. Since the opening of Southampton Art Gallery in 1939, the National Gallery has been an essential partner. In both the exhibition and this book, the fruits of this alliance can be seen in the pairings of paintings from the collections of the two galleries; these works exemplify the excellence of both collections. The narrative of interpersonal collaboration that has been so important between the two partners is clearly evident, too. Art Fund is proud to have been involved in this project and this partnership. One of our first, and still most famous, campaigns was to 'save for the nation' Velázquez's *Rokeby Venus* in 1906. This remarkable painting and the ambition to make it available for public view heralded the beginning of Art Fund and the National Gallery's partnership, which has spanned more than a century.

Art Fund's work is made possible by the generosity of our supporters, whose passion and commitment to the artistic and cultural life of Britain has so far made thousands of works of art available for free public view in museums and galleries around the UK. Art Fund also makes grants to museums and galleries for the loan and exhibition of artworks as well as developing curatorial practice and engaging young people and communities with their collections. The Curatorial Traineeship Programme is funded with the generous support of the Vivmar Foundation, one of our closest partners. Curatorial Traineeships provide essential development opportunities for the next generation of curatorial leaders. The vital experience gained through this programme enables young curators to develop new, exciting ideas and thinking that enrich our public collections. Art Fund is proud to be able to continue this spirit of collaboration by funding the Curatorial Traineeship which produced this exhibition concerning the long partnership between the National Gallery and Southampton City Art Gallery.

This book, produced to accompany the exhibition, will be a lasting tribute to the partnership it explores. Through its human stories of teamwork and cooperation, it also affirms the vital importance of curatorial training and the role the curator can play in enriching regional collections, which is central to the mission of Art Fund.

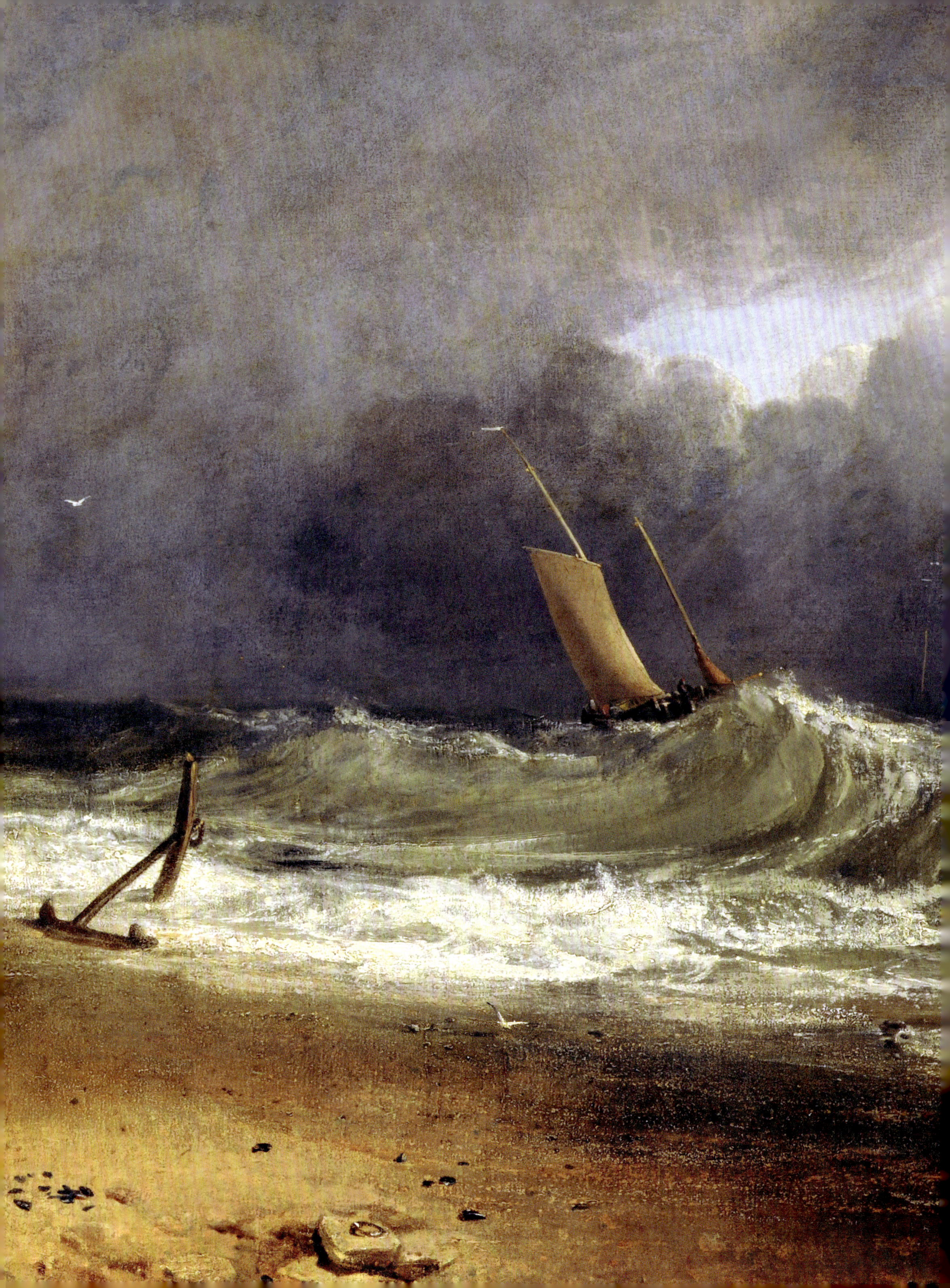

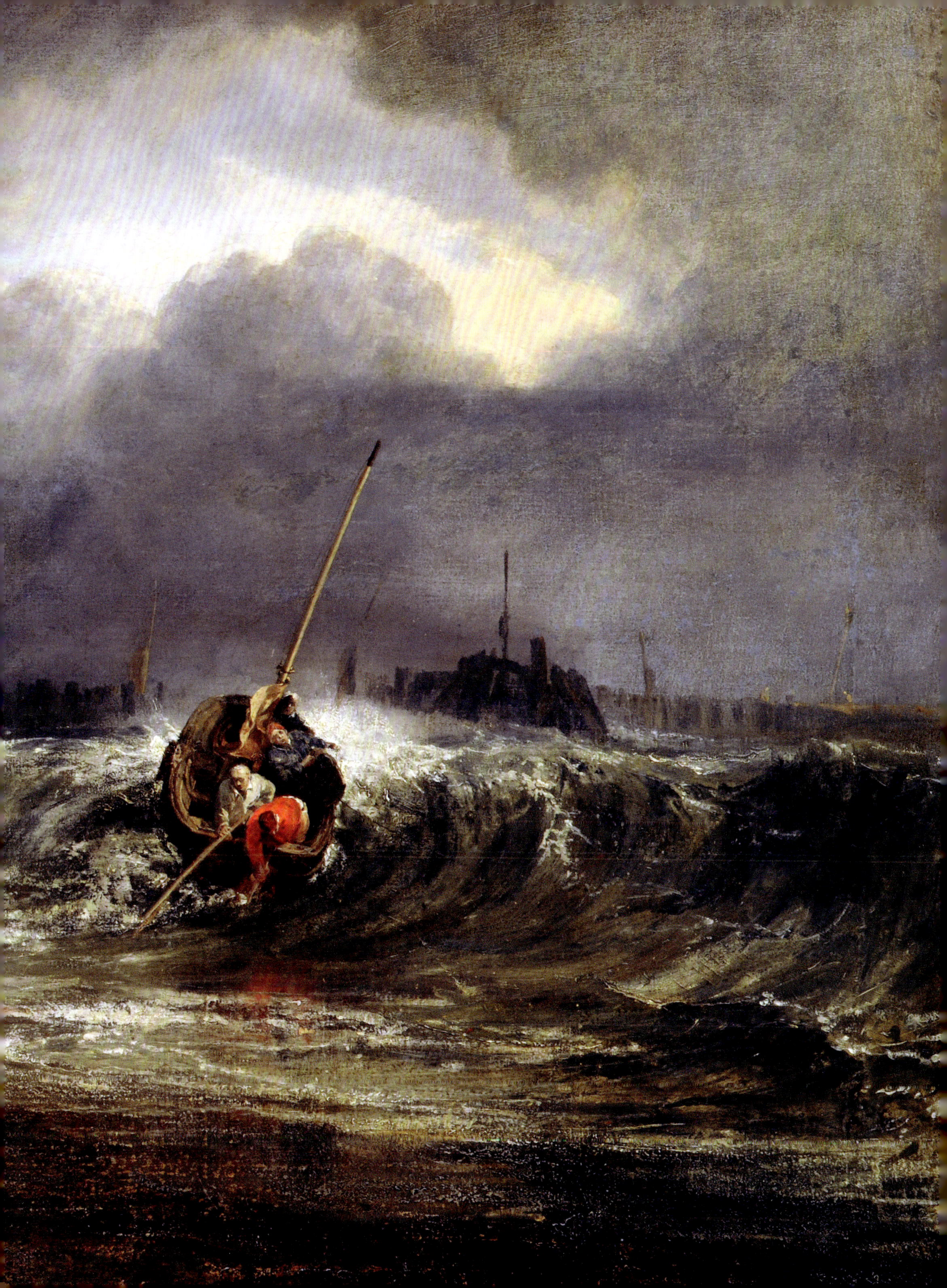

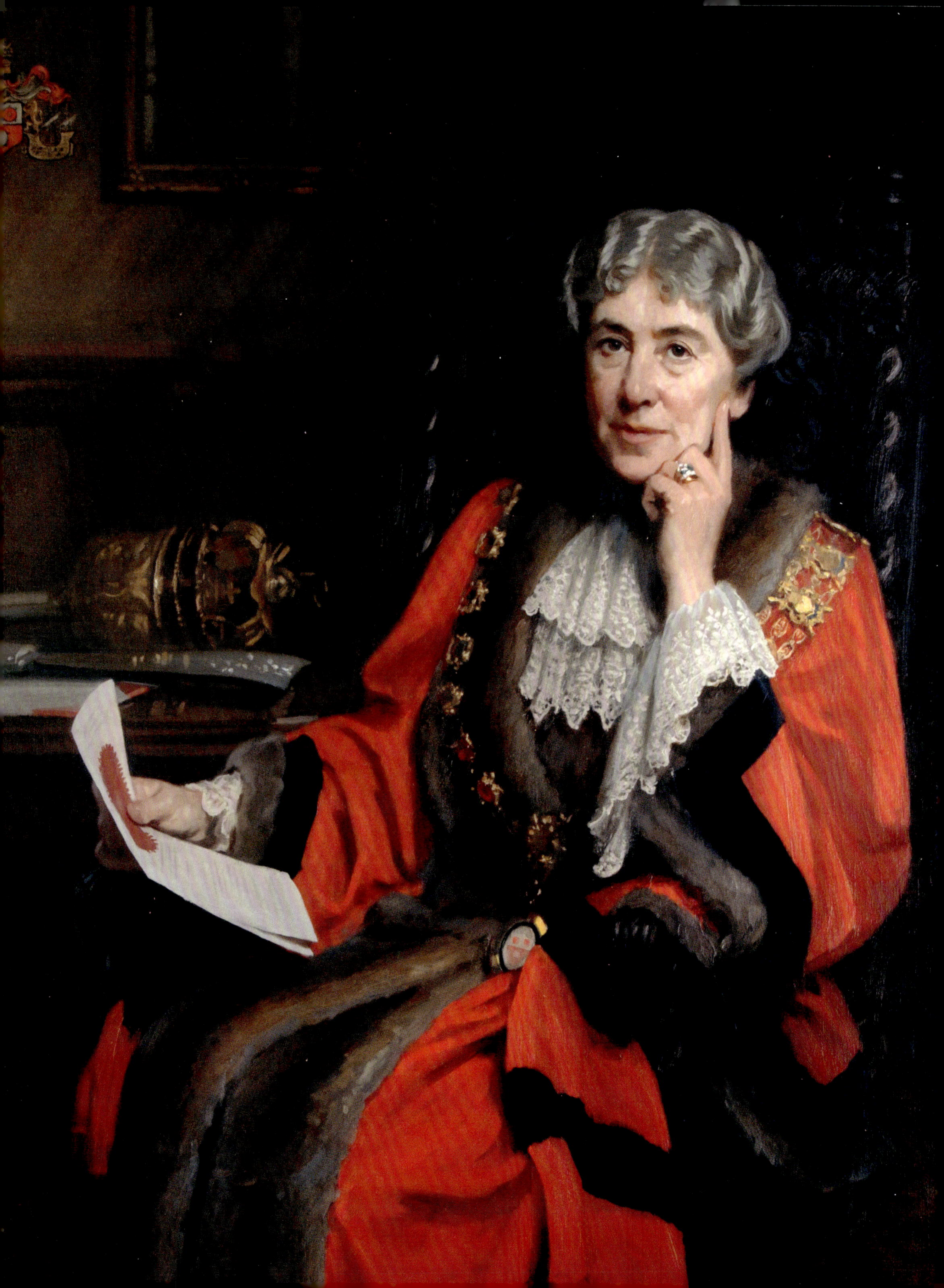

ORIGINS

1

Robert Chipperfield's Bequest and the Earliest Acquisitions (1911–1928)

In 2019, Southampton City Art Gallery* celebrated its eightieth anniversary, and the exhibition *Gallery 80: From Generous Beginnings to Lasting Legacies* gave an overview of its remarkable history. The current exhibition, *Creating a National Collection: The Partnership between Southampton City Art Gallery and The National Gallery*, is the first to focus on the unique and fruitful relationship that Southampton's art gallery has enjoyed with the National Gallery in London throughout its entire history.

The National Gallery has been seminal in the development of Southampton City Art Gallery's permanent collection. Furthermore, it has assisted with drawing up its policies for acquisitions and loans and has offered advice over both the building and key staff appointments. More recently, the two institutions have fostered productive collaborations over learning and conservation (see the four 'In Focus' sections). For the current exhibition, eight paintings and one print have been loaned from the National Gallery and paired with works in Southampton to chart the institutions' shared history and common goals, and to demonstrate the quality of works in Southampton – thereby proving why Arts Council England chose to designate it a pre-eminent collection of national and international importance.[1]

Southampton's early promotion of the fine arts

Southampton's earliest involvement with the National Gallery long predates the foundation of the city's art gallery. Since 1868, arts institutions throughout the country had been encouraged to borrow watercolour and pencil sketches from what was called the 'Travelling Provincial Collection' of works by J.M.W. Turner, formed from the painter's

* Originally named Southampton Art Gallery, it officially became Southampton City Art Gallery in 1986/7.

(PREVIOUS PAGE)
Frank Brooks (1854–1937)
Alderman Mrs L. Foster Welch, JP, 1928; detail, fig. 9
Oil on canvas, 122.3 × 101.6 cm
Southampton City Art Gallery, SOTAG 93

bequest to the National Gallery in 1856. In 1874, Thomas W. Shore, Executive Officer of the Hartley Institution (one of Southampton's earliest cultural establishments), wrote to the National Gallery's trustees to request the loan of one of the three groups of Turner's works on paper. Southampton had to be patient as all three were on loan elsewhere at that point.[2] In 1875, the Institution managed to borrow one set,[3] and went on in 1878 to borrow another.[4] A third approach was made in 1880 concerning the set that had been on loan to Dublin since 1871.[5]

Apart from these efforts, Southampton was comparatively slow off the mark in providing its citizens the opportunity to engage with the visual arts. This was rather anomalous, given that by the nineteenth century it was a wealthy port city. Indeed, the port was a crucial part of Southampton's success: it was a centre for naval shipbuilding and a thriving hub for importing luxury goods. Although its first period of great prosperity had been during the fifteenth century, when trade with Genoa and Venice flourished, the necessity of forming a Harbour Board during the nineteenth century witnesses to Southampton's second great period of commercial activity. At its Victorian-era peak, the port was handling many valuable commodities including Spanish and Portuguese wine and fruit, Baltic timber, Irish grain, Scottish slate and building stone and coal from Newcastle. Southampton also expanded rapidly through the development of the railway in the nineteenth century. The formation of a line to London, commenced in March 1836 and completed in 1840, boosted the city's commercial prosperity and also brought increasing numbers of tourists to the town by train.

By the late 1870s, other major industrial centres across Britain, including several port cities, had established art collections of varying importance: Manchester opened an art gallery in 1823, Leicester did so in 1849, and Leeds in 1876. In the latter two cases, core collections derived from eclectic holdings built up by each town's Literary and Philosophical Society. Other galleries were founded on different models, like the Shipley Art Gallery in the important dock city of Gateshead, opened in 1917, which had as its nucleus a wide-ranging collection of 504 paintings amassed by local solicitor Joseph Shipley. Yet another (unique and remarkably early) model was the activity of the town council in Glasgow in 1856, which agreed to spend £44,000 from the rates to secure the art collection of Archibald McLellan as the core of its City Art Gallery. Even on a regional level, other far smaller urban centres were ahead of Southampton: Brighton received some early Netherlandish, Dutch and Italian old masters from Henry Willett in 1903; Bournemouth benefited in 1908 when Sir Merton and Lady Russell-Cotes gave their house and its contents, and Eastbourne received the Towner Bequest of Victorian paintings in 1920.[6]

One of Southampton's first artistic associations was its School of Art, co-founded in 1855 by retired Major-General William Lacy (1809–1892), a skilled watercolour artist with a keen interest in the visual arts.[7] The School of Art changed location several times from its first home in the Royal Victoria Assembly Rooms on Portland Terrace. Pupils, who included the future Royal Academicians Hubert von Herkomer (1849–1914) and Edward John Gregory (1850–1909), were given an art education typical of the day, which included sketching expeditions – in their case, to Southampton Common and Woodmill.

In 1862, the Hartley Institution came into existence; its modern descendant is the University of Southampton (while the School of Art is a predecessor of Solent University). Henry 'George'

Robinson Hartley (1777–1850)[8] wanted his town house to be turned into a museum to encourage the study of classics and natural sciences. There was a flurry of local interest when Hartley's legacy first became known. Henry Moody, who had worked as a curator at nearby Winchester Museum, wrote to offer his expertise, informing Southampton's Mayor 'that a Museum in your large and populous borough will be an advantage all will admit, but I think no one can tell how it will be appreciated and enjoyed better than myself.'[9] The lack of progress with implementing the Hartley Bequest was also commented on in certain quarters. Local Southampton artist, printer, architect, civil engineer and guidebook writer Philip Brannon voiced his frustration in a letter to *The Times* of December 1855 declaring:

> The bugbear to silence all appeals for a long time past has been the Hartley Bequest. To the eloquent orators and influential men of the borough it has afforded the delightful opportunity of making fine speeches and fair professions in favour of libraries, museums ... and at the same time of effectually quashing every attempt at their extension and establishment.[10]

A major delay was caused by different interpretations of Hartley's will; while one side took a more wide-ranging view which involved educating the many, the other side interpreted Hartley's original wording to indicate his wish to form a more elite college. Despite early complications, the Hartley Institution soon became a focal point for intellectual activities, offering a public events venue and a library. It was officially opened in 1862 by Lord Palmerston at the site of Hartley's own town house, centrally located on Southampton's High Street. A year later, it moved from the town centre to larger premises further out in Highfield. At this point, the council invited local literary, scientific and educational societies to apply for accommodation in the Institute's former premises. Bodies such as the Southampton School of Art, Polytechnic, Chamber of Commerce, Medical Society and Choral Society thereby came under one roof. This bringing together of various institutions in one place reflects Prince Albert's contemporary ideas for developing an intellectual and cultural hub for the country's leading scientific and artistic bodies in South Kensington, an area of London consequently nicknamed 'Albertopolis'.

In addition to the School of Art, several other amateur art associations were established in Southampton at the end of the nineteenth century including the Ordnance Survey Art Association, founded in 1882, and the Southampton Amateur Art Society, which emerged from the earlier Pen & Pencil Club.[11] Apart from founding the Southampton School of Art, William Lacy was responsible for setting up the Amateur Art Society in 1885. It expanded its membership to include professional artists and soon mounted exhibitions, the first of which was held at the Philharmonic Rooms in Above Bar Street. After the Society became known to the Ordnance Survey Art Association, the two groups amalgamated to become the Southampton Art Society in 1887.

To oversee Southampton's developing cultural life, the Free Library Committee was established in 1883, with Timothy Falvey (1813–1898) from the council of the Hartley Institution as its first chair. This committee of 15 original members was composed of eight councillors and seven others outside the town council's ranks. Two of the town councillors, Robert Chipperfield (1817–1911, cat. 1) and Thomas Morgan, were particularly supportive of the arts – both were art collectors, and both were keen to see a permanent art gallery established in Southampton. Among the seven non-councillors were Surgeon-General William Campbell Maclean and the Hartley Institution's Executive Officer, Thomas Shore.

Morgan advocated that some of the Hartley Bequest funds should help finance the establishment of a permanent art gallery and the nucleus of an art collection.[12] Although Morgan received vocal support from the Southampton Labour Party and councillors like Chipperfield, the Free Library Committee only formally responded six months later. This tardiness was probably intentional since the deputy chair wished to delay committing the town council to any further expenses – establishing a public art gallery was not deemed a top priority. What preceded the art gallery was a central public library. The first such purpose-built edifice was erected in the town centre on the New Place House Estate, on the corner of London Road and Cumberland Place. Sir James Lemon, then mayor, laid the foundation stone on 31 August 1892, and, after designs were advertised for, those by A.E.J. Guy were chosen.[13] The Central Library opened on 29 July 1893 (fig. 1). A set of architectural plans, signed by Guy and dated 12 February 1902, show that a room was set aside specifically for an art gallery on the first floor (fig. 2), a decision presumably arrived at due to the persistent influence of Morgan and Chipperfield.

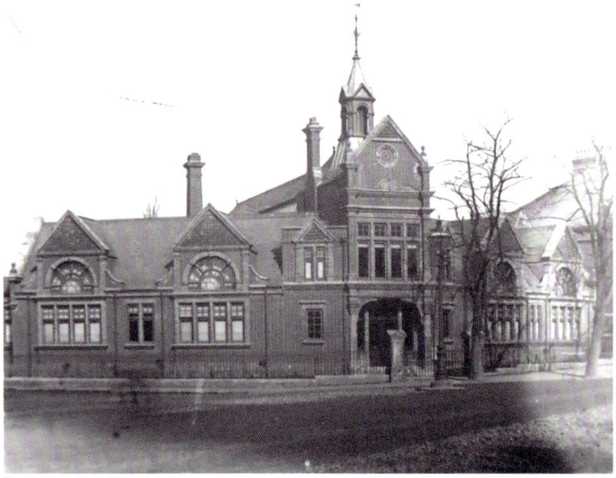

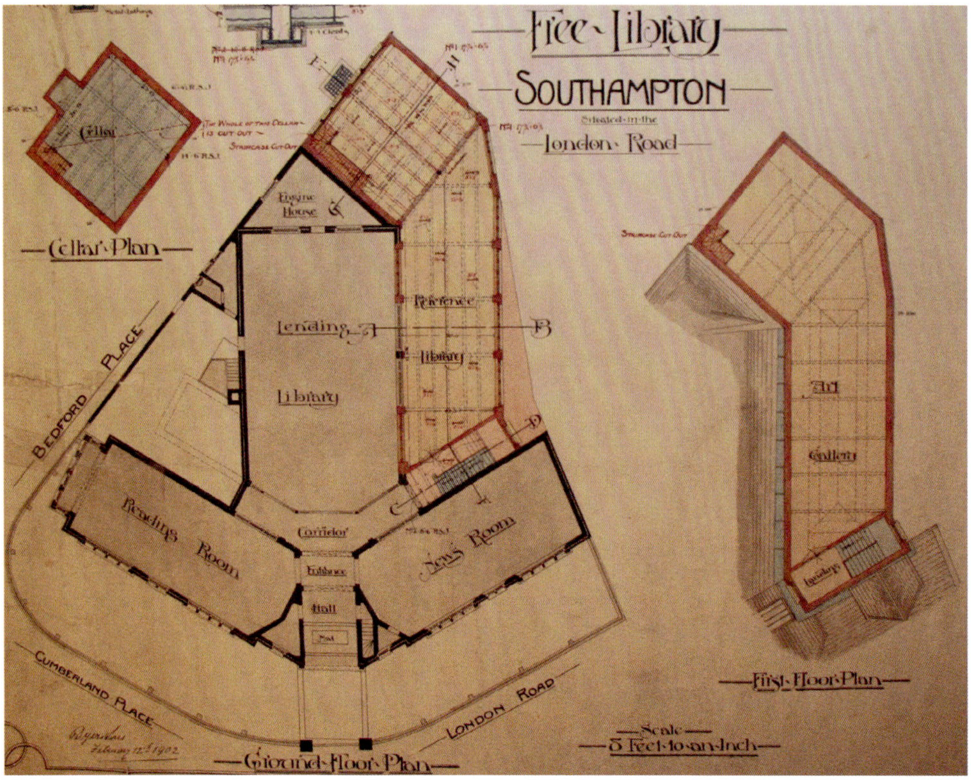

FIG. 1
The Central Library on London Road. Photograph taken after it had opened in 1893. Southampton Central Library.

FIG. 2
A.E.J. Guy, plan of the Central Library showing proposed Reference Library and Art Gallery on the first floor, 12 February 1902.

Robert Chipperfield's 'encouragement of art in Southampton'

Councillor Robert Chipperfield (cat. 1) had been involved in these discussions because he sat on the Free Library Committee between 1883 and 1909. He was also a member of the Hartley Institution's council, and from 1897 to 1908 of Southampton Art Society. Due to the foresight and generous provision in his own will, Southampton's artistic fortunes were established on extremely solid foundations. Although a Londoner by birth, Chipperfield moved in 1842 to Southampton, where he practised as a pharmacist. His first chemist shop, located in Richmond Place, Shirley, was opened by 1845. Then, in March 1846, he advertised in the *Hampshire Advertiser* that he was taking over the pharmacy of a certain Mr Beedle. From this date, he operated from Hamilton Place, Commercial Road, until his retirement in 1879. Thereafter, Chipperfield became increasingly involved in local affairs as a councillor, magistrate, Justice of the Peace and school governor.

Hartley's earlier gesture may have influenced Chipperfield's own philanthropic motivations towards the arts, with his generosity predicted in a letter to the *Southampton Times* on 27 January 1903. 'It has been for some time a growing desire of mine to do ... something calculated to substantially benefit the town of my adoption', Chipperfield noted, explaining that his particular ambition was 'the encouragement of art in Southampton', which he defined as 'the special thing, or one special thing, which I think our town lacks'.[14] True to his word, when Chipperfield died at the age of 93 on 3 August 1911, Southampton benefited in various ways: while he made other charitable donations – for instance, the hospital received an annual sum of £100 – his generosity benefited the arts most of all.

His express wish was to give 'the whole of [his] collection' to the town, which comprised 183 works

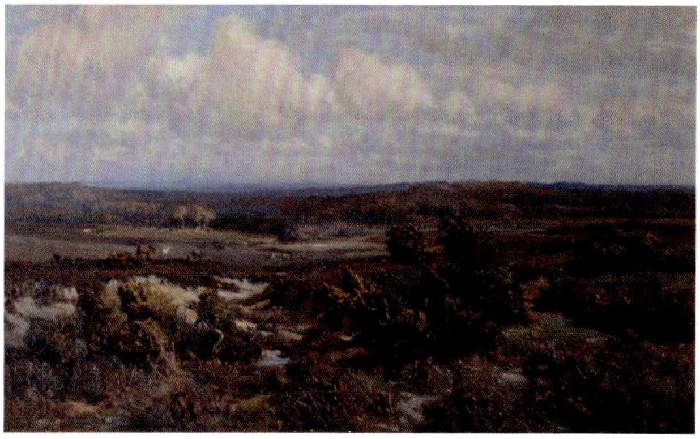

FIG. 3
Frederick Golden Short (1863–1936)
New Forest, 1900
Oil on canvas, 47 × 76.2 cm
Southampton City Art Gallery, SOTAG 507

of art. The paintings from Chipperfield's private collection are characteristic of Victorian taste. The majority are nineteenth-century British pictures, full of detail and painted in bright colours, many depicting sentimental subjects. Quite a number are by local painters, including Frederick Golden Short (1863–1936) from Lyndhurst, who became known for his accomplished scenes of Hampshire's famous woodland, including *New Forest* (fig. 3 and cat. 2). Chipperfield gave exclusively pictures to the town, and unlike those of many earlier regional museums, Southampton's fine art collection was never mixed with scientific specimens, natural history or even much decorative art.

Chipperfield's vision and generosity, however, went further than his donation of paintings. As stipulated in his will, he left money to 'build an art gallery ... and also establish a Southampton School of Art which shall be worthy of the name.'[15] There was also a trust fund for purchasing works of art. Chipperfield's wealth, which derived from his lucrative pharmacy business, was valued at the time of his death at £79,276 2s 6d, equivalent in 2021 to over £9 million. After settlement, £35,000 worth of funds (over £4 million today) were given to the

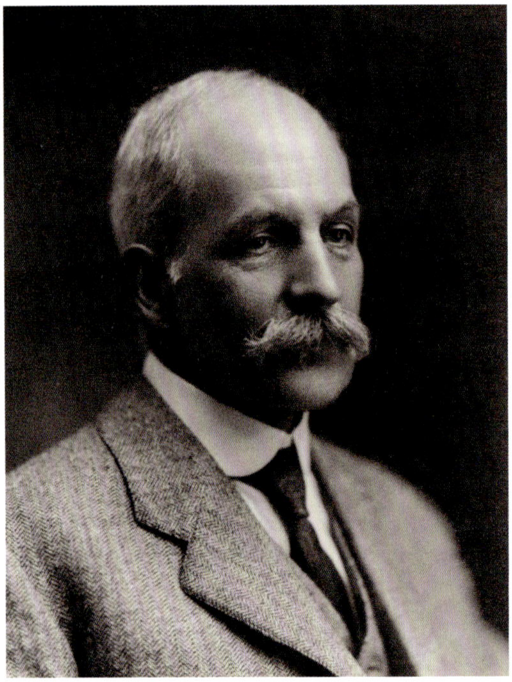

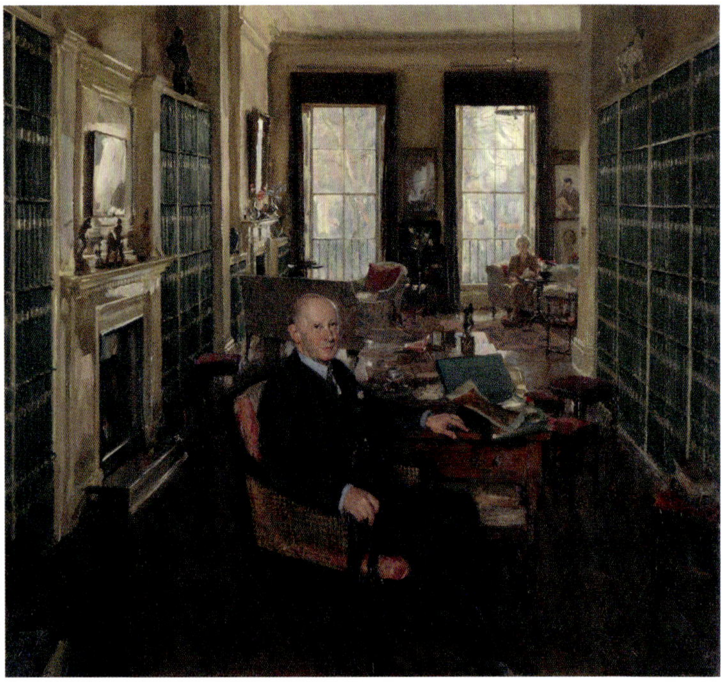

city to build a gallery and fund an art school, while Chipperfield's bequest fund for purchasing works of art amounted to £10,000 (£1,185,000 in 2021). This financial stability was the bedrock from which Southampton's art collection and eventual art gallery flourished; indeed, few other regional galleries have ever benefited from such levels of generosity – one that has is the Ferens Art Gallery, Hull.

Two further directions in Chipperfield's will were deeply beneficial to the development of the public art collection in the long term: first, the provision that the future art gallery should always be free to enter, and second, that any acquisitions made using the Chipperfield Bequest Fund should be overseen by the director of the National Gallery. The latter stipulation was a bold and insightful move and was the origin of Southampton's unique and long-standing relationship with that institution.

Although the settling of Chipperfield's will was started in 1911 by his executors – the mayor and Corporation of Southampton, in conjunction with his son Edmund – his trust only gained charitable status in 1916, and it was not until 1930 that all the legalities were finally sorted out. These delays meant that another museum opened in Southampton before the Art Gallery. Tudor House, one of the finest buildings in the town, having been the setting for various businesses over a long history, was sold to the town council. It was converted into a museum in 1912, the same year that several hundred of the town's residents, who had crewed the *Titanic*, were lost when the ship sank.[16]

Frederick William Smith's 'promotion of education in the art of painting' in Southampton

Southampton's evolving art collection was boosted in 1925 by another significant financial bequest from a councillor – Frederick William Smith (1861–1925; fig. 4). He was a timber merchant born in Birmingham whose many services to Southampton included work for the Rotary Club and University.

FIG. 4
Councillor Frederick William Smith (1861–1925). Southampton Cultural Services

FIG. 5
Thomas Cantrell Dugdale (1880–1952)
Sir Robert Witt in his Library at 32 Portman Square, 1931
Oil on canvas, 90 × 97.5 cm
The Samuel Courtauld Trust, The Courtauld Gallery, London, P.1952.RW.99. Bridgeman Images

FIG. 6
John Emms (1843–1912)
Rest after Sport
Oil on canvas, 63.3 × 76 cm
Southampton City Art Gallery, SOTAG 176

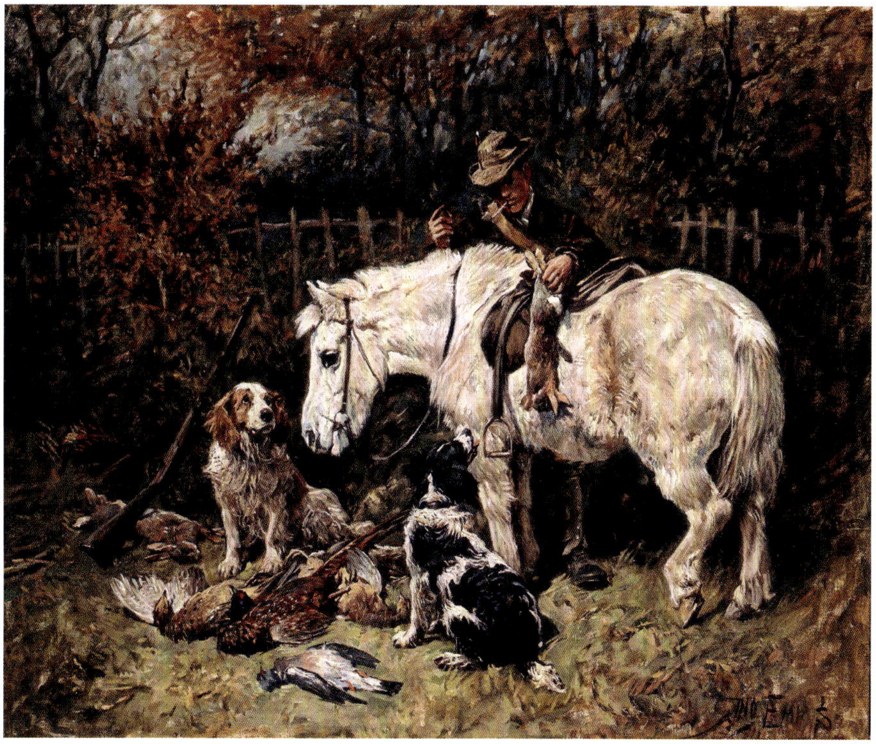

Smith had also become involved with the Public Libraries Committee and with the sub-committee responsible for the Chipperfield Bequest, associations which seem to have inspired his own subsequent generosity. Smith determined that his gift of money to Southampton should be used in the same vein as Chipperfield's, stipulating: 'My residuary estate shall be for ever devoted to the promotion of education in the art of painting; and the public opportunity of seeing good pictures.'[17] This was before death duties, legacies and pensions were taken account of, but nonetheless Smith's final legacy brought Southampton another substantial sum with which to purchase works of art – about £1,000 each year. Likewise, Smith required that acquisitions be made through a purchasing committee whose board members should include representatives from the University, the Chamber of Commerce and the Rotary Club with 'not more than two members of the City Council'. Smith hoped:

> that some good men [could] be induced to go on the Committee, men of experience in art matters and with no axes to grind ... *great* care and *experience* would be required in using this restricted amount to advantage, but *with* care and experience really good works could be obtained [Smith's emphasis].[18]

In relation to acquisitions, Smith hoped that '"freaks" [would] not be purchased, but this [did] not mean that "new ideas" must be avoided.'

The art historian Sir Robert Witt (1872–1952; fig. 5) was the first 'good man' with whom Southampton councillors got in touch. Witt, best remembered for having co-founded the Courtauld Institute of Art in 1932, was at the time a preeminent trustee of the National Gallery and had become second chair of the National Art Collections Fund (NACF, now Art Fund) in 1921. The NACF had been established in 1903, partly to raise and distribute funds to help public

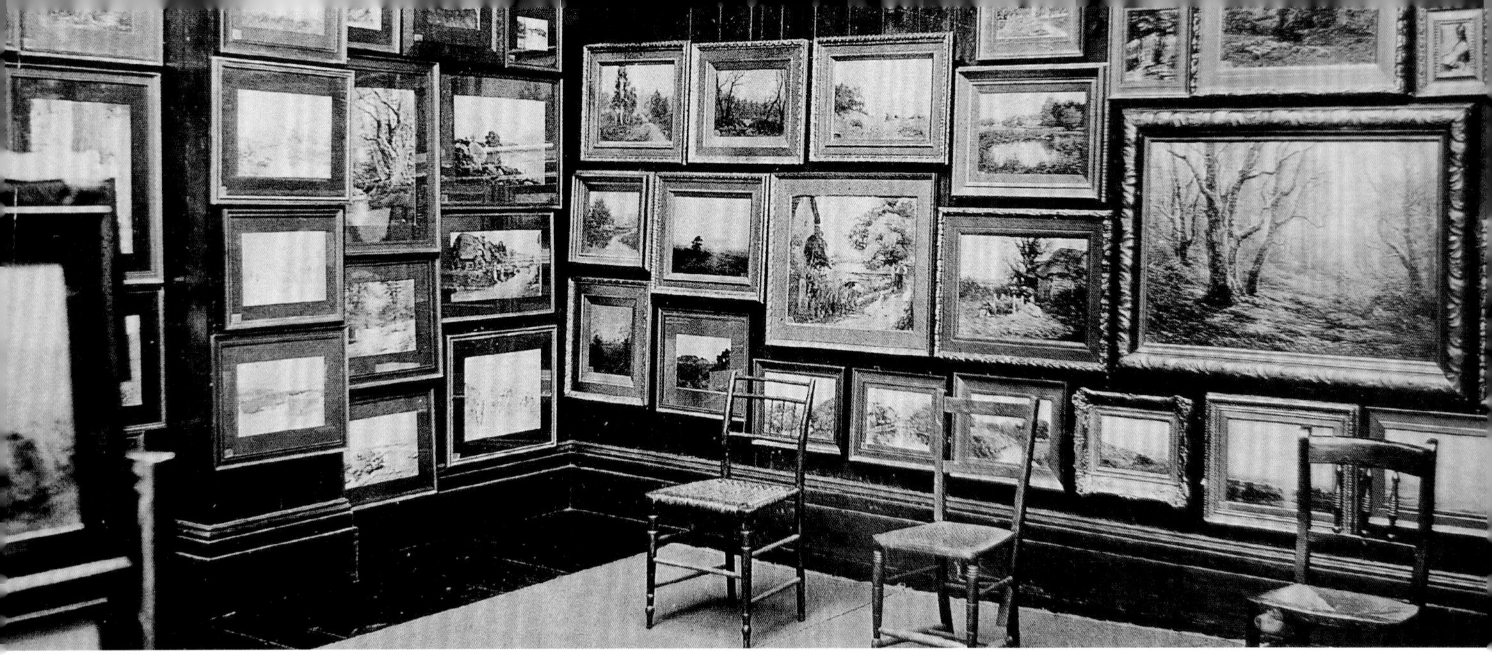

museums and art galleries acquire works of art. All told, Witt was an excellent choice as an adviser for Southampton's art gallery at this crucial early stage of its development.

Smith's will called for the council to select four pictures from his private art collection, a task which in February 1926 was delegated to Witt.[19] He was assisted by three others, including local art collector William Burrough Hill and Alderman Thomas McDonnell, who acted as chair of this sub-committee. Ultimately, five works were selected by local painters: three by Frederick Lee Bridell, John Emms's *Rest after Sport* (fig. 6) and a *Coast Scene* by William Shayer.

The Southampton solicitors, Page, Gulliford & Gregory, were able to report that as of 31 March 1931 there was £2,801 17s 6d available in the Smith Bequest Fund to spend on works of art. They submitted a memorandum about the intentions laid out by Smith in his will in relation to 'the purchase of pictures'. The document noted Smith's desire that potential purchases 'should be selected by the decision of a majority', and that spaces on the committee might appropriately be filled 'for the time being' by those in the roles of 'President of the Royal Academy, or Director of the Tate Gallery in London (or anyone they nominated to appoint).'[20] However, as the solicitors pointed out in a letter of 27 May, this was not a legal requirement. Whether based on Chipperfield's earlier decision to nominate the director of the National Gallery as an art adviser, or simply building on the earlier connection that the Smith Bequest Sub-Committee had forged with Witt, his name came up again as a possible candidate. The solicitors reported that Witt had 'been good enough to say that he would be willing to bring suitable pictures to the attention of the Purchasing Committee and render them assistance in the selection of them.'[21]

In just over a decade, Southampton had received two significant financial bequests which ensured it was now in a strong position to start catching up with other regional galleries. In fact, Southampton had accumulated a small group of pictures before it received Chipperfield's original bequest or purchased others using funds from the Chipperfield and Smith Bequests. There had been gifts and bequests to the city from the later nineteenth century, albeit this original grouping was of a very different kind to the works of art that started to be pursued once representatives of the London art world became involved in shaping Southampton's art collection. The original rag-tag collection was displayed in a room in the Central Library on London Road, until Southampton Art Gallery opened in 1939 in a purpose-built city-centre home – the Civic Centre on Commercial Road – also a new home for the Central Library. A photograph survives which records the interior crammed floor to ceiling with paintings, as was the custom of the day (fig. 7).

Southampton's earliest art collection: portraits of local dignitaries and local landscapes

A good proportion of the earliest paintings acquired were portraits of aldermen, mayors and council members, often presented to the city by the sitter or members of their family, a few of which found temporary accommodation originally in council chambers and other civic buildings. In parallel, the Hartley Institution built up its own set of portraits of worthy Southampton citizens, including one of Charles Darwin's eldest son, William, who was their treasurer for 41 years.[22] These portraits formed a commemorative collection, valued as much for being an historical record as for possessing any perceived aesthetic merit. Among the earliest examples is a portrait of Alderman Samuel Michael Emanuel and an accompanying one of his wife, both given to Southampton in 1894 – the year Emanuel died so perhaps a bequest – while a likeness of Alderman Sir George Hussey by Hubert von Herkomer was given by the sitter in 1901. A portrait of Robert Chipperfield (cat. 1) was donated in 1912 by its creator, Leonard Frank Skeats.

In 1904, another portrait by Skeats, in this instance of Sir James Lemon (1833–1923) (fig. 8), was presented by the sitter's wife. A Londoner by birth, Lemon had worked as a civil engineer in Southampton, improving the town's inadequate sewerage system after two cholera epidemics in 1849 and 1866. He was involved in other improvements to two central roads, East Street and the High Street, as well as railway projects and extension schemes for Southampton's dock, including the Royal Pier, which was rebuilt in the 1890s. He became mayor, alderman and Justice of the Peace in 1891–92, and chair of the Harbour Board in 1892.[23] In recognition of his contributions to Southampton, he received a knighthood in 1909.[24] Of most significance for the cultural sphere, and in the tradition of Chipperfield and Smith, Lemon left Southampton a group of paintings along with a few prints and engravings on his death.

The practice of donating portraits of public benefactors continued at least until the opening of Southampton Art Gallery.[25] A comparatively late example of this custom occurred in 1931, when an

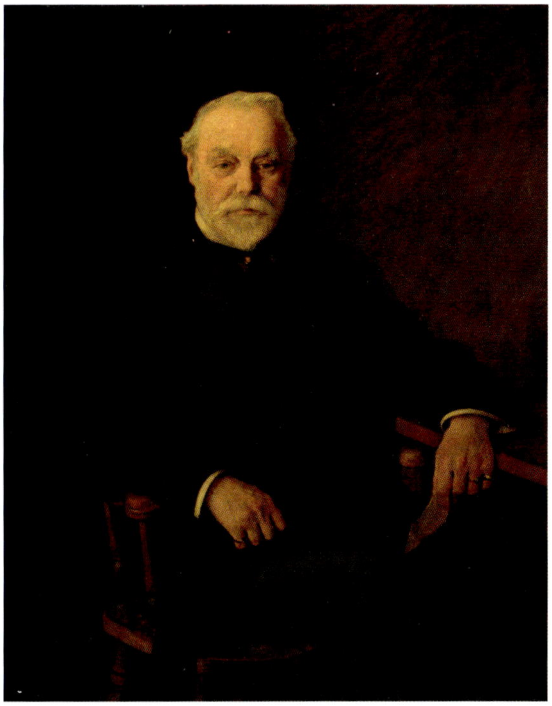

FIG. 7
Picture Gallery (interior) rented with money from the Chipperfield Bequest Fund. Photograph, about 1920. Southampton Cultural Services

FIG. 8
Leonard Frank Skeats (1874–1943)
Sir James Lemon, JP
Oil on canvas, 126.8 × 101.6 cm
Southampton City Art Gallery, SOTAG 528

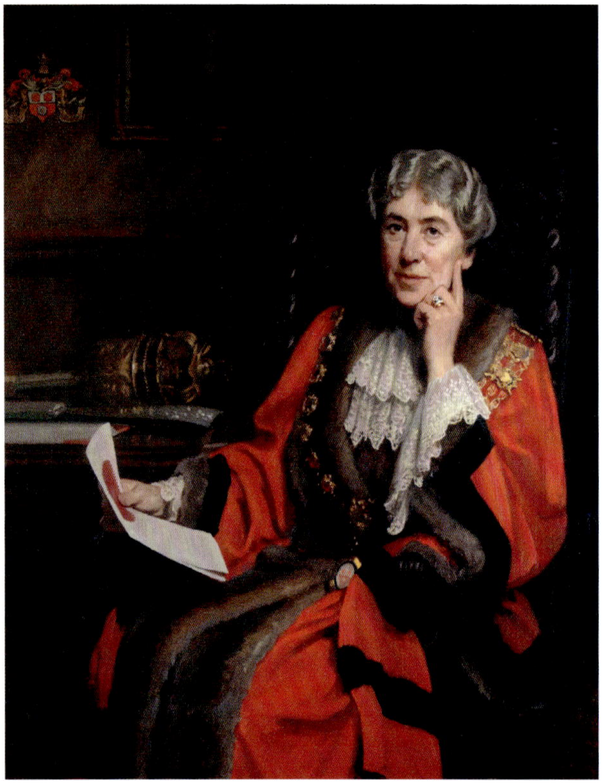

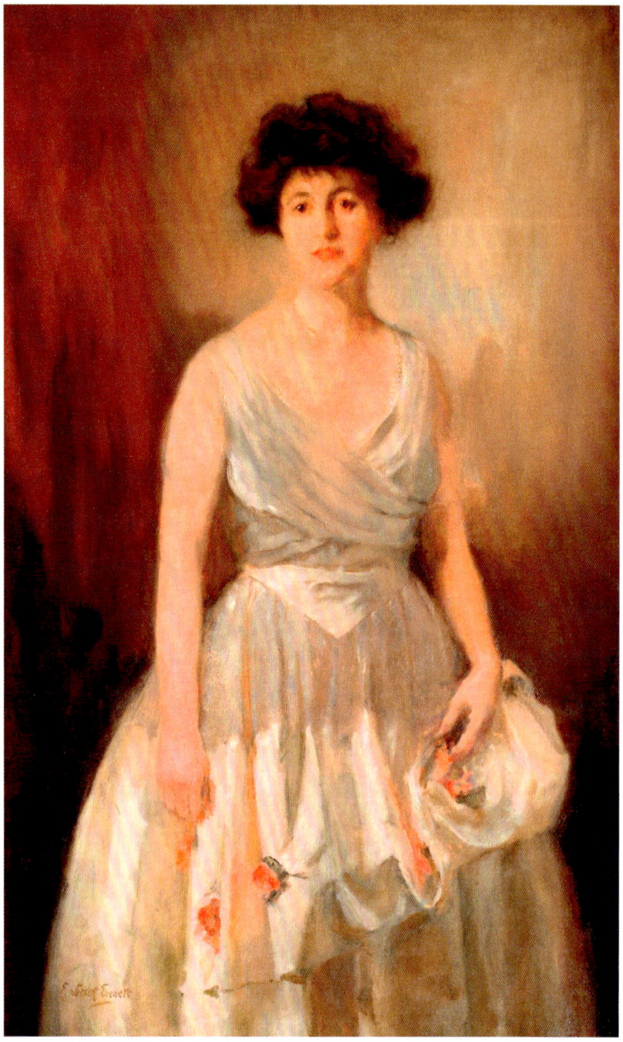

FIG. 9
Frank Brooks (1854–1937)
Alderman Mrs L. Foster Welch, JP, 1928
Oil on canvas, 122.3 × 101.6 cm
Southampton City Art Gallery, SOTAG 93

FIG. 10
Edith M. Leeson Everett (1881–1965)
Lady Swaythling
Oil on canvas, 132.7 × 87 cm
Southampton City Art Gallery, SOTAG 189

unknown donor presented Frank Brooks's likeness of Alderman Mrs L. Foster Welch, JP (fig. 9). The sitter had been very active in the suffragette movement nationally but had also shown a keen interest in local politics and social welfare in Southampton, where she had moved in 1903. She became Southampton's first female councillor, alderman, sheriff and eventually mayor in 1927.[26]

A second likeness of a local female benefactor is that of Gladys Montagu, Lady Swaythling, who donated a portrait of herself by Edith M. Leeson Everett in 1927 (fig. 10). The donor had been born into one wealthy banking family and married into another. She and her husband were leading figures in Southampton's Anglo-Jewish community (as the Emanuels were) and English society more generally. Their home, Townhill Park House, was the backdrop for entertaining elite visitors including Queen Mary, who was a lifelong friend.[27] As liberal philanthropists, the Swaythlings helped improve amenities and opportunities not only across the nation but also locally in Southampton.[28]

The majority of Southampton's early collection comprised the usual miscellaneous accumulation of gifts and bequests found in most regional art galleries. In Southampton's case, this included, apart from portraits, pictures by popular British painters who were either still living or recently deceased. In terms of subject matter, most were easy-on-the-eye landscapes or sentimental genre scenes of the type favoured by the Victorian art-loving public. Taking the work of Frederick Golden Short as characteristic, Southampton received early examples through the bequest in 1906 of H.L. Saltern, and through the bequest in 1908 of Morris Miles, while, as noted, it received yet more of Short's views of the New Forest from Chipperfield's own collection in 1911. Other works by the same painter would be gifted in 1940.

As for genre painting, a good example of a local artist whose work was eagerly collected from the start is John Emms (1843–1912). For instance, the 1906 Saltern Bequest included Emms's *Shepherd and Dogs* (fig. 11), a picture influenced by the celebrated animal painter Sir Edwin Landseer. Having exhibited several times at the Royal Academy from 1866, Emms moved to Lyndhurst, Hampshire, in 1880, where he remained for the rest of his life. Earlier, in 1895, through Lucy and Alfred Fellows of Birmingham, Southampton's Library Committee had received 26 accomplished watercolours painted by Lucy's brother C.F. Williams, a well-respected landscape artist of Southern English coasts who had died in 1891. Another landscape artist, William Sidney Goodwin, (1833–1916) donated five of his own works in 1916.

An important episode in the story of early acquisitions for Southampton concerns the collection amassed by the aforementioned William Burrough Hill (1845–1941), a Southampton businessman, art critic and fine art and antiques collector. He built up a comprehensive collection of works by local artists including by Frederick Lee Bridell (1830–1863), after whom he even renamed his house in Regents Park Road – 'Bridell Lodge'.[29] To mark the centenary of the birth of Thomas Gray Hart (1797–1881), another of his favourite local artists, Burrough Hill organised an exhibition in 1897 entitled *Ancient Southampton* and comprising 228 oil paintings, watercolours, drawings and etchings by local artists including Hart, Tobias Young, William Pether and W.M. Cooper. Between 1906 and 1910, Southampton acquired some 24 works from Burrough Hill's private collection. Given the popularity of British landscape painting, the first purchases made using the Smith Bequest Fund were all works by nineteenth-century British painters, several of whom were already represented in Southampton's art collection. Bridell's *The Fisherman's House* is a case in point (cat. 3). Later, in 1932, the council bought Bridell's most famous work *The Coliseum at Rome by Moonlight* (fig. 12).

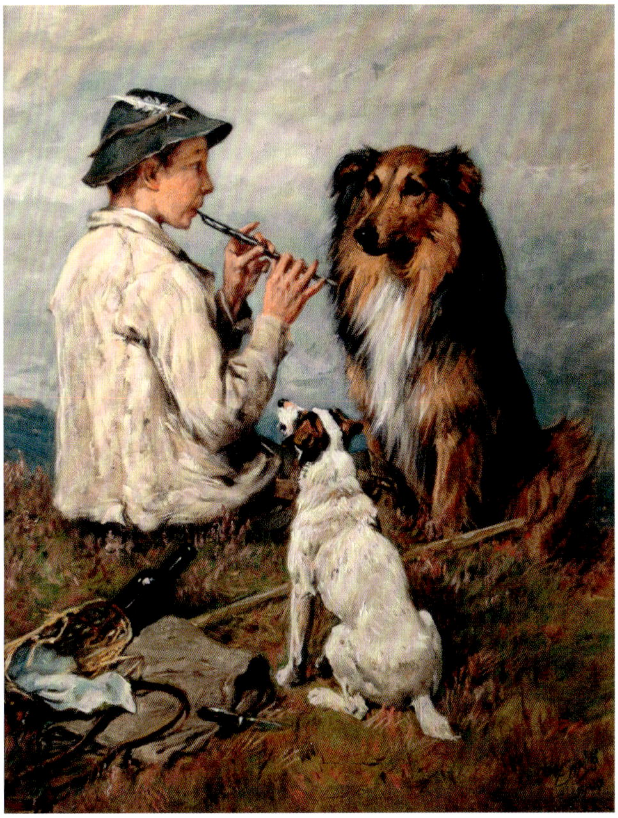

FIG. 11
John Emms (1843–1912)
Shepherd and Dogs, 1900
Oil on canvas, 50.5 × 40.6 cm
Southampton City Art Gallery, SOTAG 17

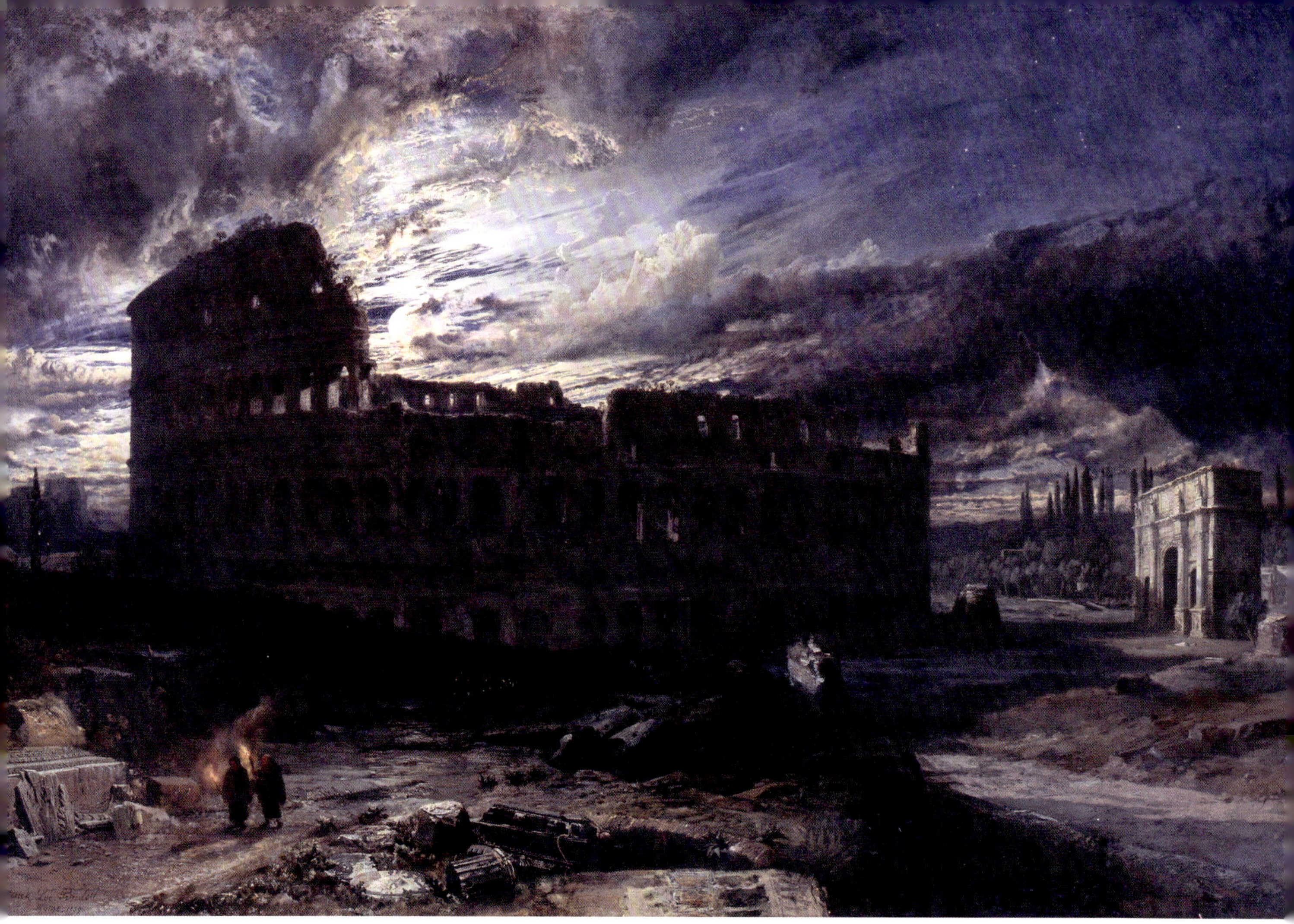

A number of these genre scenes or landscapes were by female artists. Some came as early gifts. For instance, the Chipperfield Bequest included *The New Student* by Florence Martin (1876–1893), *The Lawn Tennis Season* by Mary Hayllar (1862–about 1950, cat. 4), the latter an important work purchased through the leading London art dealer Arthur Tooth & Sons, while the Saltern Bequest included a work by Frederick Golden Short's daughter, Alice. Other examples were among the first purchases using the Chipperfield Bequest Fund, notably *Audrey* by Mary McEvoy (1870–1941), purchased in 1931, and *Timber Run in the Welsh Hills* by the gifted animal painter Lucy Elizabeth Kemp-Welch (1869–1958, cat. 5), bought the following year.[30]

By comparison, very few non-British pictures and even fewer historical works were acquired by Southampton before the National Gallery's direct involvement from 1929. In Chipperfield's own collection the only such example was a genre scene by the Dutch nineteenth-century painter Franz Meerts (1836–1896), best remembered for interiors and genre scenes, still lifes and landscapes. He often depicted the clergy and notaries in their offices in a humorous or sentimental vein as can be seen in Southampton's example (cat. 6). This parallels the situation in other regional galleries, where 'an overview of municipal collections in 1900 and even 1920 would reveal very few other works painted before 1700',[31] those few works usually

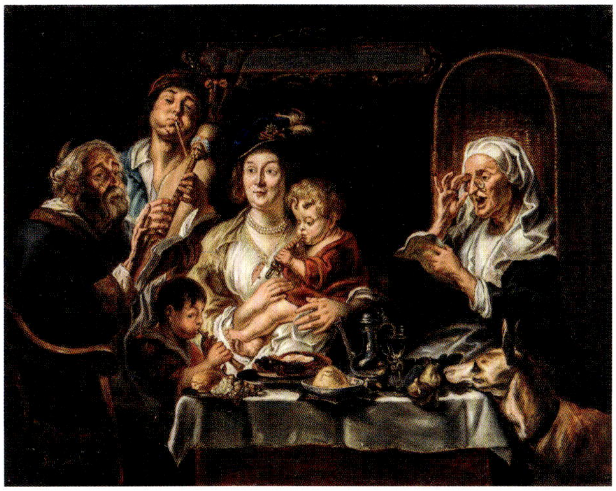

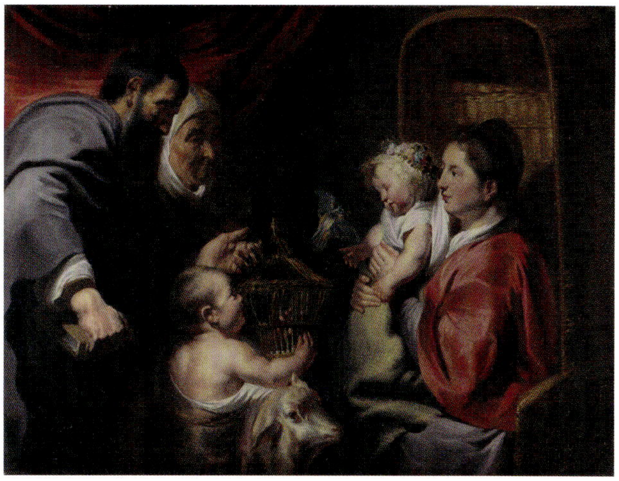

FIG. 12
Frederick Lee Bridell (1830–1863)
The Coliseum at Rome by Moonlight, 1859
Oil on canvas, 155 × 230.5 cm
Southampton City Art Gallery, SOTAG 60

FIG. 13
Michael Scholowei after Jacob Jordaens (1593–1678)
The Old Folks Sing, the Young Folks Chirp
Oil on canvas, 40.8 × 53.3 cm
Southampton City Art Gallery, SOTAG 487

FIG. 14
Jacob Jordaens (1593–1678)
The Virgin and Child with Saints Zacharias, Elizabeth and John the Baptist, about 1620
Oil on canvas, 114 × 153 cm
The National Gallery, London, NG3215

comprising Dutch paintings and seventeenth-century Italian pictures. In Southampton, the earliest such works were two of the nine pictures comprising the Mayo-Porcelli Bequest of 1914 – a pair of Italianate landscapes on copper by early eighteenth-century Austrian painter Franz de Paula Ferg (1689–1740) – and two undated copies by Michael Scholowei of works by the esteemed Flemish seventeenth-century painters Theodoor Rombouts and Jacob Jordaens, which were part of the Lemon Bequest of 1923. One of the copies was after Jordaens's *The Old Folks Sing, the Young Folks Chirp* (fig. 13), which shares compositional similarities with the artist's *Virgin and Child with Saints*, a painting the National Gallery had acquired in 1917 (fig. 14).

Donations of such pictures indicate a taste for older European art among a handful of Southampton's citizens and councillors. Such taste was rare within the tradition of assembling collections for late Victorian art galleries and museums, which generally contained no older foreign art. Giles Waterfield, the biographer of UK regional galleries, has concluded that '[t]he overall evidence suggests that it was financial problems, a desire to encourage local artists, and timidity over the acquisition of high art, that limited [regional] collections.'[32] Southampton's art gallery was comparatively well endowed financially and could call on leading artistic advisers to embolden its choice of purchases to encompass a broader range of paintings.

1

Leonard Frank Skeats (1874–1943)

Robert Chipperfield, JP, before 1911

Oil on canvas 60.7 × 45.8 cm
Donated by Leonard Skeats, 1912
Southampton City Art Gallery, SOTAG 526

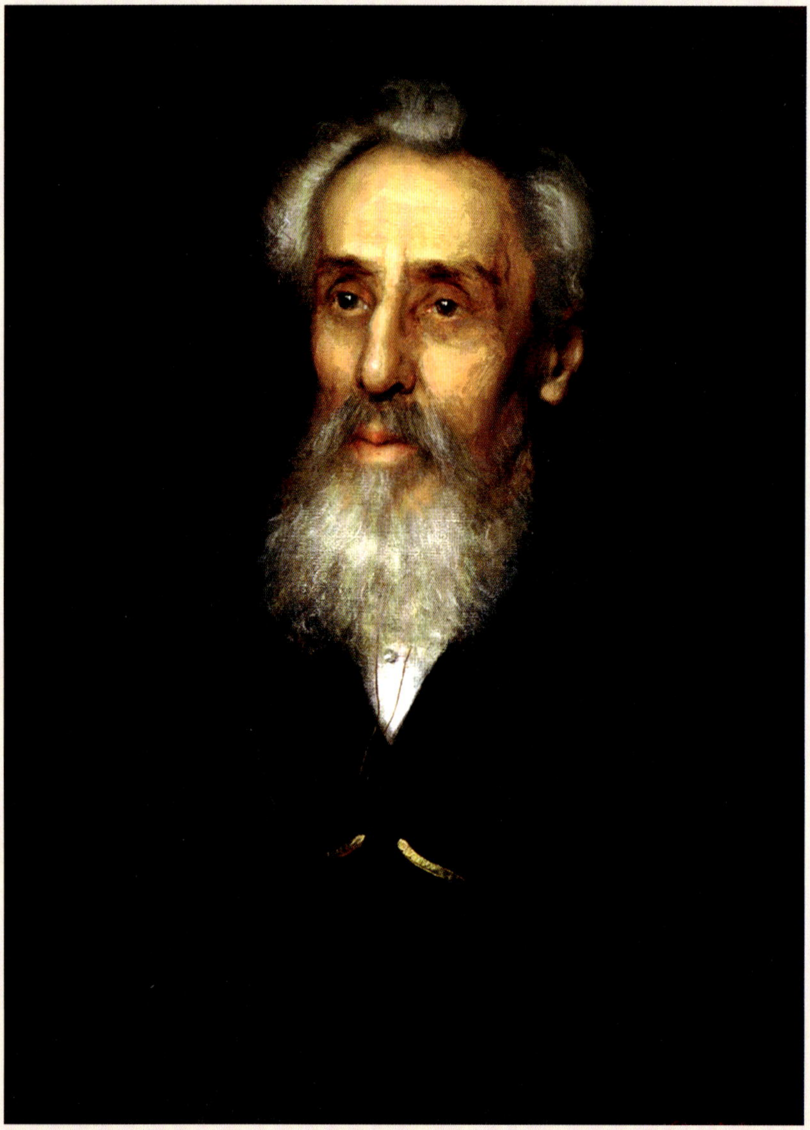

Southampton City Art Gallery is what it is today thanks to the generosity and foresight of Robert Chipperfield. Born in London, he moved to Southampton in 1842, where he ran an affluent pharmacy business from 1845 until his retirement in 1879. Thereafter, he devoted himself to public office and charitable work, serving as a local councillor for 17 years and as a Justice of the Peace for 23 years. He was also interested in local education, sitting on the boards of the Southampton Endowed Schools and on the Hartley Institution council.

Although he remembered Southampton's hospital in his will, it was the cultural institutions of his adopted city that benefited most from his wealth. He bequeathed his art collection to the city, and also left a well-endowed trust fund to pay for the purchase of further works of art and to help with the cost of erecting a purpose-built art gallery and an associated art school. Showing great discernment, Chipperfield stipulated that all future decisions regarding purchases, conservation work, loans and displays should be made with guidance from the director of the National Gallery.

Leonard Frank Skeats was a local Hampshire artist, best known for his watercolours and works in oils, although he also produced illustrations for over 20 books. He studied art at Hartley Institution (now the University of Southampton) and London's Royal College of Art, before going to Paris where he was taught by Jean-Paul Laurens, President of the Paris Salon, and Benjamin Constant. Apart from portraits, Skeats painted picturesque genre scenes, a few of which are now in Southampton City Art Gallery. Skeats's *Brittany* came as part of the 1911 Chipperfield Bequest, *The Pedlar* was bequeathed by Sir James Lemon in 1923 and *The Casualty List* was presented by Skeats's wife in 1945.

2

Frederick Golden Short (1863–1936)

New Forest, 1900

Oil on canvas, 47 × 76.2 cm
Bequeathed by Mr H.L. Saltern, 1906
Southampton City Art Gallery, SOTAG 507

Southampton's early art collection included many pictures by popular British painters of recent date. Most of them portrayed easy-on-the-eye landscapes or sentimental genre scenes. A good proportion of works were by local artists, since it was usual practice for regional galleries to acquire the work of home-grown talent – a tradition as prevalent across Europe as it was in the UK.

Frederick Golden Short was one such painter, who lived in Lyndhurst and had a studio behind his father's chemist shop on Southampton's High Street. Although he produced illustrations for books and other publications, he became best known for his bucolic depictions of the New Forest and its surrounding districts including Lyndhurst. Many of the New Forest's pub signs were also painted by him. Short's work could be seen at the leading exhibitions of his day, including those in London organised by the Royal Academy, the Royal Society of British Artists, and the New Gallery.

Southampton City Art Gallery now possesses over a dozen examples of Short's work. Two came from Robert Chipperfield's personal art collection as part of his all-important bequest of 1911, by which point the city already owned four paintings by Short as a result of the Saltern Bequest of 1906; while a fifth work was acquired through the Morris Miles Bequest of 1908. As late as 1940, two more examples were presented by a Miss A.B. Williamson. The only painting by Short to be purchased was *Whitley Road* in 1936, acquired with the assistance of the Frederick William Smith Bequest.

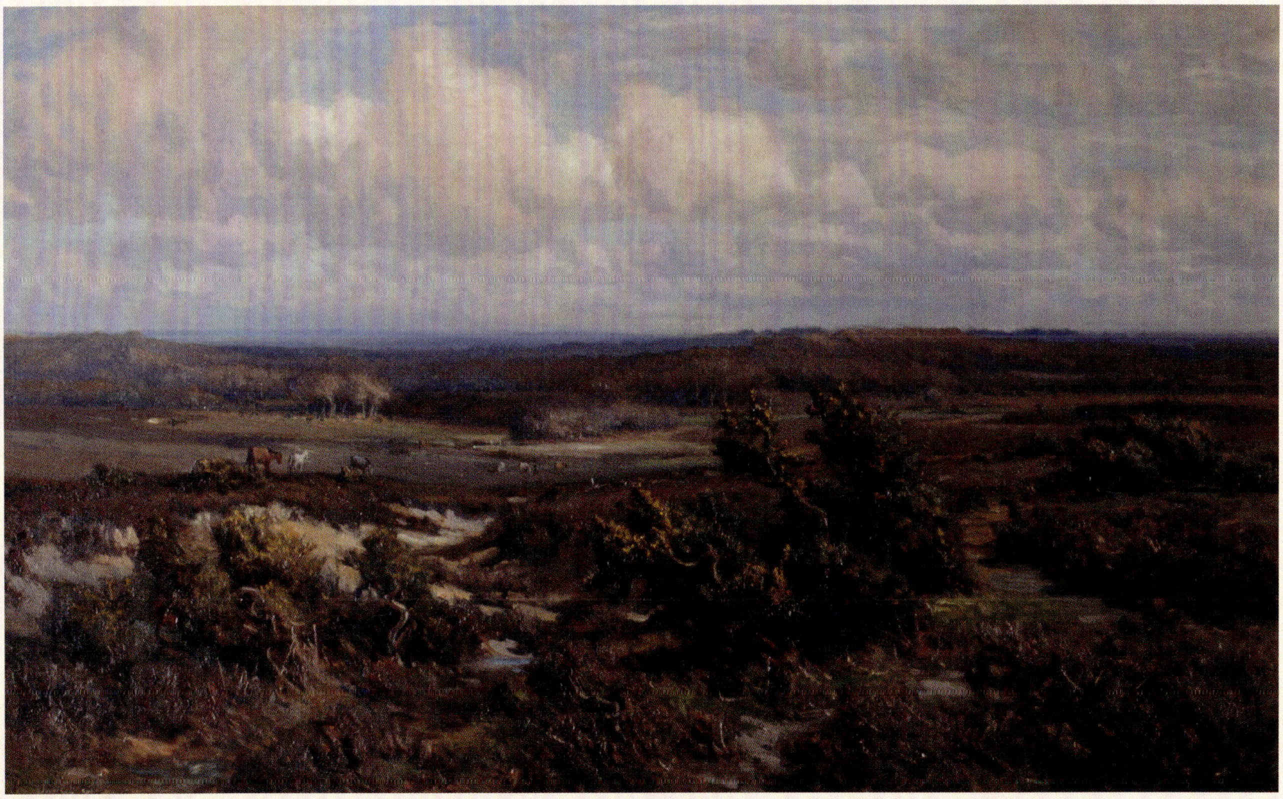

3

Frederick Lee Bridell (1830–1863)

The Fisherman's House, 1854

Oil on canvas, 49 × 39.5 cm
Purchased with the assistance of the Smith Bequest Fund, 1926
Southampton City Art Gallery, SOTAG 57

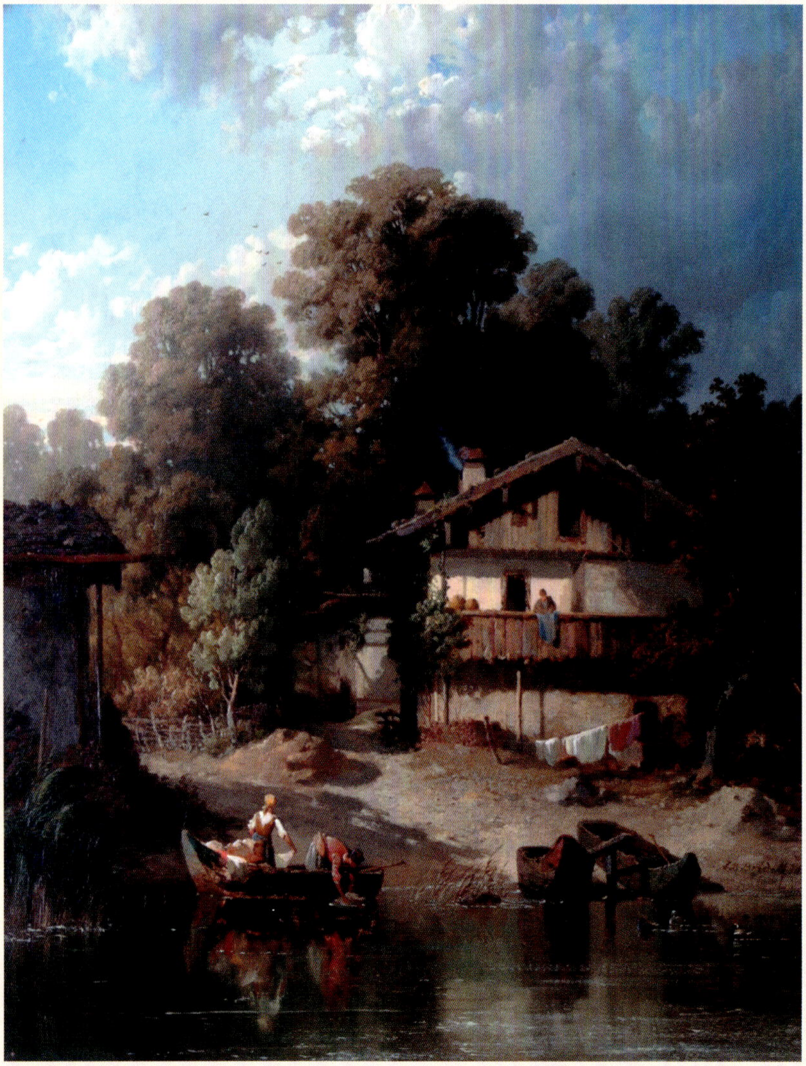

The tradition of acquiring work by local painters is exemplified by Southampton's devotion to Frederick Lee Bridell. He enjoyed a highly successful career, his poetic landscapes finding early favour with Victorian luminaries such as Robert and Elizabeth Barrett Browning. His work was exhibited at London's Royal Academy and British Institution, and at the Liverpool Academy. On his untimely death, fulsome obituaries appeared in the *Art Journal* and *Art Magazine*. The former even went so far as to state that 'Bridell had already taken foremost rank' in 'that great school of poetic landscape art in which Turner, Constable and Müller are the leaders'.[1] Bridell himself had high ambitions, hoping that his *Temple of Venus* might end up in the National Gallery's collection, displayed alongside works by Turner and Claude.

In addition to painting portraits of the Southampton well-to-do, including Mr and Mrs Day of Spear Hall, Bevois Mount, two local patrons particularly promoted Bridell's work: the shipping magnate James Wolff set up a 'Bridell Gallery' at his home, which he opened to the public, before his collection was sold in 1864. Later, another businessman, William Burrough Hill, bought numerous examples of the artist's work and named his house on Regents Park Road, 'Bridell Lodge', in his honour. In 1910, part of Burrough Hill's art collection was acquired by Southampton Council.

More than 10 of Bridell's works have been donated to Southampton City Art Gallery, while *The Fisherman's House* was purchased in 1826, followed by *The Coliseum at Rome by Moonlight* in 1932. Although his art went out of fashion during the later twentieth century, Bridell's *View of Southampton* was purchased recently in 2004. A bust of Bridell is displayed in Tudor House, another of Southampton's museums.

4

Mary Hayllar (1862–about 1950)
The Lawn Tennis Season, 1881

Oil on canvas 19.3 × 24.3 cm
Bequeathed by Robert Chipperfield, 1911
Southampton City Art Gallery, SOTAG 241

This painting by Mary Hayllar was part of Robert Chipperfield's original 1911 bequest to Southampton. Mary Hayllar was one of the four daughters of Edith Phoebe Cavell and the acclaimed Victorian genre painter, James Hayllar, himself a regular exhibitor at the Royal Academy from 1850–98. Of their nine children, several became successful artists, the best known being the eldest two daughters, Jessica (1858–1940) and Edith (1860–1948). Examples of their work are preserved in public collections in Wallingford, Oxfordshire, where the family lived before moving to Bournemouth in 1899 after the death of their mother.

Although equally accomplished, Mary was the least prolific family member, only exhibiting at the Royal Academy for five years from 1880. After her marriage, when she became Mary Wells, she gave up painting, as was often the case with women artists at that time. Her children continued to model for paintings by her sisters.

The Lawn Tennis Season, dated 1881, was probably painted at the family home, Castle Priory, in Wallingford. Domestic scenes recording leisured life in affluent Edwardian England, such as this one, became the subject of the sisters' most renowned paintings. A table laden with refreshments, perhaps a modern take on the traditional still-life genre, is a common theme of their work. In this case, we see a glass pitcher already half empty, its contents presumably enjoyed by the participants of a game of tennis, who can be spotted through the window overlooking a lawn tennis court.

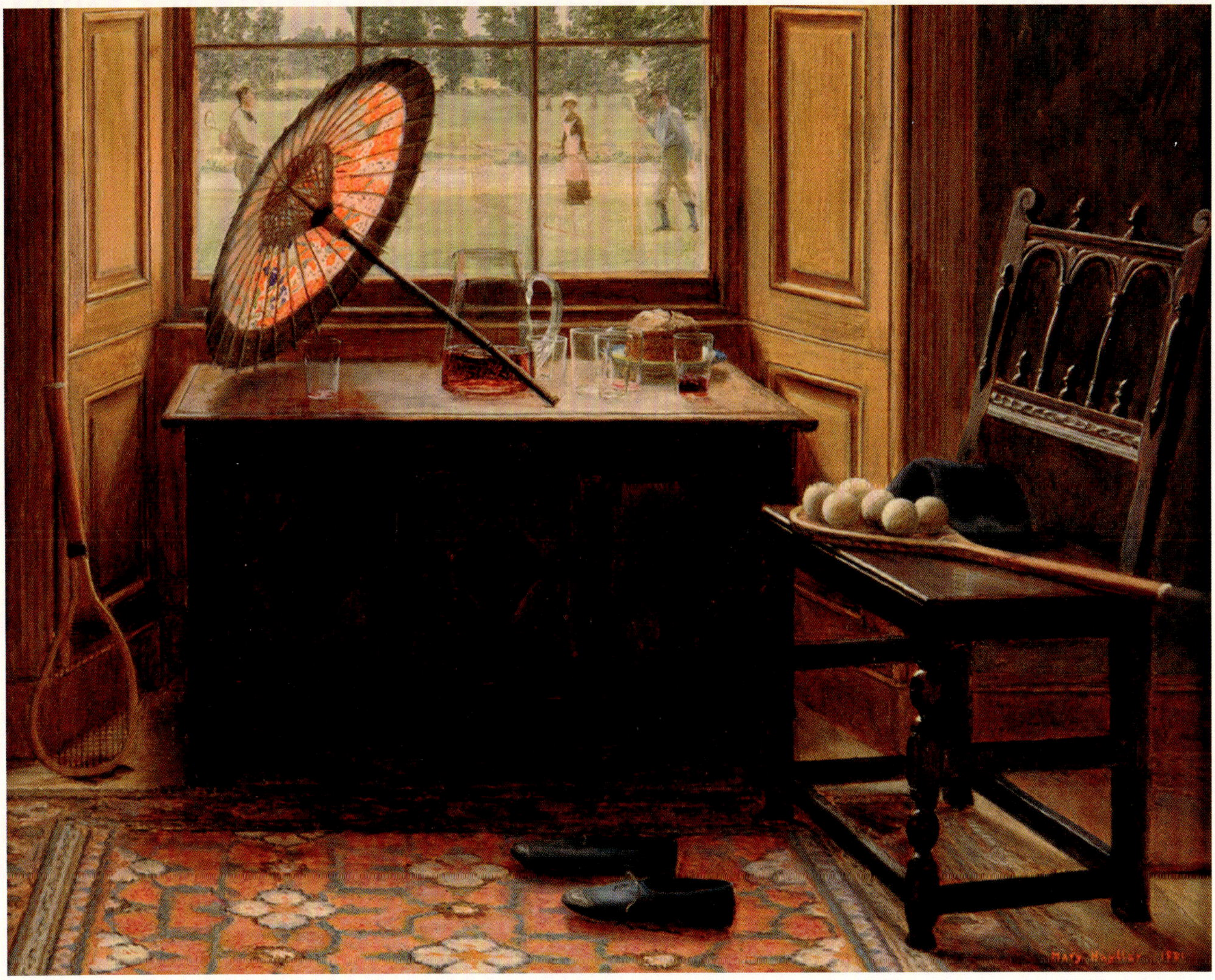

5

Lucy Elizabeth Kemp-Welch (1869–1958)
Timber Run in the Welsh Hills, date unknown

Oil on canvas, 110.8 × 155.5 cm
Purchased with the assistance of the Chipperfield Bequest Fund, 1932
Southampton City Art Gallery, SOTAG 317

Southampton is notable for several works by women painters acquired early on in the history of its public art collection. Robert Chipperfield's founding bequest included Mary Hayllar's *The Lawn Tennis Season* (cat. 4). Although some of the first purchases of paintings by women using the Chipperfield Bequest Fund were of mixed quality, this is a work of national significance.

Lucy Kemp-Welch, an expert horsewoman, also became the foremost painter of horses of her day. In addition to her well-known illustrations to the 1915 edition of Anna Sewell's children's classic, *Black Beauty*, she painted equine subjects of all kinds, including wild ponies on Exmoor, polo ponies, heavy working horses, war horses and circus horses. *Colt-Hunting in the New Forest* (1897) became her best-known picture after it was purchased for the national collection in 1897 through the Chantrey Bequest. She exhibited over sixty works at London's Royal Academy and held important positions in the art world, becoming the first President of the Society of Animal Painters and one of the first two women members of the Royal Society of British Artists. Her works can be found today in many public collections in Britain as well as Australia, New Zealand and South Africa.

The greatest collection of her work is in the Bushey Museum, Hertfordshire as she lived most of her life there. Having enrolled, aged nineteen, at Hubert von Herkomer's art school there, on his retirement in 1905 she took over its running until 1926, transforming it into a world-renowned school for animal painting.

Kemp-Welch had local connections to Southampton, an additional incentive for the Art Gallery to acquire this picture. She had grown up in Bournemouth, where she nurtured her talent by drawing the ponies of the New Forest, and received her first training at Bournemouth School of Art.

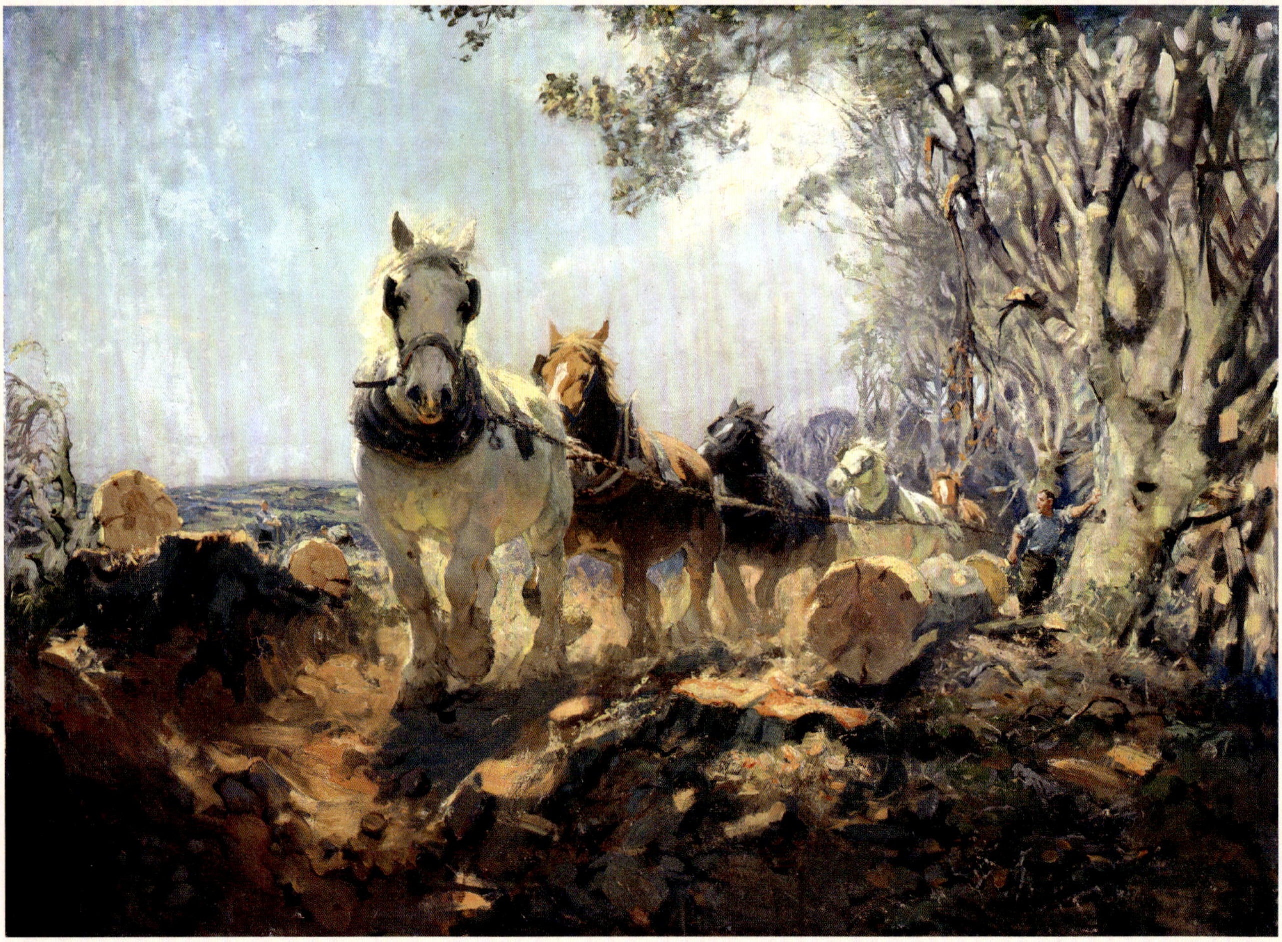

6

Franz Meerts (1836–1896)

The Old Attorney, mid-nineteenth century

Oil on canvas, 40.3 × 31.4 cm
Bequeathed by Robert Chipperfield, 1911
Southampton City Art Gallery, SOTAG 401

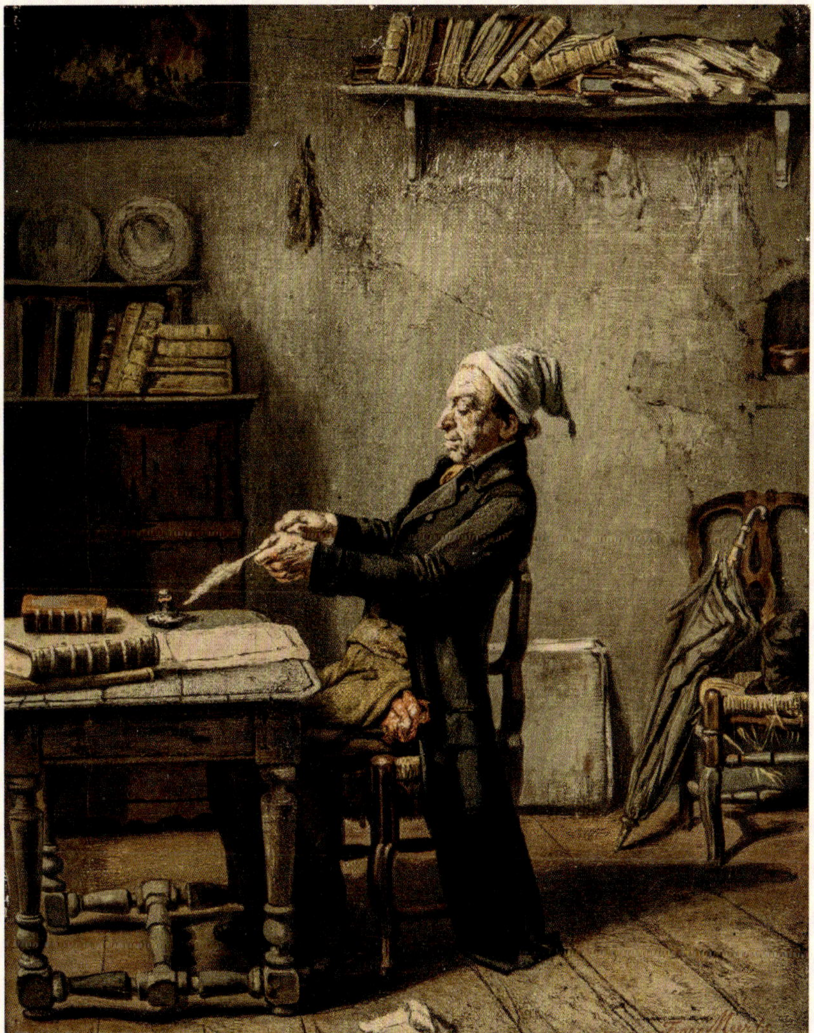

This work was in the private collection of Robert Chipperfield, bequeathed as the core of a public art collection to Southampton in 1911. The presence of a modern continental work shows that Chipperfield's tastes extended beyond collecting only the work of native talent.

The Belgian painter Franz Meerts co-founded two artist associations in Brussels. The first was *L'Union des Arts* which existed from 1876 to 1885 and held three group exhibitions in Meerts's own painting studio. In 1885, he co-founded a new society for aspiring painters called *Voorwaarts* ('Forward' in Dutch) with the motto *Hooger is ons doel* ('Higher is our goal'). He was also director of the Art Academy of Soignies, in Hainhaut, for over two decades.

As a painter, Meerts is best known for interiors, genre scenes, still lifes and landscapes. He often depicted the clergy and notaries in their offices in a humorous or sentimental vein as can be seen in Southampton's picture, which shows a notary seated at his desk, sharpening a quill pen. A badly damaged version of the work is in the Shipley Art Gallery, Gateshead, and there is a copy in Snowshill Manor, Gloucestershire (National Trust). The composition recalls seventeenth-century Dutch genre paintings. Certainly Meerts had studied the old masters because as a young artist he was commissioned by the Belgian government to travel to Italy and Spain to copy works by the most esteemed historical painters, and he was also paid by Louvain's city council to copy works by Dirck Bouts (1400?–1475) for its town hall.

In Focus:
Links between Southampton City Art Gallery and the National Gallery

Like other regional art galleries, such as the Graves Gallery in Sheffield, Southampton did not originally have a proper home to display its pictures. Instead, space was hired in the city's central public library, using money from the Chipperfield Bequest Fund to pay the rent. Plans for a new civic centre, including an art gallery, were postponed during the First World War and then delayed until agreement was reached over the site. A design competition was announced in 1928, and 47 designs were submitted.

The winner was Ernest Berry Webber (1896–1963), who had already built Peterborough Town Hall and who would go on to design civic centres in Dagenham and Hammersmith. He was also the architect of King Edward VI School in Southampton.

Southampton's Civic Centre (fig. 15) incorporated four separate elements linked by corridors. The north wing, which houses the art gallery, was the last block to be built; it was completed in 1939. To give the building a modern appearance, a stripped-back classicism was chosen as the architectural style; its pale-coloured interiors were praised for being light and airy, evoking an Italian basilica. Today the complex is Grade II* listed.

FIG. 15 Perspective drawing of the Civic Centre, Southampton (1928–39), by E. Berry Webber. Published in *The Builder*, 11 January 1929, p. 91. Southampton City Archives

FIG. 16 The Main Hall during the 1960s before its refurbishment in the 1990s. Southampton City Archives

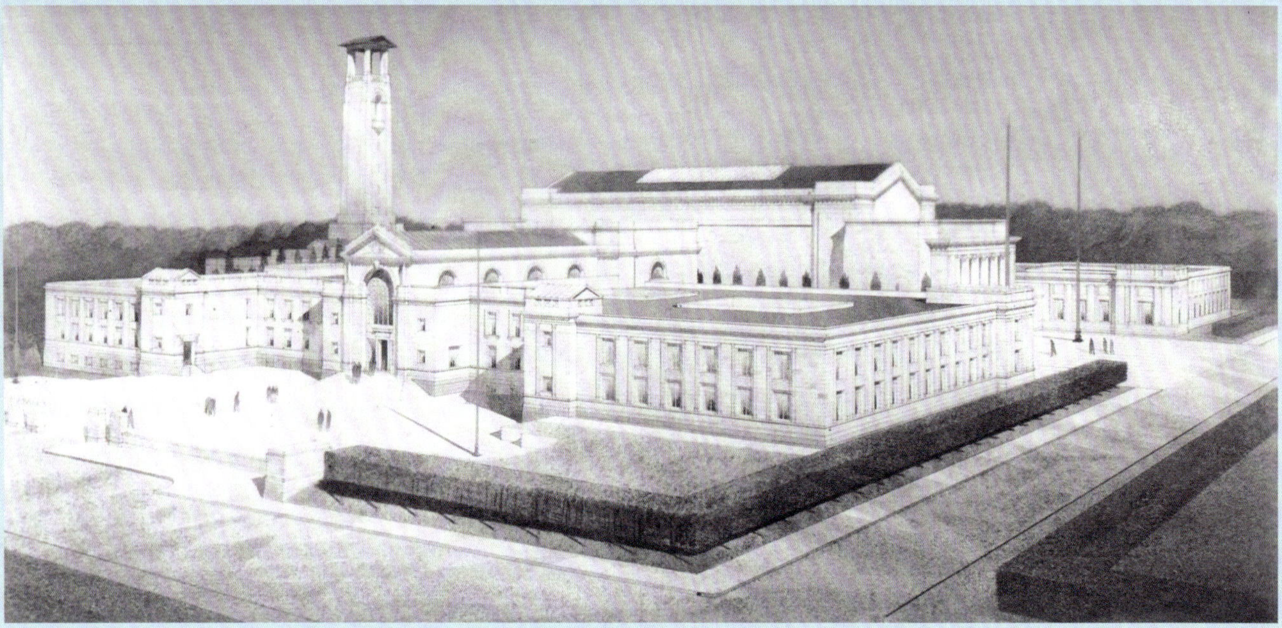

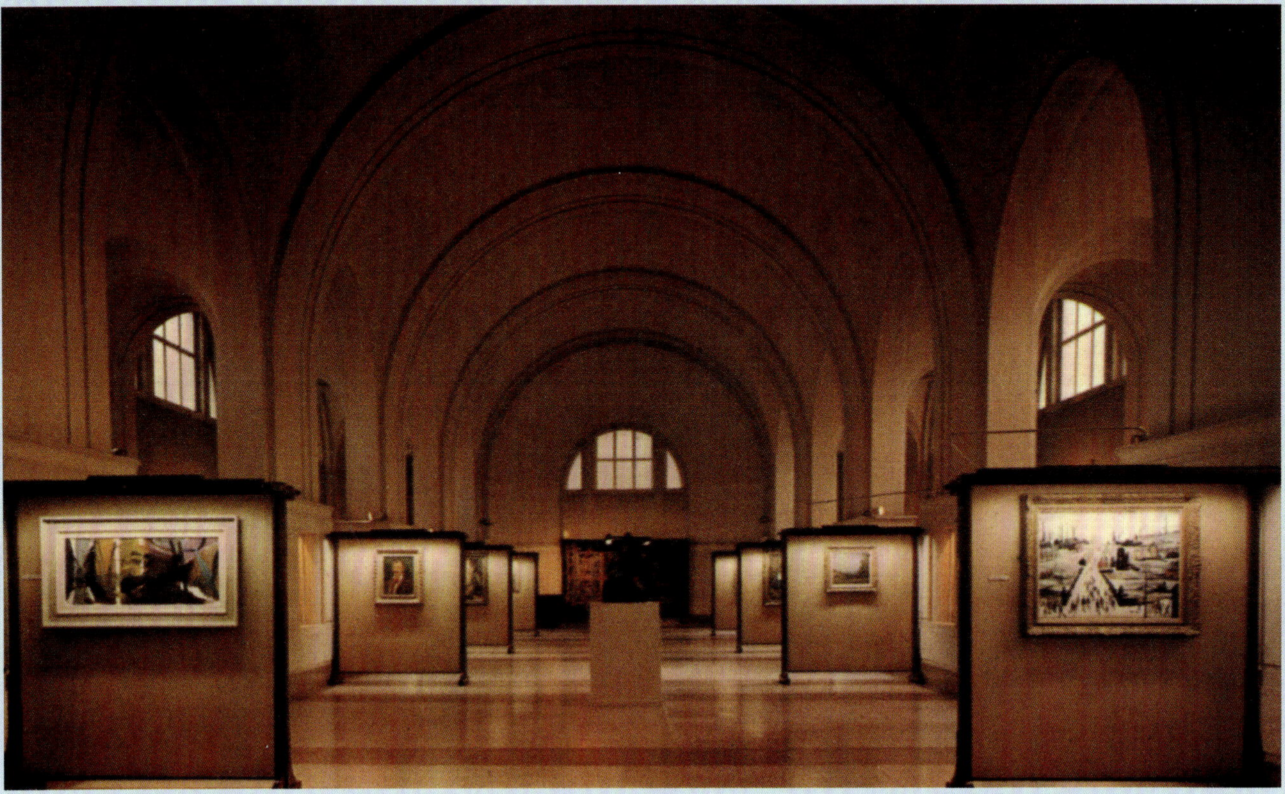

The Gallery was officially opened on 26 April 1939 by the Duke and Duchess of Gloucester, but after only a few months most of the collection was moved away for safety following the outbreak of the Second World War. For the duration of the war, the Gallery was requisitioned for use by both local and central government, with four galleries ultimately occupied as the headquarters for the 14th Major Port, US Army.

The Civic Centre received several direct hits during the Blitz of November 1940, which destroyed part of the Art Gallery's facade, its central staircase and several galleries. During its post-war rebuilding, and in consultation with Berry Webber, it was decided not to replace the grand central staircase but instead to pave over the floor to create a large hall for the display of sculpture (fig. 16). A grand event in 1950, attended by the National Gallery's then director, Philip Hendy, marked the point when the new hall was ready, and all the galleries were back in working order. The revamped art gallery was less ornate than the original building.

During the 1990s, after 15 years of persistent effort by Elizabeth (Liz) Goodall, then director, and a £7 million refurbishment project, the interior of the Art Gallery was completely revamped. This was partly to make the gallery more visible from the entrance foyer, given that since 1950 it had been accessible only by two hidden side stairs. To offer a sense of arrival, it was agreed to reinstate the central staircase, with new spaces given over for displays in the foyer. The project also provided new amenities such as a lift, café, children's activity room, art stores, and a lecture theatre whose lobby displayed a newly commissioned memorial to those killed in the building during the war.

A very visible way in which the newly refurbished space was enlivened was through the placing of innovative works specially created for the Gallery. Goodall commissioned a site-specific work for

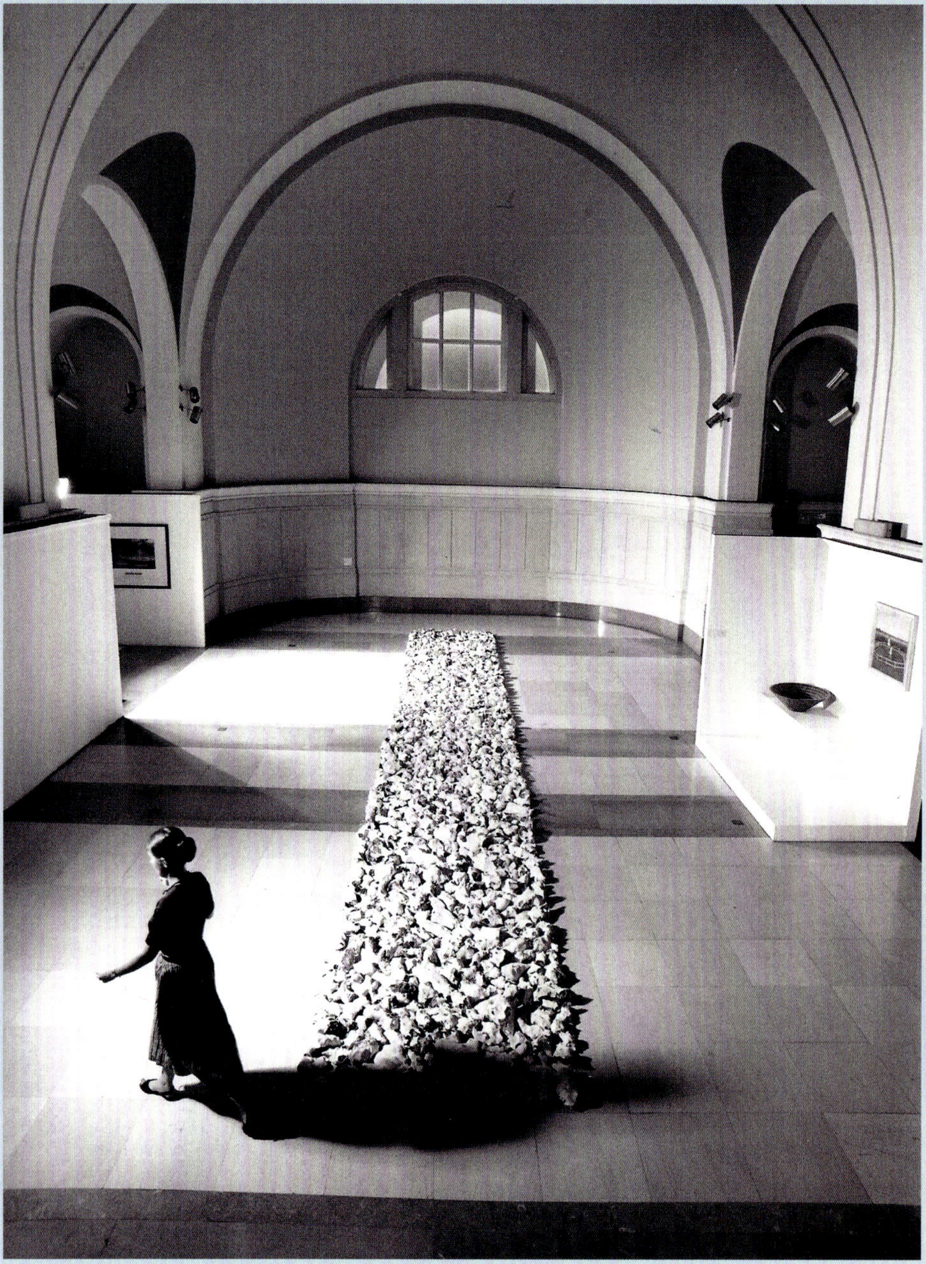

FIG. 17
Richard Long (b. 1945)
Wessex Flint Line, 1987
Flint, 1130 × 160 cm
Photograph after installation, July 1987, with Gill Hedley.
Southampton City Art Gallery, SOTAG 7/1987

FIG. 18
Daniel Buren (b. 1938)
With The Arcades, three colours, 1997
Permanent in-gallery installation
Southampton City Art Gallery, SOTAG 3/1995

Southampton in 1987 by Richard Long, the most celebrated of the British Land Artists and Turner Prize winner of 1989. He produced *Wessex Flint Line* as a commission, in which pieces of local white Hampshire flint were carefully placed to form a line 37 feet long by 5 feet wide (fig. 17). It was Long's first commission for a public collection, and the work Goodall was proudest of having acquired for Southampton. Long made it to fit within the Main Hall, its straight lines contrasting with the curves of the arches in the space. The second in-situ work came about in 1994 when the French conceptual artist Daniel Buren, amongst other artists, was invited to create art on the walls in the west wing as part of the Contemporary Art Society's *Wall to Wall* exhibition. Buren asked if he might instead use the Main Hall, and the result, produced with the help of local university students, was *With The Arcades, three colours* (fig. 18), which followed the attractive curves of the Art Deco ceiling. In an astute move by Margot Heller, then Art Gallery manager, Southampton purchased the work. It was the first public installation of Buren's work in the UK and being placed so prominently, it was spotted by the Arts Council with positive consequences for the artist's career. As recently as May 2017, Buren's signature stripes have appeared on a second permanent installation in the UK – *Diamonds and Circles* at Tottenham Court Road tube station in London, commissioned by 'Art on the Underground'. It is worth remembering that Buren had been talent-spotted by Southampton almost a quarter of a century earlier.

Once the refurbishment had been completed in 1995, the Gallery won several national awards. It was named Fine Art Museum of the year, as well as ranking as a finalist in the European Museum of the Year Award and winning a Jerwood Prize for its inclusion of artists in the project. In their summary, the judges for the Fine Art Museum Award called Southampton 'an excellent gallery with one of the most enterprising collecting policies to be carried out by a British local authority in this century'.[1] More praise came at the presentation of the European Museum of the of the Year Award to Southampton's full council meeting, when Wim van der Weidon, one of the judges, explained: 'we were impressed by the Director's dynamic and practical approach and by the way the Gallery has integrated into the social structure of the city'.[2]

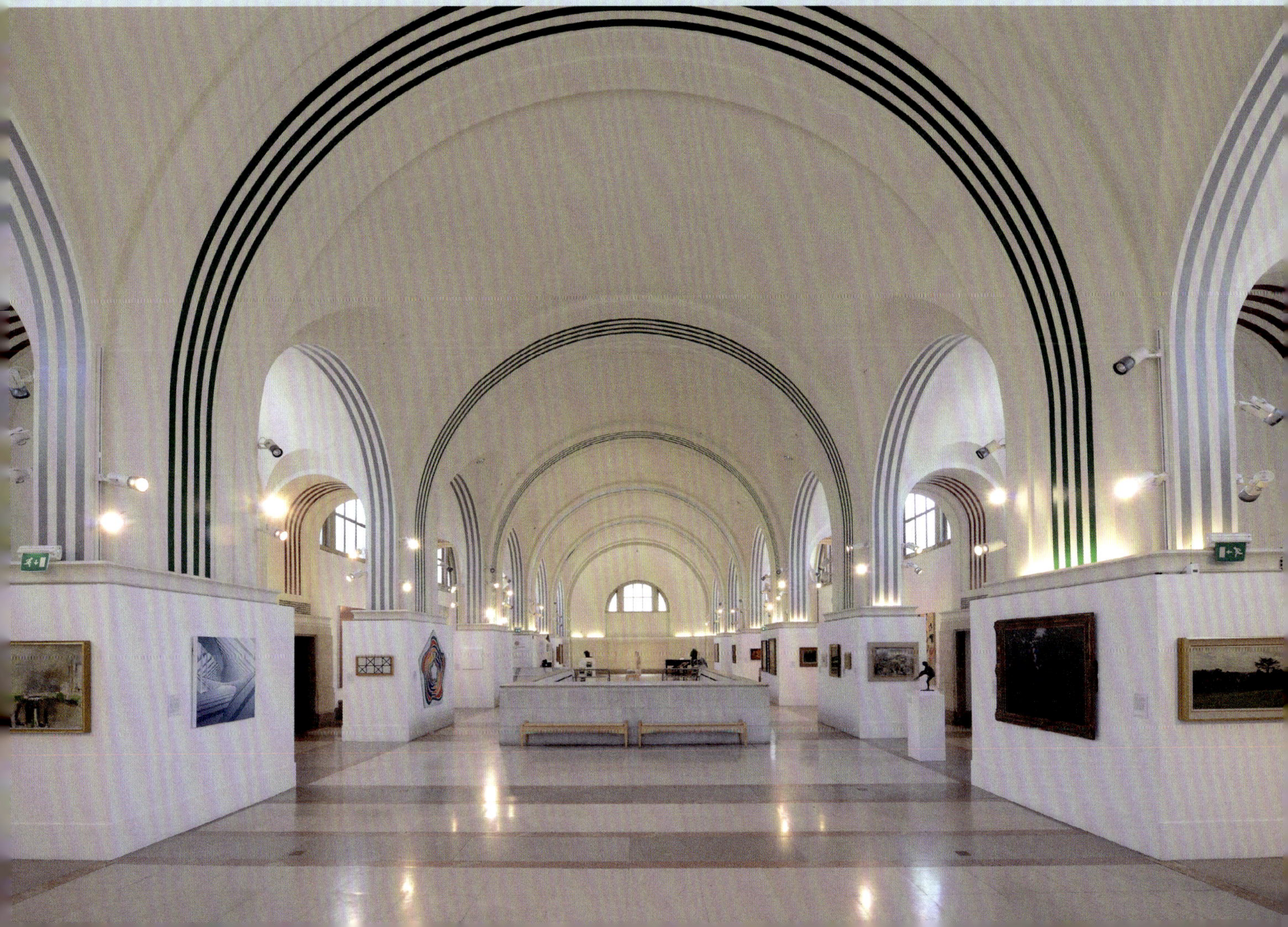

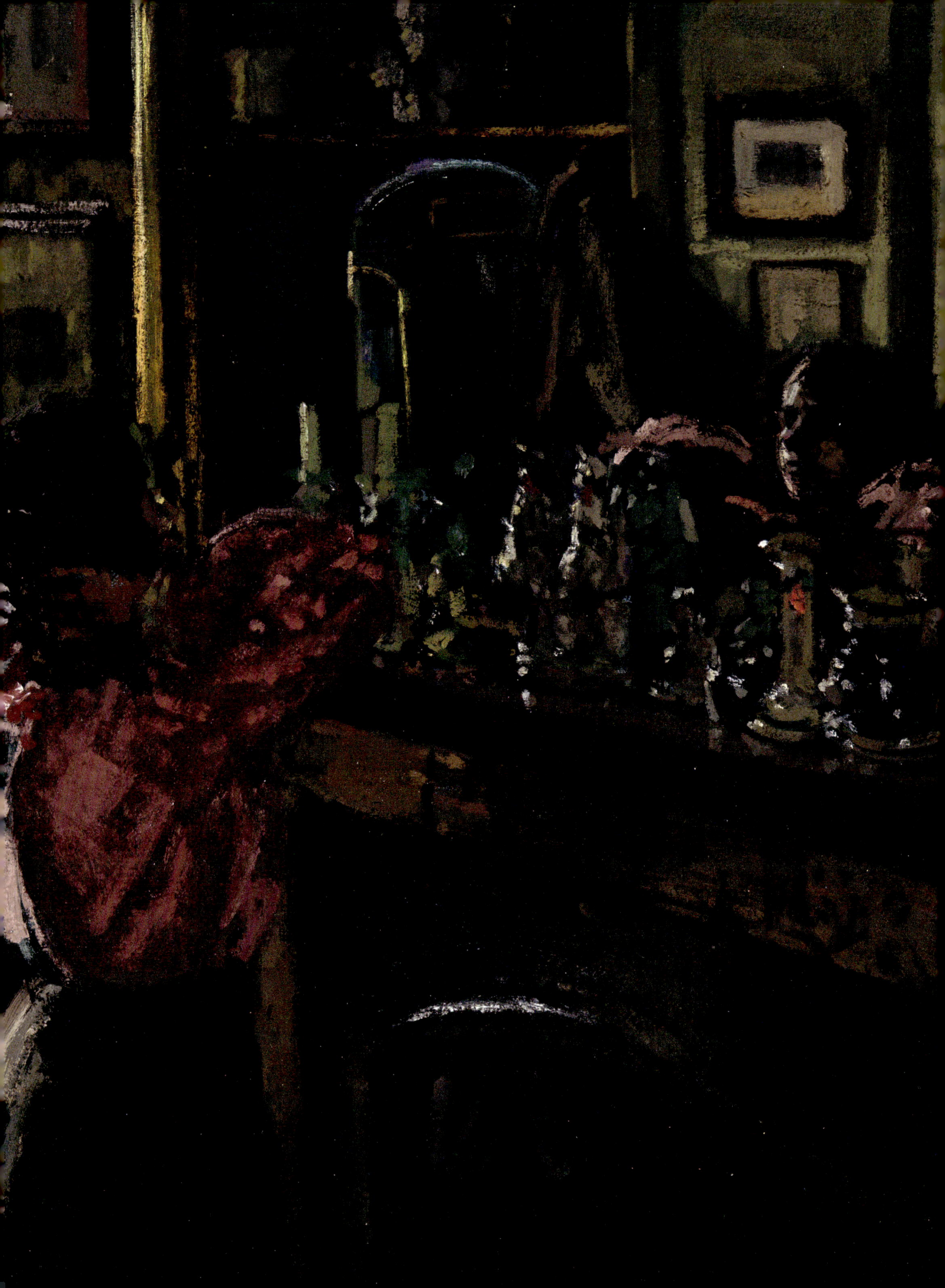

AMBITIONS

Developing a Relationship with the National Gallery (1929–1933)

2

After slow beginnings over two decades from 1911, the fortunes of Southampton Art Gallery started to rise. Matters concerning the wills of Robert Chipperfield and Frederick William Smith were resolved in 1930 and 1931 respectively, and Southampton and the National Gallery began to establish a unique and fruitful relationship from late 1929. From the mid-nineteenth century, various loans and circulating groups of J.M.W. Turner's works on paper had been shared nationwide (as noted in Chapter 1), but otherwise the National Gallery had never established formal or sustained links with any particular cultural institution. In 1928, however, it was agreed that its director would act as an adviser and trustee of the Iveagh Bequest for Kenwood House in London. Although the commitment lasted until 1949 and involved four successive directors, the evidence suggests that the assistance amounted to little more than sporadic advice about picture cleaning. Kenneth Clark, for instance, apparently took nothing more than a 'leisurely approach to his duties as a Trustee of the Iveagh Bequest.'[1] By contrast, he, as well as his predecessor and successors in post, would demonstrate a proactive and sustained commitment to Southampton. Indeed, this would prove to be the longest and most engaged relationship ever forged by the National Gallery with any sister institution.

Traditional channels for buying: London's Royal Academy and local exhibitions

On 12 November 1929 a letter from the Chipperfield Bequest Sub-Committee was read out at a National Gallery board meeting, which 'nominated the National Gallery, or such officer of the Gallery as [the Director] should appoint, to act as adviser to the Council, under a Trust, in connection with the purchase of pictures for the art gallery.'[2] The response to this request for help from an emerging regional institution was open-ended. Southampton's councillors were told that the National Gallery's director would be 'willing to act as their adviser for one year' but that the general feeling was that any duty of care towards Southampton's art collection might be delegated to someone other than the director, and 'that a better arrangement could be achieved'.[3]

The link between the two institutions was formalised following the settlement of Chipperfield's will on 23 January 1930.[4] The legal document – an Order of the Chancery Division of the High Court of Justice – stipulated the extent of the National Gallery's powers, which were, in fact, quite extensive: the director or his deputy was to help decide which of Chipperfield's works 'shall be placed and exhibited' and, in relation to the growth of the collection, 'no work of art shall be purchased, exchanged, accepted on loan or lent by the Council except on such expert advice as aforesaid'. Furthermore, it was noted that 'expert advice' should be sought in relation to 'the renovation restoration or repair of any works of art'.[5] The same document required that a full financial record should be kept and made available for an annual audit by the Council. This stipulation encouraged professional record-keeping from the start – the resulting accounts have proven an invaluable source for this narrative.

Although the assistance of the National Gallery was in theory broad-ranging, in practice – at least initially – it was limited to acquisitions. This may have been in part because the Gallery's then director was not particularly ambitious or proactive. Augustus Moore Daniel (1866–1950; fig. 19) had recently been appointed as a 'caretaker director', in January 1929. Daniel's experience of arts administration had come from serving as assistant director of the British School at Rome between 1906 and 1907, and from having acted

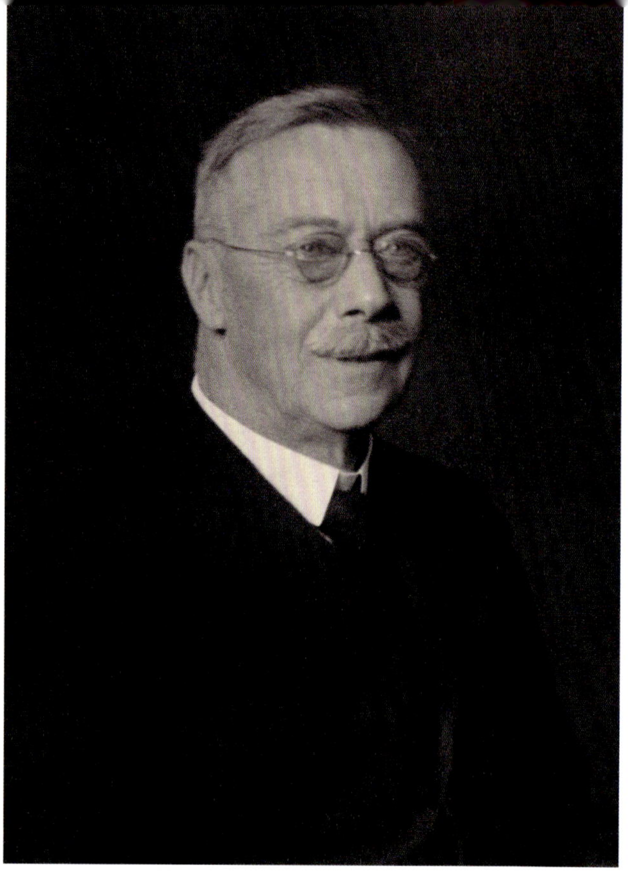

(PREVIOUS PAGE)
Walter Sickert (1860–1942)
The Mantelpiece, 1907; detail, cat. 10
Southampton City Art Gallery,
SOTAG 517

FIG. 19
Walter Stoneman (1876–1958)
Sir Augustus Moore Daniel, 1933
Bromide print, 16.3 × 12 cm
National Portrait Gallery,
London, 166977

as a trustee of the National Gallery from 1925 until he resigned to become its director, a position which he retained until the end of 1933. Daniel secured some high-profile purchases for Trafalgar Square, including *The Wilton Diptych* and Titian's *The Vendramin Family*, even though his time in office coincided with the early years of the Great Depression. Notwithstanding, Daniel is not remembered as especially dynamic or proactive; a recent biographer of Kenneth Clark dismissed him as 'probably the most inactive director the Gallery had ever appointed'.[6] However, a review of Daniel's activities on behalf of Southampton Art Gallery reveals that he was not completely 'inactive' and that he did assist with some significant purchases which helped to shift the vision and ambition of the newly established regional art collection in important new directions.

For one thing, Daniel set up the working relationship between Southampton and London on transparent and orderly foundations. A typed note in his name survives, which states: 'I have preserved a certain amount of correspondence, which may be destroyed in time, in order to show the procedure I have adopted.'[7] Fortunately, a paper trail survives in both institutions which helpfully maps the entirety of their relationship.

Certain teething problems are recorded. In an early note, Daniel referred to a particularly 'formidable' alderman, and in another he confessed: 'The whole matter is so complicated and the atmosphere in Southampton is so thunderous that a letter would not explain all the intricacies'.[8] The major bone of contention appears to have been who was in charge; clearly, certain members of the Chipperfield Bequest Sub-Committee were unwilling to cede power to an outsider from London, regardless of how qualified he was to perform his duty. Daniel, himself clearly frustrated by the situation, noted: 'the Committee are quite ignorant and not wholly satisfied with the scheme and the steps which have been taken to obtain this compulsory scheme.'[9] A related sore point was money – which Daniel defined as the struggle 'to obtain the right distribution of the capital and income'.[10] Questions arose over how much was deemed appropriate to spend on pictures, especially those which were controversial in subject matter or style, or which came with price-tags that were considered excessive. Matters were not helped by the fact that there was no curator in Southampton who could support or help to interpret positively the responses from the National Gallery.

The Chipperfield Bequest Sub-Committee, despite having the director of the National Gallery on board, showed itself keen to continue using well-trodden paths to purchase pictures. The town clerk, R.R.H. Meggeson, wrote to Daniel on 9 May 1931, announcing that the Sub-Committee had 'recently considered the subject of framing a policy under the Trust as to the purchase of pictures', and that certain councillors would be attending the annual Royal Academy exhibition in London.[11] From the mid-nineteenth century, it had become standard practice for town councils to send representatives to London to select paintings from the walls of the Academy's annual Summer Exhibition. But increasingly voices were raised in opposition, including that of Sir Charles Holmes, editor of the newly founded and scholarly art-history journal, *The Burlington Magazine*, and Daniel's predecessor as director of the National Gallery. 'Councils are free to buy what pictures they please without any annoying responsibility to art or to tradition', Holmes noted ironically in his book *Pictures and Picture Collecting* (1903), lampooning the fact that many town councils selected pictures only because they fancied their choice would 'amuse their fellow-citizens'.[12] In Holmes's opinion, an alternative approach was necessary if paintings of quality were to be collected: 'In several places, such as Glasgow, Birmingham, and Norwich, the existence of a local school, the generosity of a private donor, or the intelligence and tact of a curator, has formed a nucleus of pictures.'[13] This same battle would be played out in Southampton, with the opinion of the town councillors holding sway until the rise of the expert art adviser shifted the power dynamic in favour of the specialist.

Initially, the council remained happy to continue acquiring works that were safe and pleasing to a broad audience through well-worn channels, and Daniel had to be content to let the Chipperfield Bequest Sub-Committee have its way on numerous occasions. The town clerk sent him a letter on 6 May 1933, for instance, which included a list of possible acquisitions from the Royal Academy Summer Exhibition, drawn up by the sub-committee. The list survives with various crossings-out in Daniel's hand (fig. 20). On this occasion, he ultimately approved just two works out of a total of seven.[14]

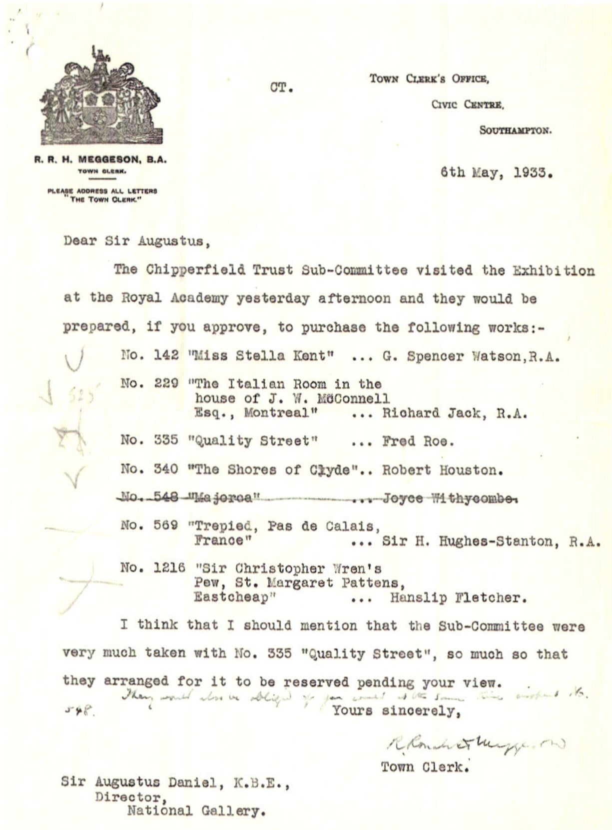

R. R. H. MEGGESON, B.A.
TOWN CLERK.

PLEASE ADDRESS ALL LETTERS "THE TOWN CLERK."

CT.

TOWN CLERK'S OFFICE,
CIVIC CENTRE,
SOUTHAMPTON.

6th May, 1933.

Dear Sir Augustus,

The Chipperfield Trust Sub-Committee visited the Exhibition at the Royal Academy yesterday afternoon and they would be prepared, if you approve, to purchase the following works:-

No. 142 "Miss Stella Kent" ... G. Spencer Watson, R.A.

No. 229 "The Italian Room in the house of J. W. McConnell Esq., Montreal" ... Richard Jack, R.A.

No. 335 "Quality Street" ... Fred Roe.

No. 340 "The Shores of Clyde".. Robert Houston.

~~No. 548 "Majorca" ... Joyce Withycombe.~~

No. 569 "Trepied, Pas de Calais, France" ... Sir H. Hughes-Stanton, R.A.

No. 1216 "Sir Christopher Wren's Pew, St. Margaret Pattens, Eastcheap" ... Hanslip Fletcher.

I think that I should mention that the Sub-Committee were very much taken with No. 335 "Quality Street", so much so that they arranged for it to be reserved pending your view.

Yours sincerely,

Town Clerk.

Sir Augustus Daniel, K.B.E.,
Director,
National Gallery.

FIG. 20

Letter from R.R.H. Meggeson, town clerk, to Augustus Moore Daniel, Director of the National Gallery, 6 May 1933. National Gallery Archive, NG16/201/1

Another tried and tested way of purchasing paintings was through local exhibitions. A strong tradition of mounting exhibitions in regional galleries had developed in Britain, usually in the autumn following the Royal Academy's Summer Exhibition. By the early twentieth century it was customary that prominent artists from London were encouraged to participate alongside local practitioners. For instance, Southampton Art Society's 41st Annual Exhibition of 1927 included works by painters of national repute including William Rothenstein, Henry Tonks and Philip Wilson Steer as well as by local Hampshire painters such as Short and Skeats. Thus, in Autumn 1930, Daniel went to Southampton to inspect a collection of pictures brought together by a local art society.[15] He subsequently reported that the committee had been happy to purchase three of his suggestions. Although he did not specify his choices, it seems likely that one of them was Jean Boswell Farquharson's *Portrait of a Young Girl* (fig. 21).

When Daniel was invited back the following year to attend the exhibitions of the Southampton Art Society and the Southampton and District Artists' Club in order to advise on another batch of purchases, he made use of his right to send a deputy.[16] Perhaps this decision is indicative of his inactivity, but Daniel hinted that he did not want to get too embroiled,[17] and at least his substitution was well made. He selected Reginald Gleadowe (1888–1944), one of the leading designers of his day and author of several art books. At the time, Gleadowe was Slade Professor of Fine Art at Oxford University and had been 'for many years Principal Lecturer in [the National] Gallery and ... in charge of the Fine Art Training at Winchester College.'[18] In fact, Gleadowe had acted as assistant to the director of the National Gallery between 1919 and 1923, before becoming the drawing master at Winchester College from 1923 to 1939 (where, from 1917 to 1922 Kenneth Clark was a pupil). Conveniently, Gleadowe lived locally, at 7 College Street, Winchester, and so was aware of the Hampshire art scene in a way that Daniel, being London-based, was not. 'My dear Gleadowe', wrote Daniel, 'Will you do me a great favour? It should not give you very much trouble and might be a little amusing ... [and it] would be politic ... to help ... until things have settled down.'[19] In a more serious vein, Daniel forewarned his colleague of the sensitivities of the situation. Meanwhile, he made it clear to colleagues in Southampton that they could not get 'a better qualified man' than Gleadowe.[20]

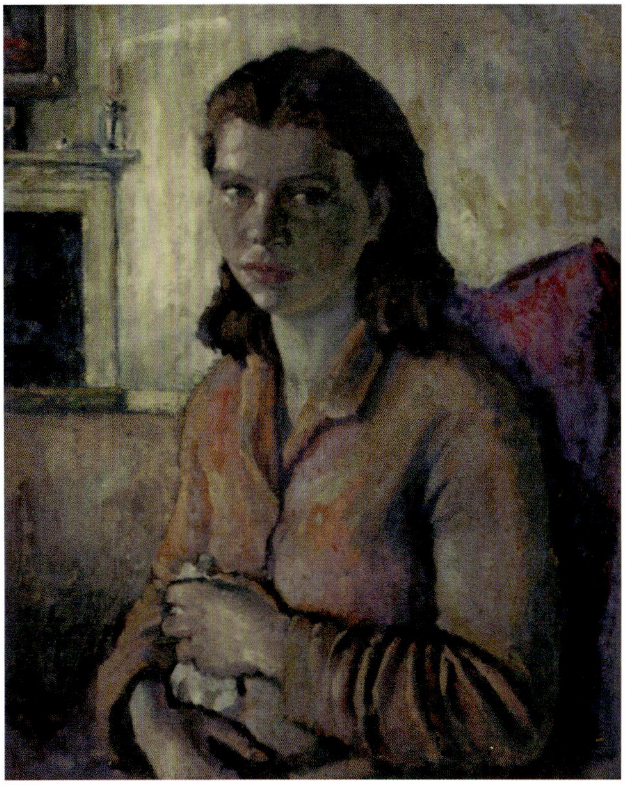

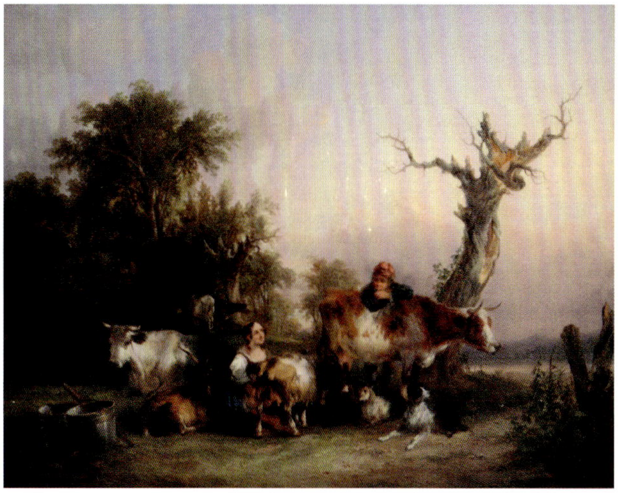

FIG. 21
Jean Boswell Farquharson
Portrait of a Young Girl,
about 1930
Oil on canvas, 56.5 × 45.7 cm
Southampton City Art Gallery,
SOTAG 190

FIG. 22
William Shayer (1787–1879)
Milking Time, date unknown
Oil on canvas, 71 × 91.5 cm
Southampton City Art Gallery,
SOTAG 501

New ambitions for Southampton's public art collection

While the Chipperfield Bequest Sub-Committee remained loyal to promoting local artists' work, Daniel remained equally committed to encouraging its members to be bold enough to set their sights in new directions. Two episodes from 1933 reveal the different points of view at play, and the shift in thinking – and thus in approach – which incrementally took place. The first incident occurred in January, when a member of the Kimber family, an influential local dynasty, offered three works by William Shayer (1787–1879). The painter was a self-taught landscape and animal painter whose output largely comprised idealised woodland scenes depicting Romany people, rustic figures and animals, set in his native Hampshire landscape of the New Forest. When Daniel asked the ever-obliging Gleadowe to inspect two of the pictures then in Winchester (the third was in London),[21] the latter had little to say in praise of either. Even the better of the two – *Gipsies in a Wood* – was condemned with faint praise: 'Nobody would notice it much in a public gallery; but if they did it could do them little harm.'[22] Daniel had already notified Gleadowe that unless Southampton was anxious to buy all three, the expert advice was not to take more than two.[23] Presumably the committee's desire to acquire works by Shayer stemmed from the fact that the painter was a Southampton success story – formerly a humble coach painter, he became a professional artist, exhibiting at the Royal Academy in 1820.[24] A single picture by Shayer, *Milking Time*, (fig. 22) was acquired in 1933, which was presumably a pleasing outcome for both parties: Southampton secured a work by a favourite painter while Daniel's guiding hand had tempered a potential buying spree. Over the years,

Southampton Art Gallery accepted several more works by Shayer as gifts, including *The Gleaners* and *The Fish Stall*, both presented by Miss E.M. Welch in 1943.

The second episode took place in May, when Gladys Montagu, Dowager Lady Swaythling, wrote to express her wish to bequeath her late husband's collection of works by another local Southampton artist, Leonard Durkin. Daniel responded firmly that 'it would be rather difficult to call them pictures'[25] – the items in question were a set of marquetry panels depicting local Southampton views – but that he would approve their purchase if the committee remained determined to obtain them. The Chipperfield Bequest Sub-Committee was resolute,[26] a stance based perhaps on a desire to keep on favourable terms with a family as eminent in local affairs as the Swaythlings. The panels by Durkin therefore joined the portrait of Lady Swaythling (fig. 10) which, as noted in Chapter 1, she had donated in 1927.

Daniel made it plain from the start that the Chipperfield Bequest Sub-Committee should raise its sights towards acquiring works by painters of national and international reputation, from the past as well as the present. Asserting his authority to help move Southampton onto new tracks, Daniel wrote in 1932 with a 'definite and independent judgement'.[27] Using the chance to respond to certain pictures sent for his assessment, he made the more general point: 'A public Gallery should last for centuries and it is a great pity to begin with slight and unimportant pictures which detract from, rather than strengthen the prestige of the Collection.'[28]

In the same year, Southampton used the Smith Bequest Fund to acquire its first work of undeniably high quality, the *Moonlight Village Scene* (*Marine effet de lune*, cat. 7) by the esteemed nineteenth-century French artist Eugène Louis Boudin (1824–1898). In spite of its small size, it was not a sketch but a work fully finished in the artist's studio. Its acquisition reflected similar purchasing activity at the National Gallery, which, in the first decades of the twentieth century, acquired three Boudins as well as three works by Camille Pissarro and its only Alfred Sisley. Southampton's purchase also set a precedent in terms of which funding stream was used for which pictures: the more modest Smith Bequest Fund tended to support the acquisition of nineteenth-century paintings, which were cheaper, while the better-endowed Chipperfield Bequest Fund was reserved on the whole for the more expensive old masters.

The following year the Smith Bequest Fund enabled the purchase of a second important nineteenth-century work by a European artist associated with the Impressionist movement: *Estuary of the Nalón, Asturias* by the Spanish painter Joaquín Sorolla (1863–1923, cat. 8). By contrast, the National Gallery had to wait until 2019 to acquire its first Sorolla, *The Drunkard, Zarauz*, paying far more for it comparatively than Southampton had done in 1933. The two acquisitions of a Boudin and Sorolla demonstrate how Southampton was starting to purchase paintings outside the conventional buying patterns of most regional UK art galleries – by artists whose work is now recognised as part of the mainstream of European art collecting.

It was the acquisition of British art that established the beginnings of a concord between councillors in Southampton and the National Gallery. As a result of Daniel's interventions, the names of several British painters with national – if not international – reputation started to enter the conversation. In 1932 Southampton bought three works by the celebrated Irish painter Sir John Lavery (1856–1941), best known for his realistic portraits, genre scenes and landscapes.[29] Two of the acquired works were portraits – *Miss Diana Chamberlain* and *Portrait of Miss Betty Shaughnessy* (fig. 23) – while the third was a landscape entitled *Monte Carlo, Afternoon*. A novelty of this group was that all three pictures came through the art market – namely, from Lavery's art agent in London, P.&D. Colnaghi. That same year Henry Tonks's *The Torn Gown* (cat. 9) was purchased. Tonks, a British surgeon, was also a draughtsman, figure painter and caricaturist as well as an influential art teacher at London's internationally acclaimed Slade School of Fine Art. The work was purchased from another leading London art dealer, Lockett Thompson of Barbizon House, for £195 in July 1932. '[A] very delicate piece of work', according to Daniel,[30] it is certainly an uncharacteristically charming image for Tonks, who is best known for tragic images of disfigured soldiers from the First World War.

Perhaps the most interesting purchase of that year was *The Mantelpiece*, painted by the British painter and printmaker Walter Sickert, who played a central role in the formation of the British avant-garde art movement, the Camden Town Group (cat. 10). The image of a woman idly regarding herself in a mirror is arguably more conventionally attractive than many of Sickert's pictures, which often focus on more unsettling emotions ranging from boredom to menacing frustration. In reviewing this group of purchases by living British painters, it is clear that the calibre of acquisitions at Southampton had risen significantly, even if the examples selected were from the least challenging part of the artists' oeuvres.

By the mid-1930s, then, Southampton had shown clear signs that it was willing to branch out in new directions in terms of acquisitions. Not only had it successfully purchased some fine works by leading British painters, notably Sickert, Lavery and Tonks, but it had also tentatively entered the international realm with purchases of works by the nineteenth-century foreign painters, Boudin and Sorolla.

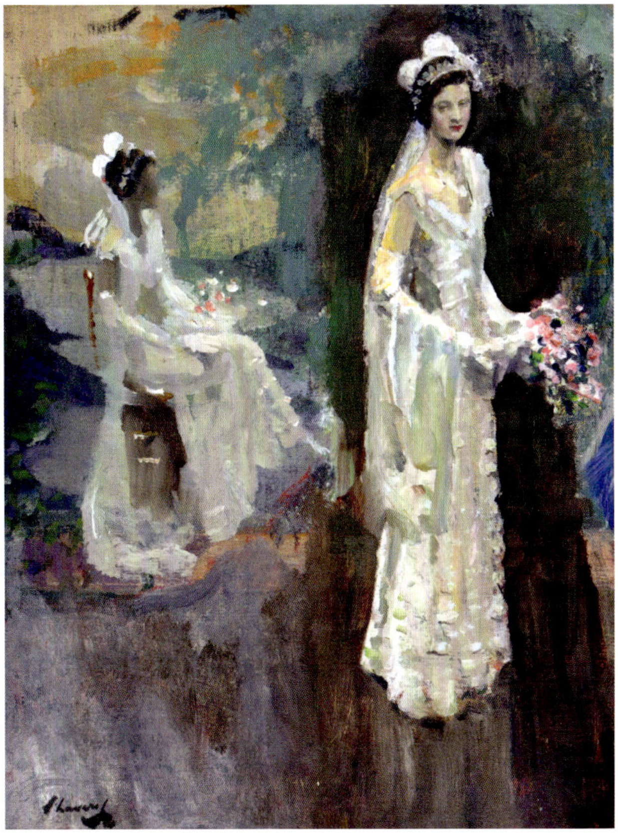

FIG. 23
John Lavery (1856–1941)
Miss Betty Shaughnessy, 1931
Oil on canvas, 50.7 × 37.8 cm
Southampton City Art Gallery, SOTAG 339

7

Eugène Louis Boudin (1824–1898)
Moonlight Village Scene, Le Faou, Brittany (Marine effet de lune), perhaps 1867

Oil on canvas, 30.5 × 46.5 cm
Purchased with the assistance of the Smith Bequest Fund, 1932
Southampton City Art Gallery, SOTAG 45

Bought in 1932, this work was one of the first important historical paintings purchased for Southampton Art Gallery. That year, Augustus Daniel, Southampton's first art adviser, wrote to encourage an ambitious purchasing policy. Explaining that a public gallery should last for centuries, he recommended that 'slight and unimportant pictures' should be avoided because they would detract from the prestige of the Collection.'[1]

The picture is certainly prestigious, given that Boudin was an important precursor of the French Impressionists. Although he took part in the first Impressionist exhibition of 1874 in Paris, he did not fully embrace the ideals of the movement. His importance lies largely in the fact that he persuaded Claude Monet, whom he met in 1858, to paint directly from nature, which became a fundamental tenet of Impressionist landscape painting. Monet later claimed, 'If I have become a painter, I owe this to Eugène Boudin and no other.'[2]

Boudin's interest in painting outdoors led him to produce countless small sketches, mostly depicting harbours and beaches of northern France, including his native Honfleur; Southampton's picture depicts La Faou, a fishing village near Brest. This night scene is unusual for Boudin, but relates to his constant interest in capturing the effects of light and weather, focused here on the play of moonlight through the clouds and on the water below.

Boudin's pictures soon became highly collectable, especially in Britain. Recognised as a key acquisition, the work was included by Southampton in two important touring exhibitions, including its inaugural one to Exeter's Royal Albert Memorial Museum in 1955. Southampton acquired its second Boudin, *Fishing Boats on Berck Beach*, over half a century later, in 1986.

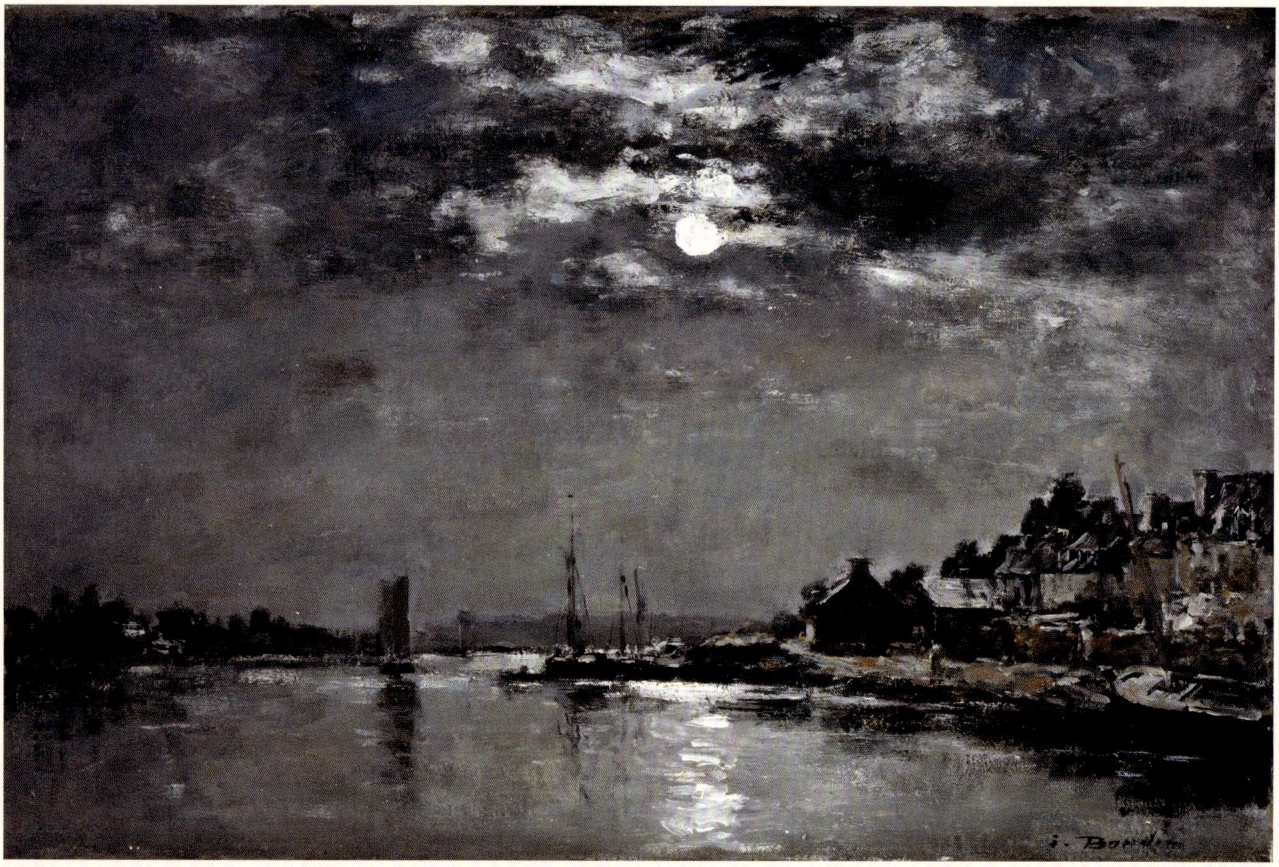

8

Joaquín Sorolla y Bastida (1863–1923)

Estuary of the Nalón, Asturias, 1883

Oil on canvas, 62 × 93.5 cm
Purchased with the assistance of the Smith Bequest Fund, 1933
Southampton City Art Gallery, SOTAG 542

By the mid-1930s, Southampton Art Gallery was showing clear signs that it was willing to branch out in new directions in terms of its acquisitions. Its decision to collect works by artists now recognised as falling within the mainstream of European art history set its purchasing policy apart from the conventional buying patterns of most regional UK art galleries at the time.

Having purchased a picture by Boudin in 1932, the following year Southampton bought a second important work by a European artist associated with the international Impressionist movement: *Estuary of the Nalón, Asturias* by the nineteenth-century Spanish painter and illustrator Joaquín Sorolla. He made his name through exhibiting large-scale, colourful paintings on themes of Spanish life at major exhibitions across Europe and the Americas, a strategy that won him prestigious awards and sales to important public and private collections. His work was often compared with that of other celebrated contemporaries, including Claude Monet and John Singer Sargent. By 1910, and until Pablo Picasso eclipsed him, Sorolla was the most famous Spanish artist in the world. When he died in 1923, he was given a state funeral.

Sorolla became renowned for evoking the play of brilliant sunlight on water, often near his hometown of Valencia. His bold handling of paint to capture atmospheric effects can be seen in Southampton's picture, which records the overcast sky and lush hillsides so typical of the wetter climate of Spain's northern coast. Sorolla's characteristic broad sweeps of paint are especially evident in passages where he blended the still-wet paint. This technique differed from the application of small dashes of paint for which the French Impressionists became known and suggests the influence of Sargent and earlier old masters like Rubens and Frans Hals.

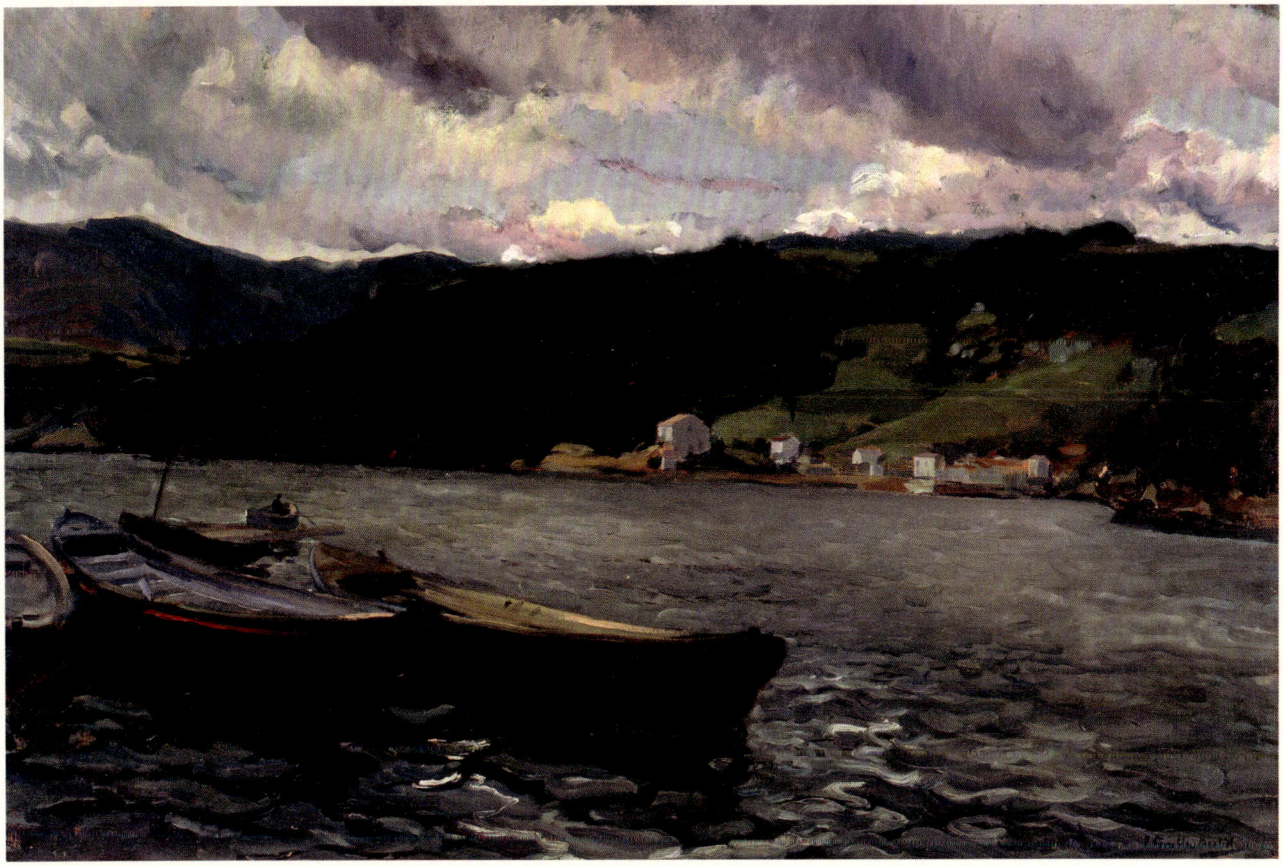

9

Sir Henry Tonks (1862–1937)

The Torn Gown, 1897

Oil on canvas, 87.2 × 72.1 cm
Purchased with the assistance of the Chipperfield Bequest Fund, 1932
Southampton City Art Gallery, SOTAG 584

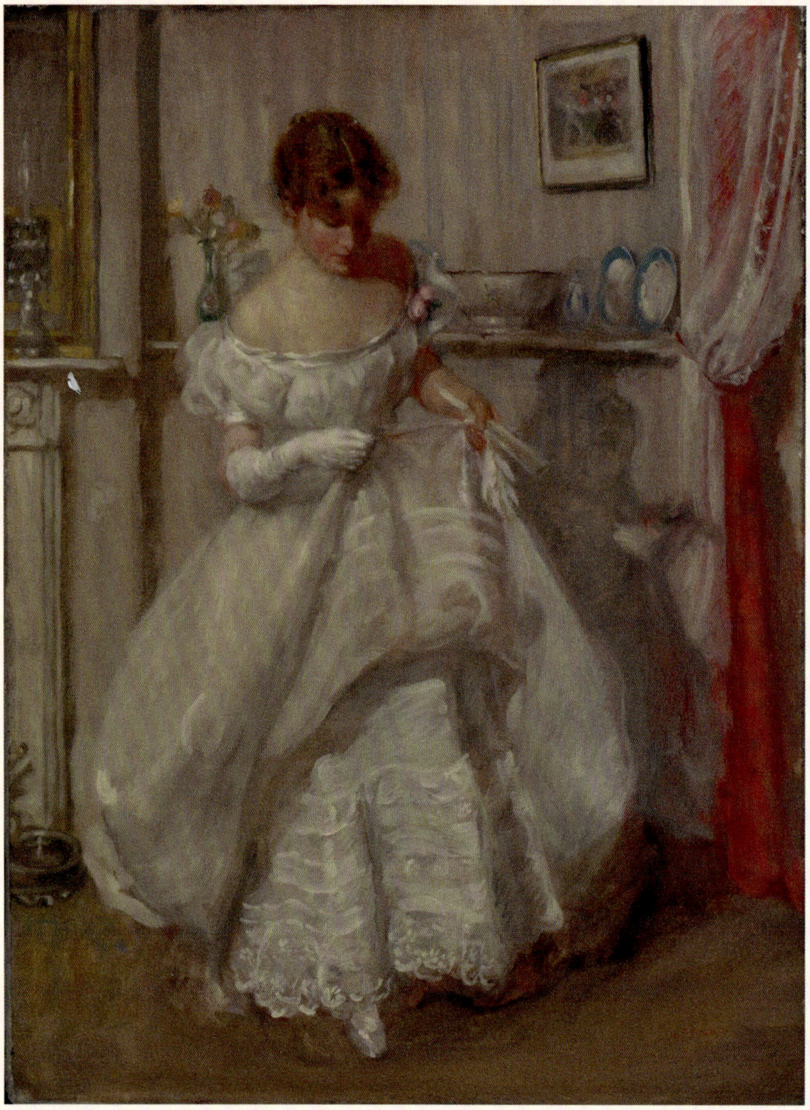

Henry Tonks qualified as a surgeon and as a teacher of anatomy in 1888, a field in which he worked until 1892, when he was appointed Slade Professor of Fine Art. He had begun studying art at Westminster School of Art in 1887, and in 1891 he exhibited for the first time at the New English Art Club, of which he became a member four years later. Tonks was one of the first British artists to be influenced by the French Impressionists, and associated with many of the more progressive Victorian British artists at the turn of the nineteenth century, including John Singer Sargent, Walter Sickert and James Abbott McNeill Whistler.

The Torn Gown is part of a series of paintings by Tonks depicting figures in white dresses. In this work, the free brushstrokes used for the dress are in contrast with the careful detail of the figure, in which the surgeon's interest in correct anatomy is evident. It was a significant early purchase for Southampton by an artist who became an influential art teacher of some of the most notable painters of their generation, namely Spencer Gore, David Bomberg, C.R.W. Nevinson, Gwen John, Paul Nash, Stanley Spencer and Mark Gertler. Largely through Tonks's teaching, the emphasis on draughtsmanship was at the heart of the Slade School curriculum at the time.

The work was purchased from the London dealer Lockett Thompson for £195 in July 1932. A label on the reverse of the canvas records that a former owner was James Staats Forbes, a Scottish railway engineer and administrator whose art collection included works by artists of the Barbizon School, Corot, nineteenth-century Dutch painters and Whistler.

10

Walter Richard Sickert (1860–1942)

The Mantelpiece, 1907

Oil on canvas, 76.2 × 50.8 cm
Purchased with the assistance of the Smith Bequest Fund, 1932
Southampton City Art Gallery, SOTAG 517

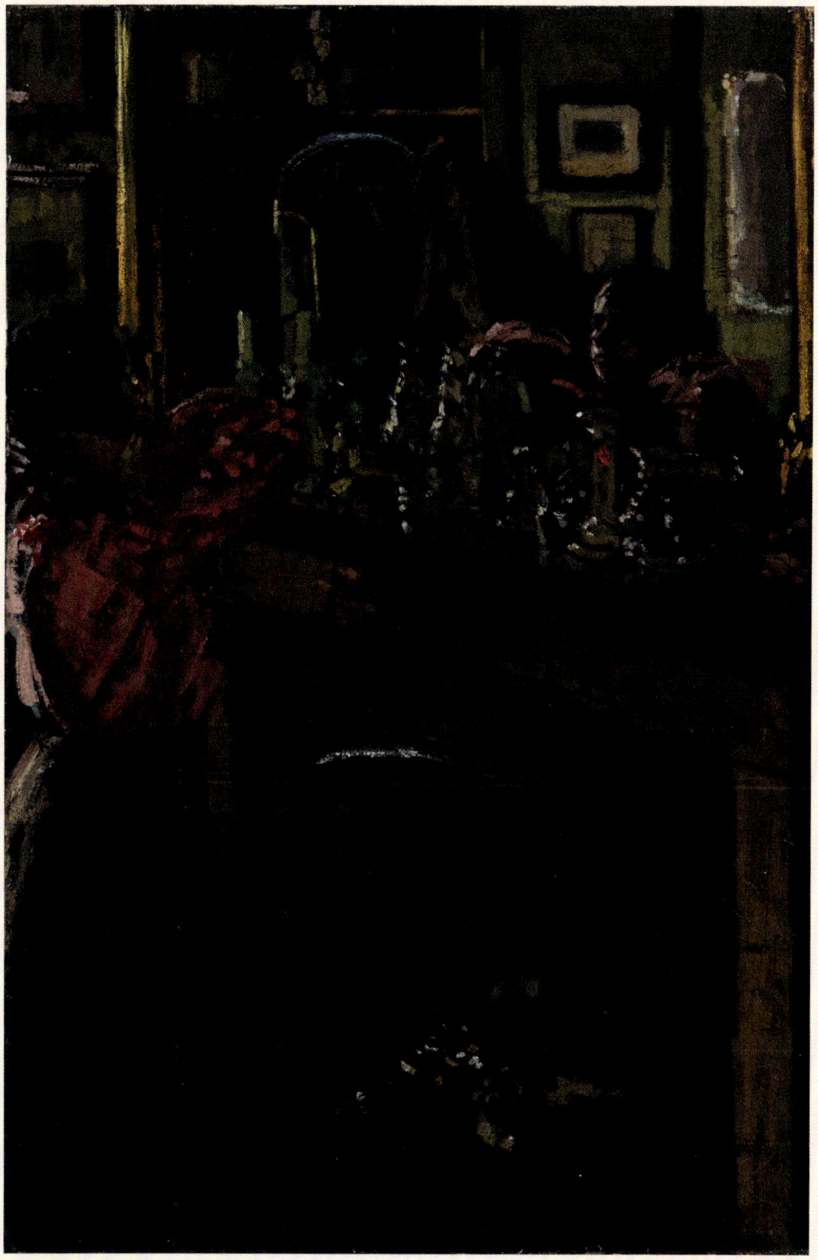

With the appointment of the director of the National Gallery as art adviser to Southampton, there was a shift away from acquiring British art with local connections. Instead, the advice from London was to think more ambitiously about buying work by native painters with national or international reputations. The purchases of the early 1930s, which included this work by Sickert and others by Henry Tonks (cat. 9) and John Lavery, set a new high benchmark.

Importantly, Sickert founded the Camden Town Group in 1911 in response to modernist art movements in Europe. The name came from what at the time was a run-down neighbourhood of London where several of the artists lived, and the group become known for painting scenes of contemporary urban life. Due to the shrewd buying by Southampton's first two curators, Southampton City Art Gallery now holds the best collection of Camden Town Group paintings outside London.

Having bought its first Sickert in 1932, Southampton's newly appointed curator, (George) Loraine Conran, secured *The Tichborne Claimant* (fig. 39) seven years later, a work that was of considerable interest, according to Kenneth Clark. Later, in 1951, Conran's successor, Maurice Palmer, purchased *The Juvenile Lead* (1908), which he described as 'a most important picture from the Gallery point of view'.[3]

The Mantelpiece has appeared in many exhibitions, including one organised during the Second World War at the National Gallery, as part of an initiative to share great art with a war-torn nation. A decade later, in 1951, Southampton dedicated one of its first home-grown exhibitions to the Camden Town Group. The event was part of the country's 'Festival of Britain' and is now recognised as having sparked a new national interest in this school of painting.

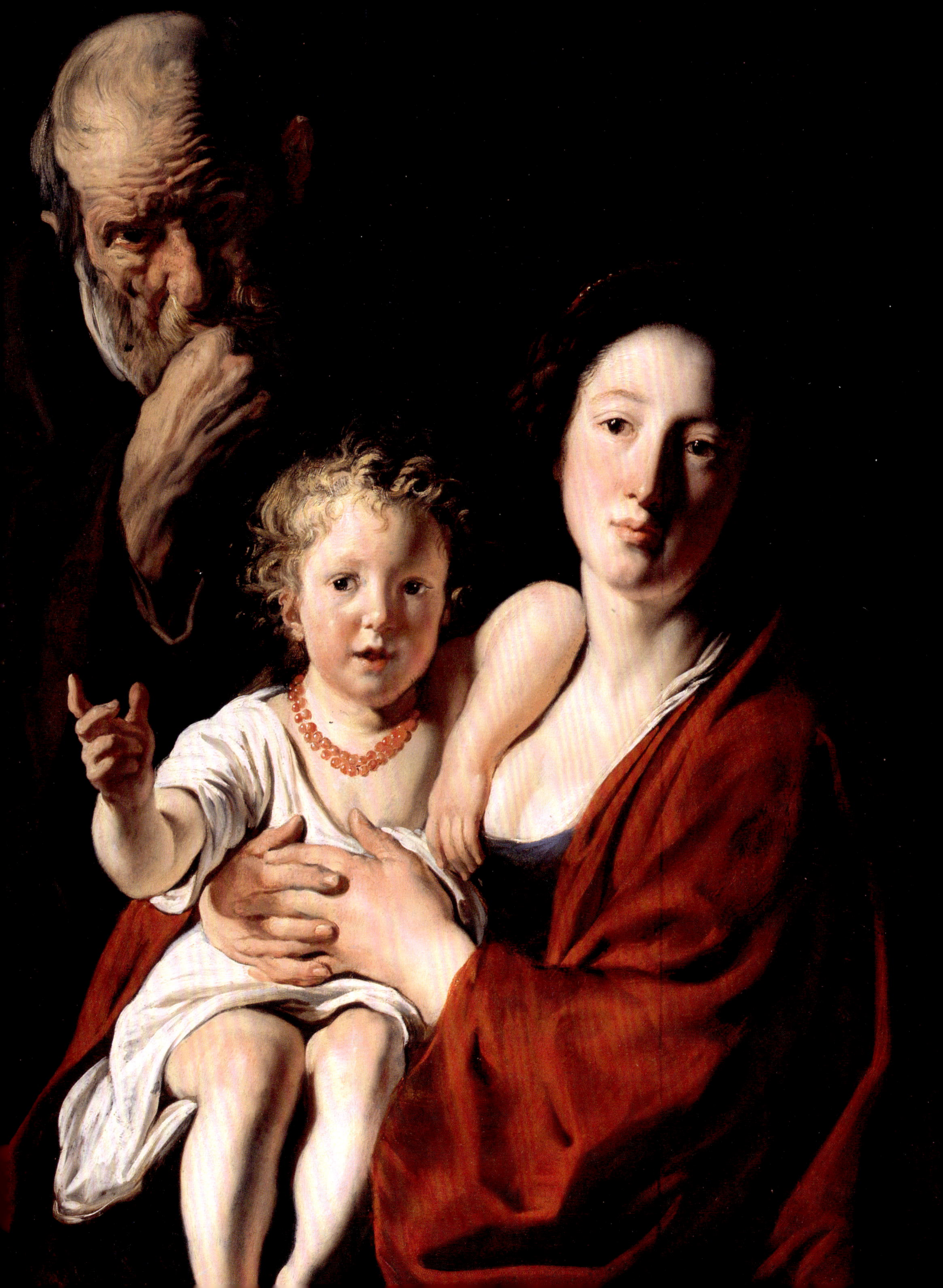

SOLID FOUNDATIONS

Becoming a Collection of National Significance (1934–45)

3

During the 11 years that Kenneth ('K') Clark (1903–1983; fig. 24) was director at the National Gallery, the relationship between the London institution and Southampton Art Gallery became much closer and more committed. The period saw Southampton develop a collection of extraordinary ambition and growing national significance.

Clark was just 30 when he took up his post at Trafalgar Square. In addition to youthful energy, he had much to offer in terms of expertise, experience, contacts and vision. The son of a wealthy Scottish businessman, Clark's artistic inclinations led him, after studying at Oxford University, to work for the eminent art historian Bernard Berenson at Villa I Tatti near Florence. Clark subsequently became celebrated for his innovative stewardship of the National Gallery during and after the Second World War. Among other things, he introduced a more modern and less cluttered hang, and set up a scientific department. After seeking advice from a PR company about how to increase visitor numbers, Clark introduced certain novelties such as putting on shorter public lectures (reduced from two hours to just one) and selling pocket guides (to counterbalance specialist official catalogues) and postcards – whose sales helped to pay for running costs associated with the scientific department.

Despite these and other significant achievements, Clark's directorship was not free from tensions with dominant trustees such as the art dealer Joseph (Joe) Duveen, and senior staff including Isherwood Kay. Other tensions arose as a result of some of his purchases. While Clark secured some truly significant pictures, notably William Hogarth's *The Graham Children*, Peter Paul Rubens's *The Watering Place* and Vincent van Gogh's *Sunflowers*, his 'Dürer' *Virgin and Child* was quickly reattributed as not by the master and, most controversially, four panels that he purchased with much pomp and ceremony in 1937, as by the Venetian painter Giorgione, were

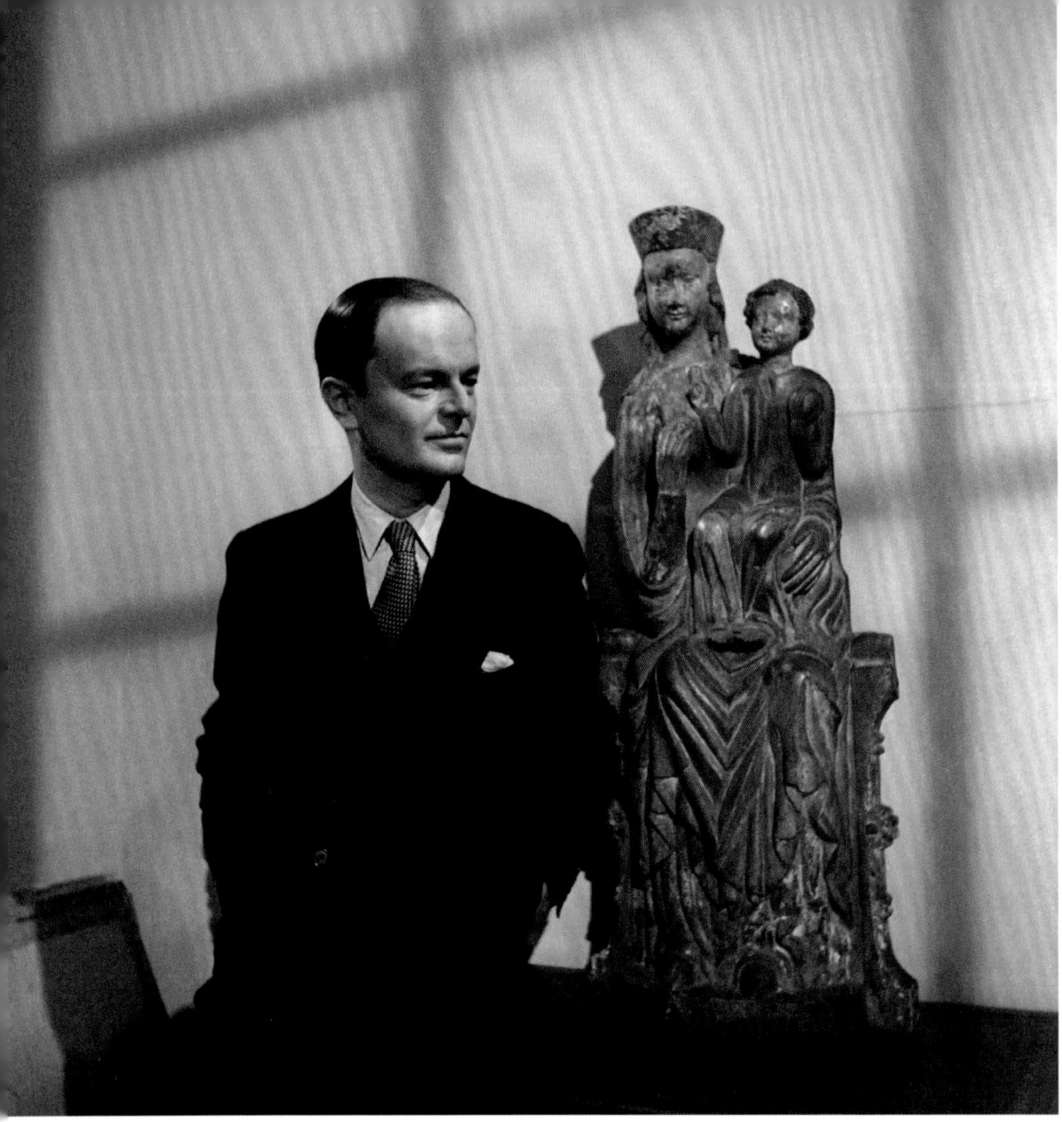

PREVIOUS PAGE
Jacob Jordaens (1593–1678)
The Holy Family, before 1628; detail, cat. 12
Oil on canvas, 105.8 × 75.5 cm
Southampton City Art Gallery, SOTAG 315

FIG. 24
Kenneth Clark, Director of the National Gallery, 1934–45. National Portrait Gallery, London

quickly downgraded as the work of a less significant contemporary, Andrea Previtali. Neither did Gallery trustees or staff approve of all his proposed purchases. For instance, Clark recalled that the board never failed to dismiss Eugène Delacroix as 'a tiresome, second-rate painter'.[1] By contrast, Clark's relationship with those in charge of running Southampton's art gallery was comparatively straightforward and harmonious.

Clark's work for Southampton is best seen as part of his larger ambition to expand a love of art throughout the nation. On one occasion, he told the art critic Clive Bell: 'Of course I don't go lecturing in Manchester for the sake of fame or fortune – in fact I am never paid, I go from the vague feeling that it encourages people to take an interest in the National Gallery and in painting generally.'[2] During his time as Southampton's art adviser, major milestones were reached: Southampton Art Gallery first opened in a bespoke building, appointed its first permanent curator and developed an ambitious new profile as the UK's leading gallery in the south of England. Having committed itself to an expanded collecting remit encompassing old masters as well as important modern British and foreign art within the figurative tradition, Southampton's art gallery came into regular contact with leading art dealers. Clark also ensured that power was largely removed from Southampton's city councillors in terms of decision-making, and vested instead in himself and Southampton Art Gallery's first curator.

From the start, Clark proved himself a staunch ally. He made a point of meeting members of the Chipperfield Bequest Sub-Committee as early as 7 May 1934 in London (he had been appointed in January),[3] and he intervened just two months later to ensure that plans for a purpose-built art gallery were not jeopardised. The problem was raised thanks to the ever-vigilant Reginald Gleadowe, who wrote, introducing himself as the person who had 'acted as Deputy for Daniel in certain matters' and therefore as knowing 'something of local tendencies and personalities'. Gleadowe explained: 'It appears that plans for a fine Art Gallery at Southampton have recently been modified as to combine a curtailed Gallery with a Public Library: and that this modification needs carefully looking into.'[4] Clark immediately wrote to Southampton, asking for clarification, stating he knew that a 'certain definite sum' had been allocated specifically for building the art gallery. He went on to say that 'any modification or diminution of the scheme' should be made in consultation with him to ensure that the construction of the art gallery would not be threatened by any other project.[5]

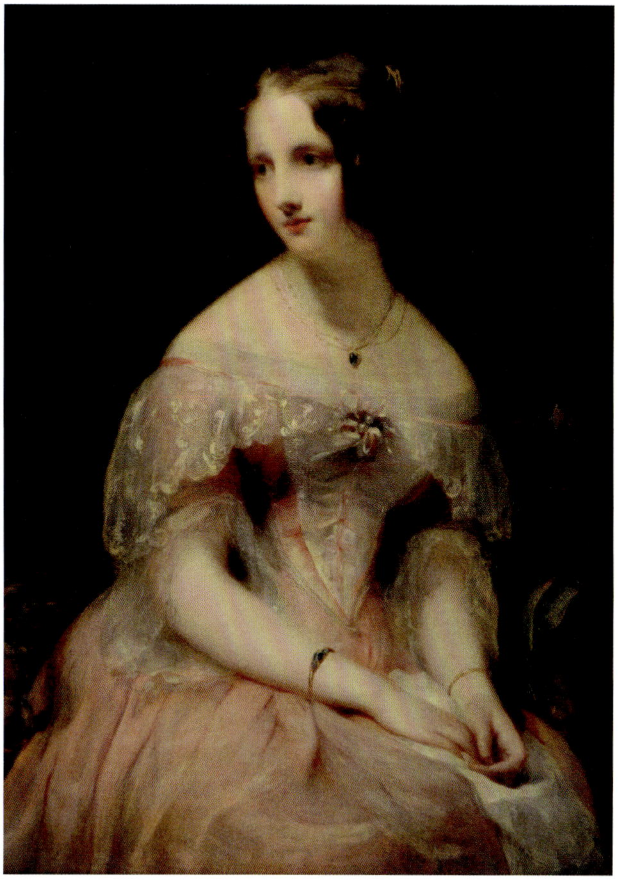

FIG. 25
Richard Rothwell (1800–1868)
Portrait of a Lady
Oil on canvas, 97 × 71.8 cm
Southampton City Art Gallery, SOTAG 482

Expanding the collection: historic and modern British art, and continental old masters

In July 1934, Clark encouraged the Chipperfield Bequest Sub-Committee to refine its collecting strategy, restating the case his predecessor Augustus Daniel had made, albeit in more forceful terms. The catalyst for his intervention was a discussion over the merits of the potential acquisition of *Portrait of a Lady* by Richard Rothwell (fig. 25), a pupil of the great Regency portraitist Sir Thomas Lawrence. The then owner, a Mr Enness, had written to the Sub-Committee that the work would 'give a great deal of pleasure in Southampton and at least will not offend or harm',[6] a verdict that encouraged Clark to submit a nuanced response. On the one hand, he confessed to not finding the work appealing on an aesthetic level, describing it as having 'many of the weaknesses of nineteenth century art', and therefore concluding, 'I should not advise a well-established gallery to buy it.' On the other hand, he said, 'it is perhaps desirable that a new gallery ... should contain a few pictures with a frankly popular appeal and I have no doubt that this picture will give great pleasure.'[7] Clark clearly believed that this type of purchase would keep the general public happy while pictures of a different

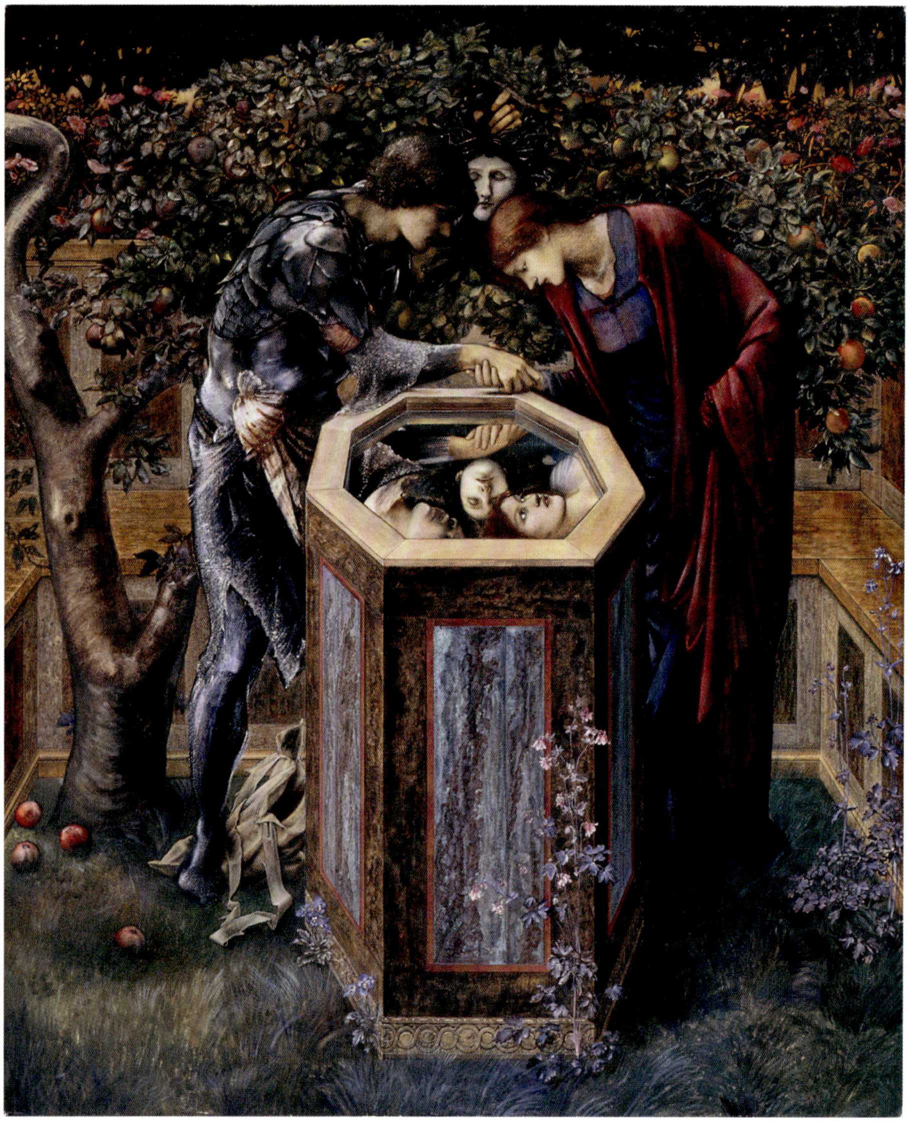

FIG. 26
Sir Edward Burne-Jones (1833–1898)
The Baleful Head (from the *Perseus Series*), about 1876
Mixed media on paper, 153.7 × 129 cm
Southampton City Art Gallery, SOTAG 108

FIG. 27
The *Perseus Series* on display in Southampton City Art Gallery. Southampton Cultural Services

kind were introduced. Southampton, presumably relieved by Clark's expedient response, snapped up the work.

Clark, however, made it clear that he felt that Southampton should refrain from purchasing what he regarded as less exciting works from the Royal Academy. In line with his predecessor's views, Clark urged Southampton to use its financial advantage to best effect by purchasing fewer, more significant works. On 21 June 1935, the Chipperfield Bequest Sub-Committee wrote for consent to acquire nine pictures from the recent Summer Exhibition, telling Clark: 'The Sub-Committee feel that if you will lend your valuable assistance in this direction, the building up of the Chipperfield collection will be proceeding on the right lines.'[8] But just the month before, Clark had boldly stated his position: 'I would like to repeat what I said last year; viz. that it is unadvisable for a growing art gallery to buy its pictures at the Royal Academy. The Royal Academy does not attract the best talent of the country and the prices are well above what they would be under any other circumstances.'[9] He would continue to state this point of view[10] – a perspective not unique to Clark.

Clark's first chance to show exactly what he believed to be a suitable acquisition came in October 1934, when he endorsed the purchase of a series of pictures depicting the story of Perseus and Andromeda by Edward Burne-Jones, one of the last of the British Pre-Raphaelites (fig. 26). This important cycle of gouache cartoons was being offered by Lady Violet Henderson, wife of a local Tory MP.[11] Recommending its purchase, Clark explained that the series would be 'a very interesting addition to, or rather nucleus of, the Southampton collection.'[12] His detailed response outlined a range of benefits that he envisaged would arise from the purchase. As a great example of historical British art, he predicted that the presence of the series in Southampton would ensure increased visitor numbers, an important incentive for any new art gallery. Clark also referred to the acquisition as financially astute. He foresaw that the fashion for Burne-Jones would experience a revival. Ever sure in his convictions, he announced that it was a 'good moment to buy', recommending that an offer in the region of £3,500 would be fair, even though the series had been valued far higher at probate at £6,000.[13] Realising that the cartoons' vast size would impact on the building's plans since the series would best 'be treated as the decoration of a single room,'[14] Clark made it his business in November 1936 to meet with the architect, Ernest Berry Webber, who was then in the process of designing Southampton's new civic centre (fig. 27).

Soon afterwards, Clark was again asked his opinion about the *Perseus Series* when the Chipperfield Bequest Sub-Committee received its first loan request. It came from the British Institute of Adult Education (BIoAE) and concerned an exhibition it was organising at Swindon.[15] Always with an eye on promoting the collection, Clark was in favour of lending all 10 pictures until such time

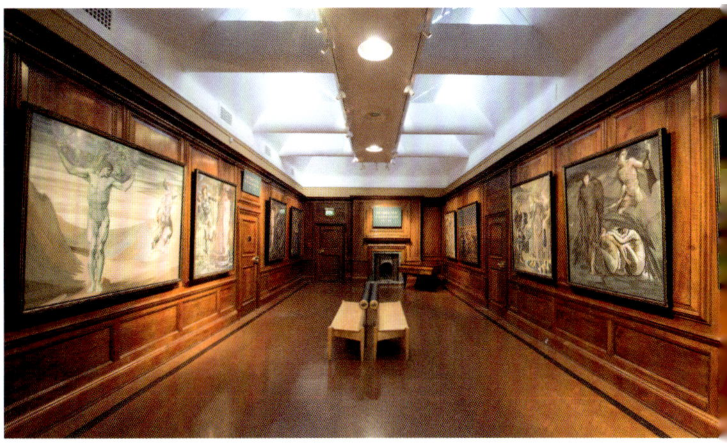

as 'it [was] possible to put them on exhibition in Southampton'.[16] Clark went so far as to send a copy of the National Gallery's 'Regulation for Loans' policy as a template. He also suggested that the Sub-Committee should visit prospective venues to check that they were fire-proof and had appropriate climate controls and security measures in place.[17]

This significant and strategic purchase was soon added to by other related purchases and gifts; time and again a key purchase acted as a starting point around which subsequent acquisitions from the same artist or school were strategically clustered. In the case of British Pre-Raphaelite art, only two years later, in 1936, money from the Smith Bequest Fund was used to buy *Cordelia's Portion* by Ford Madox Brown (1821–1893). The painter was closely associated with the original Pre-Raphaelite Brotherhood, having for a short time taught Dante Gabriel Rossetti, a founding member. Southampton Art Gallery also received two related significant gifts over the next two decades. The first was a work by one of the founders – William Holman Hunt (1827–1910) – whose *Afterglow in Egypt* was presented in 1946 by Dr H.H. Clarke (fig. 45). The second, another painting by Burne-Jones (*Launcelot at the Chapel of the Holy Grail*), was bequeathed in 1958 by the British painter, illustrator and author Graham Robertson. All of these works demonstrate typical Pre-Raphaelite qualities of medievalism, bright

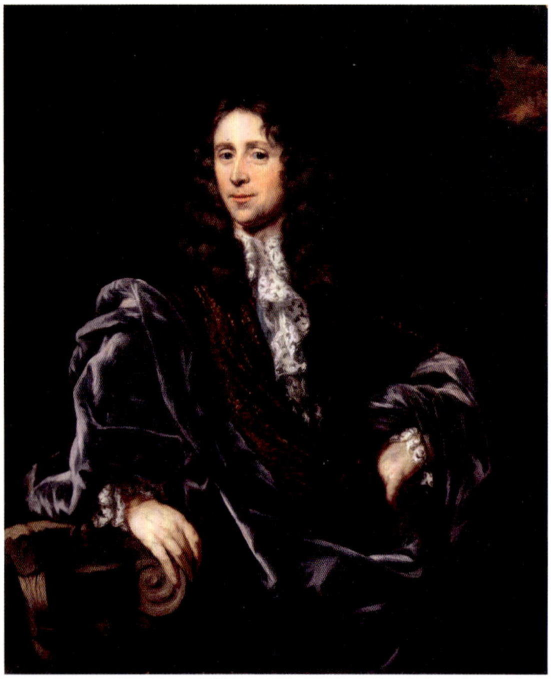

FIG. 28
Nicolaes Maes (1634–1693),
Portrait of a Man, 1670s or 1680s
Oil on canvas, 68.5 × 58.5 cm
Southampton City Art Gallery,
SOTAG 385

FIG. 29
Nicolaes Maes (1634–1693)
Portrait of Jan de Reus, 1670s
Oil on canvas, 79 × 62.5 cm
The National Gallery, London,
NG2581

colouring and fine detail. This new group ensured that Southampton's holdings of Pre-Raphaelite art was able to stand up against those which had been built up previously by the city art galleries in Birmingham and Liverpool, in the 1880s and 1890s, respectively.[18]

Alongside Southampton's entry into the field of historical British art, Clark encouraged another new acquisition track – namely, securing good quality continental art from the past. To his mind, this was to be done systematically so that a meaningful narrative of Western European art might be told on the walls of Southampton's art gallery. This was in contrast to showing a few old masters out of context in what was essentially a modern collection, as had happened earlier in Leeds when its art gallery was given a few old masters by Pietro da Cortona and Ambrogio Bergognone, and in Birmingham when its art gallery had acquired a Murillo and a Charles Le Brun.[19] Southampton's first foray into this field resulted in the purchase of three seventeenth-century paintings, albeit pictures which, then as now, were rated as of second rank. This was a deliberate ploy on Clark's part, whose initial encouragement to purchase representative works by lesser-known artists or works that may not have been considered of outstanding merit, meant that Southampton's limited funds could go further while creating a respectable foundation of historical art from which to cultivate a new and ambitious collection.

The *Portrait of a Lady* (about 1660s) was acquired as a work by Massimo Stanzione, an Italian painter whose success in Naples equalled that of his rival Jusepe de Ribera, although now the picture is catalogued as by the lesser-known north Italian artist Girolamo Forabosco. The other two acquisitions were both Dutch seventeenth-century works of more significance: Nicolaes Maes's *Portrait of a Man* (fig. 28; cat. 11) and Jan Hackaert's *The Avenue*, the latter sold at a reduced price thanks to Clark's intervention.[20]

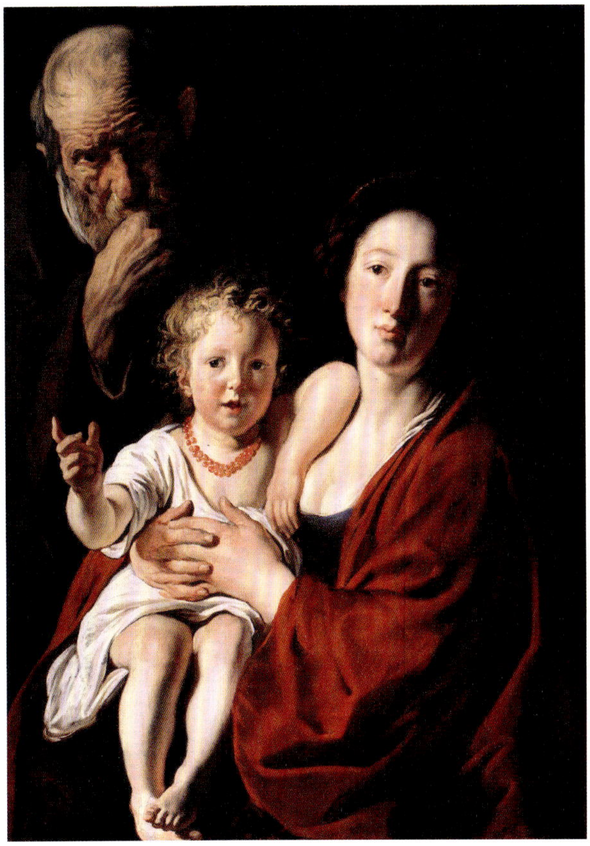

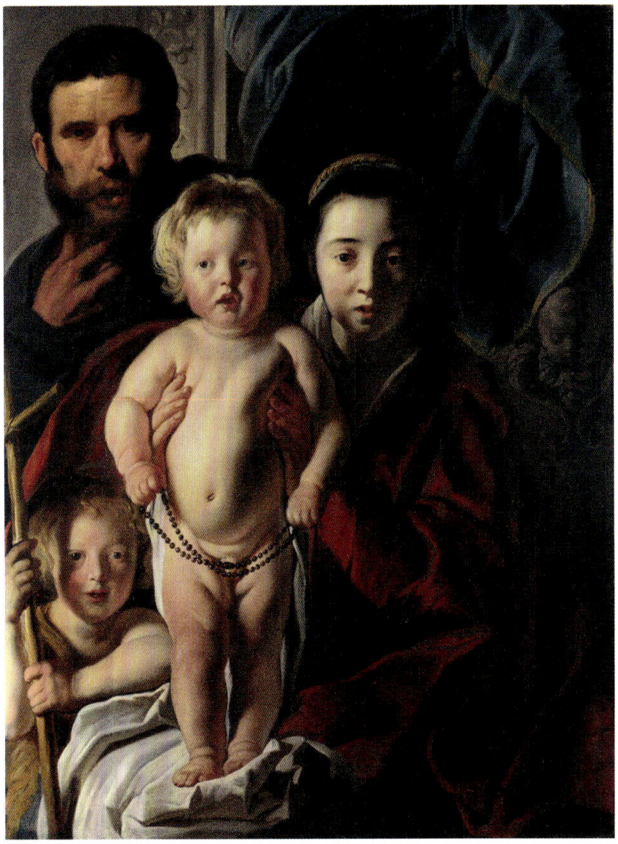

FIG. 30
Jacob Jordaens (1593–1678)
The Holy Family, before 1628
Oil on canvas, 105.8 × 75.5 cm
Southampton City Art Gallery, SOTAG 315

FIG. 31
Jacob Jordaens (1593–1678)
The Holy Family and Saint John the Baptist, probably 1620–25
Oil on oak, 123 × 93.9 cm
The National Gallery, London, NG164

By this time, the National Gallery owned seven works by Maes, including three half-length male portraits; of these, two had been acquired relatively recently through bequests of the 1910s. Its *Portrait of Jan de Reus* (fig. 29), a Rotterdam silk merchant and a director of the Dutch East India Company, is a particularly fine and striking image.

The historical European collection at Southampton reached a milestone the following year with the very important purchase of Jacob Jordaens's *Holy Family* (fig. 30; cat. 12). This work has clear visual links with the National Gallery's own Jordaens, *The Holy Family and Saint John the Baptist* (fig. 31), acquired half a century earlier in 1883. Clark himself proposed the Jordaens for Southampton as a potentially eligible purchase to show how committed he was to offering alternative suggestions whenever the proposals he received from the Chipperfield Bequest Sub-Committee were not to the mark. On this occasion, the Jordaens was a substitute for the nine works noted earlier, which had been proposed as potential purchases from the Royal Academy's Summer Exhibition. Keen to promote this single old master in their place, Clark speedily announced he would contact the London dealer Arthur Tooth and 'instruct [him] to send you a photograph of it, giving the price and dimensions.'[21] Outmanoeuvred by Clark's nimble footwork, and perhaps reassured by the reasonable price tag of £450, the Chipperfield Bequest Sub-

Committee fell into line. The town clerk admitted to Clark that 'in view of your recommendation, I feel sure that the Town Council will purchase it.'[22] This acquisition of an acknowledged continental old master is a prime example of the activity that took place early on in relation to Southampton Art Gallery as a result of the National Gallery's timely interventions. Indeed, these first old master acquisitions were not only intrinsically important but also historically significant, because they sent out a clear signal about the new direction in which this particular regional art gallery was heading.

An acquisition policy for Southampton Art Gallery

No doubt it was partly to encourage further boldness in the old master art market that Clark wrote a letter on 14 March 1936 to Councillor George Waller, chair of the Chipperfield Bequest Sub-Committee, following on from an earlier discussion between its members and Clark on 26 February. This letter is of vital historical importance because its contents became the basis of a new acquisition policy for Southampton Art Gallery. Clark laid out four areas which he thought should comprise its future acquisition policy – with a hint of how much time, money and hanging space should be dedicated to each. Based on the assumption of an annual income of about £1,200–1,500, he suggested that:

> [...] the gallery ought to comprise the following: -
>
> (i) A large and continually growing collection of modern painting in oils, occupying perhaps one large and one small gallery;
>
> (ii) A smaller and comparatively static collection of nineteenth century painting of a popular (Royal Academy) kind. Examples can be bought for next to nothing, and if carefully chosen, this section of the Gallery could be popular without being disgraceful. It could occupy one fair-sized room.
>
> (iii) A collection of old masters. The extent of this would depend entirely on the opportunities which offered themselves. While the collection was still small, it could be helped out by loans.
>
> (iv) A collection of watercolours and drawings. These could be had very cheaply and are always a popular feature of a gallery, as they appeal to the small private collector.[23]

Clark anticipated that council members would not object to points 2 and 4 given that they were both traditional areas of British collecting, and ones with which Southampton was already familiar. The novel aspects were modern art (but not abstract art which Clark never took to) and especially the old masters. Realising the likelihood of potential opposition from councillors, Clark attempted to alleviate anticipated concerns. To counter any idea that collecting historical art might be expensive and risky, Clark noted that 'old masters, if prudently bought, are the cheapest of all works of art.' Elsewhere, he would underscore the fact that it was an optimum time for Southampton to acquire old masters given 'the falling off of the American market'.[24] Arguing the point from the opposite angle, he reminded the Sub-Committee: 'your resources are very much greater, for example, than those of the Tate.' To defend such art against the accusation that it would not attract visitors, Clark argued that it would, on the contrary, open up the art gallery to new sorts of highly desirable visitors from beyond the local Hampshire area: 'although [old masters] may not have an immediate popular appeal, [they] can give a gallery great prestige and make it an attraction to visitors from other parts of England, or from abroad.'

Clark ended his letter by suggesting that the art collection would benefit from having a 'first-rate adviser' until such time that its collection was sufficiently large to warrant the appointment of a 'director'. If the adviser were given 'a comparatively free hand', they would be able to 'create a gallery which would be the envy, not only of all provincial towns, but of the London galleries.' Clark, a natural orator, clearly wished to paint a picture of a bright and financially secure future for Southampton Art Gallery, so long as it followed the path he suggested. In a subsequent letter of 1 April 1936, he reiterated this message, noting that if the Chipperfield Bequest Fund was appropriately deployed, it 'should be possible to make the Southampton Gallery one of the finest in England outside London'.[25]

Clark's suggestions were taken up in their entirety, both in relation to the type of paintings that should be acquired and the necessity of appointing a 'technical adviser'. The paperwork also confirmed that 'the selection and purchase of pictures' would be undertaken by the National Gallery director 'with the help of the Technical Adviser'.[26] These points became the core of a 'Policy for the Purchase of Pictures', proposed by the Chipperfield Bequest Sub-Committee (2 April), and then ratified first by the full committee (7 April) and then by the borough council (25 April).

Clark's help was as practical as it was theoretical. In the meeting between him and the Chipperfield Bequest Sub-Committee of 26 February 1936, he expressed himself 'very willing' to 'take a more active part in the consideration and selection of pictures' and 'made suggestions to that end, including an offer to acquaint [the Sub-Committee] with suitable pictures he might find on his visits to Paris, etc.'[27] Clark's suggestion was gratefully accepted and over the next few years, true to his word, he informed the Chipperfield Bequest Sub-Committee of eligible paintings for sale abroad.[28] Recommending that it was 'usually better [i.e. cheaper] to buy at sales in London than from private collections in the country',[29] Clark occasionally arranged for bidding to take place on Southampton's behalf at London auctions,[30] and regularly arranged for London dealers to send pictures to Southampton for first-hand inspection. However, believing that opportunities were lost whenever a dealer could not be persuaded to 'send the original down to Southampton', Clark suggested that the Sub-Committee should start making 'periodical visits to London'.[31] Furthermore, he tutored the Sub-Committee on how to secure the most favourable deals: on a case-by-case basis, he would explain how particular dealers and artists should be handled. As part of his overarching plan 'to get satisfactory pictures for much smaller sums than has hitherto been possible',[32] Clark also suggested that he should be authorised to purchase pictures up to a certain amount rather than having to wait – and thereby lose precious time – for the Sub-Committee's permission to proceed. The initiative was adopted with £300 set as the first cap from September 1937;[33] thereafter the matter was regularly reviewed to take account of rising prices and inflation. Generally open to suggestion, Clark was, however, never afraid to use his power of veto to block works of art that he deemed were unsuitable for Southampton's collection – usually because he regarded them as unimportant, badly painted or overpriced. For such reasons, pictures by Lawrence Alma Tadema (1836–1912) and James Ensor (1860–1949) were not pursued.[34]

The results of the new acquisition policy were quickly apparent.[35] In 1936 Southampton secured several other interesting and good historical pictures – even if their modest prices indicated that they were then not considered outstanding. R.E.A. Wilson, a London art dealer based in Ryder Street, St. James's, approached the Chipperfield Bequest Sub-Committee with three works, including Sofonisba Anguissola's *The Artist's Sister in the Garb of a Nun* (fig. 32, cat. 13). That picture was purchased for the modest sum of £60.[36] Anguissola, a late Renaissance painter from Cremona in Northern Italy, was one of the first and few known women to have established

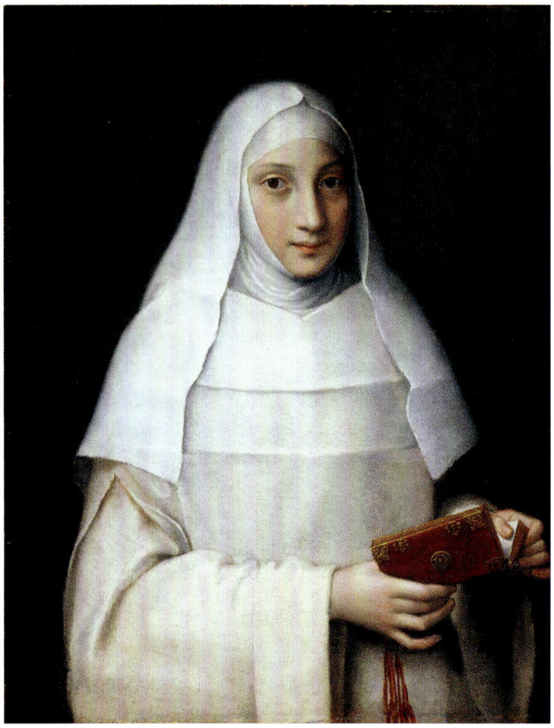

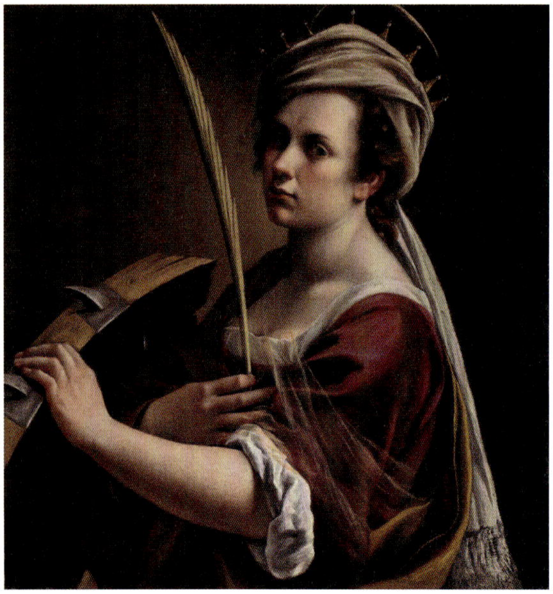

FIG. 32
Sofonisba Anguissola
(about 1532–1625)
The Artist's Sister in the Garb of a Nun, 1551
Oil on canvas, 68.5 × 53.3 cm
Southampton City Art Gallery, SOTAG 3

FIG. 33
Artemisia Gentileschi
(1593–1654 or later)
Self Portrait as Saint Catherine of Alexandria, about 1615–17
Oil on canvas, 71.4 × 69 cm
The National Gallery, London, NG6671

an international reputation as an artist; she was even praised in Giorgio Vasari's celebrated *Lives of the Most Excellent Painters, Sculptors and Architects* (first published in 1550). This painting is the only one by Anguissola in any public UK collection, and is the artist's earliest known dated work. Despite an inscription on its reverse confirming the painting to be by Anguissola, it was attributed for years to Titian due to its exceptional quality. Indeed, it is only recently that other outstanding portraits, previously misattributed to celebrated male artists such as El Greco and Antonis Mor, have been correctly reassigned to Anguissola.[37] Although the National Gallery has never owned an example of Anguissola's work, in 2018 it did acquire a significant work by another 'old mistress': Artemisia Gentileschi's *Self Portrait as Saint Catherine of Alexandria* of about 1615–17 (fig. 33). The recent turn in art history to challenge the parameters of the 'old master' canon has started to encourage the rediscovery of accomplished female artists such as Anguissola and Gentileschi.

Two other painting were also acquired in the same transaction with R.E.A. Wilson: Domenico Feti's *Rebecca at the Well* for £60 and *The Young Poet* (cat. 14) for £100, the latter as a work Jan van Bylert but now catalogued as by his contemporary and a fellow Utrecht painter, Johannes Moreelse.[38] Clark commented on the high quality of the frames round all three works and how they 'form[ed] part of the charm of the pictures'.[39]

The Chipperfield Bequest Fund was dipped into again the following year for *Allegory of Winter* by another Dutch artist, Caesar Boëtius van Everdingen (fig. 34, cat. 15). In this instance, it was Clark who put forward the painting, describing it as an 'unusually attractive work by a painter whose reputation will stand much higher in the future than it does to-day.'[40] He suggested that it would appeal to the general public and scholars alike, and that an additional advantage was its modest asking price.[41] The memorable image, depicting a young woman warming her hands above a

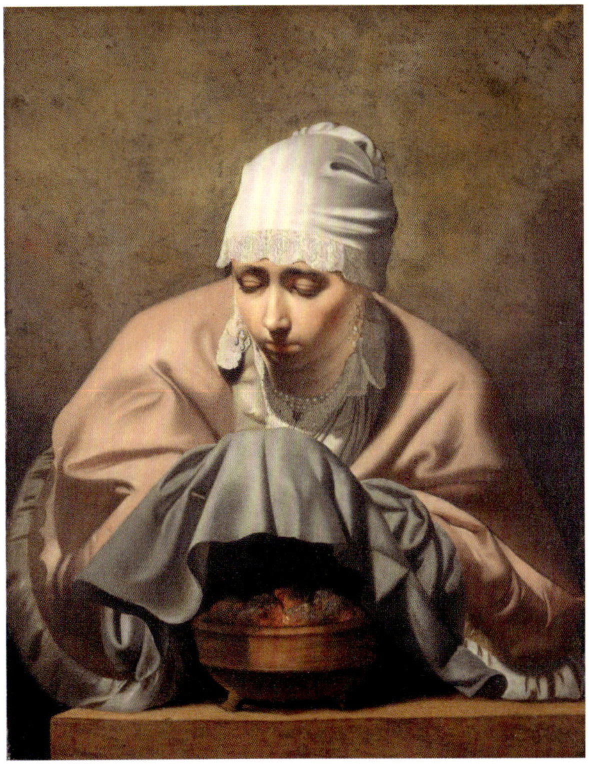

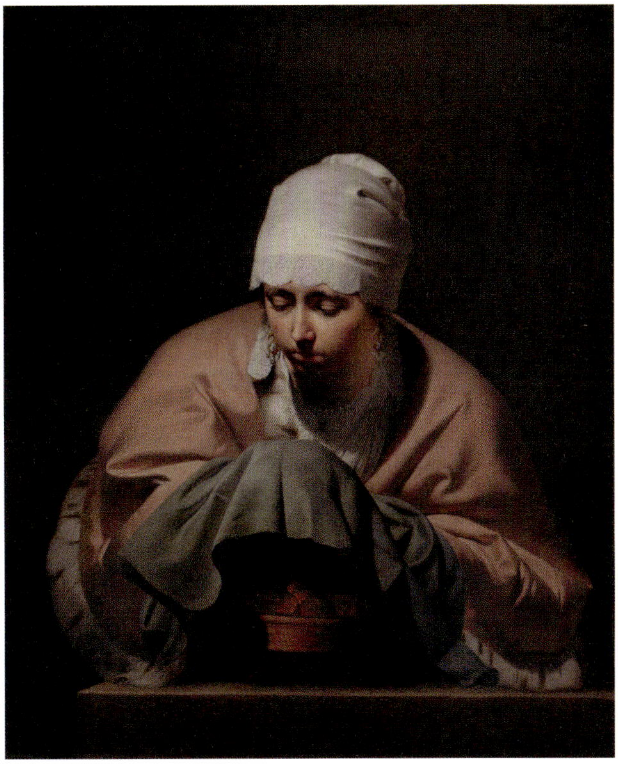

dish of glowing coals, personifies the season of Winter. This purchase was a coup given that the Rijksmuseum, Amsterdam, had also considered the work. Presumably, the Dutch institution regretted not having secured the painting for it went on to purchase a version in 1991 (fig. 35). Although the Dutch museum considers its version to be the original and Southampton's to be a replica on which pupils may have collaborated, van Everdingen's originality can be seen in the Southampton picture in the exquisite rose colour of the woman's dress and her gentle, almost sultry expression.

FIG. 34
Cesar Boëtius van Everdingen (about 1616–1678)
Allegory of Winter, 1650
Oil on canvas, 91.8 × 71.2 cm
Southampton City Art Gallery, SOTAG 188

FIG. 35
Caesar Boëtius van Everdingen (about 1616–1678)
A Young Woman warming her Hands over a Brazier: Allegory of Winter, about 1644–48
Oil on canvas, 97 × 81 cm
Rijksmuseum, Amsterdam, inv. no. SK-A-4878

Clark also oversaw the purchase through the Chipperfield Bequest Fund of some significant nineteenth-century pictures. In terms of modern French art, Clark helped Southampton to acquire a strong nucleus of Impressionist painting, building on the Boudin purchased during Daniel's directorship (discussed in Chapter 2). In 1936, Southampton bought Alfred Sisley's (1839–1899) *Avenue of Chestnut Trees near La Celle-St-Cloud* and Camille Pissarro's *View from the Versailles Road, Louveciennes* (cat. 16), works painted within a few years of each other. Both were created outdoors – a radical innovation in painting practice of the 1860s, when most painters still usually only made sketches outside, producing finished works for exhibition and sale in their studios. It was also in 1936 that Southampton bought *Vue de la Butte, Montmartre* by Stanislas Lépine (1835–1892), directly from Kenneth Clark.[42] In the following decades, Southampton would continue to expand its Impressionist collection, buying a Corot in 1947, a Renoir in 1964, a Vuillard in 1968 and a Monet (fig. 64, cat. 41) in 1975.

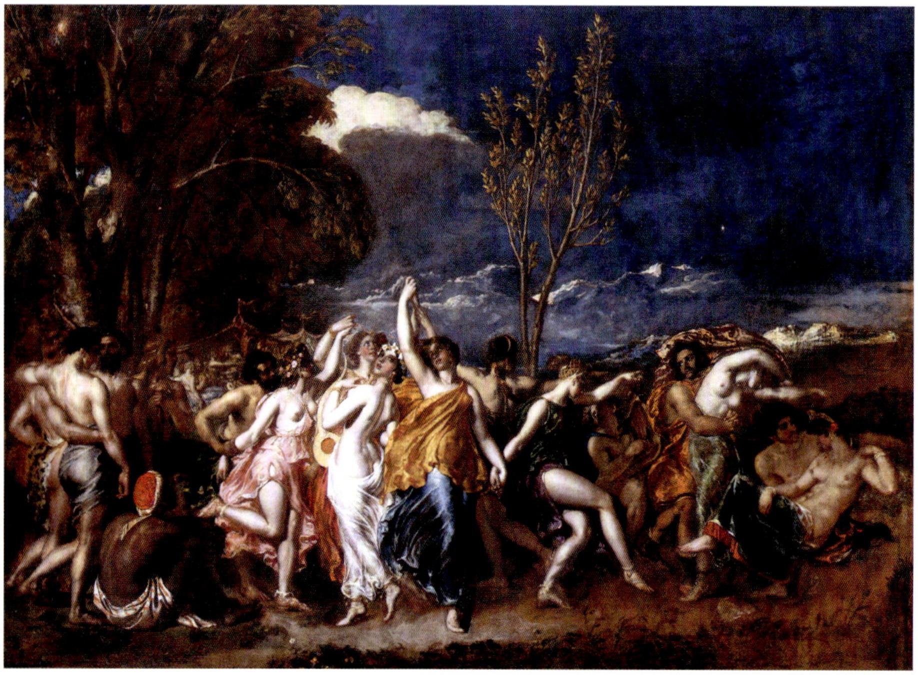

FIG. 36
William Etty (1787–1849)
The World before the Flood, 1828
Oil on canvas, 202.3 × 140 cm
Southampton City Art Gallery, SOTAG 186

FIG. 37 (OPPOSITE)
Claude Rogers (1907–1979)
Spiral Staircase, 1936
Oil on canvas, 61.3 × 51 cm
Southampton City Art Gallery, SOTAG 478

In Clark's view, his most significant acquisition for Southampton in the late 1930s was William Etty's *The World before the Flood* (fig. 36). He boldly informed the Chipperfield Bequest Sub-Committee in December 1937 that the work was 'generally regarded as the painter's masterpiece. It is a large picture ... and will make a centre for a room of 19th century English painting. I consider it to be the most important purchase I have yet been able to make for the Chipperfield Trustees.'[43] In fact, he regarded it 'so grand', that he even 'thought it ought to be considered for the national collections [i.e. the National Gallery and Tate] before being sent to Southampton'.[44] This episode may strike us as surprising today, when Etty's reputation is no longer what it once was.

The third area of collecting at Southampton masterminded by Clark was influential modern and contemporary British art. This was a field represented in Clark's own private art collection, and one connected to other aspects of his public-facing work, not least his role during the Second World War as Chair of the War Artists' Advisory Committee (WAAC), which appointed official war artists to compile a full record of Britain and its armed forces during the war. Clark's specific links with Southampton allowed him to encourage and support its Gallery's purchase of top-rate examples of modern British art, in a way that was not directly open to him in London given that the National Gallery's collection stopped, date-wise, about 1900 (later art came under the direction of the Tate Gallery of British Art, now Tate). A significant, if little recognised, legacy of Clark's work on behalf of Southampton Art Gallery is that he was able to influence some collecting for the nation in terms of modern twentieth-century art.

Southampton's first contemporary British art purchase was Claude Rogers's *Spiral Staircase* (fig. 37), bought in 1936, the year it was painted. Despite acknowledging that the artist was 'young and little-known', Clark recommended the picture as a 'beautiful piece of painting and the sort of picture which I believe the modern section of the Southampton Art Gallery ought to collect'.[45] With

William Coldstream and Victor Pasmore, Rogers went on to establish the Euston Road School in 1937. Although abstraction would become more important to his later work, Rogers remained a leading upholder of British art's sober figurative tradition.

Clark's newly gained authority to spend up to £300 on any one work was used to build up this part of Southampton's art collection. The first picture he purchased using his new powers was Harold Gilman's *Interior* of 1907, from Adam Brothers for £28, in November 1937.[46] Just one month later, he informed the Chipperfield Bequest Sub-Committee that he had bought two more twentieth-century British pictures, both from the Leicester Galleries and each costing £45: Spencer Gore's *View from a Window* (cat. 17), and Sir William Nicholson's *A Glade Near Midhurst*.[47] A third purchase in the same vein followed swiftly in February 1938. This was Henry Lamb's *Edie McNeill* (cat. 18), which Clark pronounced to be 'one of the most attractive of the artist's early works', adding: 'The chief value of the picture would be its popular appeal.'[48] A few years earlier, when asked to recommend a portrait painter to University College Southampton, Clark had singled out Lamb as 'one of the few men now painting portraits whose work is likely to survive.'[49] This important group of acquisitions by Gilman, Gore and Lamb, masterminded by Clark in 1937-38, solidified Southampton's representation of the Camden Town Group by building on earlier purchases, such as Sickert's *Mantelpiece*, discussed in Chapter 2. The National Gallery's director also secured works by artists associated with other avant-garde early twentieth-century art movements in Britain, a case in point being the Bloomsbury Group and Clark's purchase in quick succession of two works by Duncan Grant: *Thames Wharves*, purchased in 1938, and *Mrs Hammersley*, which was bought the following year because it was 'one of the best of [Grant's] small works and reasonably priced at £45.'[50]

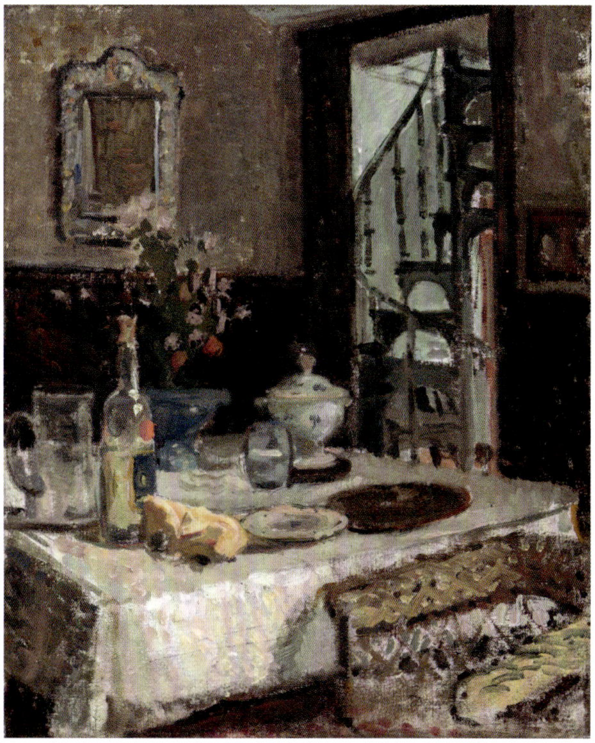

Southampton's first curator and the opening of Southampton Art Gallery

It was also with contemporary British art that Southampton Art Gallery's first curator, (George) Loraine Conran (1912–1986, fig. 38), initially made his mark. Conran, who had been deputy director of the Walker Gallery in Liverpool, was selected (with Clark's approval) in July 1938 and started work on 17 October that year.[51] The two men shared the same vision for the growth of Southampton's collection, and the management of the Chipperfield Bequest Sub-Committee. As Clark summed up in an early letter to Conran of 2 December 1938, his ambition was to acquire pictures of 'outstanding merit and a reasonable price'.[52] Their joint commitment to acquisitions explains why one of the first matters Conran attended to was increasing the amount of money that the art adviser and curator could spend without needing authorisation from the sub-

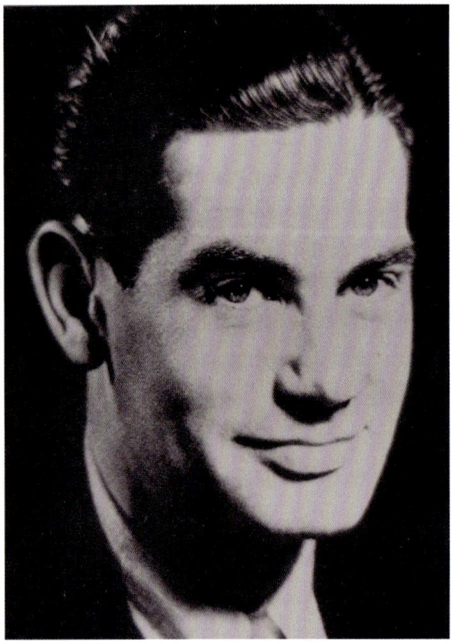

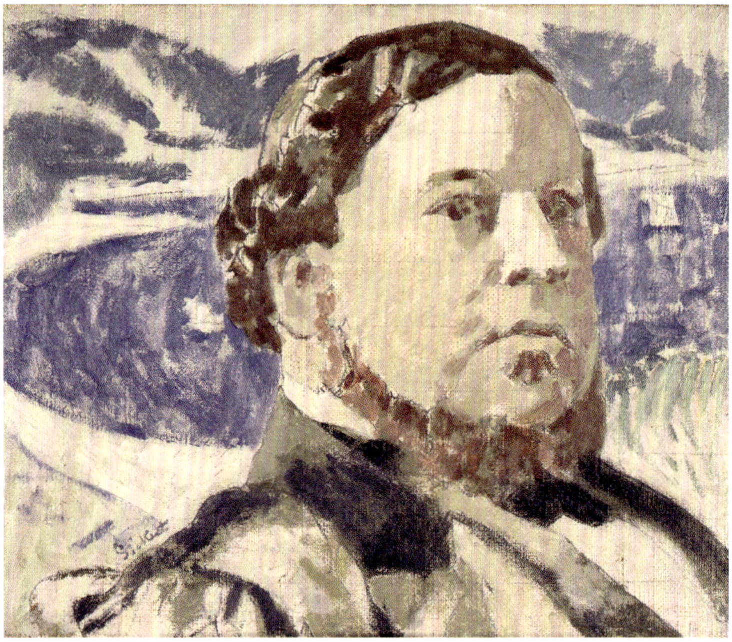

FIG. 38
Southampton's first curator, (George) Loraine Conran, photographed in about 1936. Elizabeth Conran

FIG. 39
Walter Sickert (1860–1942)
The Tichborne Claimant, 1931
Oil on canvas, 50.8 × 61 cm
Southampton City Art Gallery, SOTAG 516

committee. Conran was able to inform Clark that at his very first meeting with that body, 'it was agreed to authorize me to spend up to an aggregate of £1,000.'[53]

One of Conran's first purchases was Sickert's *The Tichborne Claimant* (fig. 39), purchased at Christie's for 34 guineas in March 1939, which perfectly fulfilled Clark's brief. While confessing that it was not the kind of Sickert he liked, Clark congratulated his protégé on an acquisition which he noted was 'of considerable interest' and had been bought 'very cheaply.'[54] It was undoubtedly of considerable *local* interest given that the portrait concerned a legal *cause célèbre* of the 1860s and 1870s, in which 'the Claimant' of Sickert's title put himself forward as the missing heir to the Tichborne baronetcy, and hence the rightful heir of Tichborne Park, a country house and estate near Alresford, Hampshire.

Conran also included examples of progressive British art in the loan exhibition he was planning to mark the grand opening of Southampton Art Gallery. To this end – but also with the permanent collection in mind – he made a point of visiting artists' studios and galleries to inspect and choose paintings.[55] Clark was consulted over a loan list because Conran, wishing to keep the examples of High Victorian paintings from the original Chipperfield Collection to a minimum, wanted to borrow some top-ranking modern and contemporary national pictures to fill the walls.[56] One way in which Clark assisted was by lending two works from his own private collection, including a picture of olive trees by Frederick Gore (1913–2009), son of the acclaimed Camden Town Group painter Spencer Gore.[57] On seeing the draft list, Clark's verdict was that it was a mixed bag 'swamped by a number of mediocrities, but on the whole ... as representative of modern English painting as one could desire.'[58] In its final iteration, the exhibition included numerous loans from private lenders and public art galleries including Birmingham, Bristol, Cardiff, Liverpool and Manchester. It remained an eclectic gathering of works, ranging from old-fashioned portraits of local worthies, including a specially commissioned portrait of Councillor Sir Sidney Kimber by Thomas Cantrell Dugdale (in the tradition of portraiture of local worthies discussed in Chapter 1), through modern British figurative painting, to examples of abstract Surrealist painting. Conran defended his choice by explaining that he had aimed to give 'a cross-section of the work that is being done to-day, without laying emphasis on any particular aspect of it', and that had he followed Clark's suggestion of introducing more examples by 'Steer, Sickert and John', he would have felt compelled to include more works by 'prominent [Royal] Academy painters'. Conran concluded: 'I thought it as well for this first exhibition in Southampton, to point no moral at all, but to leave that to later specialised collections',[59] a comment which revealed where his future collecting and display strategies lay.

On view were two striking portraits of female sitters: Augustus John's *Brigit* and a portrait by Stanley Spencer of his second wife, Patricia Preece. The former work had been purchased in 1939,[60] but the latter was a top-quality loan, hinting at the type of picture Southampton would henceforth be pursuing. In fact, it would be purchased, using the Smith Bequest Fund, some 14 years later, in 1954.[61] Yet more avant-garde was Conran's inclusion of British Surrealism, with the loan of two botanical paintings by Ithell Colquhoun. Anticipating an uncomprehending response from certain quarters, Conran introduced these works in his catalogue, with the statement: 'They will not meet with universal approval, but the collection of this exhibition was made in the belief that it is only knowledge and familiarity, even with styles of painting that are not liked, which can give a real discrimination in the arts.'[62] This focus on contemporary British art was prescient of Conran's future work at Southampton,

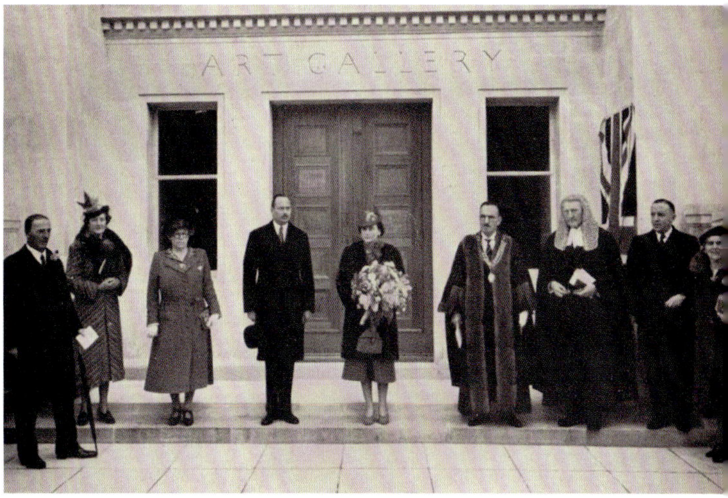

FIG. 40
Photograph of the opening of Southampton Art Gallery showing the Duke and Duchess of Gloucester. Southampton Cultural Services

and signalled areas of the collection which later generations of curators would develop. Colquhoun's *Rivières tièdes (Méditerranée)*, for instance, was purchased in 1977. Furthermore, his assertion that an art gallery should encourage visitors to broaden their artistic horizons set the tone for public engagement which has been followed by curators at Southampton ever since.

Southampton Art Gallery was officially opened by the Duke and Duchess of Gloucester on 26 April 1939, with Clark in attendance as another honoured guest. Hampshire's *Daily Echo* recorded on 6 May 1939 that the opening was 'a proud and high-spirited affair' (fig. 40). In the very same issue, it announced that Britain was ready for talks with Germany's Chancellor Adolf Hitler and that the UK's prime minister Neville Chamberlain had announced conscription for all 20- and 21-year-olds. The storm-clouds looming over Europe did not stop visitors from going to inspect Southampton's new art gallery and its ambitious opening show. Conran happily reported to Clark that nearly 35,000 people had come during the period that the exhibition was open.[63]

Conran had hoped that the exhibition would be the first in a series of impressive loan shows, and consequently one of the first matters he sorted out with Clark was where responsibility should lie for deciding such matters. In December 1938, Conran reminded Clark that the Chipperfield Bequest Sub-Committee could currently not 'either make or receive loans without your permission' and that, given his own ambitions for Southampton, this restriction would 'involve a lot of additional correspondence'.[64] Clark responded that he would be happy to be kept posted 'with a list of loans every month.'[65] Things were formalised in January 1939 when, to satisfy the town clerk's desire for correct procedure, the director of the National Gallery formally 'deputed [his] right in the matter' to Southampton's curator.[66]

Conran lost no time in planning his second loan exhibition. He got as far as putting out an open call in the local *Evening News* on 11 August 1939 to all Hampshire residents and those born in Hampshire to lend paintings of local scenes for an exhibition proposed to open on 6 October. However, international events prevented it from ever taking place. He had also begun to think of longer-term loans for Southampton Art Gallery. In February 1939, he approached Clark about the possibility of borrowing works from the 'National Gallery's Loan Collection', a notion made more concrete the following month when he submitted a list of 10 mainly Dutch and French seventeenth-century works.[67] Although the initiative was not taken forwards at this point – presumably the rumours of war were to blame – it did bear fruit later on.

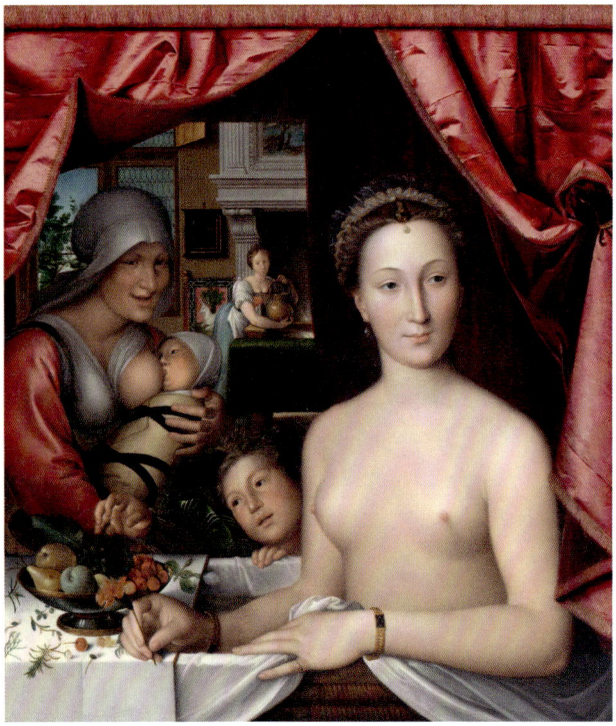

FIG. 41
François Clouet (before 1520–1572)
A Lady in her Bath, about 1571
Oil on oak, 92.3 × 81.2 cm
National Gallery of Art, Washington, 1961.9.13

Conflict over Southampton Art Gallery's future direction

Conran's first attempt to purchase a top-rate historical painting failed, despite full backing from Clark, because he got no support from the Chipperfield Bequest Sub-Committee. In June 1939, Conran flagged *A Lady in her Bath* (at the time said to represent Diane de Poitiers, the aristocratic mistress and adviser of Henry II of France) by the sixteenth-century French court painter François Clouet (1510–1572) (fig. 41) as a potential purchase, suggesting a sum of £10,000. Conran thought it would be 'good policy to acquire at least one picture of outstanding importance', and added that while it was of 'world-wide interest' it would also 'appeal to the general public'.[68] The painting was then in the Cook Collection at Doughty House in Richmond, Surrey. Ever since Sir Herbert Cook's death earlier in 1939, the art world had been anticipating that certain works from his collection (which included important Renaissance paintings and Rembrandt's *Portrait of Titus*) would become available. Clark himself had his eye on several for the National Gallery, but since he no longer enjoyed the same good relations with Cook's executors and trustees he had had with the late owner, the National Gallery ended up with nothing but Titian's *La Schiavona.*[69]

Conran reported dejectedly to Clark on 1 July 1939: 'There was no word in support of the proposal whatever' and that '[t]here was however a general agreement that the Gallery should acquire works of international importance, but certainly for not more than £1,000. How this can be done, I don't know.' Conran concluded: 'It is a dispiriting position to have a Committee appointed to buy pictures which does not consider that they have any real value. However, I shall try them again when the next opportunity arises.'[70]

In addition to the steep asking price, the subject of a naked woman in a bathtub, considered risqué, may have been another contributing factor which told against the picture. Indeed, most regional galleries had traditionally avoided acquiring or displaying works of art showing nude subjects, largely because nudity was generally frowned upon in Victorian and Edwardian Britain. Local councillors in Sunderland, for instance, refused to acquire *Love Tunes the Shepherd's Reed* by Richard Jack (1866–1952) as late as 1920 because of the painting's scantily clad figures.[71] Clark, 'all too familiar with the views of town councillors',[72] however, was of a different mind. Of the works in his private art collection, his favourite was a female nude, *La Baigneuse Blonde* by Auguste Renoir (1841–1919), and one of his most celebrated books was *The Nude: A Study of Ideal Art* (1956), in which Clark investigated the representation of the nude form in art from the ancient Greeks to Picasso.[73]

Clark did what he could to bolster Conran's resolve after this setback. In the midst of the Clouet episode he had written defiantly:

> It is essential that the Southampton Gallery should contain several pictures of European reputation, which would bring visitors, both lovers of art and scholars from all over the world and it would be disastrous if it were laid down as a principle that only pictures of moderate cost could be bought, for in that way the greater part of the Gallery would inevitably be filled with bargains and mediocre works. Southampton has the great opportunity of making a really fine collection which will distinguish it from the average mediocre collections in provincial towns and I think that the purchase of the Clouet 'Diane de Poitiers' would be the first step in the right direction.[74]

The understandable mismatch of expectations between a group of local councillors, who preferred to make inoffensive and inexpensive purchases to safeguard their gallery's reputation and funds, versus Clark and Conran, who were keen to broaden artistic perspectives and make Southampton into an ambitious and leading UK collection, led to this unusual and challenging masterpiece slipping through their fingers. The painting was sold to the Kress Foundation in 1955 and given to the National Gallery of Art in Washington in 1961. This would not be the last time that such diverging interests would play out, but it did not make for the happiest of starts between Conran and the Chipperfield Bequest Sub-Committee.

Southampton Art Gallery had been open for less than six months when it was forced to shut due to the outbreak of war. By that point, battles of their own were being waged in Southampton. Even before the announcement came from central government to close galleries and museums, Conran's position, along with his collecting policy, was seemingly under threat. In early October 1939, Conran informed Clark: 'I am told that during my exclusion from a committee the "Saloon Boss" [their nickname for Sidney Kimber] tried to close the Gallery & dismiss me but for the time being we are open, with the valuable pictures removed, and attracting a reasonable attendance.'[75] In a letter two months later, Conran informed Clark that, when reminded that the Chipperfield Bequest Fund could only be used to purchase pictures, Kimber had threatened that '"there may be acts of parliament and all sorts of things which will change that"'.[76] Clark sent reassurances from London that, if necessary, it would be his 'painful duty' to use his privilege to veto proposals if 'nothing but bargains unworthy of the Gallery' were proposed, [77] and that he would do his best to keep the Chipperfield Bequest Sub-Committee 'interested in painting' during Conran's absence.[78] It was agreed that, while Conran was away, Clark would make suggestions for purchases, which Mr H. Jackson Seed, the temporary 'Acting Curator', would then place before the Sub-Committee.[79]

Southampton Art Gallery during the Second World War

Conran remained steadfast in his duty of care towards the emerging art collection. He arranged for Southampton Art Gallery's art collection to be evacuated to Wicken Park House, in Bletchley, Buckinghamshire. This decision echoed Clark's in relation to the National Gallery's paintings, which were transported from central London and dispersed initially in various places across Wales and Gloucestershire, before finding permanent storage from 1941 in a former slate mine at Manod, near Blaenau Ffestiniog.[80] These were wise moves, because Southampton and London became prime targets for Nazi bombing raids. Although the National Gallery suffered several direct hits, no one was killed; in the case of Southampton, aerial bombardment of 6 November 1940 destroyed part of the Civic Centre, a tragic episode when more than 35 people (including 15 students) died from injuries sustained as they made their way from the art school in the north wing to an air-raid shelter.[81]

Before relinquishing his post to head off to war, Conran confessed to Clark that he was anxious to 'get this place doing some useful work on the "cultural front"' – noting lectures on artistic subjects for schoolchildren and concerts as potential schemes[82] – an idea that dovetailed with Clark's activity in London. Clark was keen to keep the National Gallery as a flagship for cultural activities and did not want to see the building sequestered for ministry work (which he feared might make it even more of a target for bombing), and so he readily accepted the suggestion of the concert pianist Myra Hess that the Gallery be used to host lunchtime concerts. Inspired by this initiative, Conran worked on his own series, the London concerts being 'a useful precedent'.[83] Presumably, the strong bond that now existed between the two galleries was instrumental in Myra Hess's decision to open the Southampton series – something she agreed to do 'without fee' according to the delighted Conran.[84]

Conran also played a key role in introducing to Southampton the idea of exhibitions with associated art history lectures. He directed most of his efforts through the *Art for the People* scheme, organised by the British Institute of Adult Education (BIoAE), whose aim was to bring art to everyone, especially to 'places which have no Art Gallery of their own'. Conran had been contacted by the Institute as early as December 1938 and, keen to oblige, he worked hard to enable the fledgling gallery to host one of BIoAE's *Art for the People* exhibitions the following year. Conran was able to report solid attendance figures which compared favourably with those of other towns.[85] As part of the scheme, Southampton put on its first ever public lecture series. BIoAE's original circular had noted that 'former students of the Courtauld Institute, Westminster School of Art, Slade School etc.'[86] were the type of speaker usually employed. In response, Conran brought together an impressive group of lecturers for Southampton, including the prominent artist, writer, broadcaster and art critic, Eric Newton.[87]

At Trafalgar Square, picture displays were organised by Clark of various kinds, comprising some long-term loans from the Tate Gallery, the occasional old master brought back from storage in Wales as part of the *Picture of the Month* series, and exhibitions of war artists' work. Additionally, there was a series of exhibitions of art unrelated to conflict, spearheaded by the well-known London art dealer Lilian Browse, the 'Duchess of Cork Street'. Interestingly, one of them was devoted to Walter Sickert and it featured *The Mantelpiece* on loan from Southampton. Browse praised it as 'one of the finest examples in the exhibition'[88] (although she noted, sadly, that Sickert's *The Tichborne Claimant* (fig. 39) which she had also hoped to display, 'did not hang at all well among the smaller pictures' and so was going to be returned to its wartime home at Wicken Park).

In 1947, the War Artists' Advisory Committee divided up the collection of paintings it had accrued through commissions. After the largest share had been allocated to London's Tate Gallery and Imperial War Museum, galleries around the UK and the Commonwealth were approached about potential gifts. Southampton was allocated nine pictures, eight of them wartime subjects by Patrick Carpenter, Leslie Cole, Charles Ernest Cundall, Leonard Daniel and the writer, broadcaster and noted war artist Stephen Bone (1904–1958; fig. 42). The odd-man-out was a portrait of the Dowager Queen Mary by (Dennis) William Dring (1904–1990), a painter who had taught at the Southampton School of Art until 1942, before resigning to complete several portrait commissions for WAAC. It is reasonable to suppose that the level of generosity Southampton experienced may have had something to do with the fact that Clark was essentially in charge of the donating body. This was not the last time that Southampton would benefit from the influence wielded by its supporters and allies.

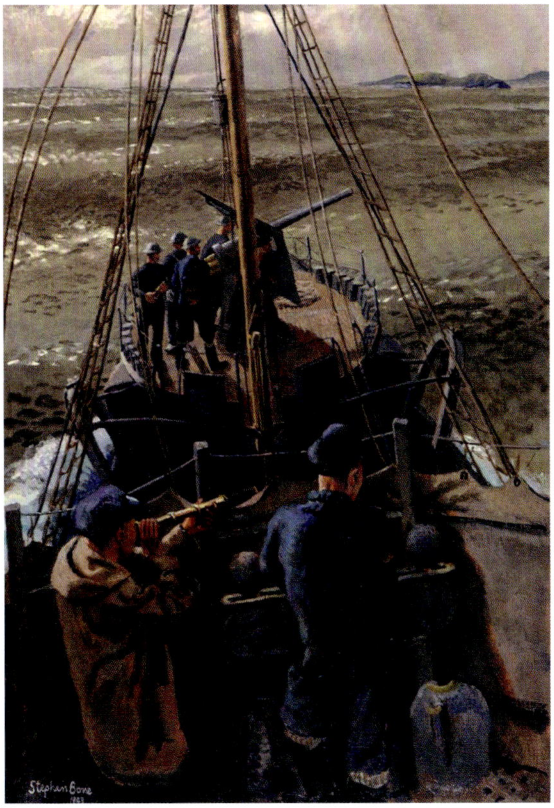

FIG. 42
Stephen Bone (1904–1958)
Trawler's Twelve Pounder, 1943
Oil on wood, 92 × 64.1 cm
Southampton City Art Gallery, SOTAG 1309

By the time Conran himself resumed his curatorial role at Southampton in 1946 (also the date when the gallery reopened – rebuilt with less architectural ornamentation), he no longer had Kenneth Clark to advise him. Clark left the National Gallery in December 1945 to become a member of the executive committee of the Council for the Encouragement of Music and the Arts (CEMA). He had in fact done much to support its establishment by the wartime government in January 1940. Later, Clark accepted the role of chair of CEMA's Arts panel when the body was reconstituted as the Arts Council of Great Britain in August 1946.

11

Nicolaes Maes (1634–1693)

Portrait of a Man, 1670s or 1680s

Oil on canvas, 68.5 × 58.5 cm
Purchased with the assistance of the Smith Bequest Fund, 1934
Southampton City Art Gallery, SOTAG 385

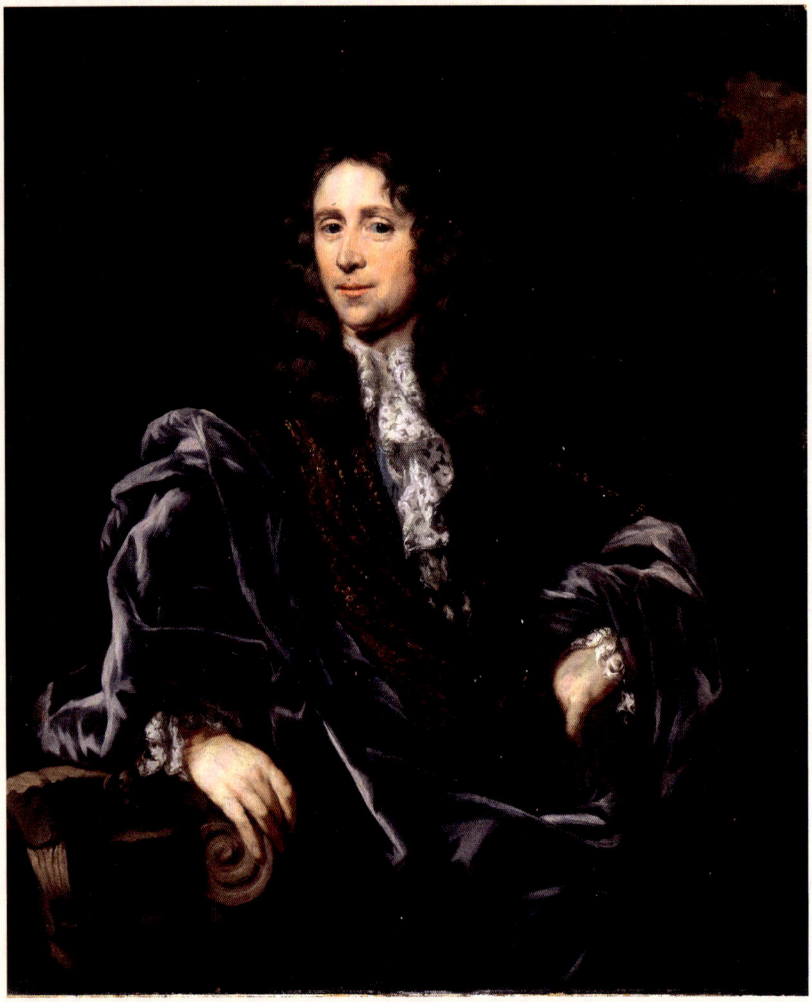

Nicolaes Maes was one of the most versatile and inventive artists of his generation in the Netherlands. He studied painting under Rembrandt, producing a number of historical and biblical scenes, before broadening his oeuvre to include genre painting. His experiments with interior space and the unusual intimacy of his domestic scenes influenced many of his contemporaries, including Pieter de Hooch and Johannes Vermeer. As was characteristic of much genre painting, many of his works harbour moralising messages, albeit expressed with humour to make them more palatable.

Shortly before 1660, Maes turned exclusively to portrait painting, devoting the rest of his long career to this profitable pursuit. He changed his style so radically that his late work has little in common with his genre paintings from the 1650s, let alone the darker tonality and rich textures of his earliest 'Rembrandtesque' works. He developed a brighter palette, reflecting an international interest in both the work of Anthony van Dyck and French portraiture. Standardised compositions, poses, costumes and accessories enabled Maes to increase his output and cope with high demand. Having painted an estimated 900 portraits, he died a wealthy man.

Over time, the identity of sitters in many of Maes's portraits has been lost, and consequently some of his portraits have been given erroneous if attractive titles to make them more sellable. Southampton's picture was traditionally called *The Duke of Portland*, referring to a Dutchman who had come to England with King William III in 1689. Looking nothing like other verified portraits of Portland, it is likely that the sitter was one of the numerous rich Amsterdam burghers who made up Maes's clientele. It was purchased with the assistance of the Frederick William Smith Bequest Fund, in 1934. Several such half-length male portraits had been acquired by the National Gallery, including a particularly arresting one of the Rotterdam silk merchant Jan de Reus (fig. 29), bequeathed in 1910.

12

Jacob Jordaens (1593–1678)
The Holy Family, before 1628

Oil on canvas, 105.8 × 75.5 cm
Purchased with the assistance of the Chipperfield Bequest Fund, 1935
Southampton City Art Gallery, SOTAG 315

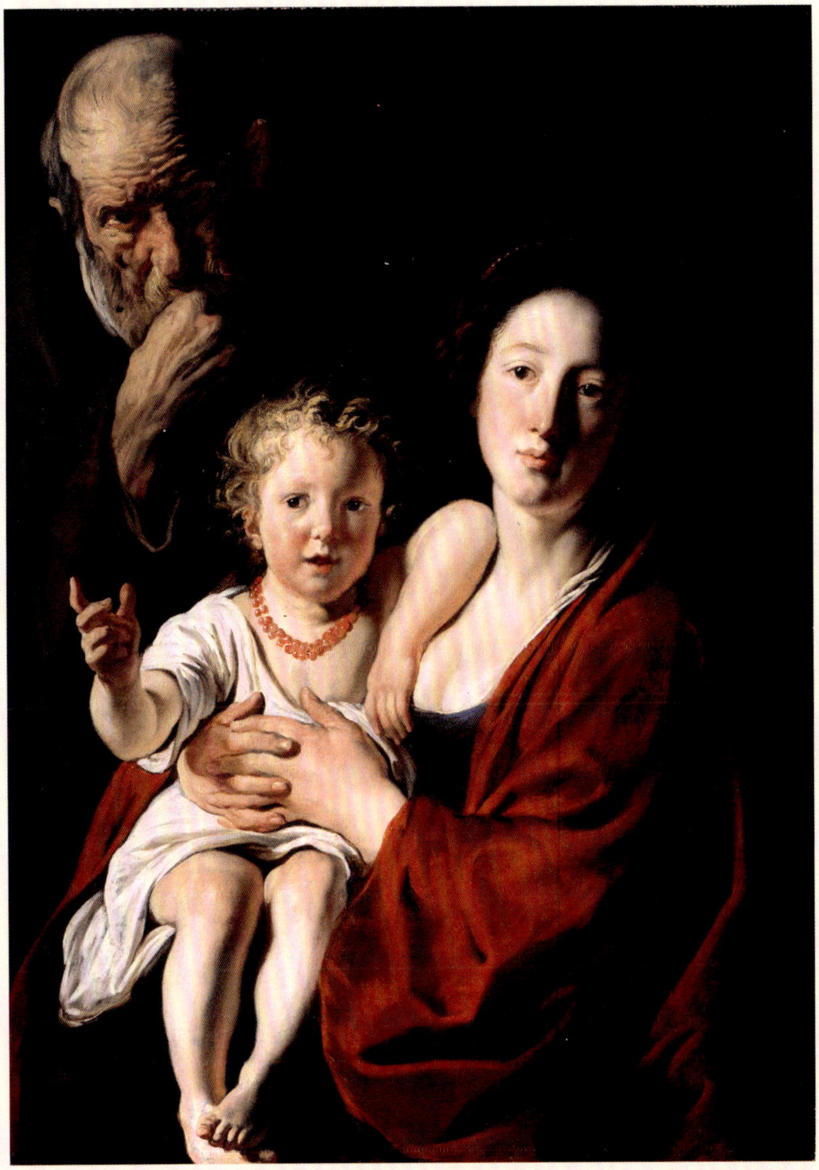

When Kenneth Clark took over as art adviser, he argued that through strategic use of the Chipperfield Bequest Fund, it would be possible to transform Southampton Art Gallery into one of the finest in the country outside London.

Clark first made his opinion felt when he assisted with the purchase of three old masters in 1934, including a portrait by Nicolaes Maes (cat. 11) and a landscape by Jan Hackaert. The following year he rejected as unsuitable nine works from the Royal Academy Summer Exhibition that the Chipperfield Bequest Sub-Committee had put forward as potential acquisitions, instead suggesting Jacob Jordaens's *Holy Family*. It was through Clark's robust and rapid intervention that Southampton Art Gallery secured this important painting.

Jordaens was a leading Flemish painter and designer of tapestries, whose international patrons included Queen Christina of Sweden and Charles I of England. Although Jordaens converted to Reformed Protestantism later in life, he mostly painted for Catholic patrons in his native Antwerp. His paintings are notable for their exuberant compositions, lively colouring and flamboyant handling of paint. The artist produced a number of intimate depictions of the Holy Family; the National Gallery owns another version, which depicts the Christ Child's earthly father Joseph as a far younger man than the elderly figure portrayed here. It has been suggested that the model for the child in both pictures may have been one of Jordaens's own children.

13

Sofonisba Anguissola (about 1532–1625)

The Artist's Sister in the Garb of a Nun, 1551

Oil on canvas, 68.5 × 53.3 cm
Purchased with the assistance of the Chipperfield Bequest Fund, 1936
Southampton City Art Gallery, SOTAG 3

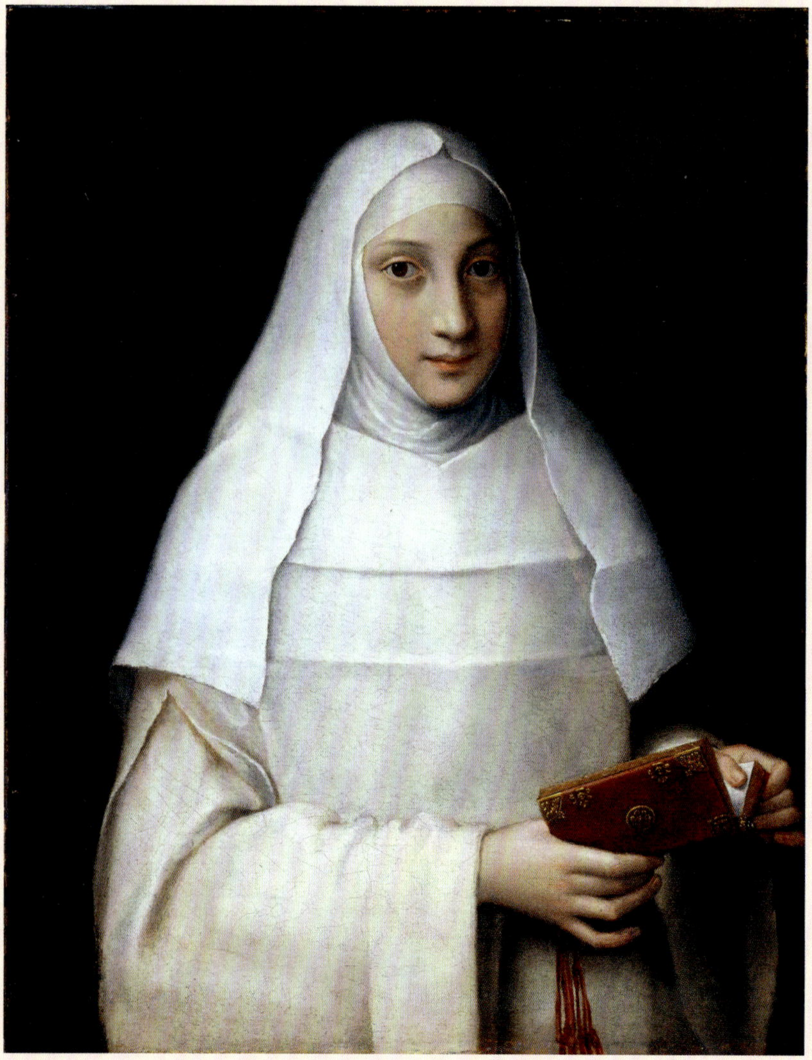

Sofonisba Anguissola, a late Renaissance painter from Cremona in Northern Italy, was one of the first women artists with an international reputation. Anguissola's family were members of the Cremonese nobility. Painting was an acceptable part of a young noblewoman's education, but to train professionally in an artist's studio (as Anguissola and her sisters did) was almost unknown. Her abilities were praised by her contemporary Giorgio Vasari in his celebrated *Lives of the Artists*. She was invited to be a lady in waiting, court painter and art teacher to Elizabeth of Valois, wife of King Philip II of Spain. Decades later, the young Anthony van Dyck made a portrait sketch and a small painting of her when she was very old, marvelling at her skill and her commitment to art.

Anguissola fell into obscurity, and many of her paintings were subsequently attributed to celebrated male artists. This portrait, due to its high quality, was once thought to be by Titian, despite the presence of an inscription on the back recording Anguissola's name and the date of 1551. It is her earliest known work, and is thought to show her sister Elena, who became a nun in Mantua.

Kenneth Clark, determined to acquire notable old masters and nineteenth-century paintings for Southampton, purchased this picture in 1936. It had once been part of the esteemed collection of the Earls of Yarborough. When Southampton purchased Gwen John's *Mère Poussepin* (cat. 36) in 1956, another sensitive portrait of a nun was brought into the collection.

14

Johannes Moreelse (after 1602–1634)

The Young Poet, about 1630

Oil on wood, 70.5 × 54.3 cm
Purchased with the assistance of the Chipperfield Bequest Fund, 1936
Southampton City Art Gallery, SOTAG 110

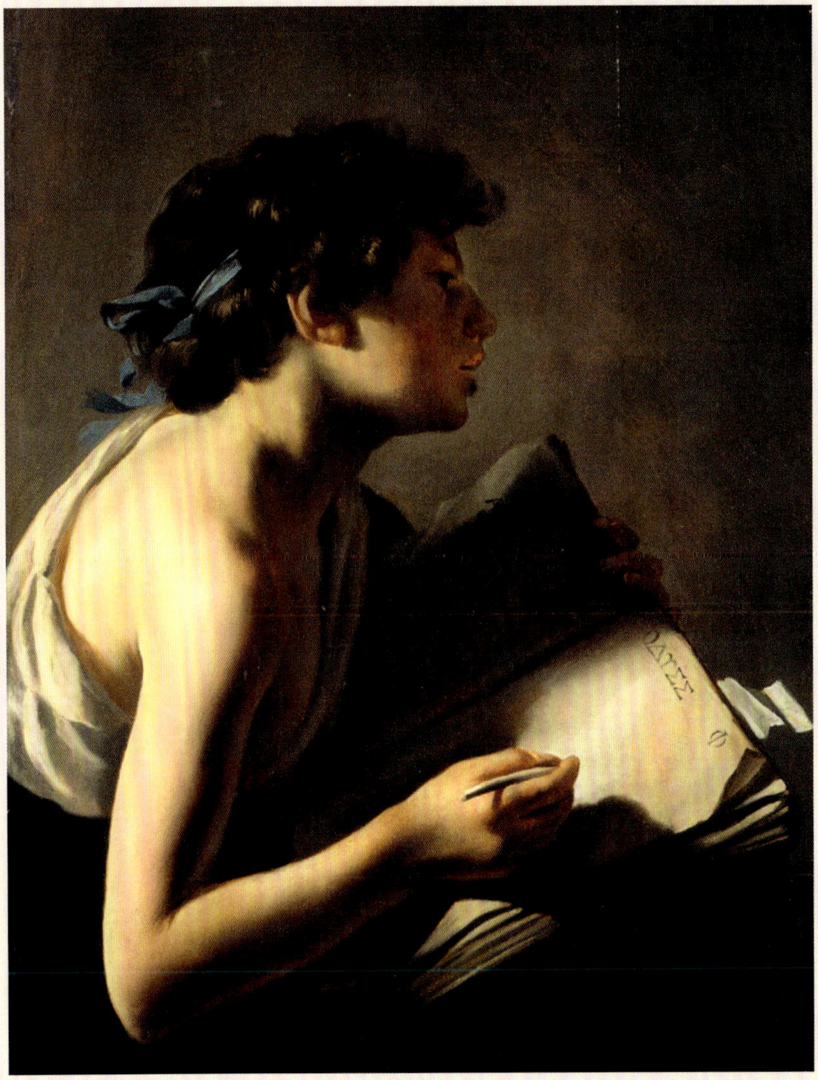

Johannes Moreelse was active in Utrecht during the seventeenth-century Dutch 'Golden Age' of painting. His father was a well-known portraitist, but little is known about Johannes himself. A number of works attributed to him are portraits, and he also painted images of saints and classical figures, including muses and figures with exaggerated facial expressions. Moreelse created likenesses of Greek men of learning such as Democritus and Heraclitus (for instance, his *Heraclitus, Ancient Greek Scientist* is in the collection of Museums Sheffield). This interest in the classical world can be seen in *The Young Poet*, which depicts a boy in the act of taking a dictation from the work of Homer, the celebrated blind poet of two ancient Greek epics, *The Iliad* and *The Odyssey*. There are humorous overtones to the narrative, given that the sentence from *The Odyssey* the pupil is in the process of writing (the only decipherable part of the text), appears to be a mild remonstrance from the great master: 'But if you listened to me it would be much more use.'

This was a relatively early old master purchase for Southampton. It was bought after Kenneth Clark became Southampton Art Gallery's art adviser in 1934, and was part of his drive to encourage the gallery to expand its collecting remit by acquiring good and affordable historical art. It was purchased from R.E.A. Wilson, a London art dealer and restorer, together with Sofonisba Anguissola's *The Artist's Sister in the Garb of a Nun* (cat. 13) and Domenico Feti's *Rebecca at the Well*. It was significantly more expensive than the other two pictures, notwithstanding the fact that Southampton had negotiated a reduction in the original asking price. It entered the collection as a work by Jan Van Bylert (1597/8–1671), another painter from Utrecht, whose work was indebted to that of Caravaggio.

15

Caesar Boëtius van Everdingen (about 1616–1678)

Allegory of Winter, 1650

Oil on canvas, 91.8 × 71.2 cm
Purchased with the assistance of the Chipperfield Bequest Fund, 1937
Southampton City Art Gallery, SOTAG 188

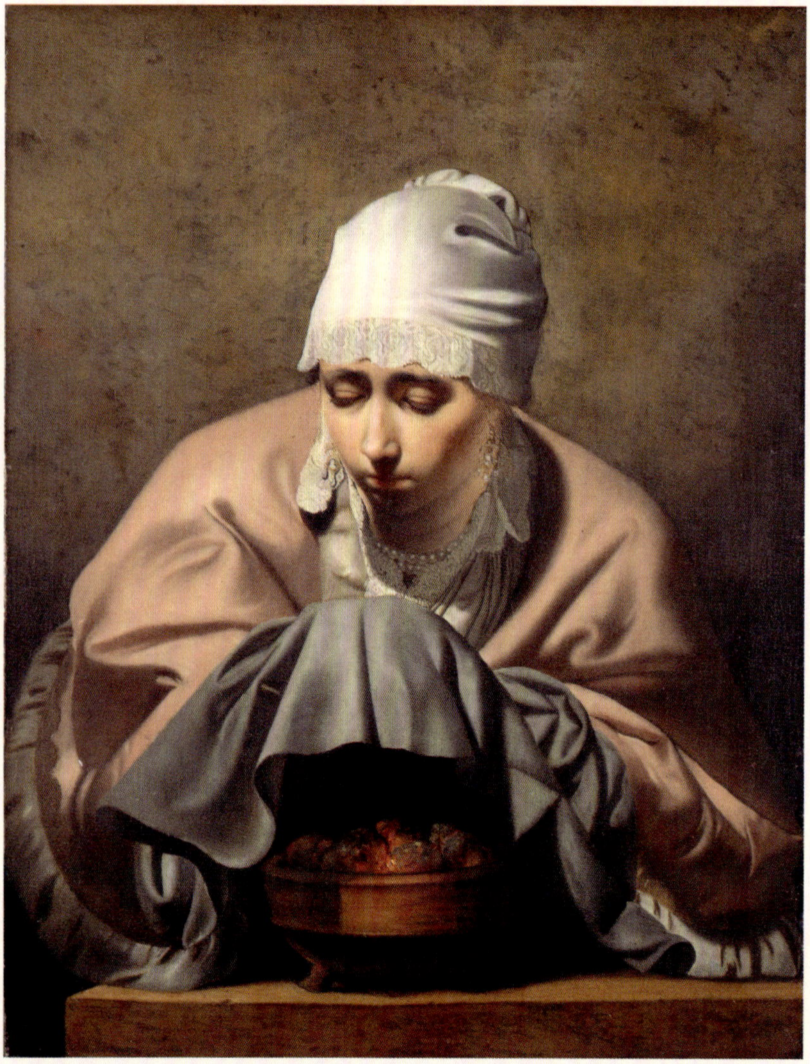

Caesar van Everdingen hailed from a distinguished family of painters from Alkmaar in the Netherlands. He became associated with the Haarlem School of painters, renowned for idealised, classicising history paintings and genre scenes in the mid-1600s. Van Everdingen's work is distinctive for the prominence given to his figures, many of whom exude a palpable sensuality.

In addition to portraits, van Everdingen produced many mythological and allegorical pictures, including this work. Other Dutch artists usually portrayed Winter as an elderly figure, often in rags and warming their hands to indicate the harshness of the end of the year. For instance, Abraham Bloemaert personified Winter as a hoary old man, as did his son, the painter Hendrick Bloemaert. Depicting 'Dame Winter' as a well-dressed, alluring young woman was unusual.

Kenneth Clark urged Southampton to purchase this work when it came on the art market in 1937. He noted several advantages: it was an unusually attractive work by a painter whose reputation would surely rise, it would have universal appeal, and was on offer at a bargain price. That Clark appreciated the painting's quality in 1937 demonstrates what an astute connoisseur he was. Indeed, van Everdingen was only recognised as a major artist much later in the twentieth century.

Before Southampton, this work was offered to the Rijksmuseum, Amsterdam, but turned down. More recently, the Rijksmuseum acquired another version of slightly higher quality, which, on account of its pentimenti must have preceded the Southampton painting. Occasional doubts have been raised about whether the Southampton version can be attributed to van Everdingen, but its quality suggests that this is probable. Furthermore, the artist is known to have painted replicas of his own works, with two depictions of Winter by the artist listed in his estate inventory.

Allegory of Winter was lent to the National Gallery's *Art in Seventeenth Century Holland* exhibition in 1976 (see Appendix).

16

Camille Pissarro (1830–1903)
View from the Versailles Road, Louveciennes, 1870

Oil on canvas, 45.8 × 55.7 cm
Purchased with the assistance of the Chipperfield Bequest Fund, 1936
Southampton City Art Gallery, SOTAG 461

As well as developing a purchasing strategy, Kenneth Clark took a key role in sourcing and securing acquisitions for Southampton Art Gallery. For instance, he told the Chipperfield Bequest Sub-Committee in April 1936 that he would happily inform them of any suitable pictures he found on his business trips to Paris.[1] This painting was one of the first to reach Southampton from the international art market, purchased in Paris in 1936.

There are closely related paintings by Pissarro in collections in Europe and America, including the Nationalgalerie, Berlin and the Clark Art Institute, Massachusetts. The small scale of these works suggests that they were painted directly from nature (rather than created in the studio), a practice for which French Impressionist painters became famous.

Southampton's picture shows Pissarro moving from the style of his teacher Corot towards a more pronounced naturalism, exemplified in the sense of movement evoked by the racing clouds. The suburban house at the left is cropped, rather as if the scene were captured through the lens of a camera, a still novel invention at the time. This quiet sunlit landscape, with its two figures contemplating the view, reflects the Impressionists' fascination with contemporary life.

Pissarro moved to Louveciennes in 1869, but the outbreak of the Franco-Prussian War the following year and subsequent siege of Paris forced him to leave. On his return after the war, he found that his house had been used by Prussian troops and over a thousand paintings left behind were lost. Hindsight gives the painting the character of a poignant farewell.

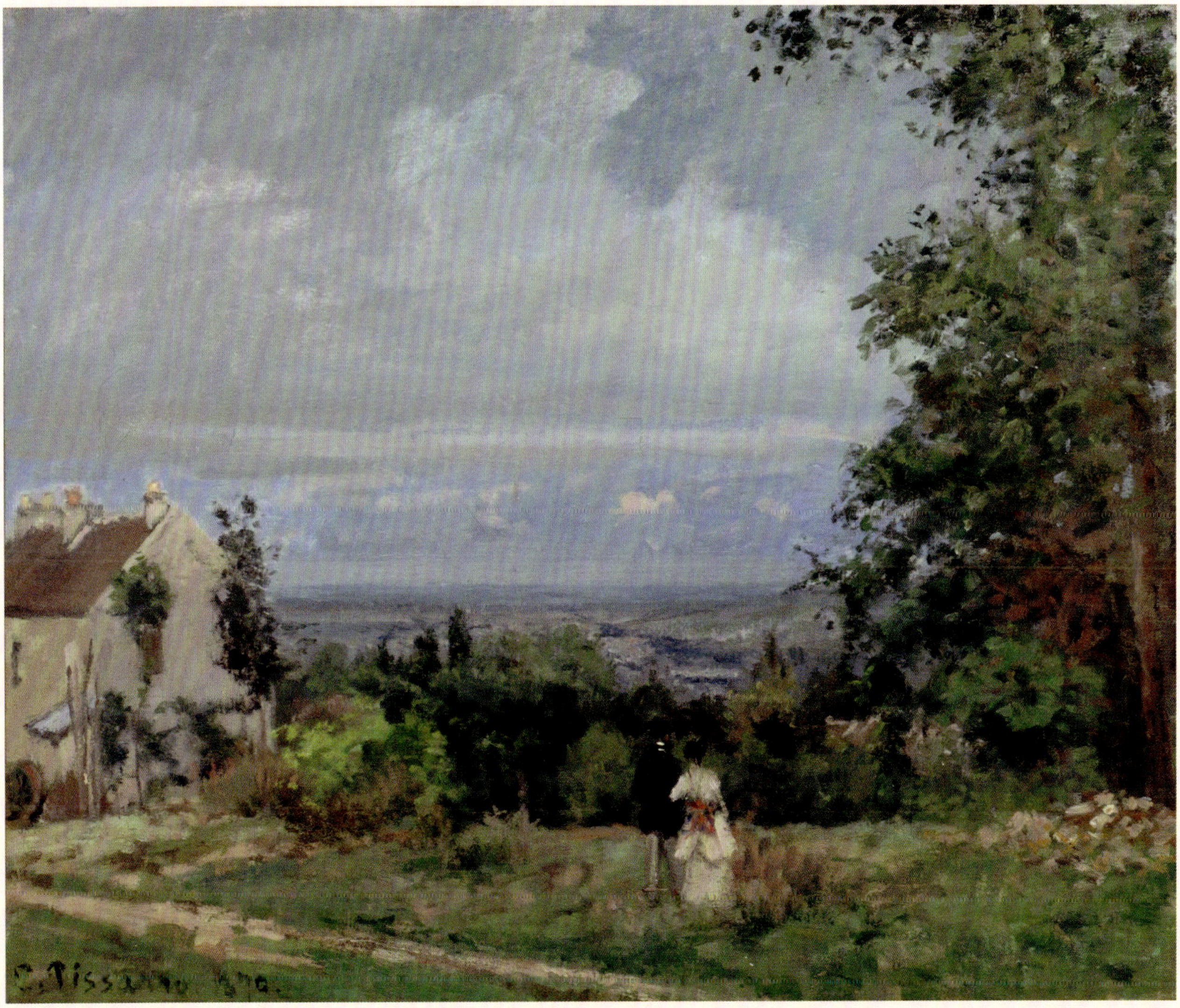

17

Spencer Gore (1878–1914)

View from a Window, 1909

Oil on canvas, 50.8 × 40.3 cm
Purchased with the assistance of the Chipperfield Bequest Fund, 1938
Southampton City Art Gallery, SOTAG 221

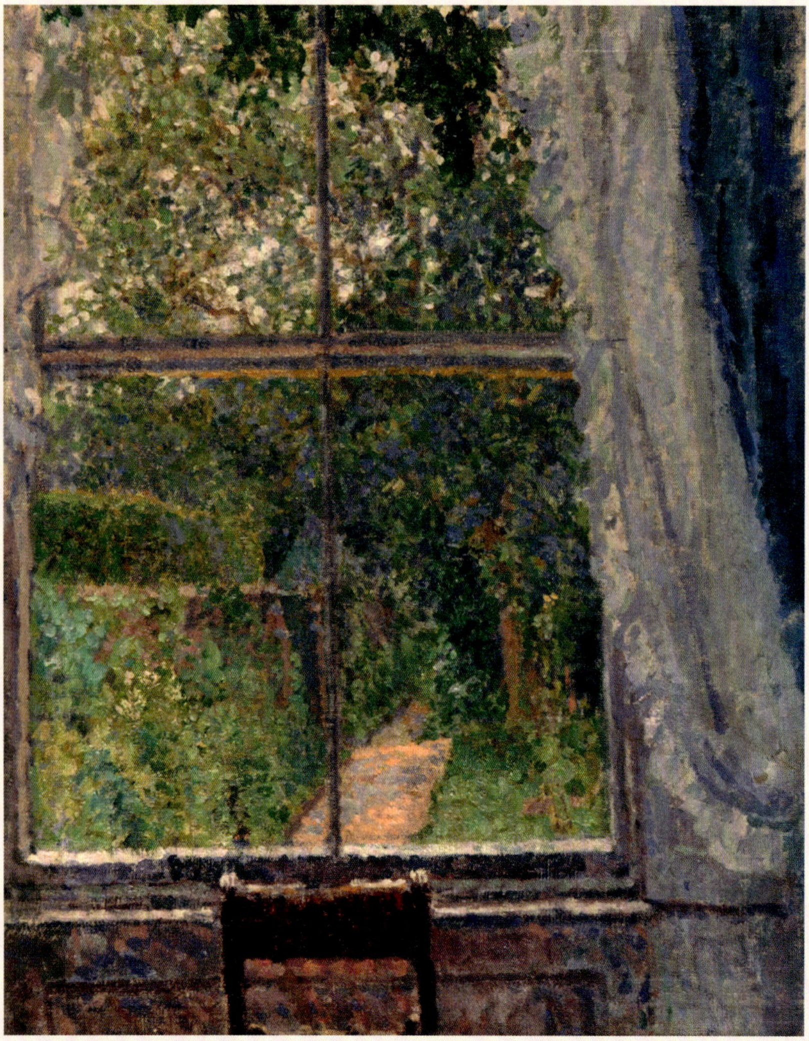

As a young boy at Harrow School, Spencer Gore won the first Yates Thompson Prize for drawing. After studying at the Slade School of Fine Art (1896–99), he quickly established himself as a painter of landscapes, interiors and music-hall scenes. Gore became the first president of the Camden Town Group, a group of painters who lived and worked in the Camden Town area of London, who made a name with depictions of urban life in the years before the First World War. Gore was particularly close to the Group's members Harold Gilman, Charles Ginner and Lucien Pissarro (son of Camille Pissarro, cat. 16) as well as Walter Sickert, its founder. Importantly, Gore encouraged Sickert to use a brighter palette, which became a hallmark of the Group's style.

For decades, two other British art movements – the Bloomsbury Group and Vorticism – were considered more stylistically innovative and responsive to avant-garde European trends and they eclipsed the Camden Town artists. However, in 1951 Southampton Art Gallery reignited national interest in the Camden Town Group through an ambitious exhibition of their work, organised as part of the Festival of Britain. The display showcased important works from Southampton's permanent collection which had been acquired intermittently, including a cluster of works by Gilman, Gore and Lamb, purchased by Kenneth Clark in 1937–38.

This painting depicts a view from the window of the home of Gore's mother in Hertfordshire, where he stayed during the summers of 1908–09. Dabs of colour used to express the garden owe more to Impressionism, and perhaps fellow Camden Town artist, Lucien Pissarro, than to Gore's later landscapes of Letchworth and Brighton, strongly influenced by Paul Gauguin and Paul Cézanne.

18

Henry Lamb (1883–1960)

Edie McNeill, 1911

Oil on canvas, 127.5 × 76.2 cm
Purchased with the assistance of the Chipperfield Bequest Fund, 1938
Southampton City Art Gallery, SOTAG 330
Bridgeman Images

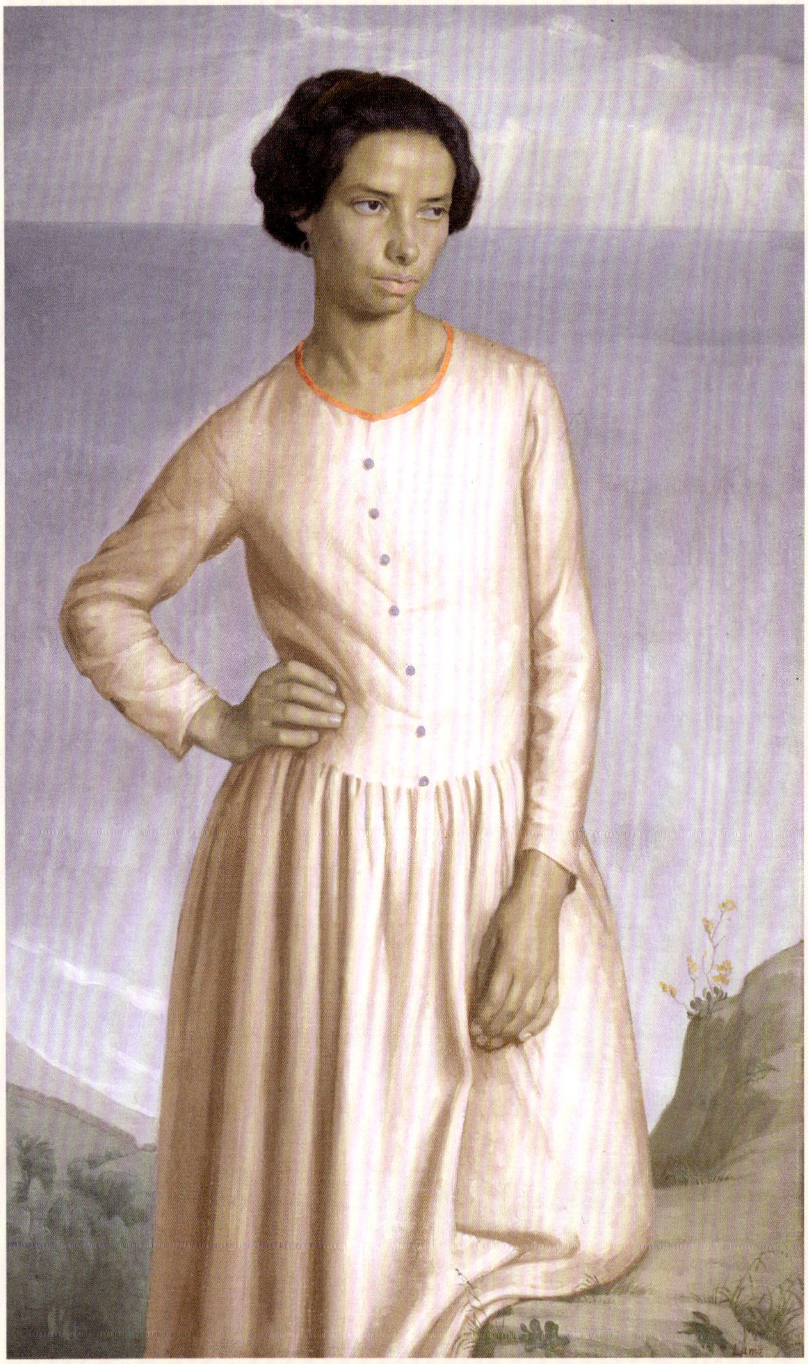

Henry Lamb was an Australian-born British artist who, having abandoned medicine as a career, studied painting at the Chelsea School of Art in 1906 under William Orpen and Augustus John. In 1911, he became a founder member of the Camden Town Group, a short-lived association of English Post-Impressionist artists who gathered frequently at Walter Sickert's studio in the Camden Town area of London. Although the group was best known for its scenes of contemporary urban life, Lamb made his name with striking portraits, including a memorable likeness of the writer and critic, Lytton Strachey. Lamb saw active service as a doctor in the First World War; during the Second World War, however, he was appointed an Official War Artist.

Edie McNeill posed for Lamb on several occasions; she was also a regular model for other artists, including Derwent Lees and Augustus John (her sister Dorelia was John's second wife). Of all the versions of this composition, this is the earliest, most significant and most expressive. Lamb captures the strength of Edie's character in her forceful stance, dominating a clifftop and calm sea below.

Acquired in May 1938, the purchase was masterminded by Kenneth Clark, who declared it to be 'one of the most attractive of the artist's early works' and predicted it would have popular appeal.[2] It was accessioned as 'Portrait of a Girl' because the identity of the sitter was not known. Decades later, in 1973, Southampton's curator Anthony Howarth purchased another of Henry Lamb's portraits in oil – a head of Lady Mary Packenham (1929) – thinking it would 'well complement' *Edie McNeill*.[3] Drawings by Lamb were acquired later still, in 1975 and 1988.

In Focus

Links between Southampton City Art Gallery and the National Gallery

During Kenneth Clark's time in office (1934–45), Southampton Art Gallery opened in a purpose-built edifice, developed an ambitious acquisitions strategy and appointed its first permanent curator. (George) Loraine Conran was one of two candidates shortlisted by Clark in 1938, the other being Albert Charles Sewter. Clark had met both men and believed they had good knowledge and understanding of painting, along with relevant administrative experience.[1] Conran was backed by the Byzantine historian Robert Byron, who declared that Conran 'knew a good picture when he saw one'.[2] Another advantage was Conran's curatorial experience, gained from senior posts he had held at the leading UK public art galleries in Birmingham and Liverpool. Conran secured the position.

Clark and Conran discussed the acquisition policy and management of the Chipperfield Bequest Fund, first by letter, then in person. Clark was keen to continue helping Southampton acquire pictures of outstanding merit yet of reasonable price. Honesty was encouraged, with Clark telling Conran to 'say so without fear that it will hurt my feelings' if their verdicts disagreed, and stating it was more important for potential acquisitions to please Conran.[3] Correspondence even shows Clark advising on the best type of paint to use on gallery walls.[4]

On Conran's return to work after the Second World War in 1946, a new era dawned. Philip Hendy became Southampton's adviser after he was appointed director of the National Gallery in January 1946. Conran wrote to Hendy explaining his advisory duties and power 'to veto all purchases made from the monies of the Chipperfield bequest'.[5] Hendy also had much to do with choosing Conran's replacement in 1950: he met the chairman of the Chipperfield Bequest Sub-Committee to review the applications and was delighted when Maurice Palmer, then curator at Bedford's Cecil Higgins Museum of Art, secured the position.[6]

The long-lasting partnership between Hendy and Palmer during the 1950s and 60s benefitted Southampton's collection enormously through their highly prestigious acquisitions, including works by esteemed old masters such as Anthony van Dyck and J.M.W. Turner. Strategic acquisitions of modern British art and sculpture followed; indeed, most of Palmer's acquisitions were British works produced in the first half of the twentieth century, which led to Southampton holding unrivalled collections of both the Camden Town Group and St Ives School.

Southampton Art Gallery experienced a new wave of optimism and excitement when Anthony Howarth was appointed curator in 1971. He was put in charge of all the city's museums from 1974, the same year that saw a radical restructure within both local government and the education system. With no precedent to guide him, Howarth boldly hired a team of visionary young staff. He advertised two positions and hired Elizabeth (Liz) Goodall (then Ogborn) and Helen Luckett to fill them, letting them choose which post they preferred – they became keeper of art and keeper of education, respectively.

Goodall remembers how Howarth inspired his staff by encouraging them 'to do what they could to make [the gallery] a really great place.'[7] According to John Hoole, Assistant Keeper of Art (1974–78), Howarth encouraged and supported without steering, trusting in the staff's capabilities and ideas. Likewise, Les Buckingham, who held the same role from 1975–83, has reflected that without Howarth's 'constant moral support and fighting for our independence with the politicians plus genuine ability to employ real talent, we would not have been able to be as experimental as I believe we were.'[8] Creating a united front, the staff felt empowered 'to question the status quo, even the art world establishment'.[9]

Experimenting in terms of public outreach resulted in the development of a ground-breaking gallery education programme; as one member of staff memorably put it: 'We broke so many moulds, it is difficult to count!'[10] The education department nurtured by Luckett (fig. 43) was innovative in the way that it 'worked seamlessly with the curatorial division.'[11]

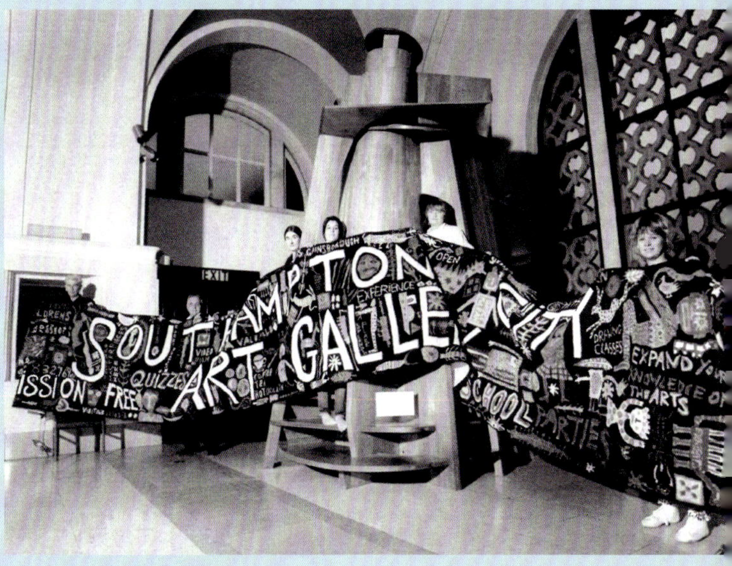

FIG. 43
Southampton City Art Gallery's staff in the Main Hall, displaying a banner designed by Charlie Hackett for a community project, 1987.

Michael Levey, appointed director of the National Gallery in 1973, became another crucial friend to Southampton. Levey promoted public outreach, which baffled some senior staff and trustees in London, but he felt at home with like-minded colleagues in Southampton and regarded them as kindred spirits. Howarth thanked Levey for supporting Southampton's strategic decision to start acquiring contemporary art, while acknowledging the growing involvement from the Tate. Southampton began buying in new areas and Dr David Brown from the Tate Gallery soon became Southampton's advisor, helping navigate less-assured colleagues through uncharted territories given he constantly had 'his eye on all that [was] going on in London.'[12] As one door was shutting on the historical partnership between the National Gallery and Southampton, Levey expressed a desire to think creatively about finding new openings for future collaboration between the two institutions.

Although from this point onwards the National Gallery's director no longer acted as art adviser to Southampton, there are nonetheless important episodes when expertise was shared and ideas were exchanged between colleagues from both institutions – in particular concerning educational initiatives and conservation work.

More recently, there have even been instances of overlap between members of staff. For instance, Britta New, a conservator at the National Gallery since 2007, undertook a three-month placement as part of her conservation training at Southampton City Art Gallery in 2000. She has recalled: 'The internship was probably one of the biggest influences to my heading down the path of a career in a museum. They [Tim Craven and Rebecca Moisan] gave me a very valuable cross-section of all the different aspects of conservation within a museum setting, which was enormously useful.'[13] Such interconnections ensured that the longstanding partnership between London and Southampton did not completely fade away, but rather found new modes of expression.

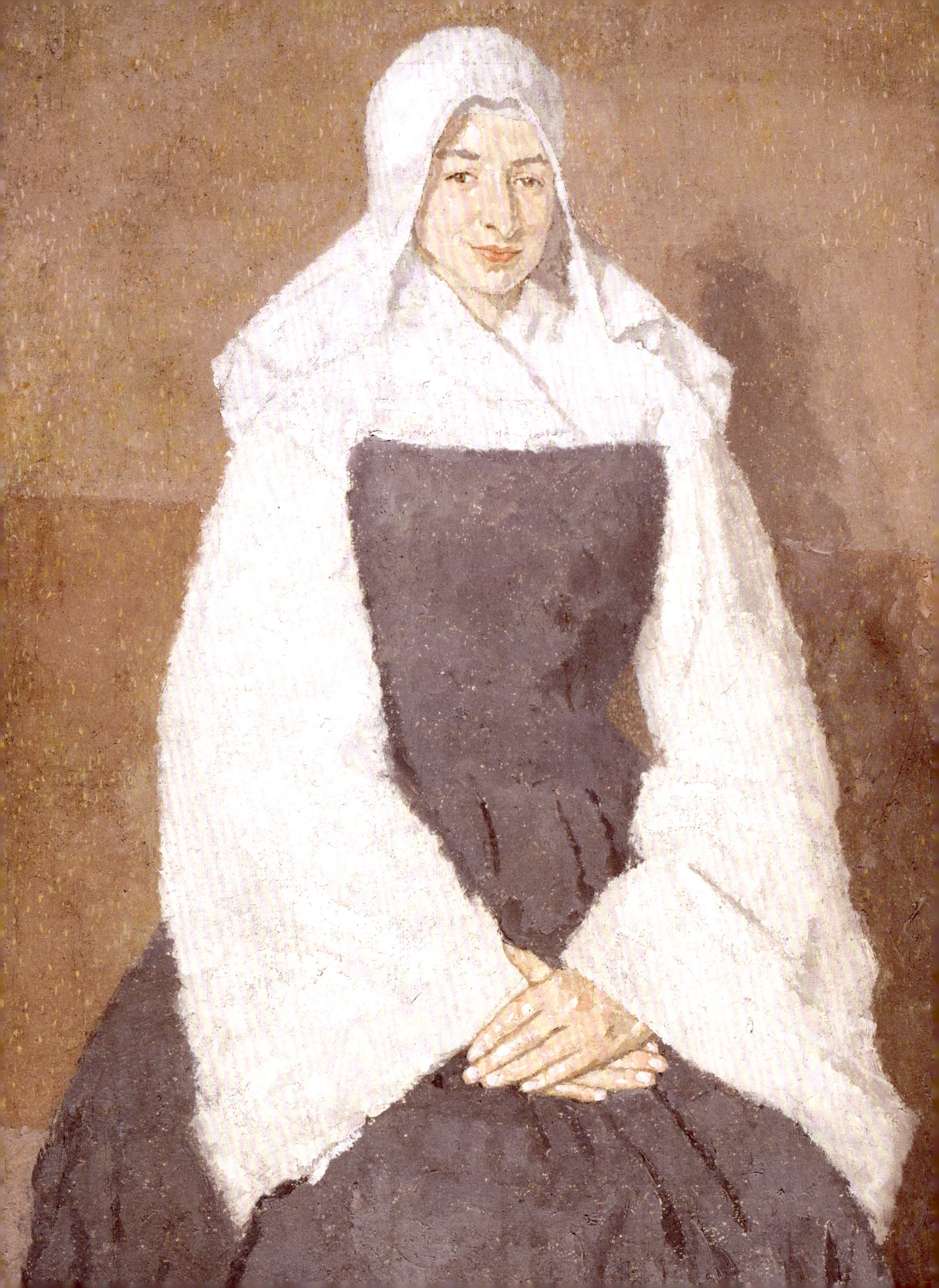

REPUTATION

4

Flourishing with the National Gallery's Support (1946–70)

The dynamic and fruitful relationship between Southampton Art Gallery and the National Gallery nurtured by Kenneth Clark was further developed by his successor, Philip Hendy (1900–1980; fig. 44), the Gallery's longest-serving director, who was in office from January 1946 for 22 years. In the post-war years, Southampton's curator, (George) Loraine Conran, continued to develop the Gallery's collections and exhibitions with great energy, and Maurice Palmer, who replaced him in 1950, was equally effective in pushing Southampton's interests forwards.

Hendy was an experienced museum professional by the time of his appointment in London, as he had worked in the USA and had run Leeds Art Gallery since 1934. He had become known for his entrepreneurial spirit and his outspoken support for the decentralisation of culture in Britain. At the outbreak of the Second World War and after Leeds Art Gallery had been closed and its collections removed, Hendy explored new ways to reshape the public's experience of art. He redisplayed the collection in Temple Newsam House, four miles east of the city, and organised exhibitions of contemporary art in this traditional country house setting. The most important of these, which took place in 1941, showcased the work of Henry Moore, Graham Sutherland and John Piper.

Once at the National Gallery, Hendy's most urgent tasks were to oversee the return and redisplay of the collection after the war and to rebuild galleries destroyed by bombing. As part of his interest in scientific advances for the benefit of the arts, he piloted air conditioning in the galleries so that the paintings could benefit from a stable climate, furnished the scientific department with spacious laboratories and established an in-house conservation department in 1946. Well known for his demands to improve the Gallery's yearly acquisition

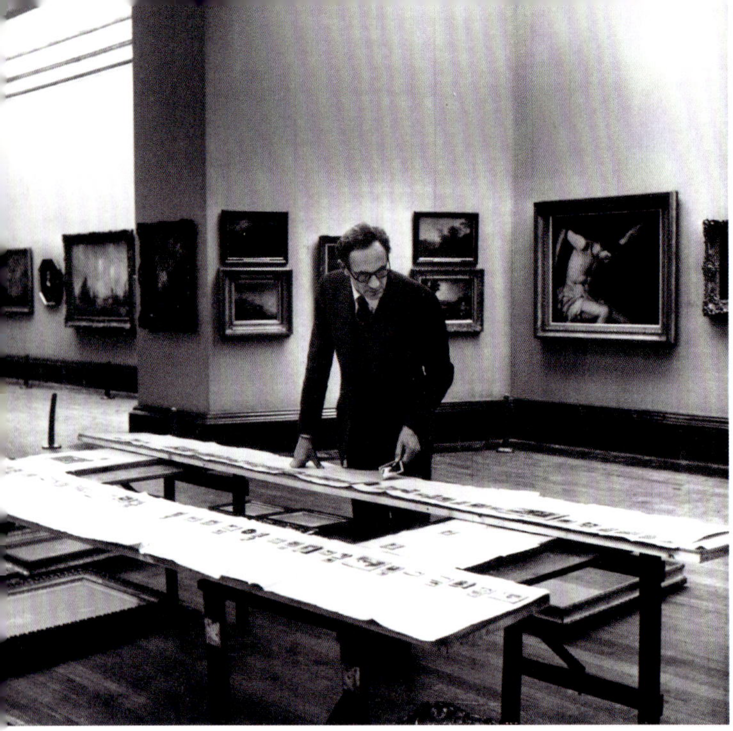

(PREVIOUS PAGE)
Gwen John (1876–1939)
Mère Poussepin, 1920; detail, cat. 36
Oil on canvas, 86.7 × 51.2 cm
Southampton City Art Gallery,
SOTAG 1456

FIG. 44
Philip Hendy, Director of the National Gallery (1946–67) rehanging paintings in the Duveen Room, 1956. The National Gallery, London

grant, Hendy succeeded in increasing the risible pre-war sum to an annual £100,000. He utilised this new wealth to fill gaps in the Gallery's holdings of French eighteenth- and nineteenth-century paintings by acquiring works by Cézanne, Monet and Renoir. He also made some celebrated old master purchases, notably Leonardo's 'Burlington House Cartoon'. From a curatorial point of view, Hendy challenged traditional types of display at Trafalgar Square, just as he had done at Leeds, by mixing up chronologies and geographies in 'daring juxtapositions' to encourage visitors to see new artistic dialogues between unlikely conversation partners. Hendy made great strides in public outreach at the National Gallery, partly by establishing a publications department in 1949 and an education department in the 1960s. Despite what are now seen as positive innovations, Hendy's approach was not regarded with approval by all of the trustees or staff, and his relations with the board were strained, especially in his early years.

A revised purchasing policy for Southampton Art Gallery in 1946

By contrast, Hendy enjoyed harmonious relations with Southampton's curator, Conran, who returned to his post at much the same time that Hendy started in London. Perhaps it was Conran's memories of his own fraught relations with the Chipperfield Bequest Sub-Committee that encouraged him to underscore Hendy's power 'of veto on all purchases made ... from the monies of the Chipperfield bequest', when he wrote to him on 19 March 1946 to explain the duties connected with his role as Southampton's art adviser.[1] His letter also detailed the healthy finances relating to the Chipperfield Bequest Fund. Although no purchases had been made during the previous six-and-a-half years – the collection had expanded through gifts – the sub-committee was now asking 'for a report on the policy to be adopted when buying is resumed'.[2]

In early July 1946, Conran informed Hendy that the Chipperfield Bequest Sub-Committee had agreed to two new resolutions concerning future acquisitions:

> (i) that the main portion of the annual income of the Trust Fund (approximately £3,000) be devoted to the purchase of works by past and present painters of the British School, and that the remainder (approximately £300) be reserved for the purchase of Victorian subject paintings, and that, when conditions permit, consideration be given to the purchase of sculpture and also Continental and American works of art and
>
> (ii) that the Art Curator be authorised, in conjunction with the Director of the National Gallery, to purchase pictures and other works of art up to an amount of £2,000 on any one occasion ... .[3]

Comparing the points raised here with the four areas of growth outlined a decade earlier in Clark's

1936 acquisition policy, ideas appear to have shifted. In reality, however, little changed. For instance, although nothing was said about it, European art of the past would continue to be pursued by Conran and his successors. Again, although two novel elements were introduced into the equation – American art and sculpture – only the latter would be pursued to any extent.

A post-war focus on contemporary British art including abstract art

During the remainder of Conran's time in office – he resigned at the end of 1949 to become curator at Kenwood House, London – he acquired for Southampton Art Gallery a number of important British pictures. In a letter of 5 December 1946, Conran referred to his hopes of securing two paintings by William Hogarth from the Cook Collection. In another of 11 December, Conran and Clark mulled over possible purchases from a Sotheby's sale, including Mark Gertler's *Portrait of a Young Girl* (now Tate). Even though none of these works was acquired, this correspondence reveals how keen both men were to maintain the high standards of acquisition of the pre-war era. An important Pre-Raphaelite work came Conran's way during his first year back in office: Holman Hunt's *The Afterglow in Egypt* (fig. 45) was presented in 1946, adding lustre to a part of the collection initiated with the *Perseus Series*.

In the immediate post-war years, Conran built up a solid core of British abstract art. This helped to transform Southampton Art Gallery into a centre for collecting modern twentieth-century art of all kinds – not just works in the figurative tradition. In the later 1940s, Conran added some notable pictures by abstract painters who had taken the English Romantic landscape tradition in new directions: John Piper's *Portland Foreshore* was acquired in 1946, Paul

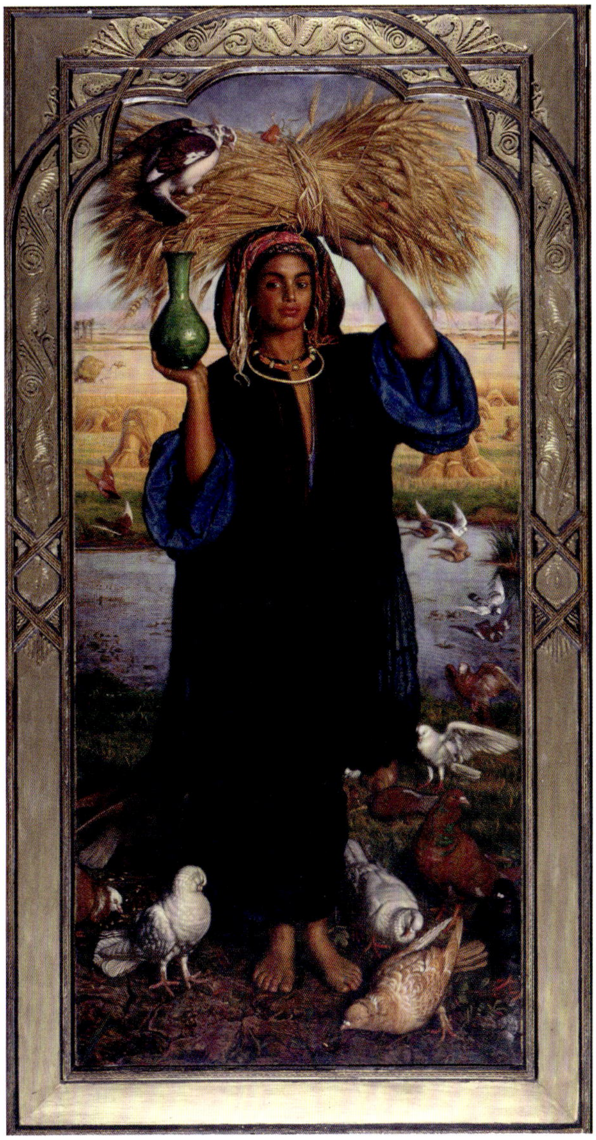

FIG. 45
William Holman Hunt (1827–1910)
The Afterglow in Egypt, 1854
Oil on canvas, 185.4 × 86.3 cm
Southampton City Art Gallery, SOTAG 1280

Nash's *Landscape of the Malvern Distance* and Graham Sutherland's *Green Lane* both in 1947, and Graham Sutherland's *Red Landscape* in 1949 (fig. 46, cat. 19).

These purchases were supplemented by gifts from the Contemporary Art Society (CAS), founded in 1910 to encourage interest in contemporary art in Britain, partly through donating works to public galleries. In

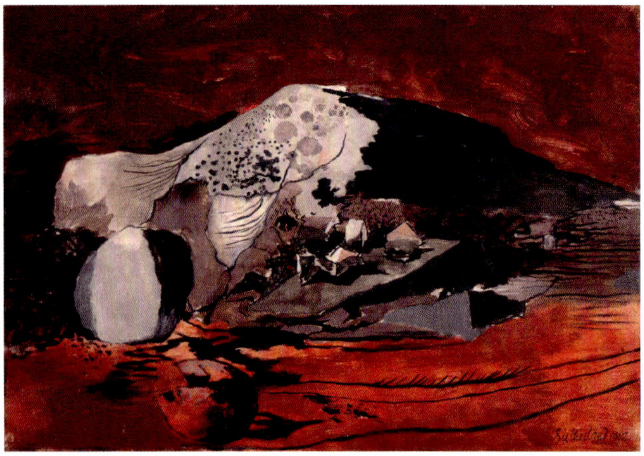

FIG. 46
Graham Sutherland (1903–1980)
Red Landscape, 1942
Oil on canvas, 68 × 99.8 cm
Southampton City Art Gallery, SOTAG 1369

1948, Southampton Art Gallery became an institutional member and two years later received its first gift from CAS of two oil paintings, both exemplifying aspects of contemporary British neo-Romanticism: John Craxton's *Dark Landscape* (cat. 20) and John Minton's *Rotherhithe from Wapping*.[4] The work by Craxton had previously belonged to Clark. It certainly did not do Southampton any harm that both Clark and Hendy were on the Executive Committee of CAS in 1949–50.[5]

Another new area of acquisition: continental modern art

Conran's self-appointed task to revitalise the gallery led him to approach local collectors for loans from Spring 1946 onwards. One who would play a particularly crucial role in bringing important foreign art to Southampton was Arthur Tilden Jeffress (1905–1961). He had started to collect art seriously from the mid-1930s and, from 1946, became an important dealer of modern art. Jeffress tried to sell *The Painter's Family* by Giorgio de Chirico to Southampton for the modest sum of £200 but, as the Chipperfield Bequest Sub-Committee was not 'dashing enough' to purchase it, the work ended up in the Tate Gallery.[6] However, Jeffress lent a considerable number of paintings by leading modern foreign painters, including the de Chirico (painted in Paris), to a pioneering exhibition at Southampton, *French Pictures from the Collection of Mr Arthur Jeffress, Southampton Art Gallery* (19 August–21 September 1946). It was a great success with more than 14,000 visitors, many of them encountering pictures by Picasso, de Chirico, Georges Rouault, Amedeo Modigliani, Chaïm Soutine, Balthus, Raoul Dufy, Édouard Vuillard and Maurice de Vlaminck for the first time. Jeffress also loaned, from November to June 1948, *Abstraction* by Jackson Pollock to Southampton (probably an ink drawing). This was the first occasion that work by this pioneering American painter was shown in a British public art gallery.[7]

More old masters for Southampton

Jeffress was also interested in art of the past. In 1948, he approached Conran about a painting of uncertain attribution and unusual subject matter, which he wondered if the art gallery might be interested in buying. The dramatic work, *The Martyrdom of Saint Catherine* (fig. 47), was offered at the low cost of £250, largely because it was unattributed. Conran recognised its 'bizarre quality'[8] and acquired it: it is now accepted as a work by François de Nomé. The following year Conran built on the purchase, acquiring two more old master paintings: John Martin's *Sadak in Search of the Waters of Oblivion* and Philip de Loutherberg's *The Shipwreck* (fig. 48). Both added to Southampton's growing collection of dramatic subjects, which would be further enhanced in 1963 with pictures from the Jeffress Bequest (after his tragic suicide in 1961), including Aldo Pagliacci's 1951 fantasy of St Peter's, Rome in flames, and two eighteenth-century scenes of sorcery by Stefano Orlandi.[9]

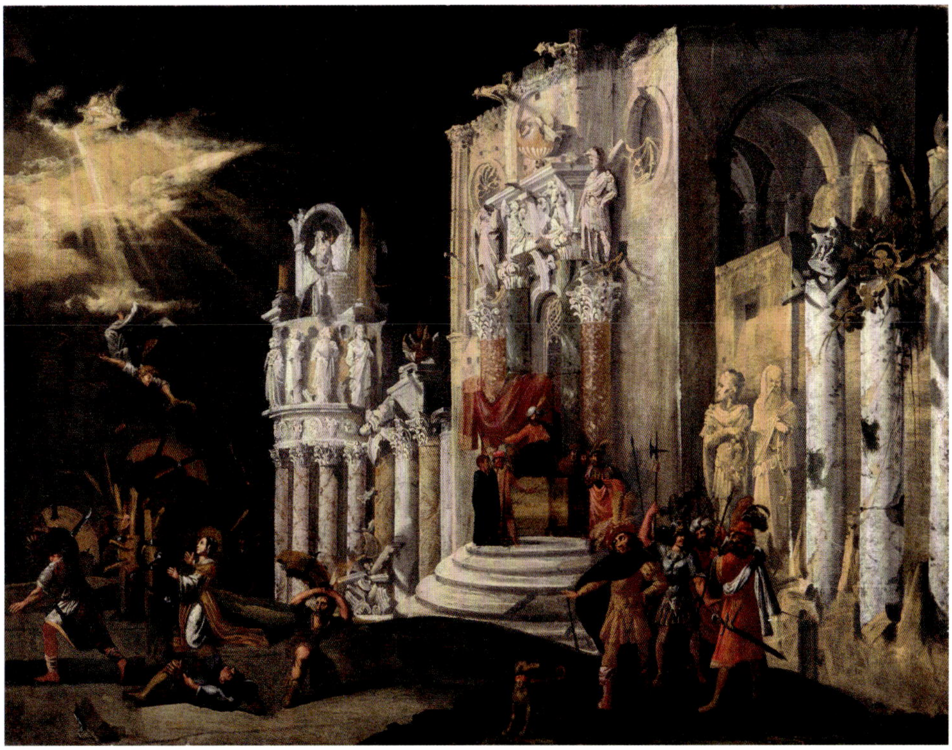

FIG. 47
François de Nomé (about 1593–after 1644) and Didier Barra (about 1590–after 1652)
The Martyrdom of Saint Catherine, 1617
Oil on canvas, 95.8 × 126 cm
Southampton City Art Gallery, SOTAG 1359

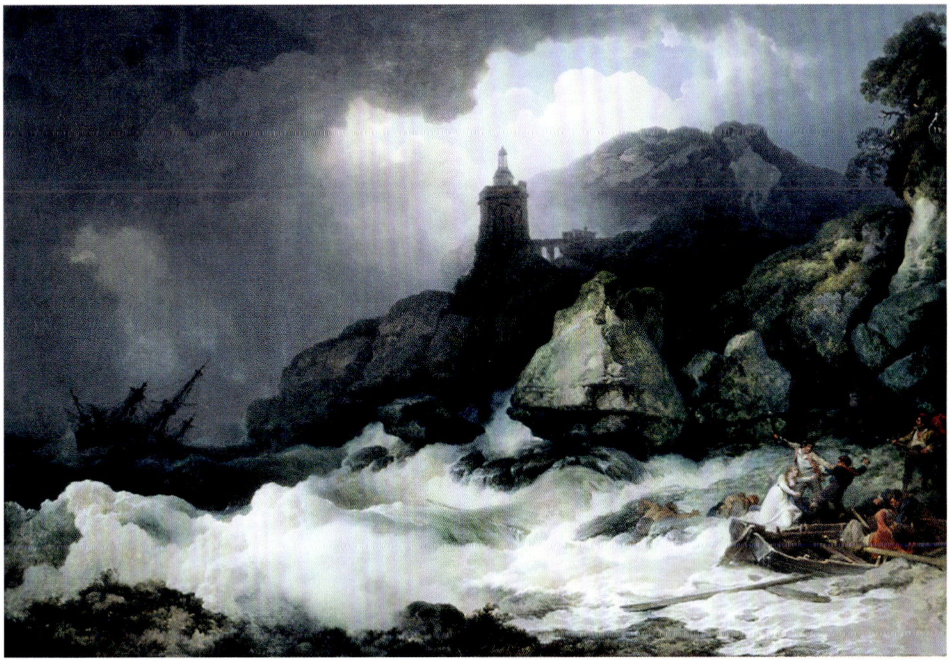

FIG. 48
Philip de Loutherberg (1740–1812)
The Shipwreck, 1793
Oil on canvas, 109.8 × 160.5 cm
Southampton City Art Gallery, SOTAG 1365

Conran's pioneering temporary exhibitions and touring shows

An important second prong of Conran's activity was to extend his pre-war initiative of mounting first-rate temporary exhibitions. In 1946, Conran was quoted in a local newspaper as hoping to bring a series of 'the very best available' shows to Southampton, and in July that year, an article in the *Southern Daily Echo* stated that it was 'the first month ... the Southampton Art Gallery has not had a loan exhibition. The previous six months have seen no less [sic] than thirteen loan exhibitions.'[10]

Two old master exhibitions represent milestones in terms of Conran's pioneering loans-in programme. In 1946, 24 Spanish paintings toured to five UK centres outside London. All 'the undoubted pictures by Velázquez in this country' were displayed, including five from the National Gallery, the artist's *Old Woman Frying Eggs* from the Scottish National Gallery and Goya's *Charles III of Spain in Hunting Dress* (Prado, Madrid). The newly formed Arts Council organised the event with Southampton as the first venue and the National Gallery as the last.[11] The decision regarding the choice of venues may have had something to do with the fact that at the time Clark was chair of the Arts Council's Arts Panel.[12]

The second significant old master exhibition was *Primitive and Early Renaissance Paintings from the Cook Collection*, which in 1947 toured to venues in Manchester, Brighton and Southampton. Presumably, it was partly due to this association that Southampton found itself the recipient of a semi-permanent loan of five works from the Cook Collection: Poussin's *The Plague of Athens*, Isenbrant's *Virgin and Child*, a study by Ribera, a portrait of a boy by Titian, and an early work by Giorgione. It is clear that by this point Southampton was considered a suitable venue for national touring exhibitions and important long-term loans.

The quantity and quality of Conran's exhibitions helped to familiarise the local gallery-visiting public with historical art, and to raise the reputation of Southampton's art gallery. This transformation was alluded to by Alderman J.H.J. Matthews, JP, when he spoke in 1953 about the unusual opportunity 'to make the acquaintance of both modern and medieval art' which the gallery offered to the public through its permanent collection and loan programme, remarking that 'forty years ago, you had to go to London for such an experience'.[13]

The appointment of Maurice Palmer as Southampton's second curator (1950–70)

Just as Clark had been involved with the appointment of Southampton Art Gallery's first curator, his successor Hendy had much to do with the choosing of Conran's replacement. In December 1949, the town clerk wrote to ask for 'the benefit of [Hendy's] experience and advice',[14] and in February Councillor Matthews met with him to discuss the six shortlisted candidates. Maurice Palmer (fig. 49), a 35-year-old curator from the Cecil Higgins Museum of Art,

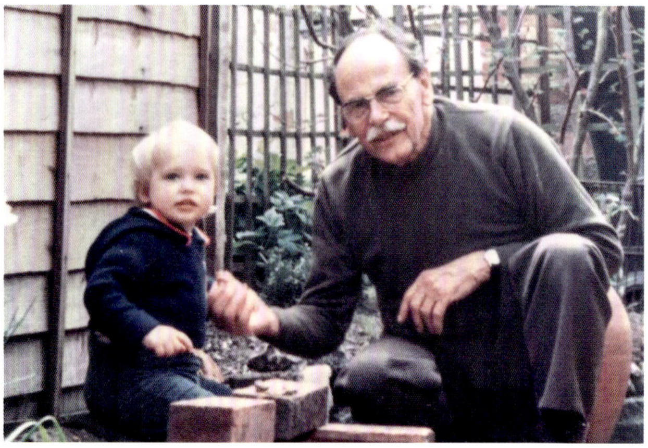

FIG. 49
Maurice Palmer (1917–2002) in Liz Goodall's garden with her daughter Laura, around 1986.

Bedford, came out on top. Several of the others went on to have distinguished careers: Henry Hanson Schubart, for instance, became director of the Bristol Museum & Art Gallery in 1953.

During two decades in office (1950–70), Palmer had a huge impact on 'rounding out' the permanent collection. Institutional records chart the various ways in which he acted boldly to secure acquisitions. He made a habit of visiting London regularly to meet the National Gallery's director and dealers in person, sent pictures to Hendy to comment on,[15] and, occasionally, felt strongly enough to go against Hendy's advice.[16] His achievements are all the more remarkable when it is remembered that he worked largely alone, his skeleton staff originally consisting of 'a conservator, a secretary and a small team of town sergeants seconded from the Guildhall, who coped with attendant duties'.[17]

With Palmer taking a strong lead, Hendy increasingly saw his role as one of support. In practice, this meant drawing attention to potentially eligible historical works and gathering opinions concerning authenticity or condition from his scholarly network. On one occasion, Hendy referred to his status at Southampton as that of 'a kind of semi-Trustee',[18] and on another he explained: 'I have been associated with many ... purchases, but have left the initiative entirely to [Palmer] and have always been very pleased with the choices that he has made.'[19] Part of stepping back also involved Hendy never utilising his power of veto[20] while relinquishing full responsibility to Palmer for certain parts of the collection, notably 'in the matter of prints'.[21]

The Chipperfield Bequest Sub-Committee was also by now less interfering. At the re-opening of the Main Hall in April 1953, Alderman Matthews could relate the happy relations which now pertained:

> [H]e could remember great battles about what pictures to buy and what not to buy! Now, however, the committee were wise enough to leave to Sir Philip ... and to the curator a great degree of freedom and responsibility. That had been a major factor in making the collection, which Southampton had today, one of the finest provincial collections in the country.[22]

Although keen to acquire paintings by esteemed names, Palmer was not averse to buying interesting pictures by lesser-known painters which needed clarification regarding authorship or subject matter, or which needed conservation treatment. He realised, as Conran had, that these matters tended to reduce the final sale price. In this regard, he had more independence than certain counterparts; for instance, curators at the Barber Institute, Birmingham, were pressurised by the terms of the foundational charter to pursue acknowledged masterpieces.[23]

Palmer's old master purchases

Although responsible for purchasing watercolours by Edward Lear and Paul Sandby and drawings by Walter Sickert, Christopher Wood, Wyndham Lewis and Duncan Grant, Palmer's most significant impact on the permanent collection was his acquisition of important historical paintings. As he wrote to Hendy in November 1957, an ambition was 'to acquire a small nucleus of really good Old Masters to take the place of our slowly diminishing Cook Collection loan.'[24] Soon, he was suggesting that a sensible approach might be 'trying to acquire some of the Cook Collection pictures rather than continuing to wait for possible purchases from other sources.'[25]

In fact, as early as 1951 Palmer had purchased a Cook Collection picture: Allegretto Nuzi's large altarpiece, *The Coronation of the Virgin* (fig. 50; cat. 21) of 1360, for £3,000 using the Smith Bequest Fund.[26] At the time of accession, it was regarded as

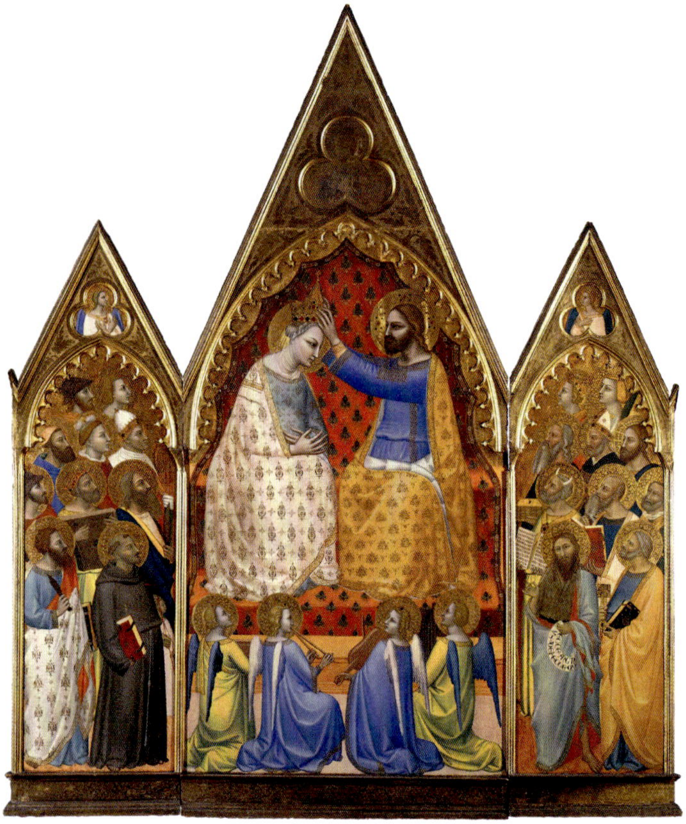

FIG. 50
Allegretto Nuzi (active 1354; died 1373/74)
The Coronation of the Virgin, 1360
Tempera on board, 245.7 × 102.5 cm
Southampton City Art Gallery,
SOTAG 1403

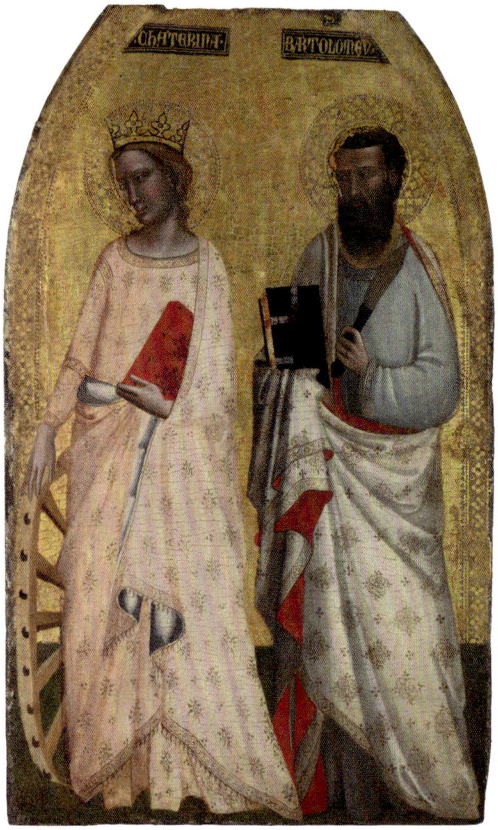

FIG. 51
Allegretto Nuzi (active 1354; died 1373/74)
and Francescuccio Ghissi (active 1345–74)
Saints Catherine and Bartholomew, about 1350
Egg tempera on wood, 83.2 × 51 cm
The National Gallery, London, NG5930

'the most important picture as yet purchased',[27] but even earlier its merits had been acknowledged. It had been described as 'one of the most important ... loans'[28] included in the Cook Collection touring exhibition of 1947, where it had hung alongside panels from Ugolino's *Santa Croce Altarpiece*, now at the National Gallery. The National Gallery had very recently – in 1949 – been bequeathed a small panel depicting Saint Catherine and Bartholomew, painted by Nuzi with assistance from Francescuccio Ghissi (fig. 51). Palmer subsequently asked Hendy for advice regarding the conservation of Southampton's triptych.[29] Although the National Gallery could not oblige, being 'swamped with work of the same kind', Hendy was able to recommend the name of a suitable conservator, William Drown & Co. of New Bond Street, London.[30]

Palmer originally hoped that 'other examples of the early Italian School or similar pictures might be 'purchased by the Chipperfield Bequest from the Cook Collection or other sources, so as to build up a small collection of "Italian Primitives", and the like in the Southampton Gallery.'[31] Although this did not happen – indeed it was rare for any regional gallery to purchase examples of early Italian art in the first half of the twentieth century[32] – Palmer did succeed in acquiring three more significant historical paintings from the Cook Collection, two in 1958 and a third in 1963.

In the 1958 transaction, Palmer secured Goswijn van der Weyden's *Saint Catherine and the Philosophers* (cat. 22) and Cesare da Sesto's *Saint Jerome* (cat. 24). Palmer had been interested also in a *Virgin and Child* by Cima da Conegliano but Hendy cautioned him against it, suspicious that it had been much overpainted, suggesting that Palmer contact Stephen Rees Jones, then head of the Courtauld Institute's technology department, to investigate further.[33] Of the two paintings purchased in 1958, Christopher Wright, author of the standard reference work to Southampton City Art Gallery's pre-1900 collection, has argued: 'Few examples of Milanese and Netherlandish pictures of such quality [are to be found] outside the National Gallery in London'.[34] Certainly, they stand up well when compared to equivalent works from the National Gallery in the current exhibition. The 1950s Cook Collection acquisitions helped to establish a strong 'nucleus' (to use Clark's and Palmer's word) of old masters in Southampton, even though extant correspondence reveals that Hendy recommended the Netherlandish triptych 'less willingly' than the Cesare da Sesto.

Palmer also made several important purchases of Baroque and later works. For instance, in 1953, he bought a pair of portraits by Anthony van Dyck, dating to 1619–20 and showing members of Antwerp's most prosperous class (fig. 52). Palmer and Hendy's pre-purchase discussion focused partly on how these works would help to illuminate the later British portraits already in Southampton's collection: 'They would be most valuable as indications of the great continental tradition from which English portraiture derived.'[35] Having sought the expert opinion of his colleague, Neil McLaren, 'our specialist on Van Dyck', Hendy was able to report that McLaren had 'no doubt about the Van Dyck attribution' and was 'enthusiastic about the pictures'.[36] Palmer ultimately secured

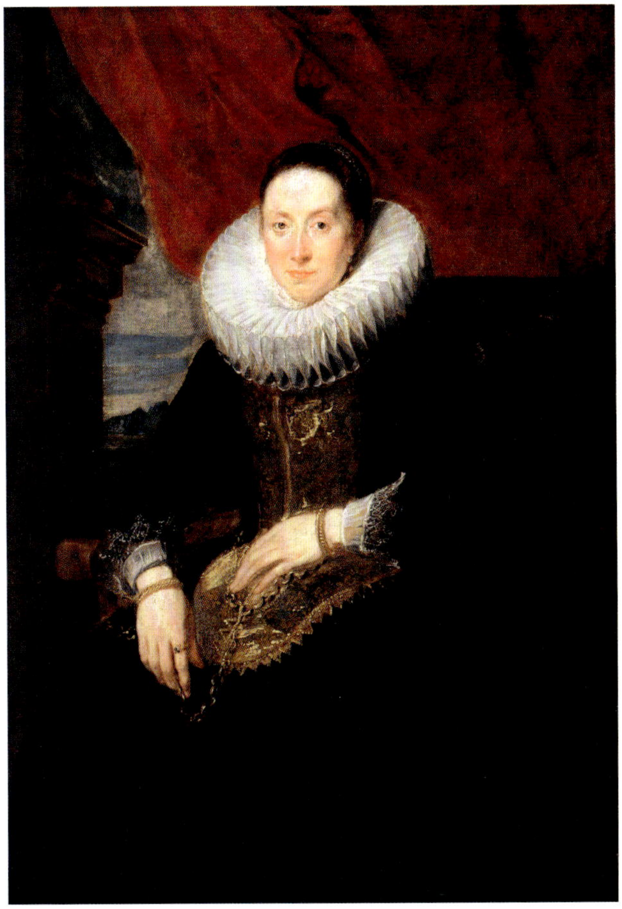

FIG. 52
Anthony van Dyck (1599–1641)
Portrait of a Woman, 1618
Oil on canvas, 127.5 × 90.9 cm
Southampton City Art Gallery, SOTAG 1431

them for only £6,500, presumably because the sitters were unidentified, and the male portrait was not in optimum condition.

Palmer made a particular point of acquiring seventeenth-century landscapes, which, although not popular among private collectors of the mid-twentieth century, were considered a fundamental addition to any public art collection desirous of plotting key moments in the history of Western European painting. Building on a gift in 1955 of Isaack van Ostade's *Travellers at an Inn*, Palmer's first such purchase, two years later, was *Landscape*

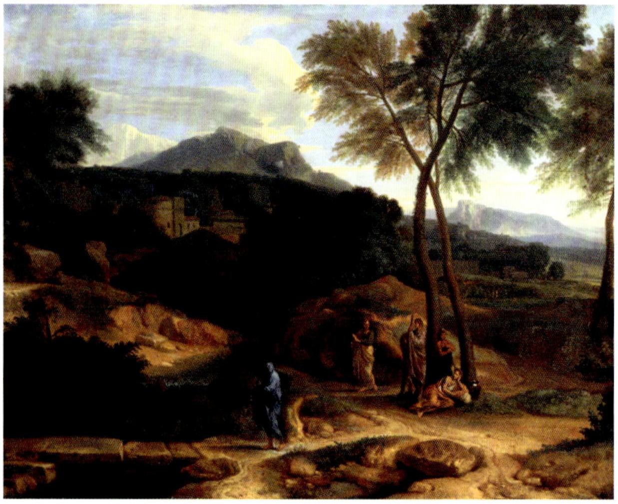

FIG. 53
Attributed to Jean François Millet (1642–1679)
Landscape with Conopion Carrying the Ashes of Phocion, about 1665–75
Oil on canvas, 112 × 143.3 cm
Southampton City Art Gallery, SOTAG 1490

with Conopion Carrying the Ashes of Phocion (fig. 53), attributed to Jean-François (Francisque) Millet. The painter had spent his short career in the 1660–70s in Paris, where he became known for his Italianate landscapes. The Southampton picture is characteristic of Millet's work, being solemn in atmosphere, dramatic in subject and demonstrating the influence of his more famous predecessors in the field, Nicolas Poussin and Gaspard Dughet. It was Hendy who drew Palmer's attention to the work and who passed on the favourable opinion of Denis Mahon, 'the best authority on such things'.[37] Southampton at that time had another landscape 'wrongly put down to Francisque Millet',[38] so the new purchase happily brought a genuine work by the painter into the collection. It was bought from Agnew's in London for an 'exceptionally good price' (£530).

Two years later, in 1959, Palmer proposed the purchase of *View of the Roman Campagna*, a classicising landscape of the 1660s by Gaspard Dughet (the brother-in-law of Poussin). He justified his suggestion by noting that it would potentially 'make an excellent pair with the Francisque Millet', adding jovially, 'What we now want are a Claude and a Nicolas Poussin!'[39] In turn, Palmer used the Dughet to argue, in 1961, for the purchase of Salvator Rosa's *A Mountain Landscape* (cat. 26), telling Clark that it 'would make a very good companion picture to the Gaspard Poussin [Dughet] which we bought ... two years ago.'[40] Both paintings were purchased from the London dealership Colnaghi's, the former costing £1,450, the latter £2,900 (employing a 40% government grant).

A fourth great landscape was purchased by Palmer in 1963: Philips Koninck's *An Extensive Landscape* (cat. 28), a huge panorama showing Dutch countryside under a vast sky, once part of the Cook Collection. Southampton's picture was bought for £9,000 from Wildenstein's in London, with the aid of a £3,500 government grant through the Victoria and Albert Museum. Fortunately, the painter's popularity had waned since the nineteenth-century or else Southampton might have had to pay far more.

The following year, Palmer purchased Jacob van Ruisdael's *Dunes near Haarlem* (cat. 30), for what Hendy referred to as 'your now splendid landscape collection'.[41] It was secured from an exhibition at the Brod Gallery, and paid for partly through a grant administered by the Victoria and Albert Museum, while according to Palmer, the Chipperfield Bequest Sub-Committee agreed to the rest largely because of 'the very valuable support which you (Hendy) gave me in your letter'.[42] Palmer was delighted with the outcome, thinking that the new work sat beautifully within Southampton's impressive group of landscapes, not least 'in company with the fine Koninck which you helped us with last year.' In 1967, Palmer acquired his sixth and final Dutch 'Golden Age' landscape. Paul Bril's *Hilly Landscape* was purchased once more from Colnaghi's and again with a government grant.[43]

FIG. 54
Joshua Reynolds (1723–1792)
Cornet Nehemiah Winter, 11th Dragoons, 1759
Oil on canvas, 113.5 × 137.5 cm
Southampton City Art Gallery, SOTAG 1482

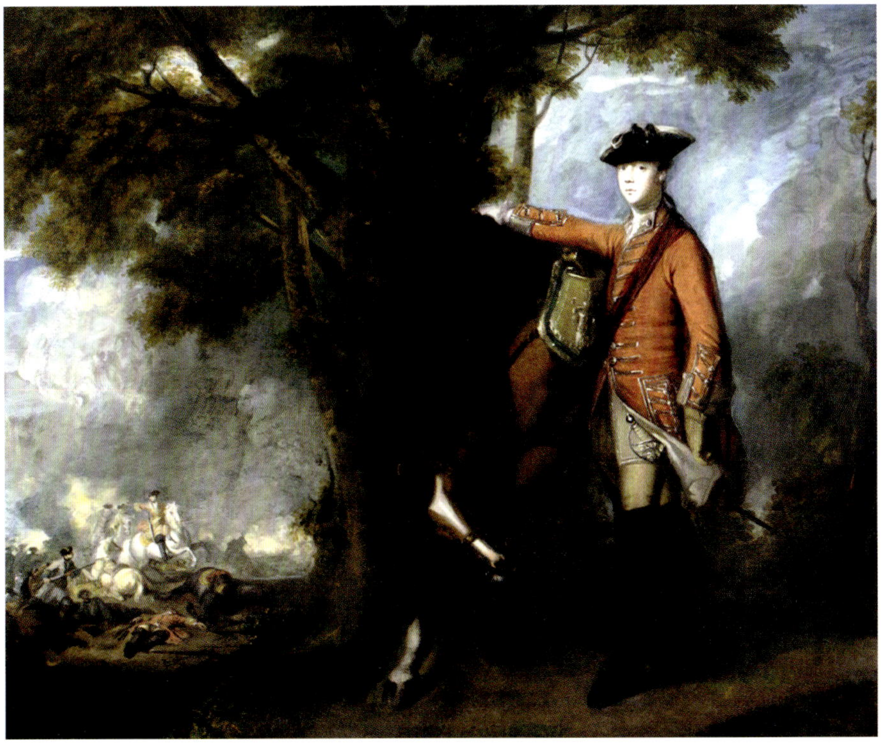

FIG. 55
Joshua Reynolds (1723–1792)
Captain Robert Orme, 1756
Oil on canvas, 239 × 147 cm
The National Gallery, London, NG681

British art acquisitions under Palmer

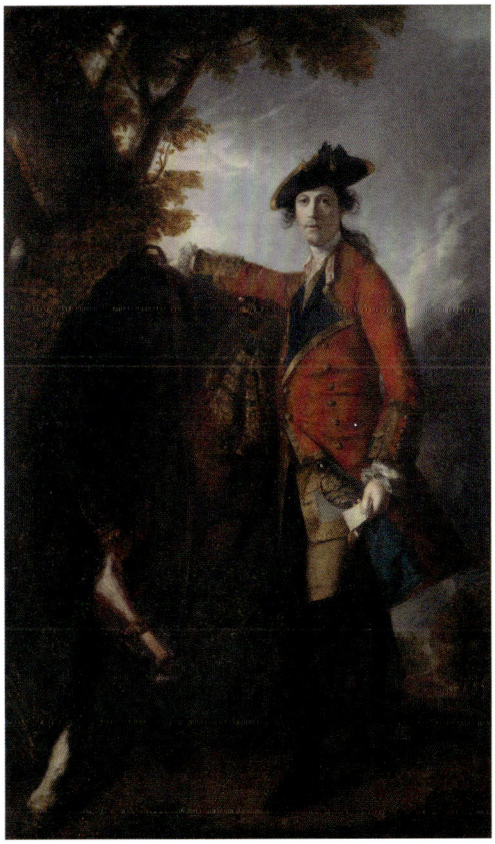

Palmer's time as curator was also important for Southampton's historic British collections. His most significant purchase of nineteenth-century British art was *Fishermen Upon a Lee-Shore in Squally Weather* by J.M.W. Turner, acquired in 1951 (cat. 31). The Chipperfield Bequest Fund also assisted with the purchase of major examples of eighteenth-century British art, including a landscape by Joseph Wright of Derby (cat. 32) – an artist then unrepresented in the collection,[44] an 'exceptionally interesting' conversation piece by Francis Hayman,[45] and a handful of prime British portraits, starting with Sir Joshua Reynolds's portrait of *Cornet Nehemiah Winter, 11th Dragoons* (fig. 54), in 1956.

Reynolds was celebrated as the first president of the Royal Academy of Arts, his lectures or *Discourses* proving hugely influential on the development of British artistic practice and theory. Being so much in

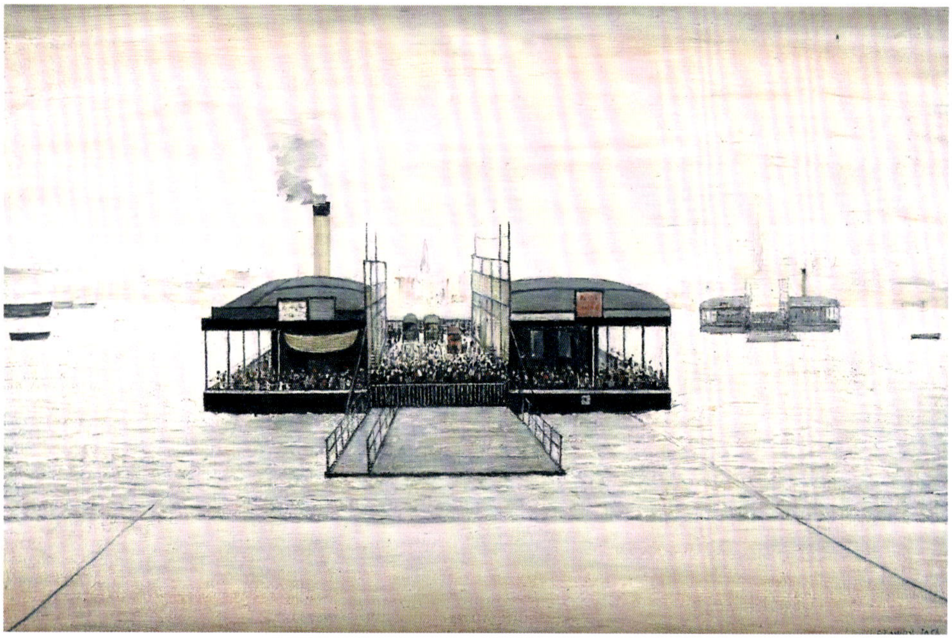

FIG. 56
Laurence Stephen Lowry (1887–1976)
The Floating Bridge, 1956
Oil on canvas, 50.8 × 76.3 cm
Southampton City Art Gallery, SOTAG 1483

demand especially as a portrait painter, Reynolds had turned to studio assistants to complete the clothing and backgrounds of his paintings, while he himself re-used poses and compositions. In Southampton's picture, the figure of Cornet Winter and his horse are based on a grouping found in Reynolds's earlier portrait of Captain Robert Orme (fig. 55), a work which entered the National Gallery's collection in 1862.[46] It was Hendy who drew the portrait of Winter to Palmer's attention, declaring it to be 'absolutely enchanting' and wishing that it belonged to the National Gallery.[47] Palmer, in response, happily reminded him that the picture had links with Southampton given that it had once belonged to Lord Swaythling of Townhill Park.[48]

The following year, in 1957, Palmer acquired Southampton's first – and only – work by Thomas Gainsborough (1727–1788), another key figure of the historical British school (indeed a rival of Reynolds). *George, Lord Vernon* (cat. 33) shows the painter's skill in capturing a natural likeness and portraying fashionable dress of his day. Although Hendy did not immediately see its merits, concerned about the sitter's waistcoat, which he thought was in 'rather a messy state',[49] Palmer thought quite differently. Since the painting had 'so much of the best and most typical of [Gainsborough's] painting',[50] he successfully argued that the Chipperfield Bequest Sub-Committee should dip into its reserves, and apply for a substantial contribution from the National Art Collections Fund.

In Conran's footsteps, Palmer continued to acquire modern British art. While the Smith Bequest Fund was generally used to pay for more modern pictures, the National Gallery still had some influence on the development of Southampton's collection in this area because the Chipperfield Bequest Fund was sometimes dipped into to support such acquisitions. For instance, L.S. Lowry's *Floating Bridge* (fig. 56) was purchased with Chipperfield money in 1956. Palmer recorded that he felt compelled to act in this way because the Lefevre Gallery 'would not reserve it at all', and '[i]t seemed a pity to miss this picture while there was a chance of securing it through the Chipperfield Bequest. My Smith Bequest machinery takes weeks to get going.'[51] The painting has always been well received given Lowry's increasing popularity and given that it depicts a local scene. Lowry first visited Southampton in 1954, while staying at Bitterne, and took the chain ferry or floating bridge across the river Itchen. On a second visit, Lowry sketched the ferry from Woolston with the city in the background. He went on to create two paintings, this one and another showing a crowd of ferry passengers spilling out.

Due to Palmer's strategic purchasing, Southampton built up one of the best groups of Camden Town Group paintings outside London. Building on the two Sickerts bought during the 1930s, Palmer purchased *The Juvenile Lead* in 1951, which he described as both '"the" Sickert self portrait' and 'a most important picture from the gallery point of view'.[52] He also bought a painting by Spencer Gore, the artist who, in 1904, had visited Sickert in Dieppe and encouraged him to come back to London, going on to rent a studio near Sickert's in Camden. As noted in Chapter 3, Gore's *View from a Window* (cat. 17) had been purchased during the 1930s, and Palmer followed this up when he bought the same painter's *Brighton Pier* in 1956. The 1950s and 60s also saw the purchase of works by other painters associated with the movement, including Robert Bevan and Charles Ginner. Adding to the purchase of *Cumberland Market* in 1947, two more works by Bevan were bought in 1952. During the negotiations for *Mydlow Village, Poland*, Palmer reminded Hendy that Southampton Art Gallery had 'specialised to some extent in the Camden Town Group' and that he felt Bevan's work 'deserve[d] to be more widely known'.[53] Southampton's curator was still using such arguments almost two decades later. In 1969, when urging the purchase of Ginner's *Early Morning* (cat. 35), Palmer recorded its 'kinship with the Camden Town Group, particularly Spencer Gore'.[54]

In 1951, one of Southampton Art Gallery's first important loan exhibitions had been dedicated to the Camden Town Group as part of the Festival of Britain. Based on Southampton's permanent collection, supplemented by a few important loans, the exhibition was positively reviewed. In the opinion of Tim Craven, a former acting director of Southampton Art Gallery, this initiative was the catalyst which sparked national interest in this school of painting.[55] Purchases of Camden Town Group pictures continued after 1970. Notably, two of Anthony Howarth's first purchases as director were Ginner's *The Barges, Leeds* and Bevan's *A Sale at Tattersalls*. In July 1974, he explained to Martin Davies, then the National Gallery's director: 'We are anxious to obtain both to augment our fairly extensive collection of Camden Town Group. Each painting is of an aspect not yet covered by the works of these artists that we already own.'[56]

Palmer also built up a strong representation of works by another looser grouping of important early twentieth-century British painters, Gwen John, Stanley Spencer and Mark Gertler, all of whom were Slade School-trained and pursued their own distinctive approaches. Indeed, what one critic said of Gertler is equally true of them all, namely that he did not 'come easily into any classification by "movements," though he may be called modern in his outlook.'[57] Spencer's paintings *Patricia Preece* and *The Resurrection with the Raising of Jairus's Daughter* were Palmer acquisitions of the early 1950s, while in 1954, he was responsible for purchasing Gwen John's *Mère Poussepin* (cat. 36). That portrait had been commissioned after her conversion to Roman Catholicism by the Sisters of Charity of the Holy Virgin of Tours – it is an imaginary likeness of their founder Marie Poussepin (1653–1744). Hendy congratulated Palmer on 'a very good buy' and stated how happy he was 'to see the best picture in the [Matthiesen Gallery] Exhibition going to Southampton'.[58] Of equally subdued tonality is John's *Girl in Mulberry Dress*, painted a few years later in 1923, which Palmer would secure in 1962.

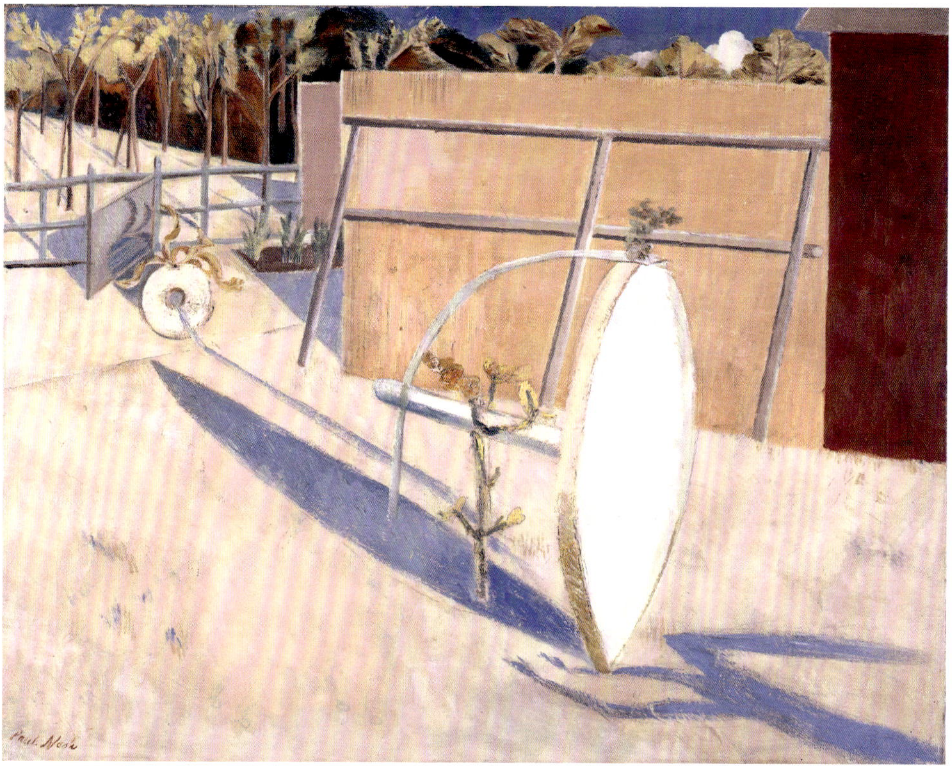

FIG. 57
Paul Nash (1889–1946)
The Archer, 1930/1937/1942
Oil on canvas, 71 × 91.5 cm
Southampton City Art Gallery, SOTAG 1415

All four of Southampton's impressive Gertlers were accessioned during Palmer's time as curator. When making a pitch in 1968 for *Rabbi and his Grandchild* (cat. 37), he drew attention to his three earlier Chipperfield Bequest Fund acquisitions of 1953–54: 'we have three Gertlers already: a very early Family Group, rather like a blue-period Picasso, said to date from Gertler's student days; a characteristic nude of 1924, and a Still Life with Guitar, typical of the 1930's. We have nothing like this picture, which seems a rather fine example of this aspect of Gertler's work.'[59] He had to work hard, however, to persuade the newly appointed National Gallery director Martin Davies of its merits, who originally dismissed it as a minor work.[60] This contrasted with Hendy's earlier enthusiastic response when Palmer had secured Gertler's *Seated Nude*: 'It was clever of you to find it, and I think it is a quite excellent buy.'[61]

A striking innovation within the British collection was Palmer's pursuit of non-figurative art. As a prelude, Paul Nash's semi-abstract *The Archer* (fig. 57) was bought in August 1952 from Arthur Tooth & Sons. Regarding it as 'one of his best pictures', Hendy, in characteristically encouraging tone, approved it 'heartily'.[62] It joined Nash's *Landscape of the Malvern Distance* which, although painted slightly later, was, according to Palmer, 'more lyrical' – and less abstract.[63] As Nash always had issues portraying the human figure, the Surrealist movement provided him with a solution in the form of the 'object personage': from 1936, he would photograph or collect objects that might stimulate his imagination and provide a cast of characters. In this instance, the abstract figure of the title is composed from an assemblage of recognisable objects.

Southampton acquired its first completely abstract paintings in 1966–67, when it purchased, using Chipperfield money, two works by Ben Nicholson: *1940–42 (two forms)* and *1966 (Greystone)* (fig. 58). Nicholson had painted many landscapes early in his

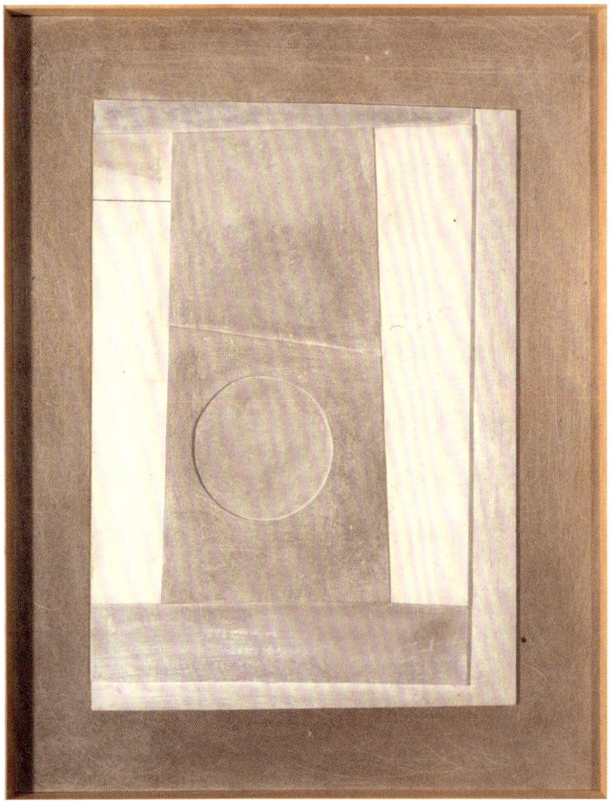

FIG. 58
Ben Nicholson (1894–1982)
1966 (Greystone), 1966
Oil on board, 56.5 × 43.9 cm
Southampton City Art Gallery,
SOTAG 10/1967

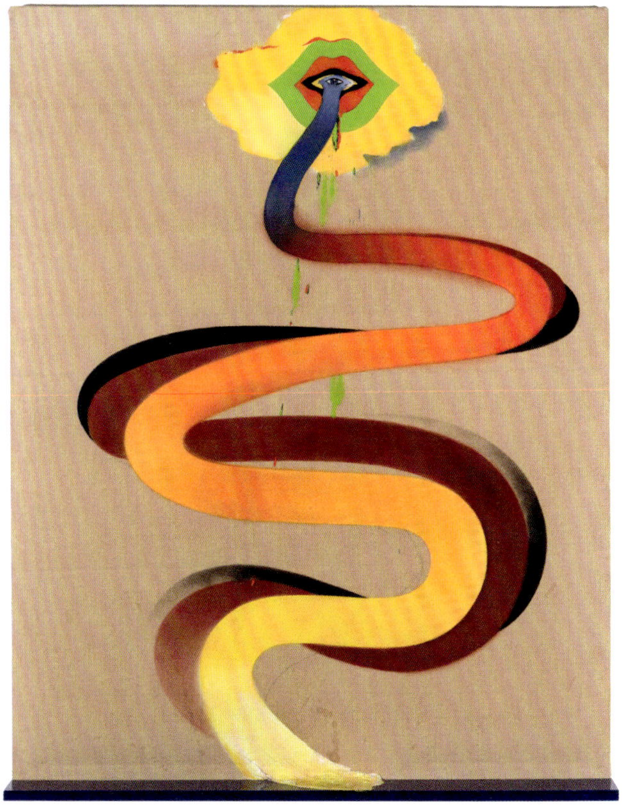

FIG. 59
Allen Jones (b. 1937)
Pathway, 1966
Oil on canvas, 127.5 × 102.2 cm
Southampton City Art Gallery,
SOTAG 4/1967

career but went on to become one of the country's most distinguished pioneers of abstract art. Palmer was pleased to secure both works, telling Hendy that he had 'been a Nicholson fan for some thirty odd years'.[64]

Southampton's collection of contemporary art was brought up to the present through a group of nine paintings paid for through a scheme organised by the Gulbenkian Foundation in the mid-1960s to encourage museums to purchase works painted within the last 15 years. The foundation offered £750 a year, the sum to be matched by funding from the city council, and Southampton participated for one year. The new pictures, showcased in Palmer's exhibition of *Recent Acquisitions, 1966–67* (3 February–31 March 1968), included works by Allen Jones (fig. 59) and Larry Wakefield, who both had local associations. The former was born in Southampton, while Wakefield was living in Southampton, his painting *Solent* referencing the area of sea between Southampton and the Isle of Wight.[65]

Just as innovatively, Palmer built up Southampton's collection of modern sculpture. This was a comparatively unusual undertaking for a UK public collection because the few regional galleries to acquire sculpture had traditionally limited themselves to works by sculptors with local roots; for instance, Liverpool's Walker Art Gallery had accepted in

1873 two statues by the renowned neoclassical sculptor John Gibson who had grown up in the city.[66] In Southampton's case, the only sculpture it had acquired since its foundation was a model for an equestrian statuette of Edward I by Sir William Hamo Thornycroft, a leading light in Britain's 'New Sculpture' movement at the end of the nineteenth century, which Conran had bought in 1946.

Between 1952 and 1970, Palmer bought six bronzes by modern artists of international standing. The impetus came partly from the resolutions passed by the Chipperfield Bequest Sub-Committee in 1946 and partly from what Palmer described in 1952 as his ambition 'to re-open our Sculpture Hall next year'.[67] Once it was discovered that the sculptures were dwarfed by the monumental proportions of the Sculpture Hall and that there were not enough of them to make an impact, the space was renamed the 'Main Hall', and moveable screens were installed for the display of mainly modern pictures.[68]

The American-British sculptor Jacob Epstein's bust of British composer Ralph Vaughan Williams was Palmer's first addition, purchased in 1952, as 'mak[ing] a good beginning from several points of view'.[69] Still in the sculptor's studio, it was the last of six original casts, and it was acquired through the Kensington Art Gallery for £210. The other purchases were by French artists: a work each by Edgar Degas, Aristide Maillol, Henri Gaudier-Brzeska, and two pieces by Auguste Rodin, both of which had originally been conceived as part of his celebrated and monumental *Doors of Hell*. Rodin's *Eve*[70] is now inside the Art Gallery for conservation reasons, but for years it was displayed outside, on the north forecourt of the Civic Centre, after an abandoned, long-standing project failed to produce a new commission for that space,[71] and after Hendy's suggestion to purchase a work by Henry Moore also came to nothing (he did, however, secure Moore's large bronze *Reclining Figure '51* for that space as a loan from the Arts Council, 1957–60).[72] Several of Palmer's acquisitions depict female nudes, including Degas's *Dancer putting on her Stocking* (cat. 38), Rodin's *Eve* and *Squatting Woman* (cat. 39) and Maillol's miniature *Woman with Crab* – the latter another work of art in Southampton's collection which had once belonged to Kenneth Clark (cat. 40).[73]

Given the quantity and quality of acquisitions secured by Palmer during his first decade in office, it is fitting that the distinguished critic Quentin Bell wrote in praise of Southampton's art collection in *The Listener* in 1959. Bell underscored Palmer's good judgement and praised the Gallery for its reliance on individual expertise:

> It is a most desirable and uncommon thing for a Gallery Committee to have the good sense to perceive that, having appointed an expert, it cannot logically do otherwise than rely upon the judgement of the man whom it has appointed. ... Where other towns rely upon the hesitant compromises of a Committee, Southampton has a Collection [sic] which has been formed by a coherent policy. Moreover, the money has been far better and more economically spent than it probably could have been in any other circumstances.[74]

Important gifts for Southampton: the Arthur Jeffress Bequest

It was largely due to his exceptional purchases that Palmer was able to attract some significant gifts and bequests. Donors recognised that their gifts would join a thriving gallery, be well looked after and promoted to the general public in exciting ways. The most important gift of paintings came from Arthur Jeffress after his unexpected death in 1961.[75] Once certain specific individuals and institutions had received named gifts, including the Tate Gallery, Southampton Art Gallery was given the opportunity to make a selection – Palmer chose 99 works by modern and contemporary British painters, including 11 by Graham Sutherland, among which was a magnificent portrait of Jeffress (fig. 60). There were also numerous views of Venice, the city where Jeffress had spent increasing amounts of time. The largest group was of French paintings, which provided 'a comprehensive range from the plein-air artists and precursors of the Impressionist movement, through the Impressionist period, to post-Impressionists and French Primitive painters.'[76]

With the Jeffress Bequest also came a few earlier historical works, including Giuseppe Arcimboldo's unusual depiction of Summer (fig. 61) dating to the 1580s, which shows a half-length man in profile, composed of plums, pears, peaches, figs, pomegranates and a watermelon. The Lombard artist, feted by the Holy Roman Emperor Rudolf II, became renowned for his portraits composed of plants, fruit, animals and other objects as well as his series depicting personifications of the Four Seasons. Jeffress, who enjoyed Arcimboldo's bizarre wit, also owned *Sense of Smell* by a follower.[77] In 1963, works from the Jeffress Bequest went on display at Southampton with a catalogue written by Jeffress's former business partner Robert Melville and a foreword by Palmer.

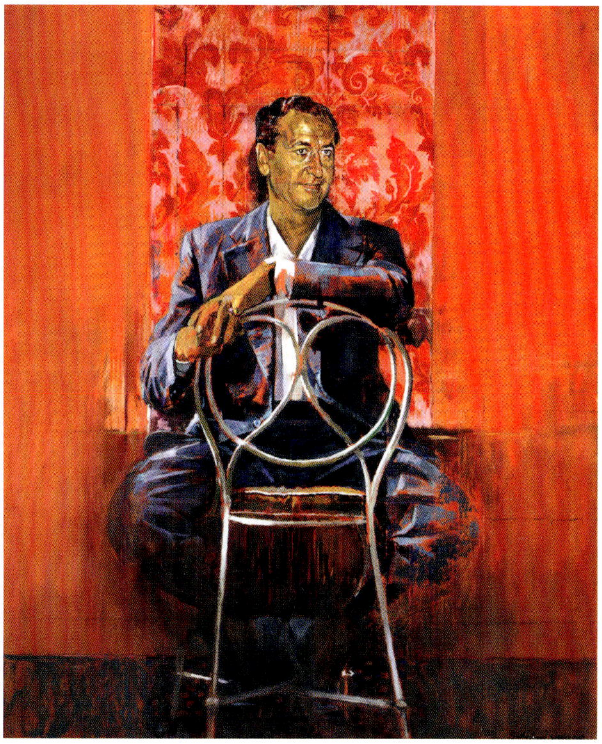

FIG. 60
Graham Sutherland (1903–1980)
Arthur Jeffress, 1955
Oil on canvas, 145.5 × 122 cm
Southampton City Art Gallery, SOTAG 71/1963

Significant loans and exhibitions to and from Southampton

In his very first letter to Hendy of 2 June 1950, Palmer asked about the possibility of borrowing works from Trafalgar Square, having heard about a new loan scheme and not wanting Southampton to miss out.[78] Thereafter Palmer's curatorial correspondence includes letters to and from the Arts Council which sent sets of paintings from both the National Gallery and Tate Gallery to regional galleries including Southampton (see Appendix). For example, in paperwork of January 1954, reference is made to the 'third distribution' of seven pictures from the National Gallery, nearly all of which were Dutch seventeenth-century works.

In addition, the Arts Council facilitated numerous national touring exhibitions which enabled Southampton Art Gallery, among other regional art galleries, to display important loans from major UK collections. By way of example, the Arts Council's *Dutch Paintings and the East Anglian School* exhibition of October 1954 included three loans from the Royal Collection, *Samuel Palmer and his Circle* (April–May 1957) had multiple pictures from the Ashmolean and the Tate Gallery, and *William Coldstream* (September 1962) showed works from

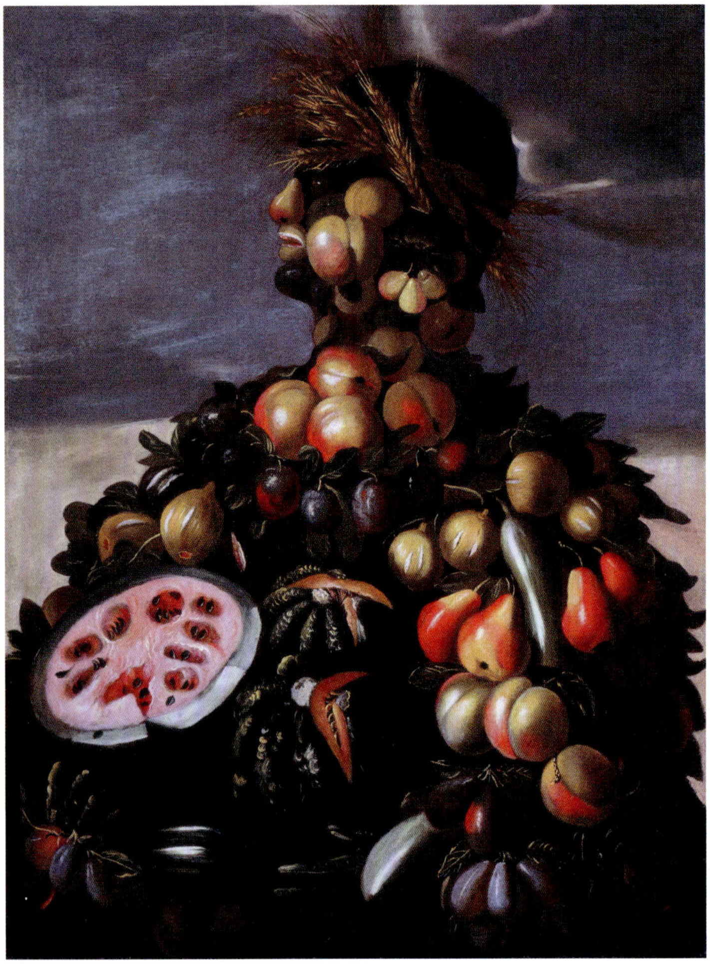

FIG. 61
Giuseppe Arcimboldo (1526–1593)
Summer, probably 1580s
Oil on canvas, 97.7 × 73 cm
Southampton City Art Gallery, SOTAG 18/1963

the Imperial War Museum and the British Council. These shows became increasingly ambitious with the introduction of international partners, such as *Eighteenth-Century Venetian Drawings from the Museo Correr* (September–October 1965) and *German Expressionism* (December 1969), which was organised with assistance from the Neue Staatsgalerie, Munich. Other sources provided further important loans of contemporary art. The Gulbenkian Foundation, for instance, lent Southampton three modern works by Ian Stephenson, Joe Tilson and Robyn Denny in 1963. Three years later, another group of modern British paintings was loaned from the Peter Stuyvesant Foundation, comprising works by Bernard Cohen, Adrian Heath and William Scott.[79] Southampton went on to acquire works by Denny, Cohen, Heath and Scott for its permanent collection.

Southampton also lent groups of works to the Arts Council's programme of touring exhibitions. The first such was *Contemporary Paintings from Southampton Art Gallery*, which took place in 1955. The venue was meant to have been Torquay, but Torquay inadvertently double-booked and so was obliged to host 'a conference of meat-traders in the gallery'.[80] Exeter's Royal Albert Memorial Museum and Art Gallery was chosen as a last-minute replacement, the exasperated Arts Council representative declaring Exeter to be 'a much more worthy place, where contemporary paintings are really appreciated'.[81] The exhibition, in its final format, ran from 18 April to 4 May 1955 and displayed 35 pictures described as 'the cream of the contemporary paintings owned by Southampton'.[82] A handful of nineteenth-century French pictures were shown alongside '27 works by British artists [including] outstanding examples by Augustus John, Matthew Smith, Graham Sutherland, Christopher Wood, J.D. Innes and [Walter] Sickert'. Other loan shows elsewhere in the UK followed. For instance, 22 twentieth-century paintings from Southampton's permanent collection were lent to Aldershot Borough Library in October–November 1955, while *Modern Paintings from Southampton* was hosted by Worthing Art Gallery in 1957. Loans from Southampton Art Gallery also featured in exhibitions with more than one lender. An early example is the Arts Council's *Exhibition of British Contemporary Paintings from Southern and Midland Galleries* (14 November 1953–24 April 1954), which toured galleries in northern Britain. Among the seven loans from Southampton was Augustus John's *Brigit*, which would also be lent to the Aldershot show.

Accolades for Hendy and Palmer

Just before Hendy resigned from the National Gallery, Palmer wrote to him in December 1967, full of praise for what his guidance over the previous seventeen years had achieved:

> When I look around the gallery as it is now and see all the pictures which in one way or another owe their place on the walls to you, I realize how inestimable the value of your advice and support have been, not least in the pictures, such as our Turner, which might otherwise [have] gone across the Atlantic. But apart from actual acquisitions, it has meant a very great deal to me to know that I had your support and could call on you and the staff of the National Gallery for advice which was always so freely given. I know that my path here has been very much smoother as a result.[83]

There were similar accolades for Palmer around the time he left Southampton Art Gallery, in 1970. A flattering article by William Gaunt appeared in *The Times* on 7 October 1969, which noted how the Gallery had been 'built up in the post Second World-War period, first by Mr. Conran and during the past 20 years by his successor, Mr. M.A. Palmer'. It summarised the clear 'directions' the Gallery had moved in regarding acquisitions. First, concerning the old masters, it noted Southampton's bias towards landscapes – 'Dutch, Flemish and Venetian works provide comparison with the English landscapes ... and those by the Impressionists and other French artists of the nineteenth century.' The 'second line of acquisition' it pointed out was modern British painting, with 'the Camden Town group [being] well represented' as well as 'other and later developments'. The acquisition of works by living painters was also highlighted as of prime importance both in encouraging painters and enabling the public 'to get an idea of the way art is going'. The only implied criticism – perhaps, a friendly goad – was the lack of scholarly literature to 'do justice to a collection expeditiously and effectively assembled, containing much of interest and value.'[84]

Publications soon followed. A detailed and fully illustrated exhibition catalogue accompanied an important loan show of works from Southampton Art Gallery at Wildenstein's, London, in 1970. Then, during his retirement, Palmer continued, as a volunteer, to 'compile the first full catalogue of the collection, spending hours in the store, measuring and recording.'[85] To mark the Queen's Silver Jubilee in 1977, the now renamed Southampton City Art Gallery mounted *The Growth of a Gallery* exhibition. Displaying many of the masterpieces acquired during Palmer's curatorship, it doubled up as a tribute to him.

19

Graham Sutherland (1903–1980)

Red Landscape, 1942

Oil on canvas, 68 × 99.8 cm
Purchased with the assistance of the Chipperfield Bequest Fund, 1949
Southampton City Art Gallery, SOTAG 1369

Southampton's first curator, (George) Loraine Conran, with encouragement from the National Gallery's post-war director, Philip Hendy, enriched Southampton's evolving collection of British twentieth-century painting with a nucleus of abstract art. Whereas Hendy's predecessor, Kenneth Clark, favoured figurative painting, Hendy promoted such pioneers of abstraction as Graham Sutherland, Henry Moore and Barbara Hepworth.

During the 1930s, Sutherland established himself as one of the most exciting talents in modern British painting. As an Official War Artist, his depictions of bombed-out buildings came to symbolise the home front, and after the war his religious paintings and portraits were equally memorable and controversial. Landscape remained a vital source for Sutherland's adventurous and often abstract works. He first visited Pembrokeshire in 1934 and revelled in what he called the 'exultant strangeness' of the untamed landscape, a characteristic that imbued many of his paintings.

Southampton built up an impressive cluster of Sutherland's work. Its first purchase was *Green Lane*, which Conran bought in 1947, followed by *Red Landscape* two years later. These works corresponded with other recent acquisitions of semi-abstract landscapes, such as John Piper's *Portland Foreshore* bought in 1946. In 1963, through the bequest of the art collector and dealer Arthur Jeffress, eleven works by Sutherland were acquired, including a portrait of Jeffress (fig. 60) and several semi-abstract landscapes. In fact, Jeffress, who preferred figurative art, admitted that a couple of Sutherland's works in his collection did 'come rather perilously close to abstraction for my own personal taste'.[1]

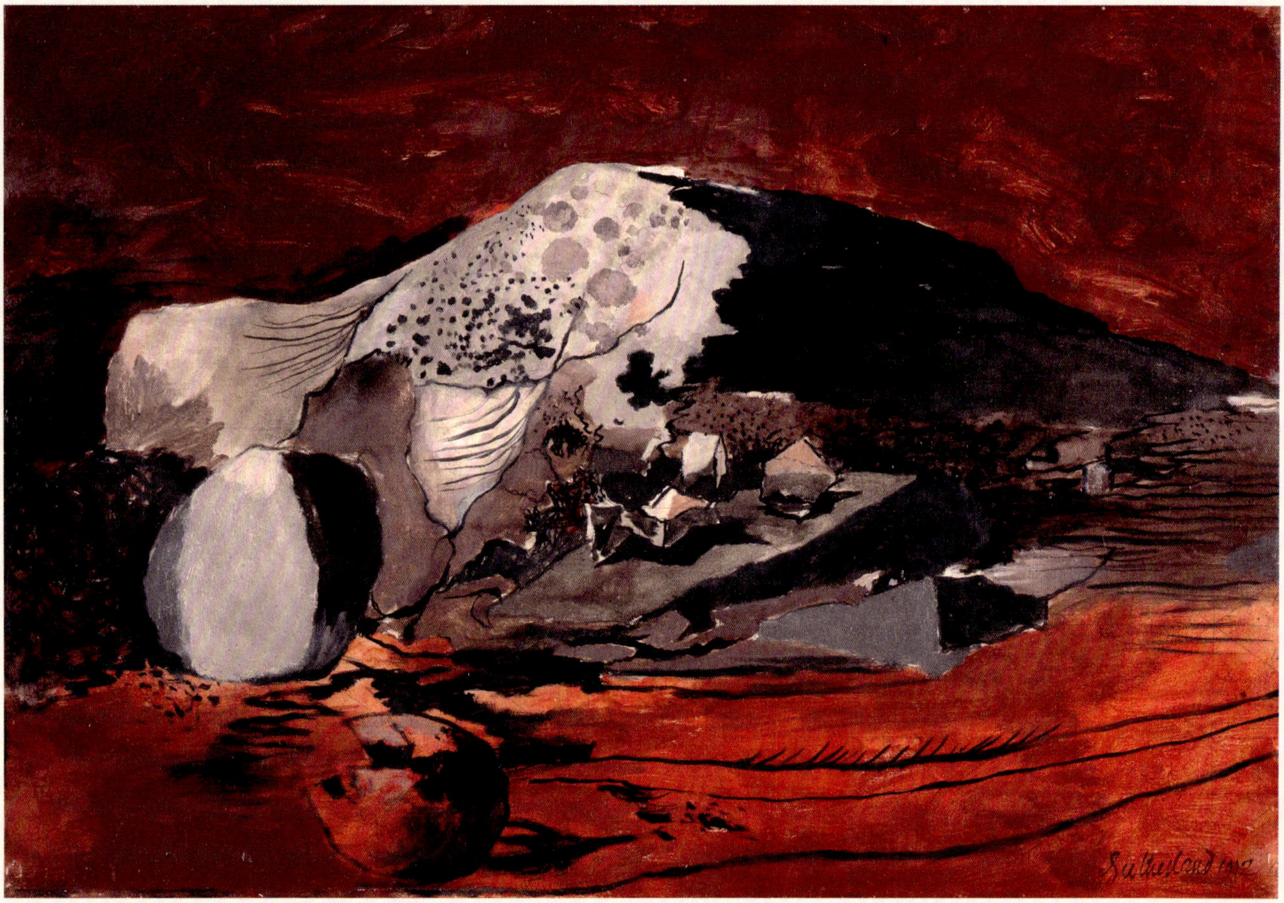

20

John Craxton (1922–2009)

Dark Landscape, 1943

Oil on canvas, 37.5 × 55.2 cm
Donated by the Contemporary Art Society, 1950
Southampton City Art Gallery, SOTAG 1378

Kenneth Clark, one-time art adviser to Southampton Art Gallery, was a patron and supporter of contemporary British art. He bought works from artists he admired, offered them commissions and worked behind the scenes to ensure their work was represented in prestigious collections. Clark was also involved with the Contemporary Art Society (CAS), founded in 1910 to encourage interest in contemporary art across the UK. In 1950 Southampton Art Gallery received from CAS a gift of two oil paintings exemplifying aspects of British neo-Romanticism: this work and John Minton's *Rotherhithe from Wapping*. Interestingly, the Craxton had once belonged to Clark.

John Craxton was championed as one of the great hopes of modern painting in Britain. He found refuge from the Second World War in creating an idealised, semi-abstracted version of the British landscape. The year after he painted *Dark Landscape*, Craxton published a series of beautiful distinctive lithographs to accompany Geoffrey Grigson's *Visionary Poems and Passages* (1944). However, in 1946, Craxton escaped to Greece, where he remained for the rest of his life, finding creative inspiration in the light-filled landscapes and easy-going lifestyle. The dark, melancholic images of the war years, exemplified by the Southampton painting, were entirely replaced by landscapes of the Aegean filled with light and life, often populated by cats and goats as well as local inhabitants.

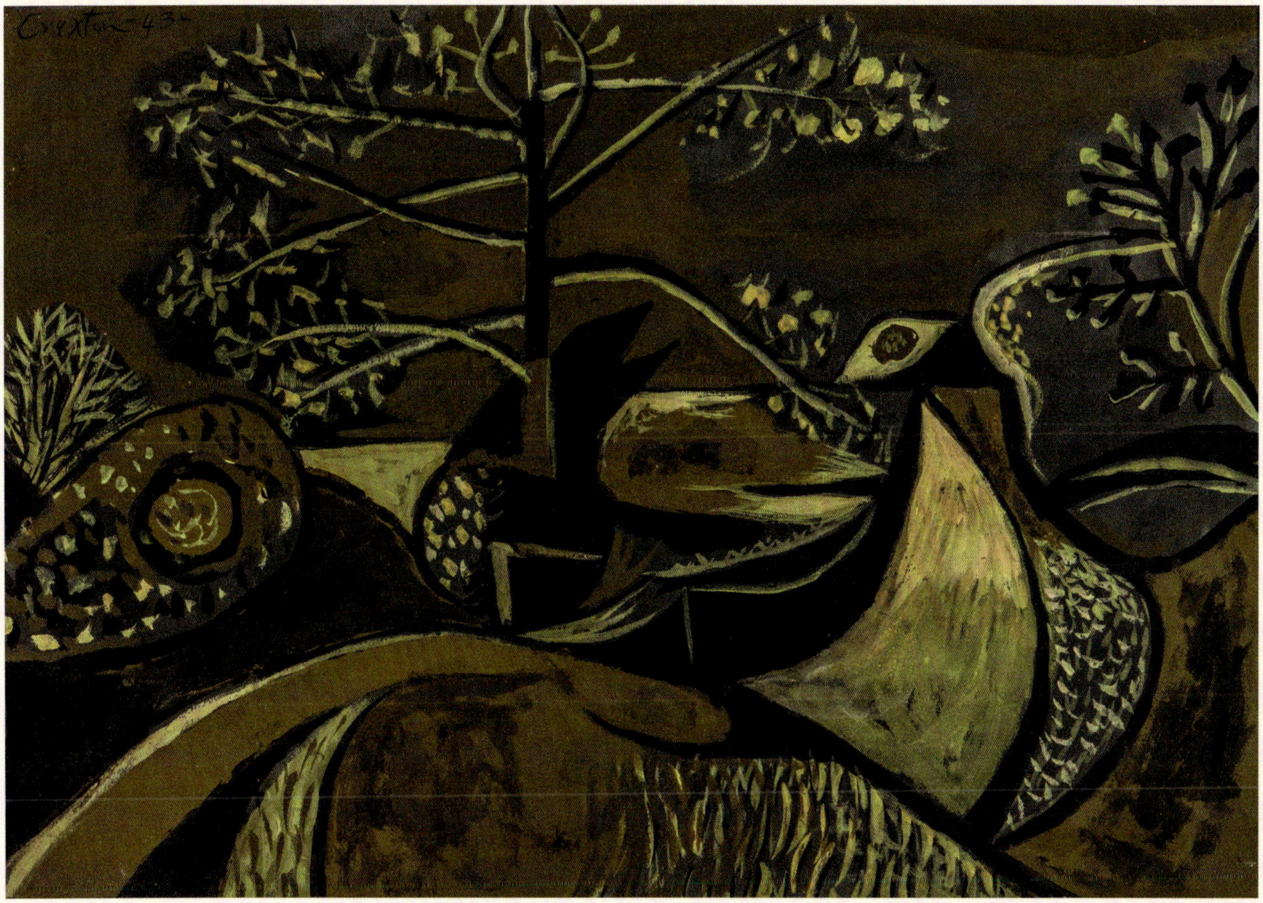

21

Allegretto Nuzi
(active 1354; died 1373/74)
The Coronation of the Virgin, 1360

Tempera on board, 245.7 × 102.5 cm
Purchased with the assistance of the
Smith Bequest Fund, 1951
Southampton City Art Gallery, SOTAG 1403

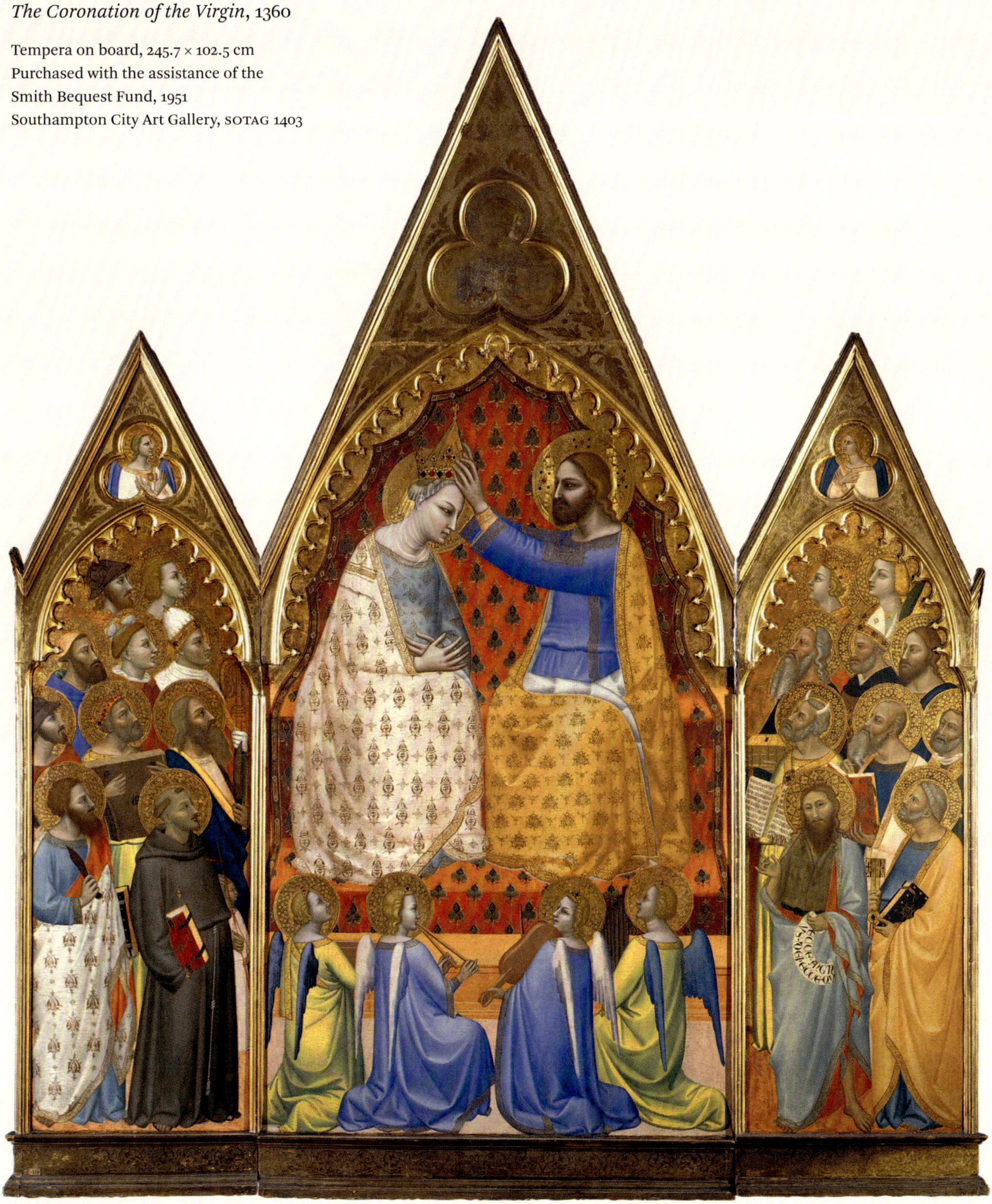

This large fourteenth-century Florentine altarpiece is the oldest work of art in the Southampton collection. It was acquired in 1951 by Southampton's curator, Maurice Palmer, after discussion with National Gallery director Philip Hendy. It had already been on show at Southampton Art Gallery, as part of the post-war exhibition *Primitives and Early Renaissance Paintings from the Cook Collection* in 1947.

It appears that Palmer had ambitions to develop this part of the collection, for he wrote to the city council about his desire to 'build up a small collection of "Italian Primitives", and the like in the Southampton Gallery.'[2] This never happened.

The central panel depicts the Virgin Mary being crowned Queen of Heaven by her son, while, in the side panels, the holy pair are venerated by adoring saints. It was a highly popular subject in Florence because both the city and its cathedral were dedicated to the Virgin – a dedication shared with many European cities. As commissioned, the altarpiece would have comprised at least five panels and been placed on or above an altar in a church. Two of the panels from the original ensemble are today in Houston's Museum of Fine Art.[3]

Although based on an earlier altarpiece by the di Cione family of painters, now in Florence's Accademia, Nuzi's interpretation, especially the mother-son relationship, is more individualised and humanised. Southampton's picture is similar in subject and composition to Florentine works in the National Gallery's collection, especially Bernardo Daddi's *Coronation of the Virgin* (about 1340–45, fig. 62), and the San Pier Maggiore Altarpiece by Jacopo di Cione and his workshop (1370–71).

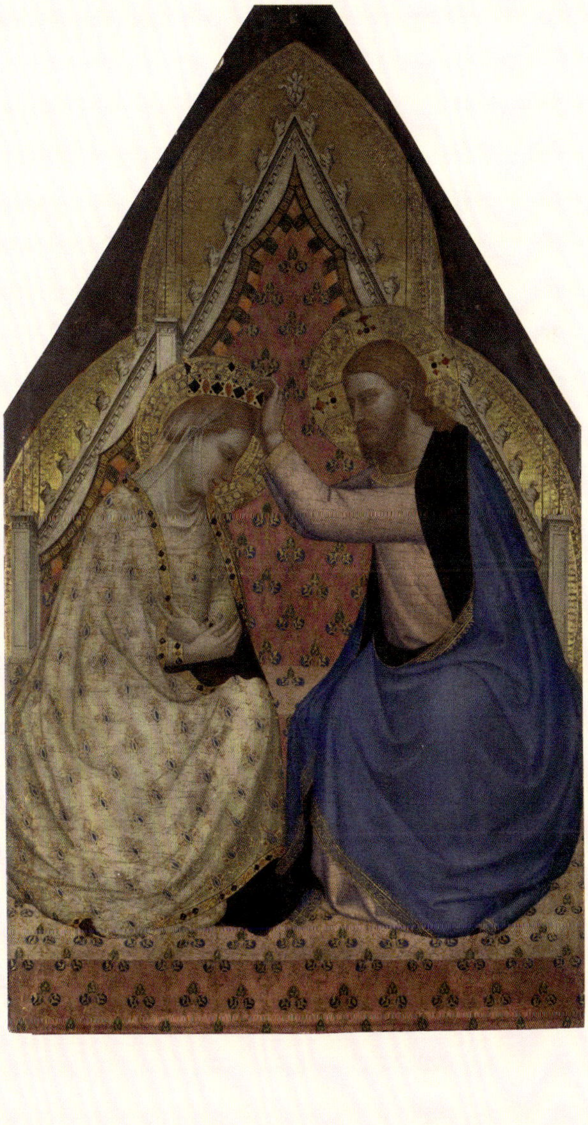

FIG. 62
Bernardo Daddi
(active 1312/20; died 1348)
The Coronation of the Virgin, about 1340–45
Egg tempera on wood, 111.7 × 75.5 cm
Bought with a grant from the American Friends of the National Gallery, London, made possible by Sir Paul Getty's endowment, 2004
The National Gallery, London, NG6599

22 (LEFT)

Goswijn (Goossen) van der Weyden (active 1492; died after 1538)
Saint Catherine and the Philosophers, 1510

Oil on panel, 108.6 × 157.2 cm
Purchased with the assistance of the Chipperfield Bequest Fund, 1958
Southampton City Art Gallery, SOTAG 1/1958

23 (RIGHT)

Workshop of Goswijn (Goossen) van der Weyden
The Visitation of the Virgin to Saint Elizabeth, about 1516

Oil on oak, 80.5 × 70 cm
Bequeathed by Mrs Joseph H. Green, 1880
The National Gallery, London, NG1082

Goswijn (or Goossen) van der Weyden was born into a family of artists. He trained with his father before establishing his own workshop in Antwerp where he developed his own style. Like most Renaissance painters, Goswijn adapted motifs and compositions from other artists; one prime source would have been the work of his grandfather, Rogier van der Weyden (about 1399–1464), a leading figure of European renown, from whom he inherited working material.

Southampton's *Saint Catherine and the Philosophers* triptych was painted in 1510 while the National Gallery's *Visitation* is a product of Goswijn's workshop of about six years later. London's picture came through a bequest in 1880, while Southampton purchased its triptych in 1958, using the Chipperfield Bequest Fund. It was one of two paintings acquired by the then curator Maurice Palmer in 1958 from the important Cook Collection, the other being Cesare da Sesto's *Saint Jerome* (cat. 24). From a surviving letter, it is clear that Philip Hendy, then director of the National Gallery, much preferred the Italian work.

Southampton's painting depicts a statuesque Catherine of Alexandria in learned dialogue with philosophers at the court of the pagan Emperor Maxentius, who can be seen seated on the right. While the central panel depicts the saint defending Christianity, the sculptural frieze embedded in the architecture narrates her subsequent story, including her imprisonment by the hostile authorities and the failed attempt to murder her on a wheel.

The National Gallery panel depicts another story in which a woman's faith in God takes centre-stage. It shows a meeting, as described in the Bible's Gospel of Saint Luke, between the Virgin Mary and her relative Elizabeth, when Mary announces

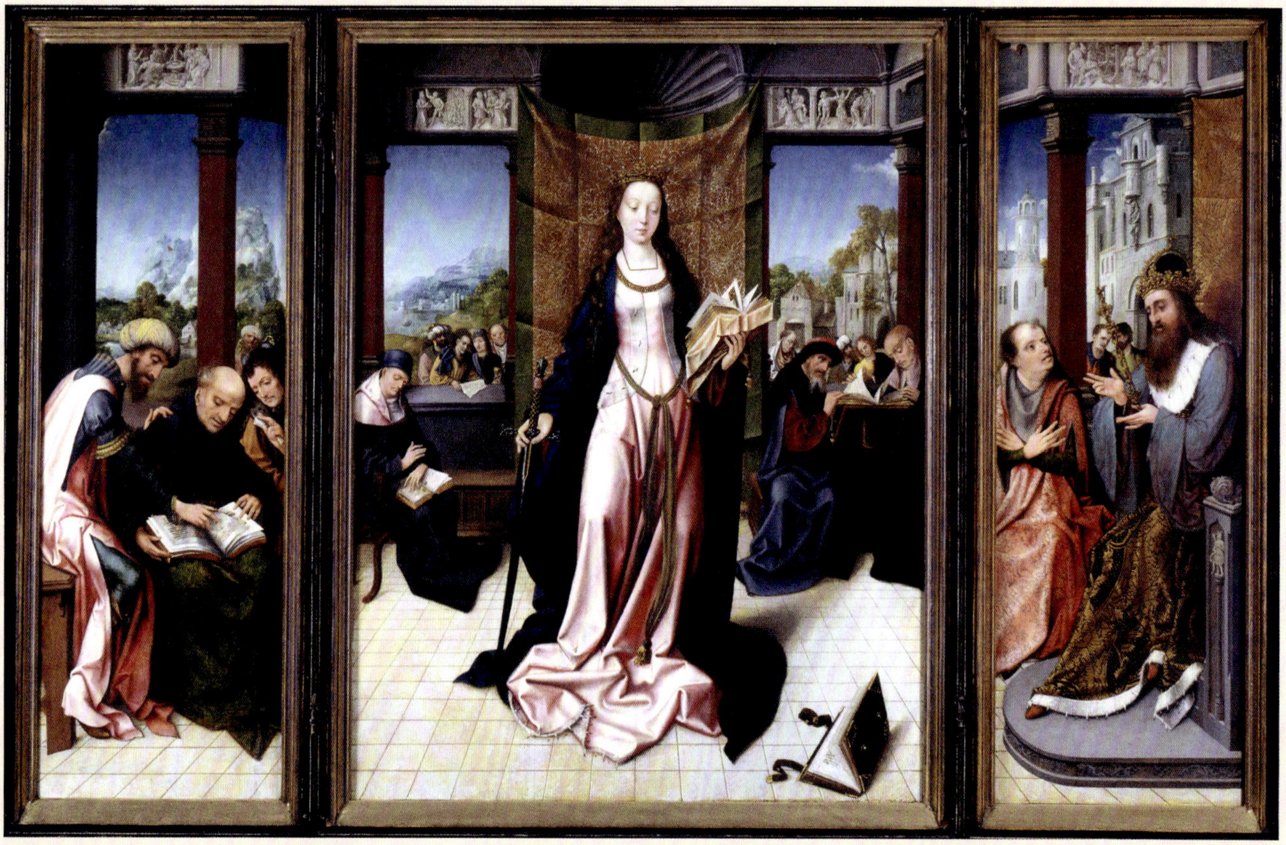

that she is pregnant with God's son and her elderly cousin responds that she likewise has miraculously conceived – her son was John the Baptist, the prophet who foretold the coming of Christ.

The Visitation relates to another panel by Goswijn in the National Gallery's collection, *The Flight into Egypt*, which narrates the story of the Holy Family's escape from the wrath of King Herod who, having learnt of Christ's birth, was determined to hunt down the baby whom he regarded as a threat to his power. These panels would have originally been displayed with others showing further episodes in Christ's life as part of a huge altarpiece, perhaps intended for export to Spain or Portugal. The small narrative panels would probably have been arranged around a large central image of Christ or the Virgin, just as the two, detail-rich wings support the central panel in the Southampton triptych.

Since its purchase, Southampton's triptych has been the subject of various collaborations with the National Gallery. About twenty years ago, a member of the National Gallery's framing department, Isabella Kocum, made it a new frame. Then, in 2003, members of the conservation department, using infrared reflectography and X-radiography, discovered the overpainted coats of arms of St John's College, Oxford on the reverse of its wings. Infrared reflectography undertaken at the same time on *The Visitation* revealed extensive underdrawing that was vastly different from the final landscapes, which suggested that at least two draughtsmen worked on it, one in charge of the landscape, the other responsible for the figures. Goswijn ran a large workshop with several assistants, which therefore makes it likely that several artists were also involved in the production of Southampton's triptych.

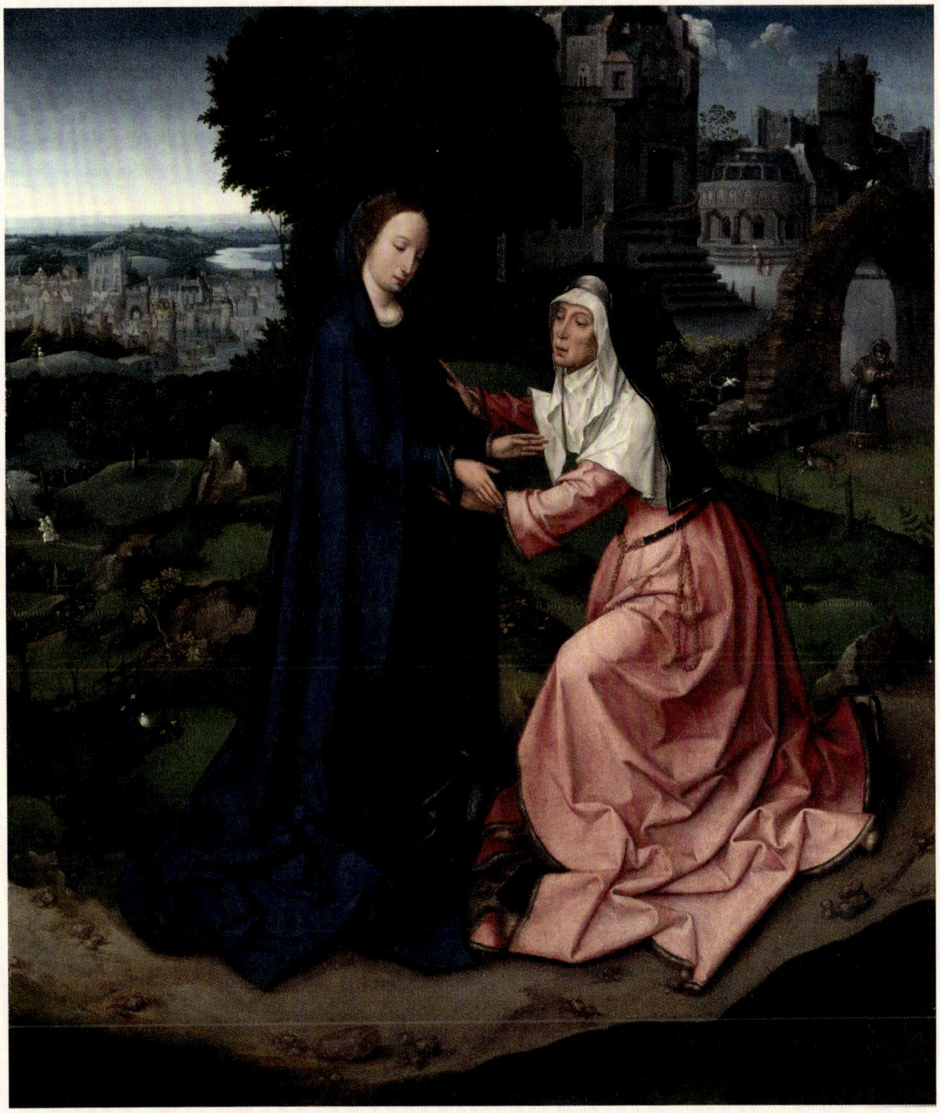

24 (LEFT)

Cesare da Sesto (about 1477–1523)
Saint Jerome as a Hermit in the Desert of Chalcis, 1520

Oil on wood, 80.3 × 60.7 cm
Purchased with the assistance of the Chipperfield Bequest Fund, 1958
Southampton City Art Gallery, SOTAG 2/1958

25 (RIGHT)

Cesare da Sesto (about 1477–1523)
Salome, probably about 1510–20

Oil on poplar, 135.3 × 80 cm
Salting Bequest, 1910
The National Gallery, London, NG2485

Cesare da Sesto, a sixteenth-century painter from Lombardy, is considered one of the 'Leonardeschi', or artists influenced by Leonardo da Vinci. In this pair of pictures, Leonardo's influence is apparent in the 'smoky' manner in which Salome's face is painted and the dramatic lighting effects, while the way that the head of Saint Jerome is set against the dark silhouette of a tree recalls Leonardo's portrait of Ginevra de' Benci (National Gallery of Art, Washington). The saint's pose, however, shows Cesare's debt to other great Renaissance painters, notably Michelangelo and his Cumaean Sibyl from the celebrated frescoes in the Vatican's Sistine Chapel.

Cesare's work is typical of much Italian Renaissance art in its conscious assimilation of sources, and its promotion of ideals of beauty of form, harmony of colouring and balanced compositions. There are interesting connections between the compositions and contents of both works. The composition of *Salome* is dominated by three bare forearms placed

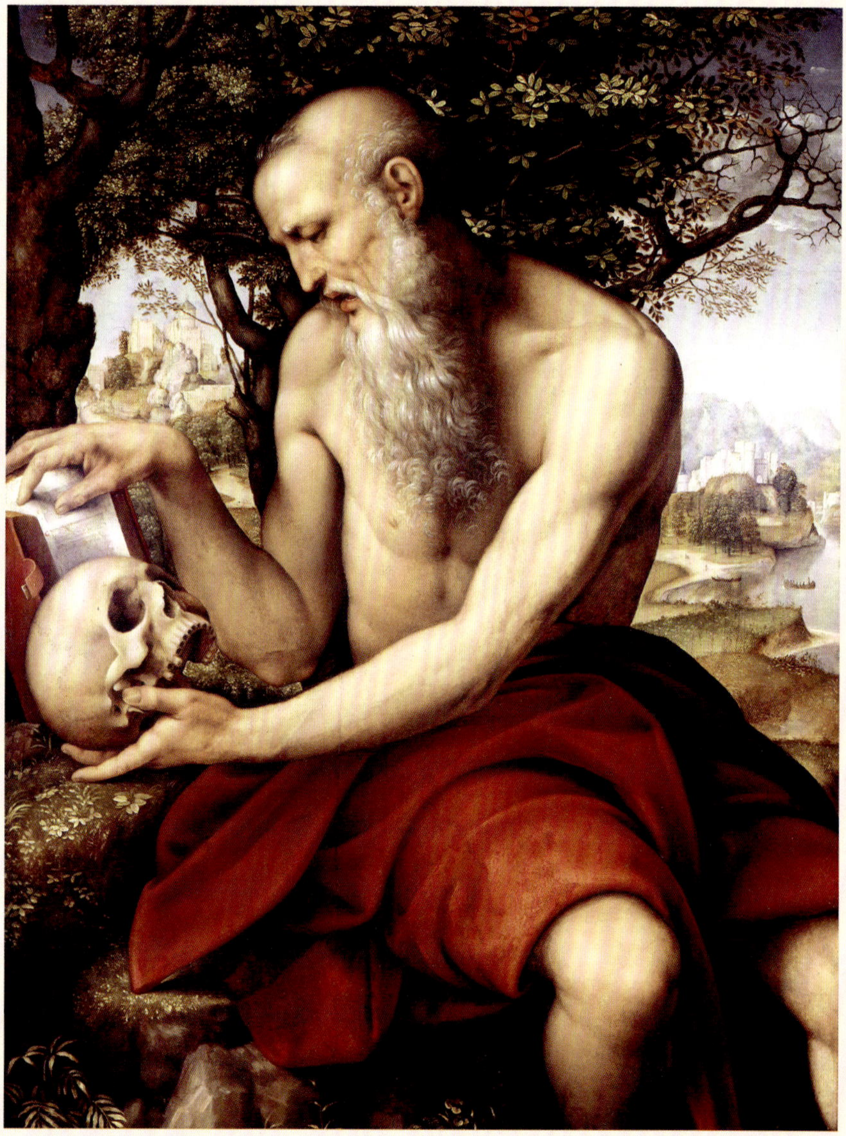

in parallel; Jerome's left arm equally cuts diagonally through the whole picture. Around these strong diagonals, the protagonists twist in elegant poses with clothing gathered in abundant swags. The centre of both compositions is empty, directing attention elsewhere to objects presented for contemplation: a decapitated head and a skull.

Salome's story is told in the Bible's Gospel of Saint Mark. She was the stepdaughter of King Herod and daughter of Herodias. With her mother, she was responsible for the death of John the Baptist, the prophet who foretold the coming of the Christ as Messiah. After her dancing at a feast had pleased Herod so much that he granted her any wish, Salome asked for the Baptist's head – her mother's idea to punish the prophet who had pronounced her marriage unlawful. While the executioner seems appalled, Salome smiles seductively, looking out of the picture, as she proudly touches the receptacle waiting for the decapitated head. Perhaps Salome's monstrous nature is alluded to by the table-leg shaped as a harpy, a rapacious half-female bird of prey from classical mythology.

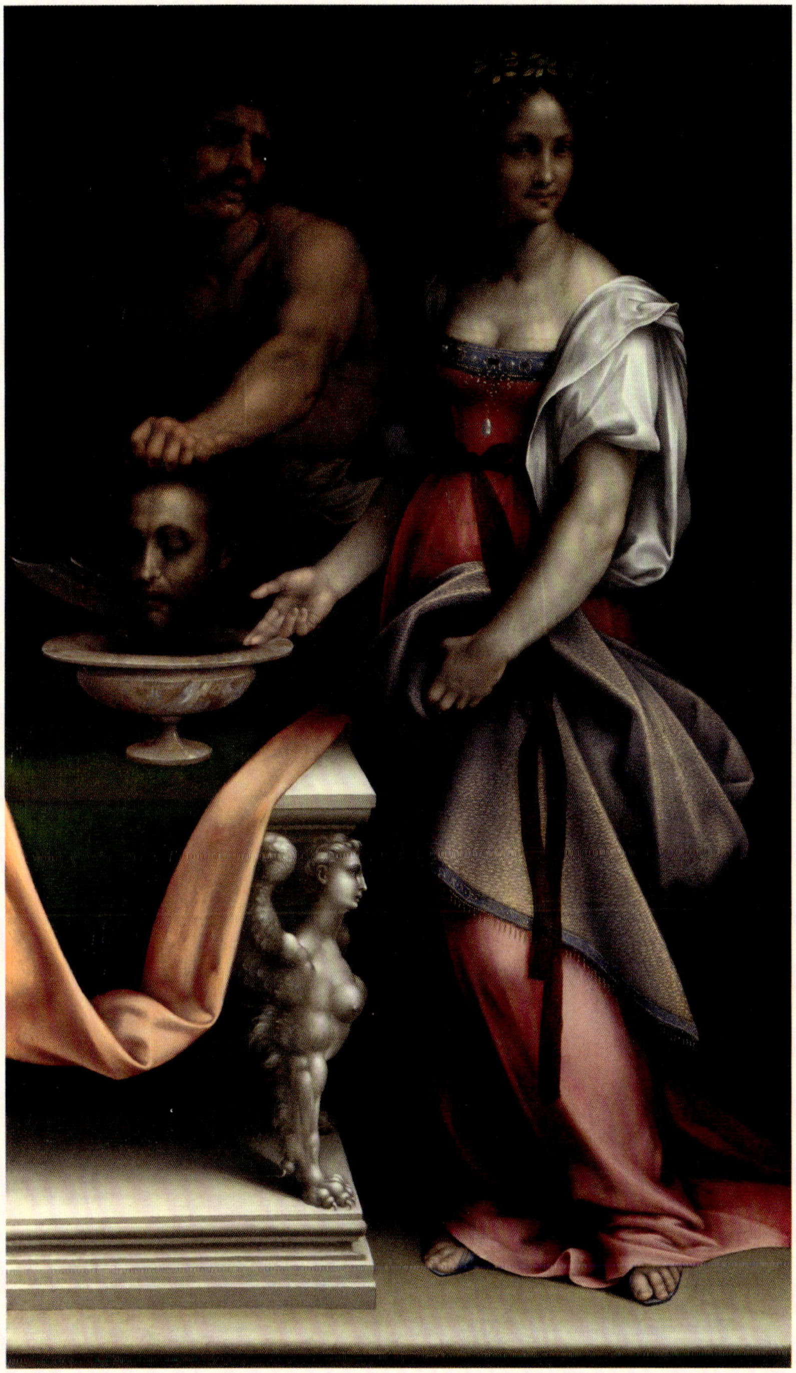

Jerome is portrayed contemplating a skull in one hand, holding open a book with the other. He was designated on account of his learning and piety as one of the four 'doctors' of the early Christian Church. His legacy was his translation of the Bible into Latin (called the Vulgate), a work he produced after five years in the desert of Chalcis, spent studying the original Hebrew text – the subject of Cesare's picture. The skull is traditionally a reminder of mortality; perhaps here it evokes the biblical message concerning Christ's role as the ultimate vanquisher of death.

The National Gallery acquired its Cesare da Sesto in 1910 through the bequest of George Salting. It is thought to be a studio version of an original once owned by the Holy Roman Emperor Rudolf II (now in Vienna's Kunsthistorisches Museum), an important art patron and collector. In the case of Southampton's picture, it was attributed to Leonardo during the eighteenth century and passed through the hands of several leading international art dealers, including Pierre Joseph La Fontaine, who sold it at Christie's, London in 1807. It was clearly a prized object: when Philippe Panné, a Flemish dealer living in London, came to sell it at Christie's in 1819, it was described as being in a 'deal case with folding doors, lock and key'.[4] In 1870, it entered the collection of the merchant and art collector Sir Francis Cook of Doughty House, Richmond, Surrey. Southampton's curator Maurice Palmer bought *Saint Jerome* in 1958, using the Chipperfield Bequest Fund for £1,750, on the recommendation of Philip Hendy, who had written in favour of it.

26 (LEFT)

Salvator Rosa (1615–1673)

A Mountain Landscape, 17th century

Oil on canvas, 98 × 136.5 cm
Purchased, 1961
Southampton City Art Gallery, SOTAG 1/1961

27 (RIGHT)

Gaspard Dughet (1615–1675)

View of the Roman Countryside, possibly Tivoli, about 1670

Oil on canvas, 71.1 × 166.9 cm
Bequeathed by Lord Farnborough, 1838
The National Gallery, London, NG161

With the encouragement of successive directors of the National Gallery, Southampton built up an impressive group of seventeenth-century landscapes. Despite modest finances and the constraints of what was available on the art market, Southampton's curators bought strategically, often seeking out affordable pictures by less well-known painters. Although such landscape paintings were not particularly fashionable among private collectors at the time, they were necessary additions to any public art collection aspiring to show key moments in the history of Western European painting.

Maurice Palmer's first such acquisition, in 1957, was *Landscape with Conopion Carrying the Ashes of Phocion* (fig. 53), attributed to Francisque Millet, a painting that demonstrates the influence of Nicolas Poussin and Gaspard Dughet. Palmer would have been familiar with Francisque Millet's *Mountain Landscape with Lightning* in the National Gallery's collection since it had been purchased as recently as 1945 from the Cook Collection, from which source Southampton bought several of its old masters. Keen to build on earlier acquisitions, he purchased a Dughet landscape of the Roman campagna in 1959. He justified his proposal to Philip Hendy stating that the Dughet would 'make an excellent pair' to the Millet acquired two years earlier.[5] Southampton's Dughet from

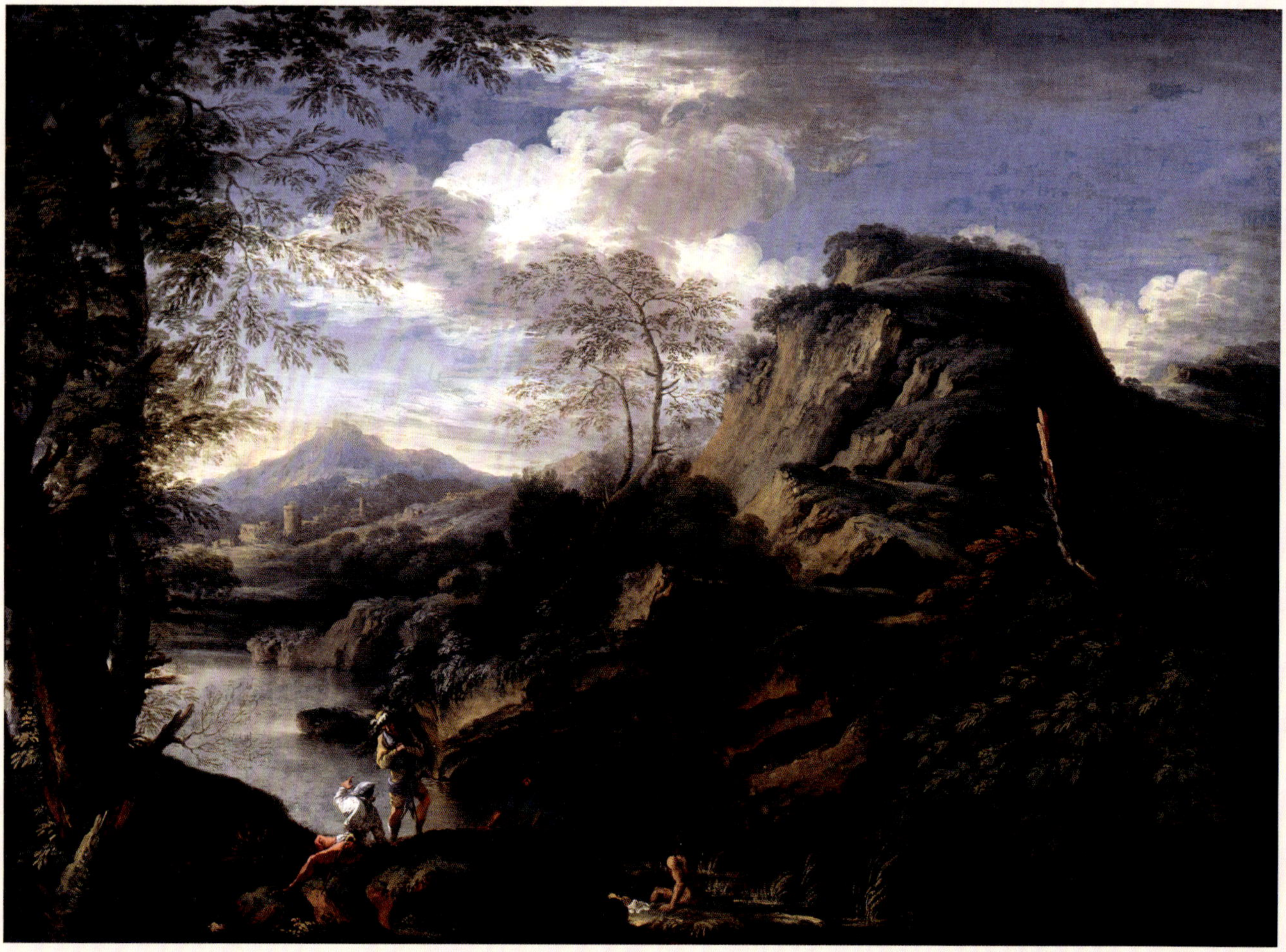

1660 is reminiscent of the National Gallery's *View of the Roman Countryside, possibly Tivoli*, another work by Dughet painted about 1670. The National Gallery's collection now holds eight works by Dughet: four were purchased between 1824 and 1884, the others were bequeathed. This work came with the bequest of Lord Farnborough in 1838. In 1961, Palmer deftly used his Dughet purchase of 1959, in turn, to justify acquiring *A Mountain Landscape* by Salvator Rosa, an Italian Baroque painter, poet and printmaker active in Naples, Rome and Florence during the seventeenth century. As was the case with Southampton's Dughet, *A Mountain Landscape* was purchased from the London dealership P.&D. Colnaghi Ltd.

Southampton's Rosa is here paired with the National Gallery's Dughet. While the location of Rosa's mountainous landscape has never been identified (if indeed it is based on a real place), the distant hillside town in Dughet's scene is probably meant to depict Tivoli, an ancient Roman city north-east of Rome, much represented over the centuries on account of its natural beauty and associations with the Classical past. Rosa's landscape is not as dark or sinister as some of his other works, including the National Gallery's *Witches at their Incantations* (cat. 56).

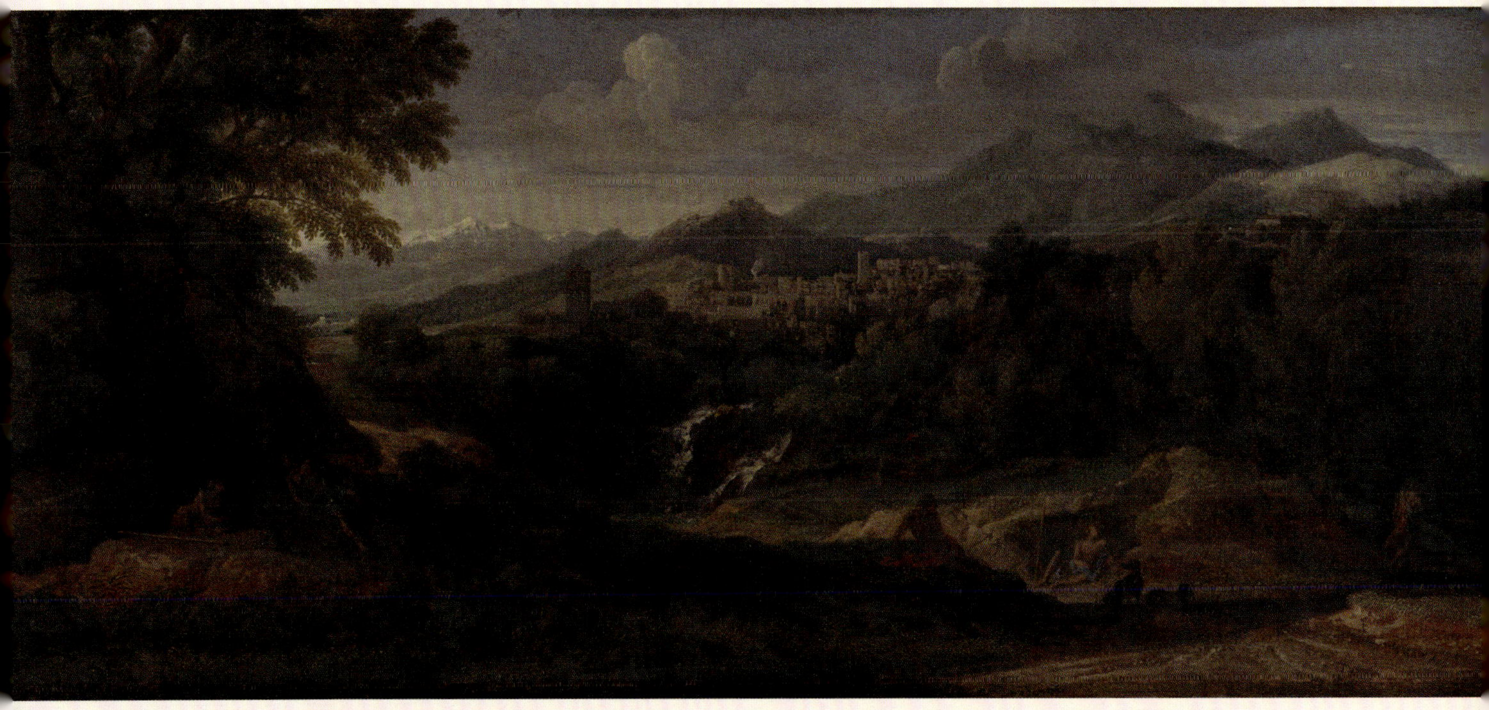

28 (LEFT)

Philips Koninck (1619–1688)

An Extensive Landscape, 1650s

Oil on canvas, 87 × 122.4 cm
Purchased with the assistance of the Victoria and Albert Museum/MGC Purchase Grant Fund, 1963
Southampton City Art Gallery, SOTAG 2/1963

29 (RIGHT)

Philips Koninck (1619–1688)

Extensive Landscape with a Hawking Party, probably about 1670

Oil on canvas, 132.5 × 160.5 cm
Bought, 1871
The National Gallery, London, NG836

Panoramic vistas showing the wide plains of Holland are often said to be the most distinctive contribution of Dutch landscape painting. Although some of these creations from the later seventeenth century look as though they could depict real places, they never aimed at topographical accuracy. As with all landscape painting of that time, they were artificial constructions, produced in the artist's studio from a patchwork of sketches.

The main exponent of this novel type of wide panoramic landscape was the Amsterdam-born Philips Koninck, which explains why Southampton Art Gallery was delighted to acquire a prime example of his work. In his own time, Koninck was also known as a painter of portraits and genre subjects. He had been trained by his elder brother, Jacob, in Rotterdam and probably became a pupil of Rembrandt after his return to Amsterdam around 1641. His ideas for a new type of landscape painting must have been encouraged by seeing Rembrandt's etchings such as *The Goldweigher's Field*, which depicts a broad sweep of country, as well as by Hercules Segers's experiments with panoramic views of the 1620s.

It was in the late 1640s that Koninck started to produce large landscapes in which almost half the canvas was given over to the sky. His attention to the clouds – their shape, density and the way they are illuminated by the sun – enabled him to convey a sense of their moving through space overhead, often producing huge shadows on the landscape below. The truthful recording of the effects of the weather by him and contemporaries like Jacob van Ruisdael would be a stimulus to

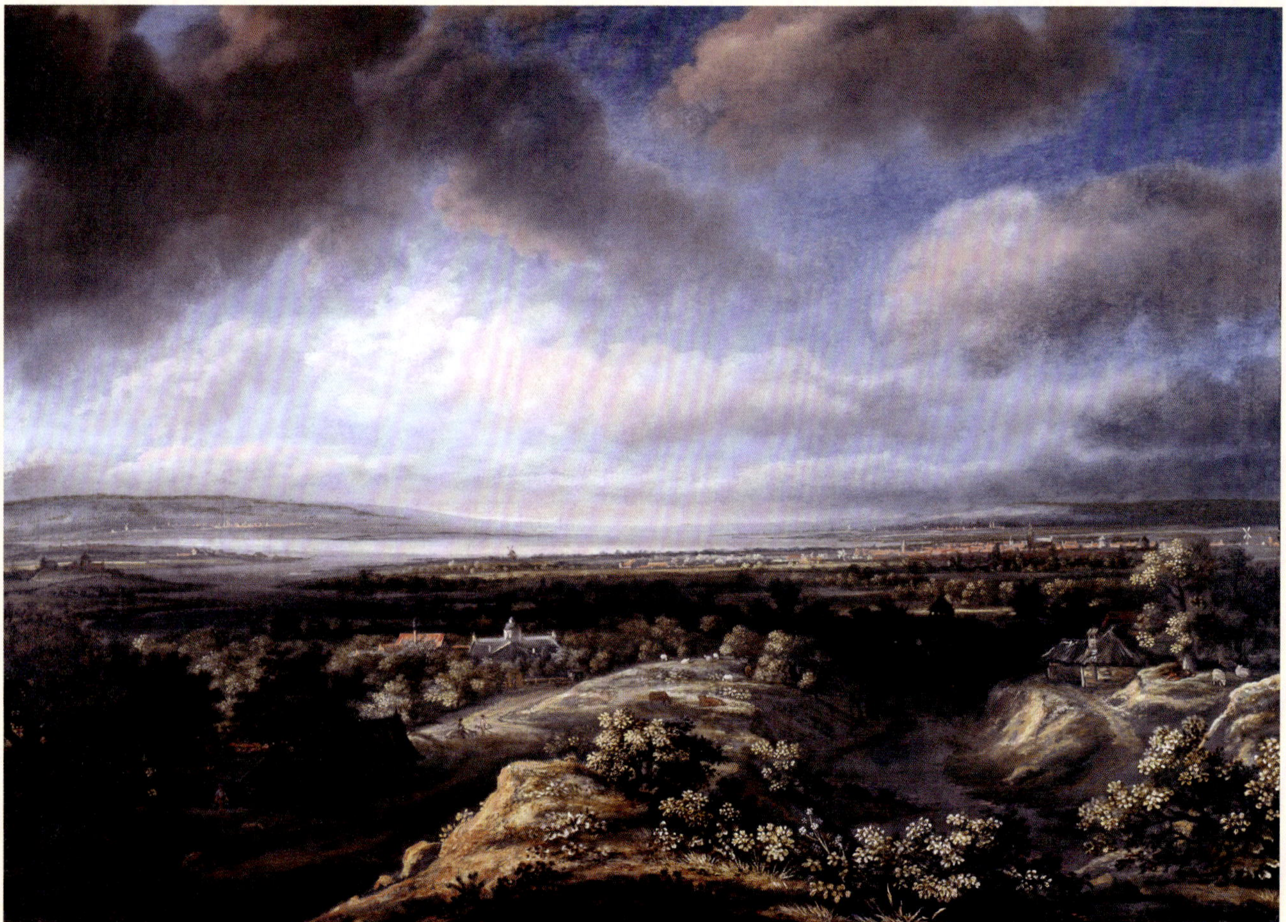

later painters, including John Constable and J.M.W. Turner in Britain.

What seems at first sight to be deserted tracts of land are in fact peopled with a small number of figures. In the London painting, for instance, we see women washing clothes in the stream, a man fishing and a child playing. On the left is the hawking party that lends the picture its title: an elegant man on horseback in a feathered hat points across the countryside to the woman riding at his side. In front, a servant carries their hooded hawks on a frame and looks after numerous dogs. Jan Lingelbach, who frequently painted figures in the landscapes of Koninck and other artists, may have been responsible for them. There is also a hawker (with hawks hanging off a frame) in Southampton's painting.

There are more of Koninck's landscapes in UK public collections than in any other country; the National Gallery alone owns four. Its *Extensive Landscape* was once owned by Sir Robert Peel, twice prime minister, a trustee of the National Gallery and a collector predominantly of seventeenth-century Dutch and Flemish works. Due to financial difficulties, Peel's son had to sell the collection in 1871. The Gallery managed to purchase most of it, including 68 Dutch and Flemish works. Southampton's *Extensive Landscape*, which had once been in the Cook Collection, was bought from the firm of Wildenstein's in 1963.

The National Gallery and Southampton City Art Gallery undertook a project to examine Southampton's Koninck, which resulted in a series of revealing X-radiographs and cross-sections of paint layers. The conclusions were shared with visitors in an exhibition, *Take a Closer Look* at Southampton (14 March–4 June 2000) and the accompanying catalogue included contributions by curators and conservators from both institutions.

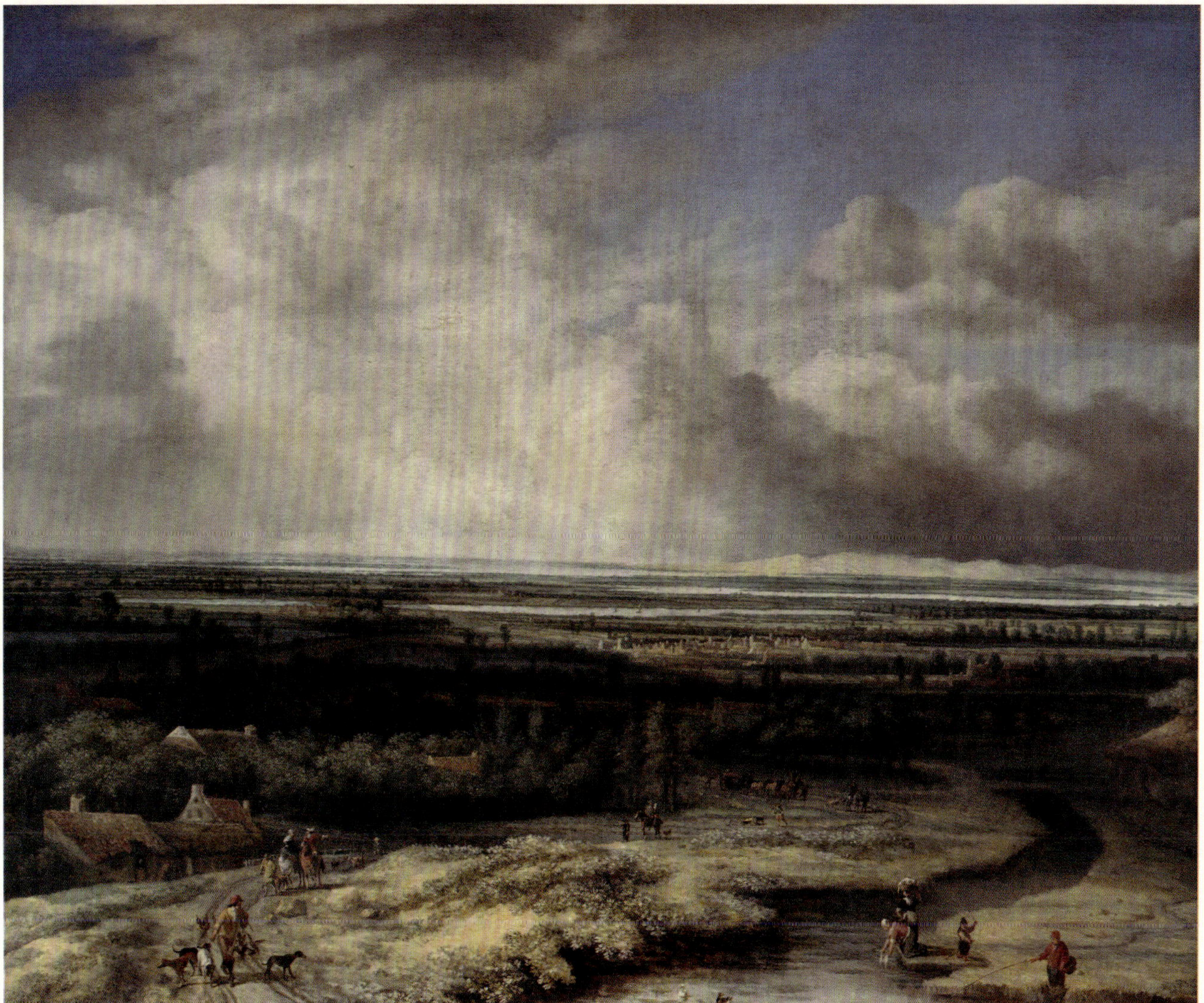

30

Jacob van Ruisdael (1628/29–1682)
The Dunes near Haarlem, late 1640s

Oil on canvas, 70 × 65.6 cm
Purchased with the assistance of the Chipperfield Bequest Fund, 1964
Southampton City Art Gallery, SOTAG 1/1964

Ruisdael, often regarded as an outstanding Dutch landscape painter of the seventeenth century, hailed from an artistic dynasty including his father Isaac Jacobsz and his uncle Salomon. Versatile and prolific, around 700 paintings are attributable to Jacob, together with about 100 drawings. Arguably, the finest collection of his work today is in London's National Gallery, which has 19 pictures. Southampton City Art Gallery's own charming example of *The Dunes near Haarlem* depicts the area where Jacob's family settled, and where the painter was buried (in St Bavo's Church), although he made his career in Amsterdam from 1657.

The expensive painting was acquired for £12,000 in 1964 with money from the Chipperfield Bequest Fund and a government grant administered by the Victoria and Albert Museum. As Palmer told Philip Hendy, the purchase was agreed largely owing to Hendy's 'very valuable support'.[6] This was the fifth notable old master landscape to join what Hendy now referred to as Southampton's 'splendid landscape collection',[7] which included a work by Koninck purchased the year before (cat. 28). It also enhanced an expanding group of important seventeenth-century Dutch and Flemish portraits, genre scenes and still lives, starting with Moreelse's *The Young Poet* (cat. 14) purchased in 1936 and van Everdingen's *Allegory of Winter* (cat. 15) acquired the following year.

The Dunes near Haarlem appears naturalistic at first glance, but the realistic observation of twisting grasses, foliage and the tree trunk are set against a poetic expanse of stormy sky which evokes the natural world in constant flux. While Ruisdael taught Meindert Hobbema, another celebrated Dutch landscape artist, his influence was wide-ranging and long-lasting, traceable across Europe in the work of Gainsborough and Constable in eighteenth- and nineteenth-century Britain and in the French Barbizon School of the 1830s–1870s. In 1986 the work was loaned to the National Gallery's *Dutch Landscape* exhibition (see Appendix).

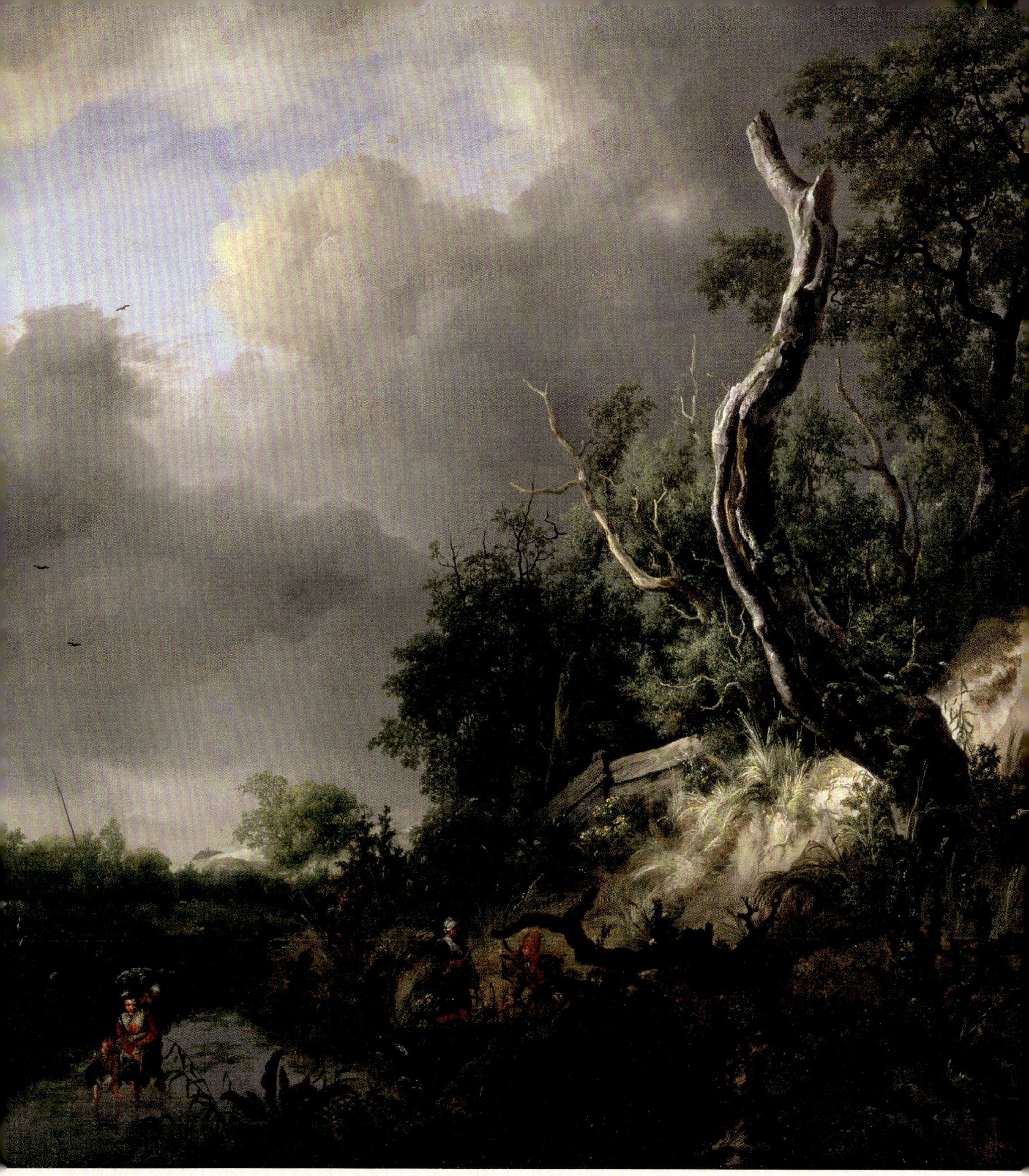

31

J.M.W. Turner (1775–1851)
Fishermen Upon a Lee-Shore in Squally Weather, 1802

Oil on canvas, 91.5 × 122 cm
Purchased with the assistance of the Chipperfield Bequest Fund, 1958
Southampton City Art Gallery, SOTAG 1396

Although Turner's more experimental paintings were not always appreciated during his own lifetime, they are now often cited as innovative forerunners of Impressionism. Turner was interested in all kinds of landscape subjects and was above all drawn to the sea for inspiration. Today we can enjoy the flashes of white paint and vigorous brushstrokes Turner used to capture the power of the waves, but at the time some critics disapproved of such effects, describing them as indeterminate and wild. Even so, such paintings established the young Turner as the most exciting and innovative landscape painter in Britain of the time.

Successful communication between Southampton, the National Gallery and the firm of Thos. Agnew & Sons in 1958 prevented this picture from being exported. Maurice Palmer noted how 'very pleased' he was with the outcome, observing that the new acquisition had arrived at 'a very opportune moment', given that certain seventeenth-century Dutch seascapes (the type of art much admired by Turner) were then on loan to Southampton Art Gallery from the National Gallery (see Appendix).[8]

Palmer worked tirelessly for two decades from 1950 to 'round out' Southampton's collection. He often told Hendy that a prime aim was 'to acquire a small nucleus of really good old masters'.[9] In relation to the British School, the acquisition of this Turner was an early coup.

When Hendy retired from the National Gallery, Palmer told him: 'When I look around the gallery as it is now and see all the pictures which in one way or another owe their place on the walls to you, I realise how inestimable the value of your advice and support have been, not least in the pictures, such as our Turner which might otherwise [have] gone across the Atlantic.'[10]

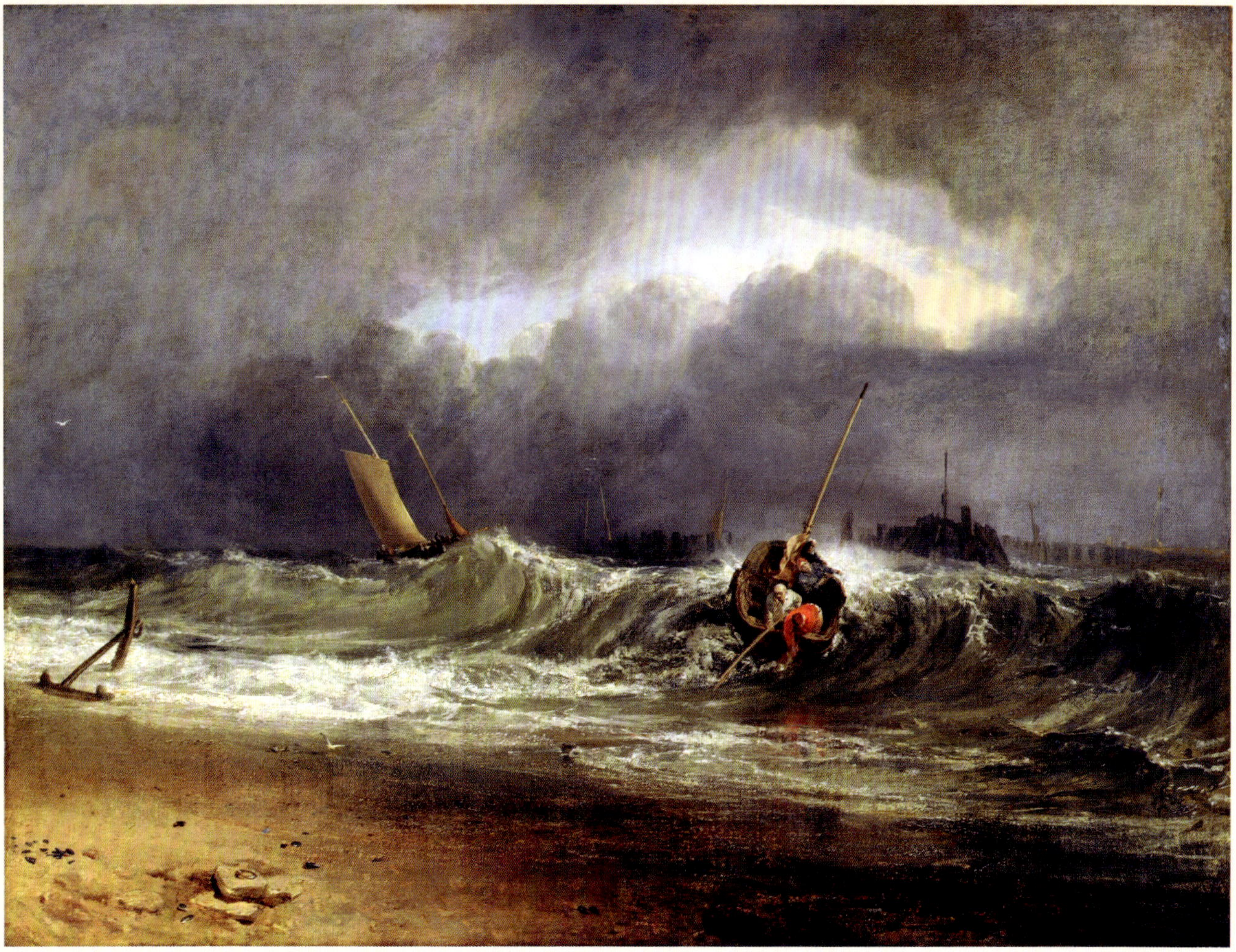

32

Joseph Wright of Derby (1734–1797)

Landscape, 1780

Oil on canvas, 101.5 × 128.5 cm
Purchased with the assistance of the Chipperfield Bequest Fund, 1952
Southampton City Art Gallery, SOTAG 1416

Joseph Wright was born in Derby, the son of a local lawyer. Like Joshua Reynolds, he was apprenticed to the London-based portrait painter Thomas Hudson. Wright then returned to Derby to set up his own studio. Among his patrons were two leading entrepreneurs of the early Industrial Revolution in Britain, the potter and abolitionist Josiah Wedgwood and the inventor Richard Arkwright. Wright's principal interest was the rendering of light and shade, often creating deliberately dramatic effects by contrasting brightly lit figures against a dark background. The National Gallery's *An Experiment on a Bird in the Air Pump* is a prime example of this technique in its depiction of an audience gathered around a lecturer to watch a scientific demonstration. It is also the largest, most ambitious and dramatic of the series of 'candlelight' pictures Wright painted during the 1760s.

Wright's interest in light is clearly evident in Southampton's painting, which depicts High Tor in Derbyshire. This location became a popular subject for artists seeking picturesque subjects during the eighteenth century. Wright painted the scene several times and this version shows the landscape bathed in the rosy light of the rising sun, making the tor glow. It was an astute purchase on the part of Southampton's curator Maurice Palmer because it was not typical of the artist's work. The result was that an outstanding landscape by an important British painter came into Southampton's collection in 1952 for a fraction of the price commanded by more characteristic, commercially sought-after paintings by Wright.

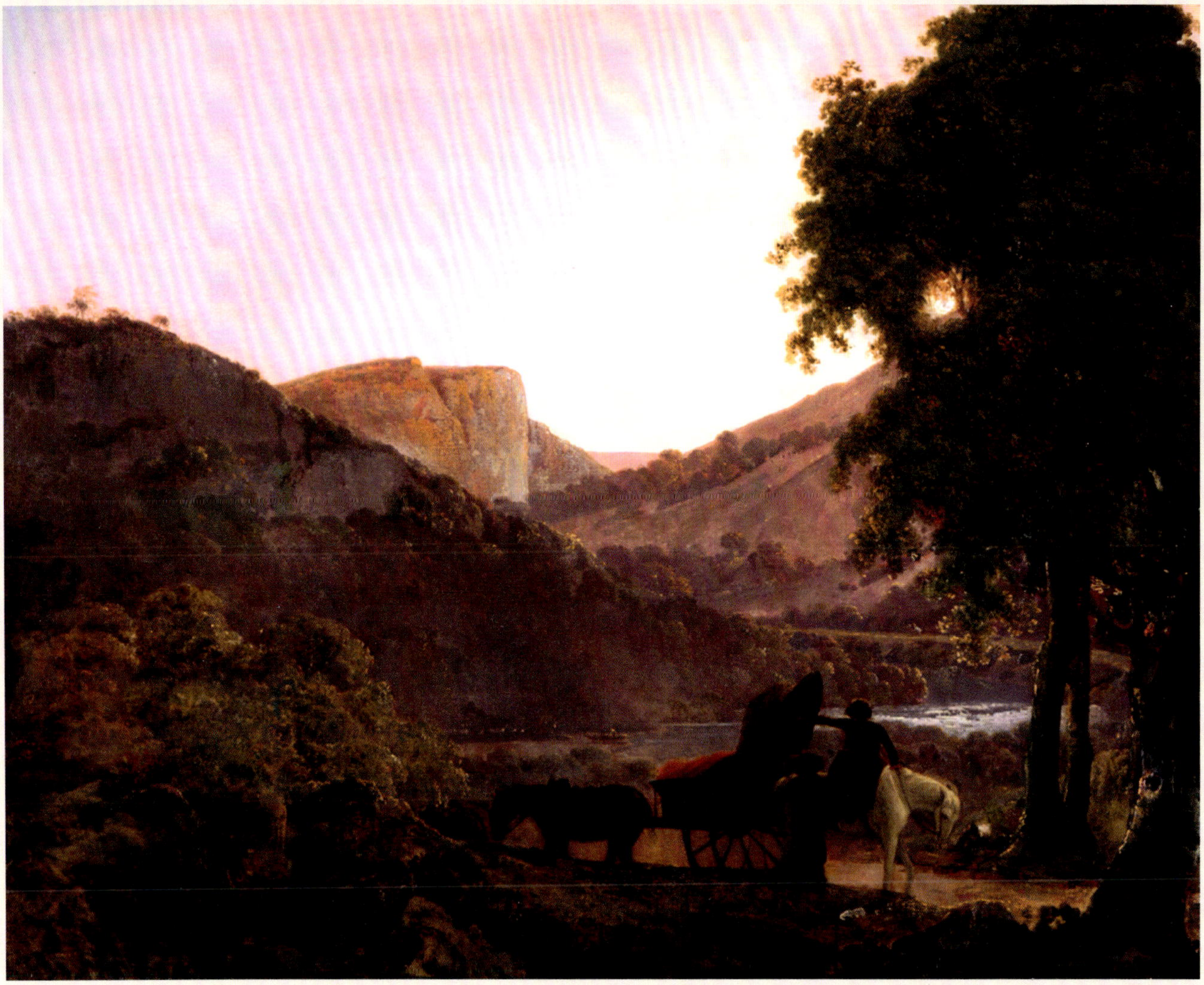

33 (LEFT)

Thomas Gainsborough (1727–1788)
George, Lord Vernon, 1767

Oil on canvas, 246.3 × 150 cm
Purchased with the assistance of the National Art Collections Fund, 1957
Southampton City Art Gallery, SOTAG 1494

34 (RIGHT)

Thomas Gainsborough (1727–1788)
Dr Ralph Schomberg, about 1770

Oil on canvas, 233 × 153.5 cm
Bought, 1862
The National Gallery, London, NG684

It was important for Southampton to acquire a portrait by a leading British eighteenth-century painter because this genre represented such a distinctive element in the history of British painting. Continental art theorists traditionally placed portraiture low down in the hierarchy of genres, and Sir Joshua Reynolds, the first president of the Royal Academy, likewise upheld history painting as the pinnacle of artistic endeavour. However, many British artists spent much of their careers producing portraits as the art form was so much in demand.

Thomas Gainsborough was a great rival of Reynolds as a portrait painter, despite his preference for producing landscapes. Unlike Reynolds, he generally avoided

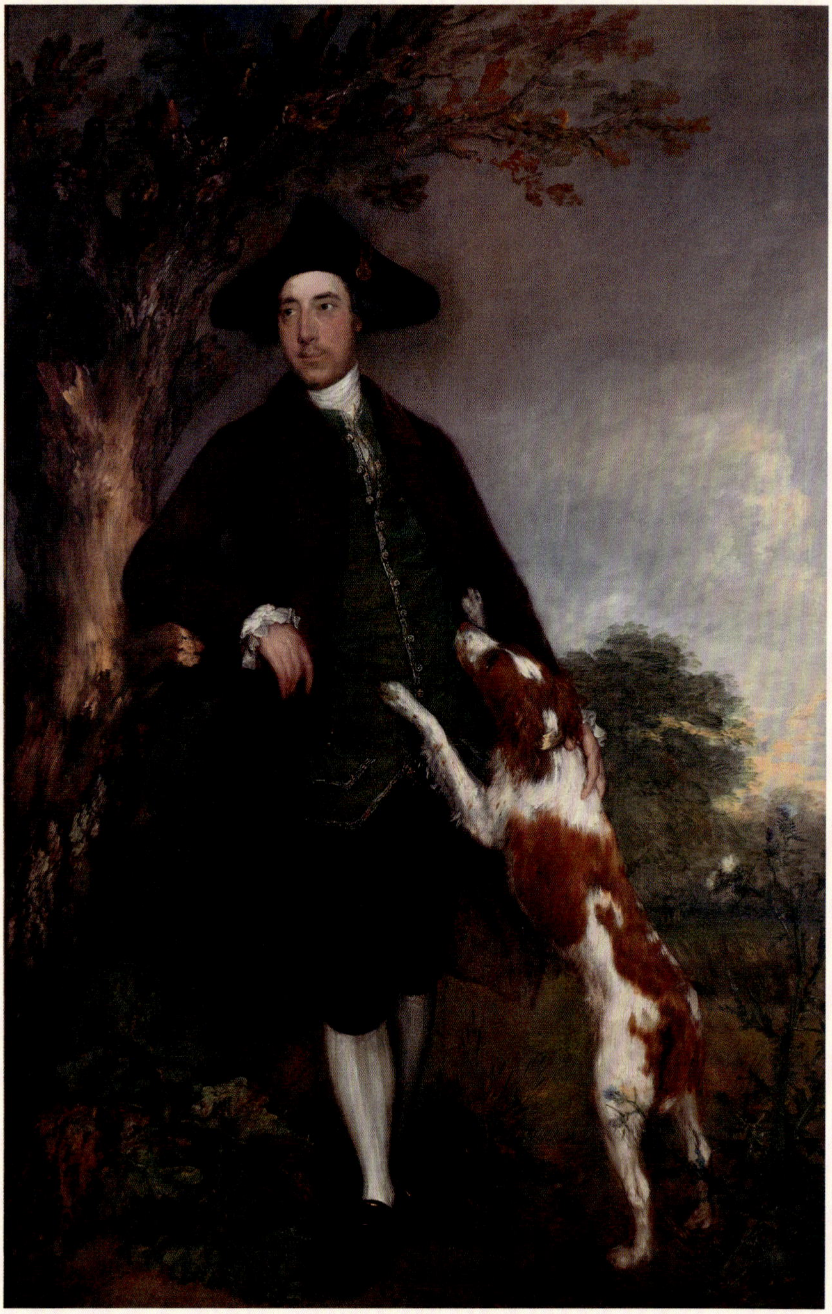

references to Italian Renaissance art or the Antique, and showed his sitters in comparatively informal poses, in fashionable contemporary dress. The feathery, vibrant brushwork and rich colours of his mature work contribute to the innate vivacity of his likenesses and their enduring popularity. After studying art in London, Gainsborough launched his career in his native Suffolk. In 1759 he moved to the fashionable spa town of Bath, where he established a successful portrait-painting practice for 15 years. From the later 1760s, Gainsborough produced a succession of likenesses of male sitters depicted full-length and outdoors: some were members of the aristocracy, others came from the professional classes.

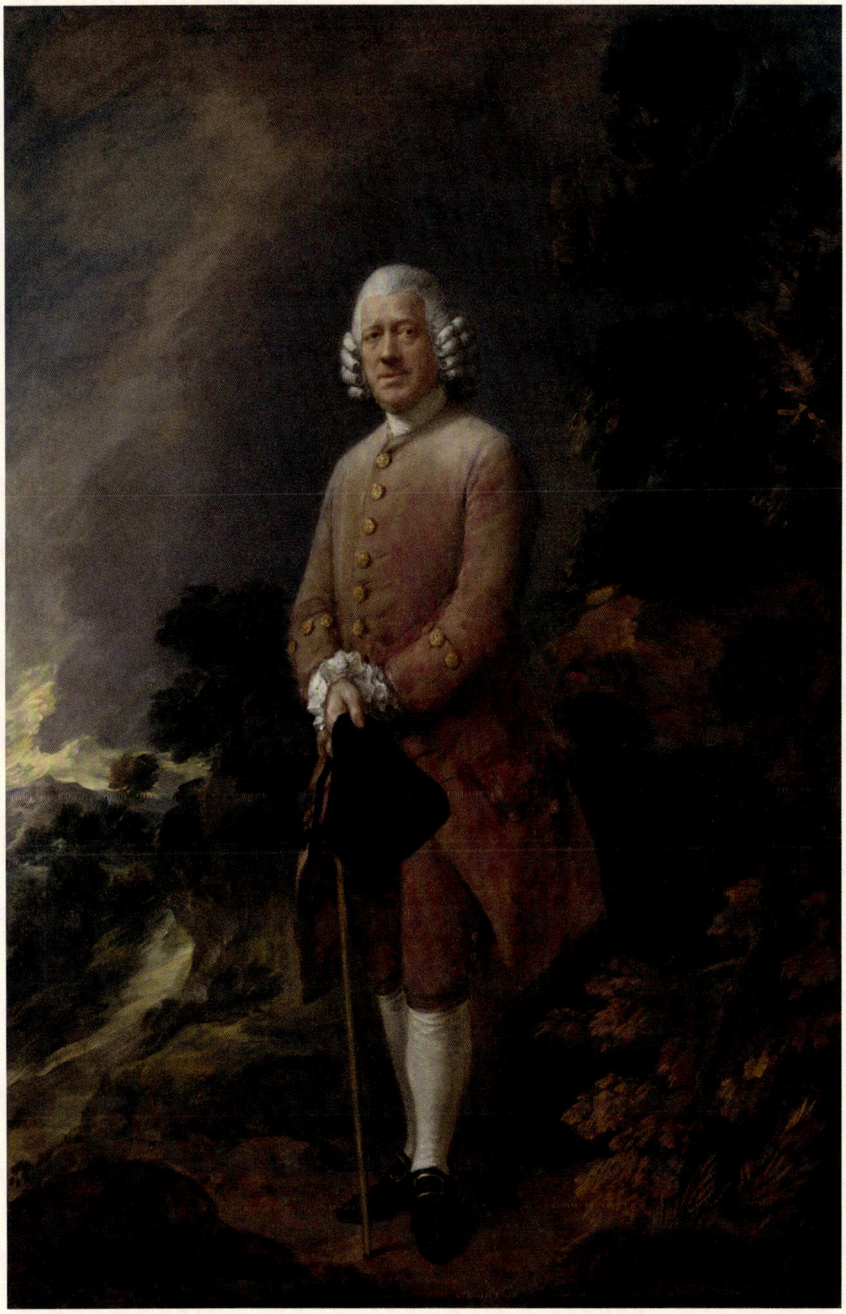

The Southampton portrait shows George Venables Vernon (1735–1830), MP for Glamorgan from 1774, and who, on his father's death in 1780, inherited the estate of Sudbury Hall, Derby, and became the second Lord Vernon. He is depicted enjoying the leisured lifestyle of a country gentleman, signalled by the presence of his gun-dog. As in many portraits of the aristocracy, the landscape is included to reinforce the sitter's identity and authority as a member of the British landed elite, a social hierarchy subtly presented as part of the 'natural' order.

The National Gallery's painting depicts the physician Ralph Schomberg, who, by contrast, looks less comfortable in a rustic setting. He came from a family of metropolitan doctors, including his father, the German-Jewish Meyer Löw Schomberg, one of London's most successful physicians. Gainsborough consulted various doctors during his years in Bath for his own medical problems, and about the mental health of his elder daughter Mary. In fact, he produced likenesses of four physicians, some of them perhaps in lieu of medical fees. Ralph Schomberg's reputation plunged some years after this portrait was finished; he was apparently frequently in debt and left Bath in shame having been caught stealing money in 1777 from the church's collection plate, intended for Bath Hospital.

Gainsborough usually painted with enormous speed and sureness; his other daughter Margaret observed that he painted with colours that were 'very liquid'. The crimson pigment in Dr Schomberg's coat has faded unevenly over time, and the physical condition of Vernon's waistcoat was also a cause for concern, with Philip Hendy describing it as being in 'rather a messy state'.[11] However, Maurice Palmer thought quite differently. Since the painting had, in his opinion, 'so much of the best and most typical of [Gainsborough's] painting', he argued that the painting should be pursued. To secure appropriate funding, Hendy suggested that not only should the Chipperfield Bequest Sub-Committee dip 'slightly into the capital' but also the NACF should be approached for 'a substantial contribution'.[12]

35

Charles Ginner (1878–1952)

Early Morning, 1917

Oil on canvas, 61.6 × 50.2 cm
Purchased with the assistance of the Chipperfield Bequest Fund, 1969
Southampton City Art Gallery, SOTAG 12/1969

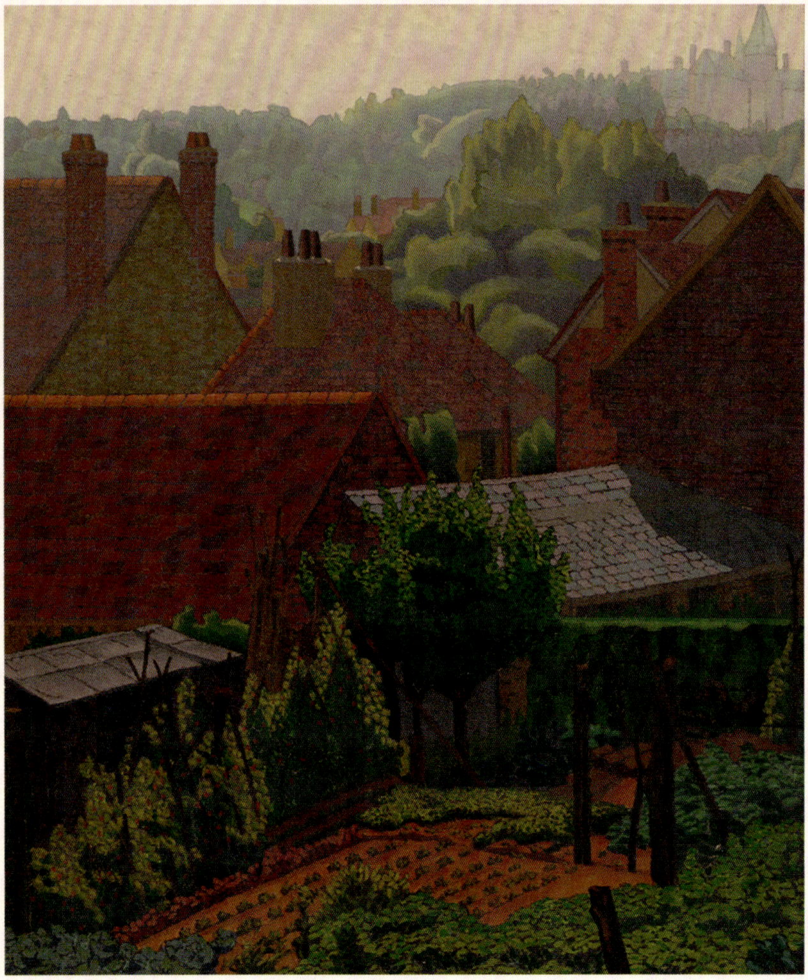

Charles Ginner was a British painter who settled in London in 1910 after growing up in France. Already a friend of artists Harold Gilman and Spencer Gore, Ginner was subsequently drawn into Walter Sickert's circle. Although he never lived in Camden – where Sickert and others had their studios – he became a founding member of the so-called Camden Town Group in 1911. Ginner painted real townscapes and landscapes, from uninhabited scenes to bustling ones, all expressed with careful craftsmanship.

Renaming themselves 'Neo-Realists' after the demise of the Camden Town Group in 1914, Ginner and Gilman fell out with Sickert, who, in a published article, criticised their use of thick paint ('impasto'). When Ginner responded, 'I shall paint as thick as I damn well please', Sickert retaliated with an article, rudely entitled 'The Thickest Painters in London'.[13] Ginner's use of impasto can be traced back to his discovery of the work of Vincent Van Gogh.

In *Early Morning*, Ginner uses a restricted palette of reds, purples and greens to evoke a calm and harmonious morning light falling over the rooftops of the town of Oxted, Surrey. His hallmark approach is evident in his meticulous depiction of individual bricks and tiles. It is seen again in *The Barges, Leeds*, a work Ginner painted in 1916 (and which Palmer would buy in 1974). Palmer was keen to acquire *Early Morning* because he felt it was nearer to the Camden Town period than Ginner's much later painting of *The Albert Memorial* (1947), which Palmer had purchased for Southampton in 1967 as its first example of the painter's work.

Southampton also owns a portrait of Ginner by Malcolm Drummond: the sitter proposed his friend for membership of the Camden Town Group.

36

Gwen John (1876–1939)

Mère Poussepin, 1920

Oil on canvas, 86.7 × 51.2 cm
Purchased with the assistance of the Chipperfield Bequest Fund, 1954
Southampton City Art Gallery, SOTAG 1456

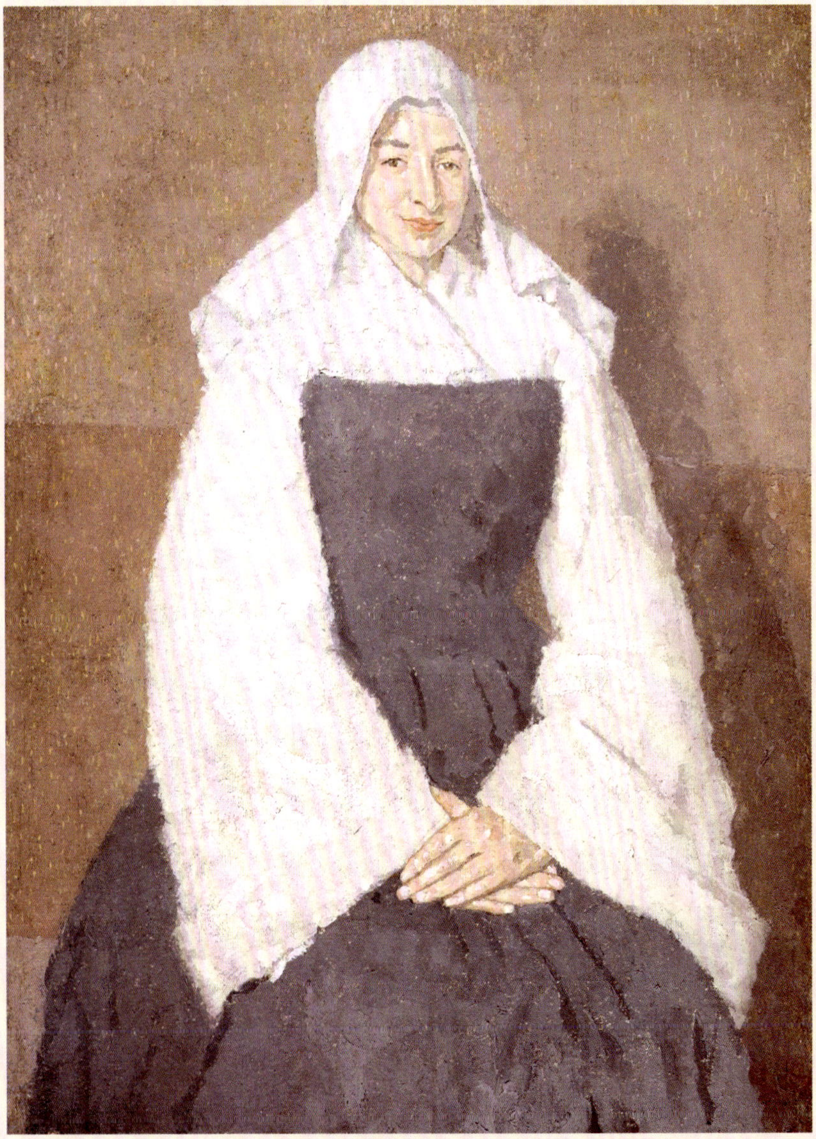

Gwen John only had one solo exhibition of her work during her life. By the time she died, living almost as a hermit in France, having ceased painting for a decade, her work was little known. However, her brother Augustus's prediction that one day her paintings would be more highly regarded than his own turned out to be accurate.[14] Exhibitions and publications about her work started to appear very quickly after her death, being given further impetus since the 1960s thanks to growing interest and scholarship in the work of women artists.

Most of Gwen John's paintings depict single figures – usually young women, women in holy orders or self-portraits. Painted within closeted interiors and often sitting or standing still, the sitters exude an unassuming dignity. This portrait depicts Marie Poussepin (1653–1744), founder of the French Dominican order of the Sisters of Charity of the Holy Virgin of Tours. After John's affair with the celebrated French sculptor Auguste Rodin ended (she had been one of his models, then his mistress for a decade), she converted to Roman Catholicism through encounters with the Meudon Chapter in 1913. The painter was subsequently asked to produce a likeness of their founder. The nuns, delighted with the result, commissioned at least five more versions. Southampton's picture, dating to 1920, is the last. Its small scale, restrained colours, simple composition and quiet intensity are characteristic of John's work.

More abstract in style is Gwen John's *Girl in Mulberry Dress*, whose sitter seems comparatively tense, her hands ill at ease. It was one of nine portraits of the same subject. Having bought *Mère Poussepin* for Southampton in 1954, Palmer purchased the second female portrait in 1962.

37

Mark Gertler (1891–1939)

The Rabbi and his Grandchild, 1913

Oil on canvas, 50.8 × 45.9 cm
Purchased with the assistance of the Chipperfield Bequest Fund, 1968
Southampton City Art Gallery, SOTAG 6/1968

The obituary of Polish-Jewish painter Gertler in *The Times* described his suicide in 1939 as 'a serious loss to British art' and 'that a considered list of the half-dozen most important painters under 50 working in England would include him'.[15] He was one of a brilliant if troubled generation of students who enrolled at the Slade School of Fine Art before the First World War, including Stanley Spencer. Despite the influences of modernist abstract art, these painters continued to produce distinctive figurative paintings.

Maurice Palmer favoured acquiring pictures by a spread of artists so that Southampton could represent milestones in the history of European painting, but he also acquired multiple examples by certain esteemed painters. He purchased three paintings by Gertler in two years: *Still Life with a Bust* and *Family Group* were both purchased in 1953 followed by *Seated Nude* the next year. *The Rabbi and his Grandchild* was purchased in the following decade, in 1968, and Gertler's *Flower Piece* was accepted in 2007 as a bequest through the Art Fund.

The Rabbi and his Grandchild is one of a series of portraits which established Gertler's reputation and reflects his interest in European painting. While possibly influenced by the *Portrait of a Lady* (about 1460) by the workshop of Rogier van der Weyden in the National Gallery's collection, the painting also charts Gertler's deepening engagement with Post-Impressionism. By making many changes and deleting various elements, his final composition was simplified and made more dramatic.

The painting draws on Gertler's Jewish roots. The child is Dora Plaskowsky, whom Gertler spotted at his family's butcher in Spitalfields, but the old man has not been identified. Contemporary reviewers understood the painting as a sympathetic allegory of youth and old age; in fact, the models never posed together nor even met.[16]

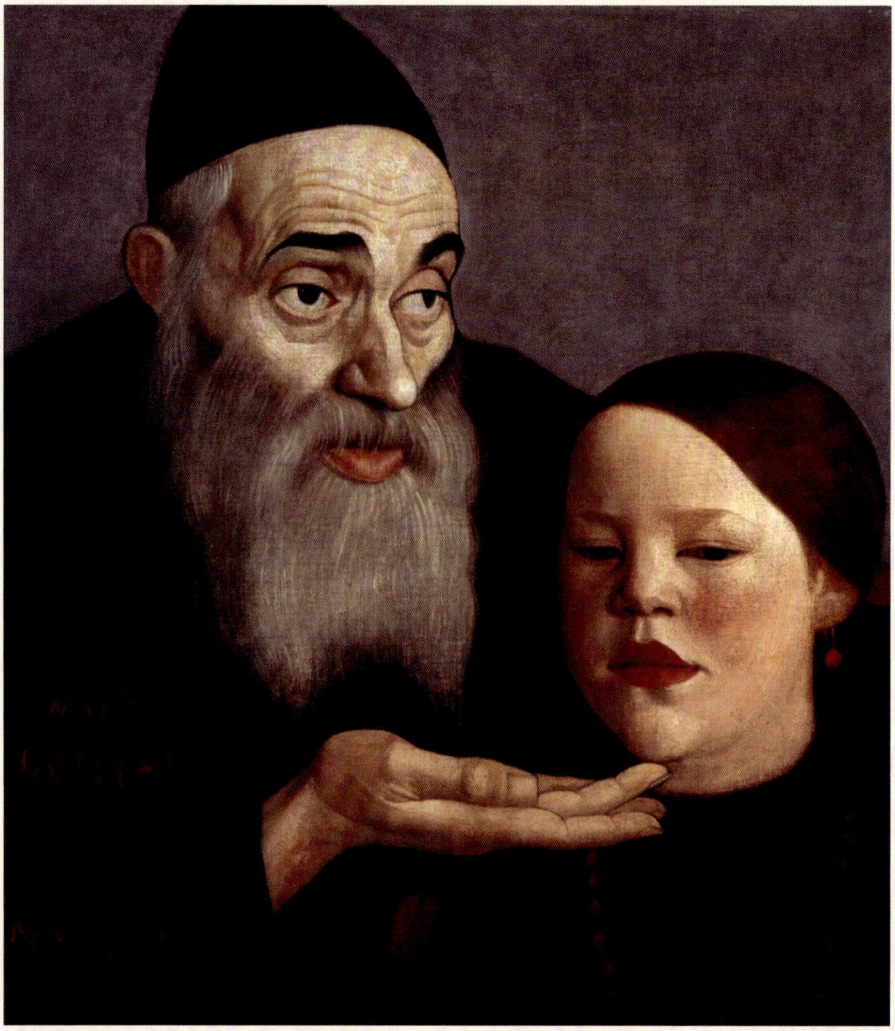

38

Edgar Degas (1834–1917)
Danseuse mettant son bas
(*Dancer putting on her Stocking*)

Original beeswax statue modelled by Degas sometime between the 1890s and 1911; cast in bronze by the Hébrard foundry (Paris) at an unknown date after 1921 and before about 1936
Bronze, 47 × 28 × 18 cm
Purchased through the Chipperfield Bequest Fund, 1952
Southampton City Art Gallery, SOTAG 1418

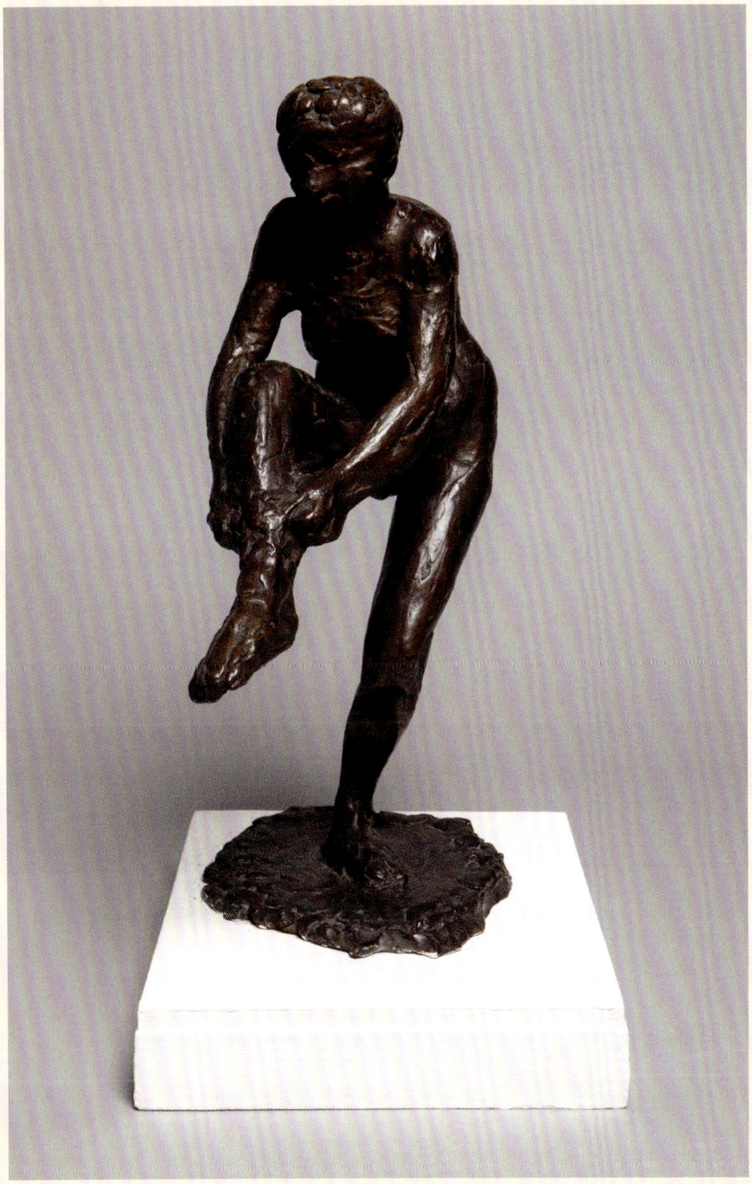

Edgar Degas devoted his ground-breaking career to depicting modern life in Paris, often from unusual viewpoints and using experimental materials and techniques. He produced countless scenes of dancers, entertainers and women at their toilette as well as jockeys, horses and racegoers. Although Degas was associated with the Impressionists, unlike other members of that group, he never painted outdoors and preferred to be called a 'Realist'.

Degas was an innovative painter, draughtsman, printmaker and photographer. He was also a talented and experimental modeller who produced small-scale figurative sculpture in a variety of malleable materials throughout his career, mainly coloured wax, Plastiline (a man-made modelling material similar to plasticine) and plaster, over shop-bought or home-made iron armatures. Unlike his 2D work which was mostly made with studio input for commercial sale, Degas's 3D work was entirely non-profit-making, made by himself, for himself. The only sculpture that Degas made for public consumption was his pioneering mixed-media polychrome *Little Dancer aged Fourteen* (National Gallery of Art, Washington), which divided opinion when shown at the Sixth Impressionist Exhibition in Paris in 1881, many critics being affronted by the girl's gaunt features. At the time of Degas's death, over 150 small-scale sculptures were found in his studio.

Although Degas had resisted the reproduction of his fragile and deliberately ephemeral one-of-a-kind sculptures in bronze during his lifetime, his heirs authorised limited edition serial casts to be made of over 70 of the most complete and attractive compositions. Although the decision was controversial, it has meant that at least a proportion of Degas's 3D compositions have been preserved and the posthumous casts can be enjoyed by the public in museums worldwide, including Southampton's version of *Dancer putting on her Stocking*, purchased in 1952.

39

Auguste Rodin (1840–1917)

Femme accroupie (*Squatting Woman*)

Original clay model by Rodin, about 1881–82;
cast in bronze by the Rudier foundry
(Paris), about mid-1950s
Bronze, 31.5 × 25 × 18 cm
Purchased through the Chipperfield
Bequest Fund, 1953
Southampton City Art Gallery, SOTAG 1422

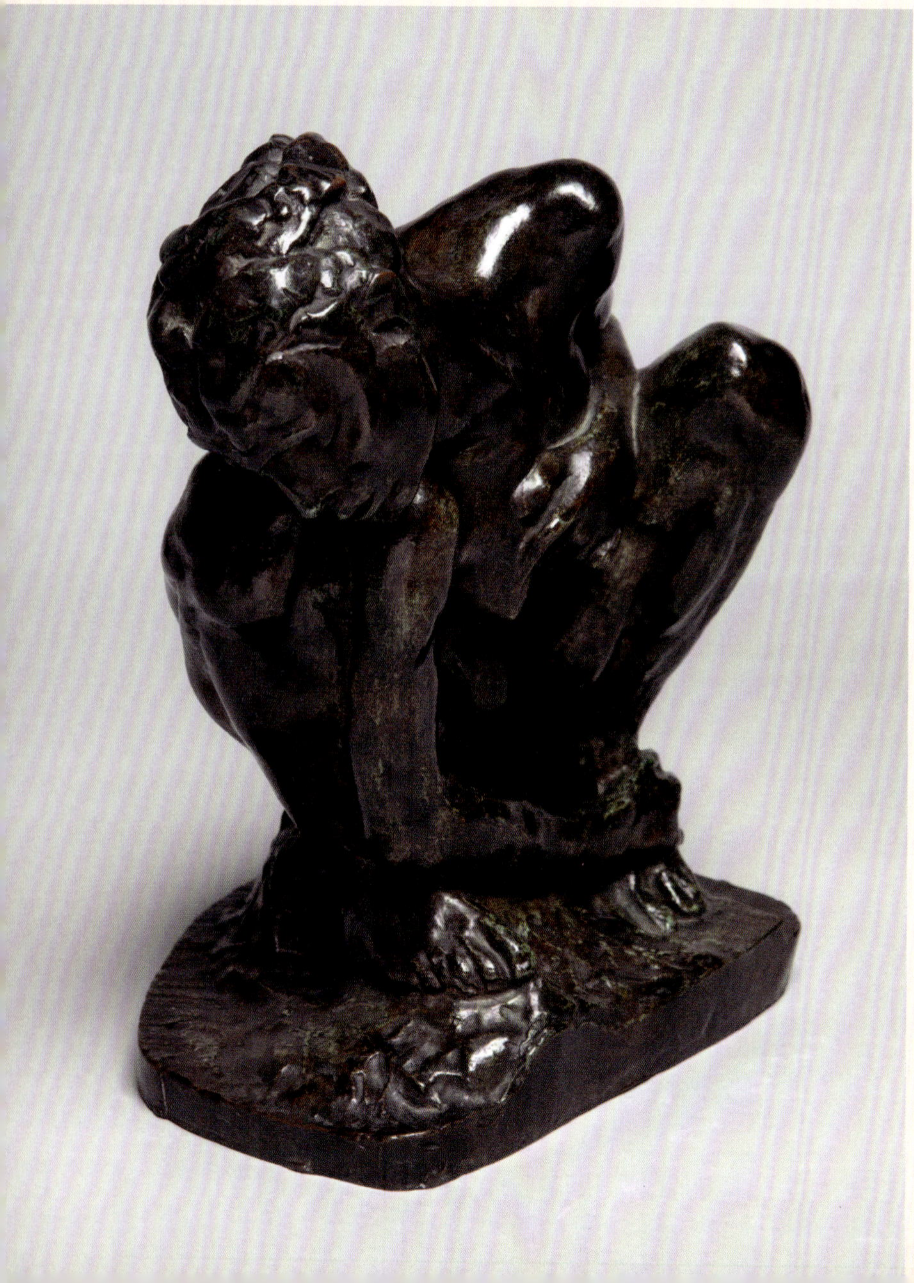

Southampton residents will be familiar with Auguste Rodin's *Eve*, displayed for many years in the courtyard outside the Gallery, opposite Watts Park. However, they may not know his *Squatting Woman*, another bronze on a far smaller scale.

Squatting Woman is a reduced-scale version of the life-sized figure that Rodin made around 1881–82 for his *Gates of Hell*, a monumental 6-metre-high bronze door for the proposed (but never built) Musée des Arts Décoratifs in Paris. Rodin had received this prestigious commission in 1880, while still relatively unknown, and used the first section of Dante's poem *The Divine Comedy* (about 1308–20) as his starting point, especially the dire warning over Hell's entrance: 'Abandon every hope, ye who enter here'. Rodin's composition was crowded with over 180 bodies, writhing in distraught, agonised and sub-human poses. Although the commission was finally abandoned, Rodin decided to extract a number of figures from the door and have his highly skilled assistants reproduce them as independent freestanding sculptures. These were mass-produced for commercial sale in limited editions, on different scales, in marble and bronze, including this *Squatting Woman*, of which several other versions in bronze are known.

The unnatural – indeed ungainly and cramped – posture of the woman and her facial expression suggest powerful feelings of pain, fear, isolation and despair, which is further emphasised by the highly agitated surfaces. Although Rodin's anti-Academic approach proved highly controversial at first, he refused to change his technique or style, and became one of the most sought-after sculptors of his day, with a large studio to meet self-generated market demand.

40

Aristide Maillol (1861–1944)
Femme au crabe (*Woman with Crab*)

Original terracotta model by Maillol in 1930; cast in bronze by the Rudier foundry (Paris), about early 1950s
Bronze and black Belgian marble, 18 × 19.5 × 15 cm
Purchased through the Chipperfield Bequest Fund, 1955
Southampton City Art Gallery, SOTAG 1464

Aristide Maillol was a French sculptor, painter and printmaker. Having moved to Paris in 1881 to study art, he was accepted at the École des Beaux-Arts four years later. He began his artistic career as a painter and tapestry designer, taking up sculpture at the age of 40. The nude female body is the subject of nearly all his mature work. He never produced the kind of emotional sculpture associated with Auguste Rodin, such as Southampton's *Squatting Woman* (cat. 39), preferring to treat his works with a greater classical poise, creating sculptures that were aesthetically pleasing and highly marketable. Though Maillol's connection to the art of the past is strong, his interest in form and geometry paved the way for the work of later abstract sculptors such as Constantin Brancusi and Jean Arp.

This small bronze, acquired by Southampton in 1955, from an exhibition at the Leicester Galleries in London, was spoken of approvingly by Philip Hendy, as 'one of [Maillol's] best'.[17] Furthermore, Southampton's curator Maurice Palmer was happy to find a visual connection between it and an earlier purchase, noting that its pose was 'almost the same as the somewhat larger Rodin [*Squatting Woman*] which we bought about two years ago.'[18] Interestingly, the Maillol had once belonged to Kenneth Clark, as had several other works of art now in Southampton's collection.

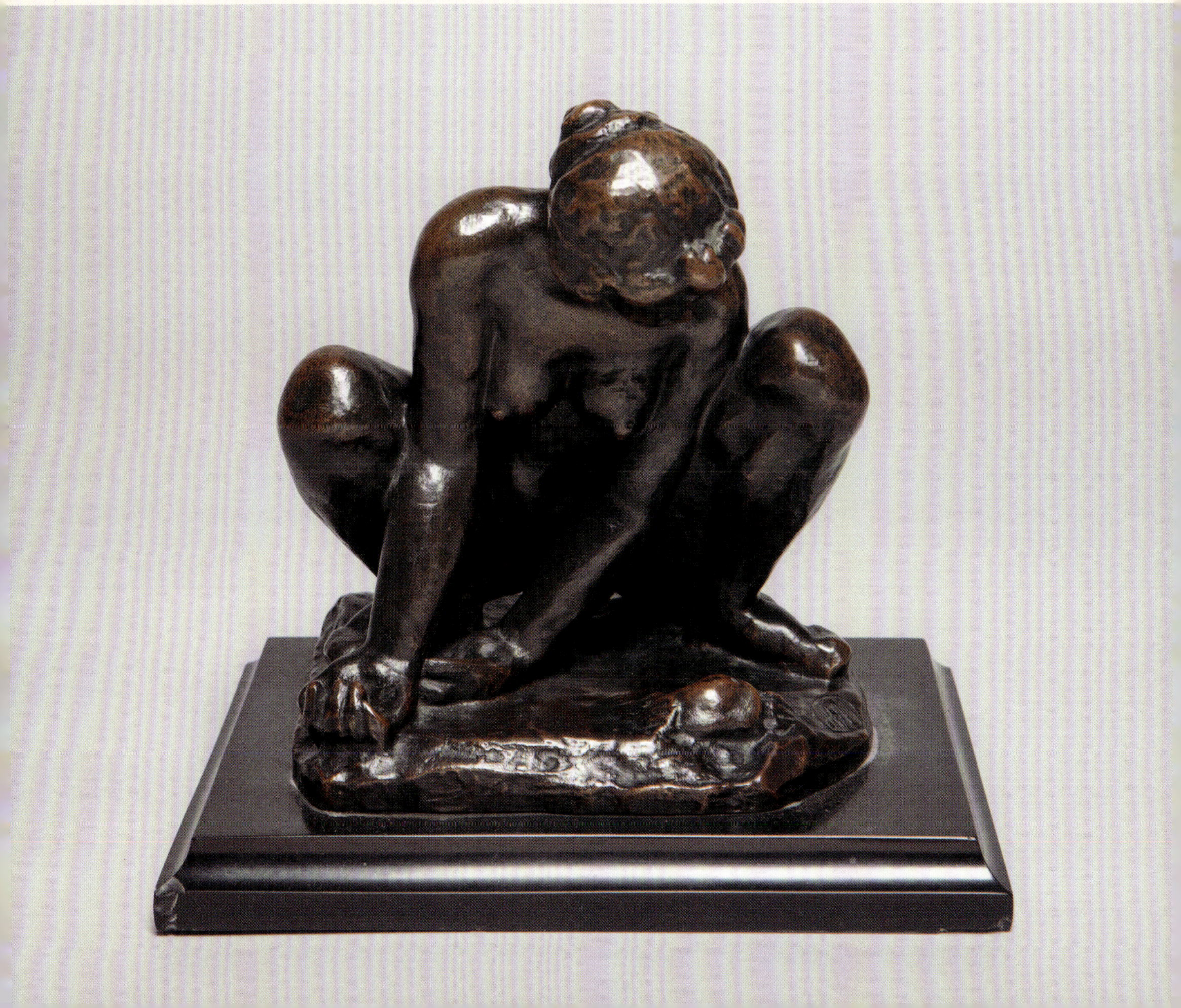

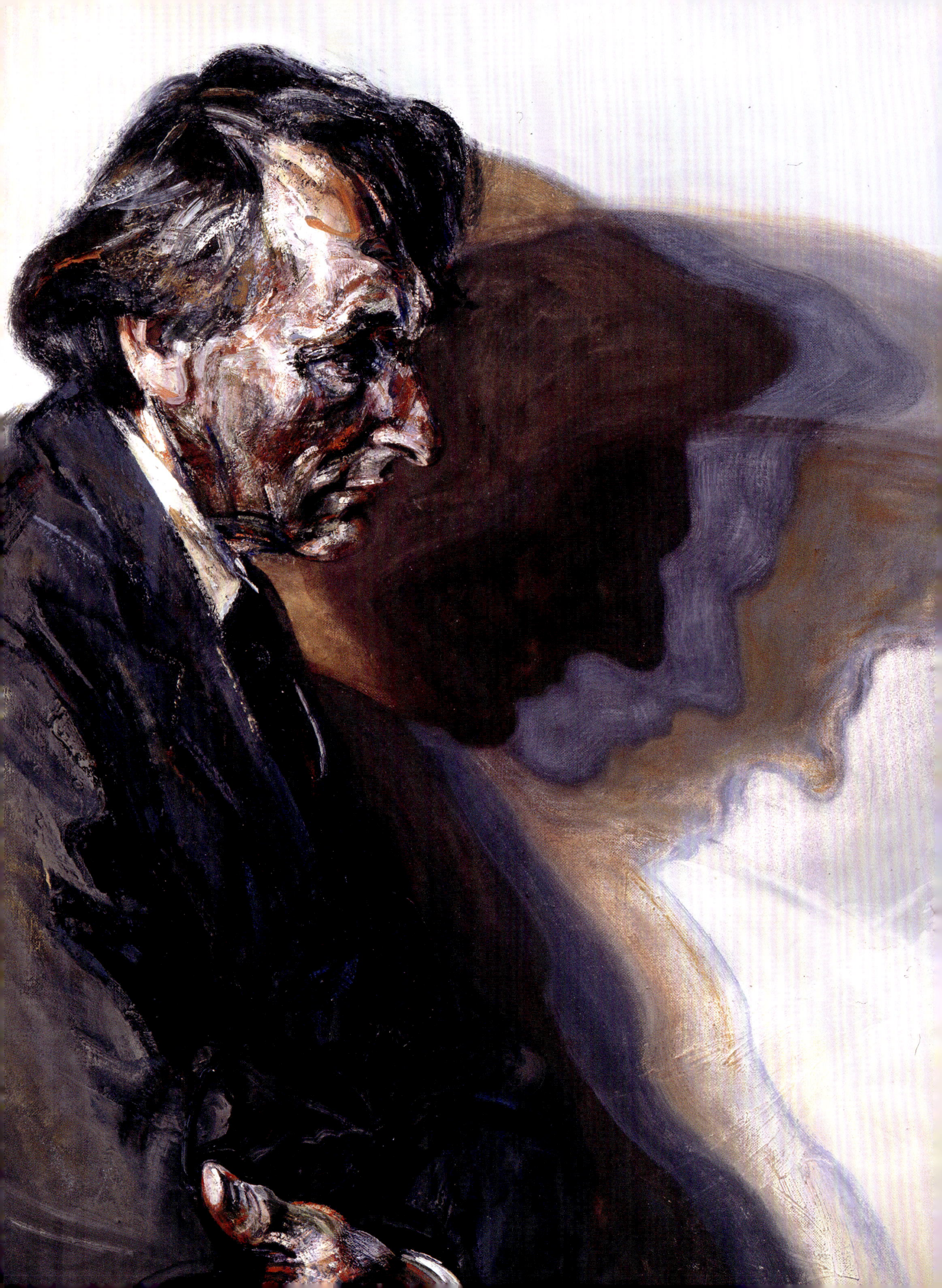

PASTURES NEW

5

Collaborating with the Tate and National Galleries (1971–present)

Southampton Art Gallery experienced a new wave of excitement and experimentation in the early 1970s. Anthony 'Tony' Howarth was appointed curator in 1971, and took the opportunity when local government and its education system were restructured in 1974 to appoint a dynamic young staff with a mandate to do what they could to 'make the Art Gallery into a really great place'.[1] Two women applied for the keeper of art role, and keen to appoint two applicants, he invited them to choose which post they wanted. Elizabeth (Liz) Goodall (then Ogborn) became keeper of art, and Helen Luckett was appointed to a new role – keeper of education. A crucial ally of the museum was the director of the National Gallery, Michael Levey, appointed in 1973 (fig. 63). He was a new kind of director because he had risen through the Gallery's ranks.

A Monet in 1975 changes Southampton's acquisition strategy

Less than two years into Levey's directorship, Southampton acquired a very important but hugely expensive French Impressionist painting – Claude Monet's *The Church at Vétheuil* (1880) (fig. 64, cat. 41) – which Howarth described as 'a sparkling example of Impressionism at its height'.[2] It was one of Monet's famous series of paintings where he viewed the same object from various positions, at different times of the day and year to capture the transient effects of light and atmosphere. Having long been in the possession of a Hampshire family, the painting was bought in 1975 for £56,284 through a combination of the Chipperfield Bequest Fund (which gave £14,000), a 50% government grant, a National Art Collections Fund (NACF) donation

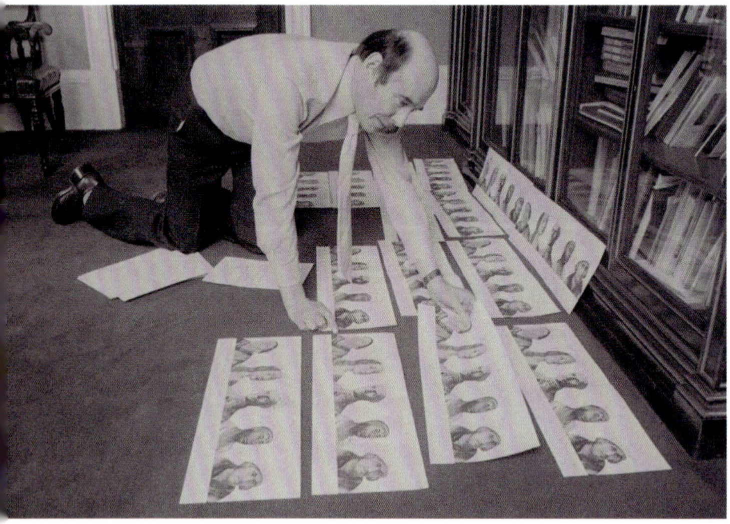

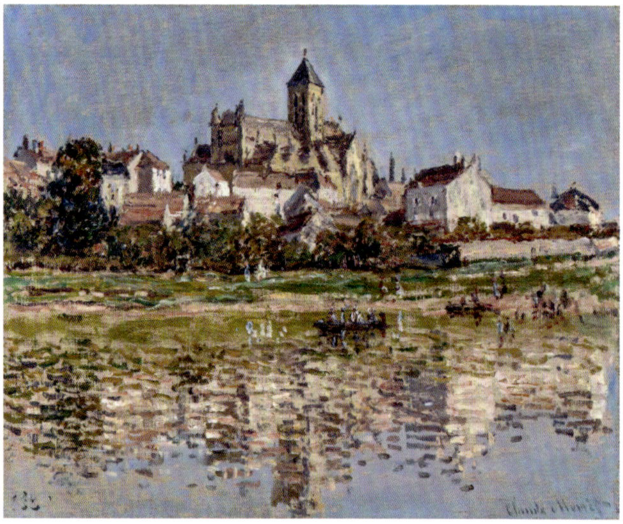

(PREVIOUS PAGE)
Maggi Hambling (b. 1945)
Mac with Shadows, 1981;
detail, cat. 52
Oil on canvas, 66.9 × 66.5 cm
Southampton City Art Gallery,
SOTAG 13/1982

FIG. 63
Michael Levey, Director of the National Gallery (1973–86) judging 'Mad Hats' Competition.
The National Gallery, London

FIG. 64
Claude Monet (1840–1926)
The Church at Vétheuil, 1880
Oil on canvas, 50.5 × 61 cm
Southampton City Art Gallery,
SOTAG 183/1975

of £3,000, and further public and private donations. It joined the ever-expanding collection of French and English Impressionist paintings at Southampton traced in this account. Goodall had argued that it was 'better to buy one important painting such as this, rather than a succession of less significant pictures'[3] – an identical attitude to that expressed by her predecessors, Conran and Palmer.

The purchase of the Monet used up much of the remaining money in the Chipperfield Bequest Fund, which meant that Southampton Art Gallery was no longer in a position to compete on the international art market for expensive historical paintings. Indeed, its final old master purchase was on a far more modest scale, and secured in 1979, with assistance from the NACF. This was John Constable's pencil sketch of *View of Southampton showing the Town Quay and the Anchorage from the Platform* (fig. 65).[4] It proved universally popular because it brought another work by a world-renowned painter into the collection, as well as having local appeal given that Constable had produced the drawing of Southampton during his honeymoon. Together with a watercolour by J.M.W. Turner of Carisbrooke Castle (ultimately not acquired), these were the last acquisitions of historical art on which the National Gallery gave advice, Levey favouring the purchase of both works.[5]

Henceforth, the few historical paintings which entered the collection did so as modest gifts or bequests – Southampton never received any important clusters of old masters in the way that other regional galleries did, such as Bristol or Manchester.[6] Thus, in 1972, the Gallery gained a Corot landscape, the *Ville d'Avray,* from a distribution by the NACF of paintings from the collection of two sisters, Rachel F. and Jean I. Alexander (the National Gallery was given 17 pictures), while in 1975, Southampton received an *Adoration of the Shepherds* by Francesco de

Mura, as part of the Wellington Bequest administered by the Art Fund. Likewise, in 1980, through the government's allocation of pictures acquired in lieu of estate duty, Southampton received a painting of *The Madonna and Child* by the great Venetian sixteenth-century painter Giovanni Bellini. Although an interesting work, it is in poor physical condition.[7]

From 1975 Howarth delegated purchasing policy and acquisitions to Liz Goodall. She was determined, despite diminished finances, to maintain Southampton's high profile as a leading regional art gallery. Goodall therefore made the pragmatic, yet far-sighted, decision, to focus on building up areas of the collection which were within their budget. It was her idea that Southampton Art Gallery should henceforth purchase mainly modern and contemporary British art, partly because it was affordable, partly because Southampton had always done so (at least to a limited extent) and also because the majority of UK public art galleries were avoiding it, after the very negative press that the Tate Gallery received in 1972 for purchasing *Equivalent VIII* by the American minimalist artist Carl Andre.[8] Levey immediately pledged his 'support for future activities concerning the Chipperfield Bequest Fund', at a meeting arranged in January 1976.[9] Goodall soon approached Levey to see whether he might be willing to be consulted about potential acquisitions in this area. Having agreed to do so, he was soon called on, in August 1976, to give advice in relation to three sculptures by the Scotsman Ian Hamilton Finlay. Stating that he knew 'a little bit about' Finlay's work, Levey was able to suggest that the prices seemed 'rather reasonable' in relation to 'other work by comparable artists about which [he had] been hearing'.[10] However, he felt increasingly out of his depth. For instance, when asked in December 1977 to comment on three contemporary works by Roger Ackling, Tony Cragg and George Fullard, Levey responded: 'I don't feel fully qualified to comment on all of these.'[11]

A new focus on contemporary art at Southampton

Extant correspondence reveals just how much Levey would learn about contemporary British art from colleagues in Southampton and the Tate Gallery.

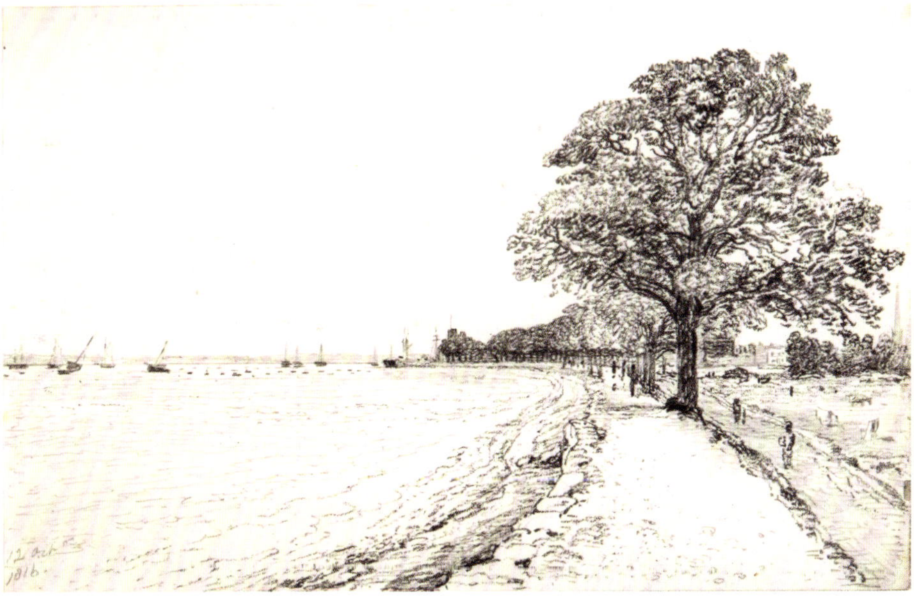

FIG. 65
John Constable (1776–1837)
View of Southampton showing the Town Quay and the Anchorage from the Platform, 1816
Pencil on paper, 11 × 18 cm
Southampton City Art Gallery, SOTAG 18/1979

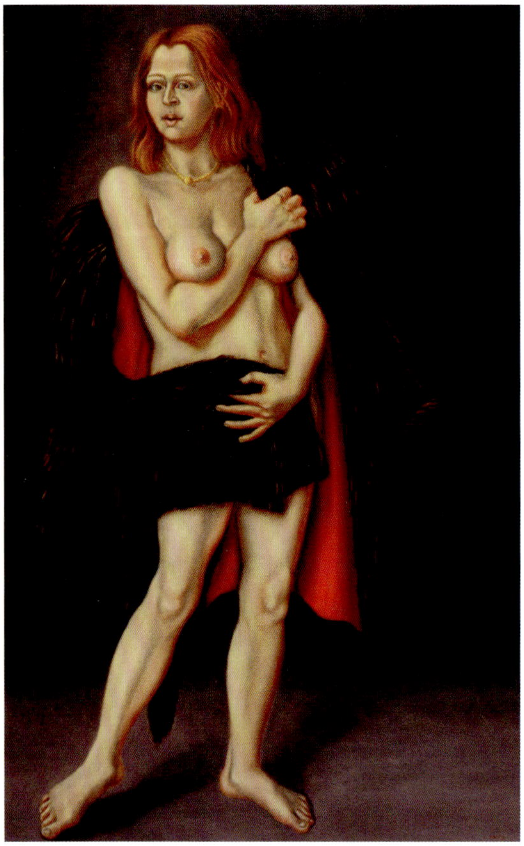

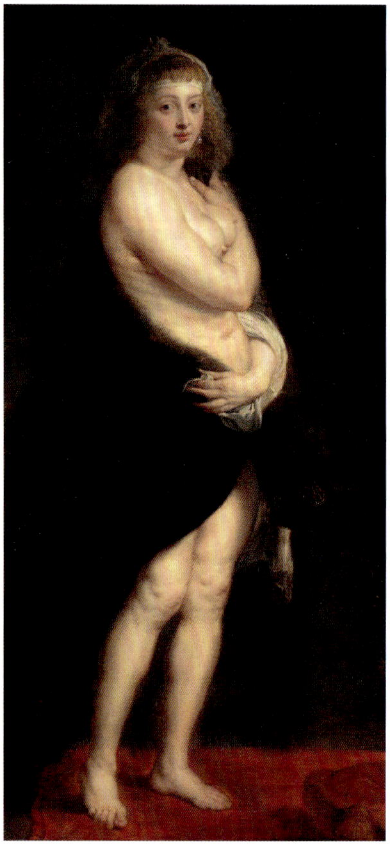

FIG. 66
Stephen McKenna (1939–2017)
Fourment, 1977
Oil on canvas, 12.2 × 8 cm
Southampton City Art Gallery,
SOTAG 24/1978

FIG. 67
Helena Fourment ('*The Little Fur Coat*'), about 1636–38
Oil on canvas, 176 × 83 cm
Kunsthistorisches Museum,
Vienna, inv. no. GG_688

FIG. 68
Maggi Hambling (b. 1945)
Portrait of Dr David Brown, 1986
Charcoal on paper, 76.5 × 56 cm
Tate, T11745

The turning point came in July 1978, when his 'considerable hesitation' over Stephen McKenna's *Fourment* (fig. 66, cat. 43), led Levey to seek out advice from another expert. Having apologised to Goodall in Southampton, 'I do not mean to question the judgement of yourself and your colleagues but ... I don't quite see what in aesthetic terms it is giving your Collection',[12] he quickly wrote again to say that he had been in touch with Dr David Brown (1925–2002), Assistant Keeper of the Modern Collection at the Tate Gallery, about the proposed purchase. He noted that the 'most useful information about McKenna' supplied by Brown had helped to contextualise the work within the European tradition (in addition to its obvious referencing of Rubens's *Helena Fourment* in Vienna; fig. 67), and had been won round. Levey concluded:

> In the light of David's information, and his views, I certainly would not wish to oppose the purchase of this picture. I rather doubt that if it is something that I personally will ever come to like, but that is a very different matter. I hardly need to say that I warmly support Southampton's enlightened policy of buying modern work.[13]

Another bold contemporary acquisition of this time was *Work* by David Redfern (cat. 44). As a reinterpretation of Ford Madox Brown's iconic painting of the same title produced in 1852–65, Redfern uses a more modern and powerful palette than the original and also weaves in contemporary cultural references. The Redfern picture was bought in 1979, the same year it was completed. By this point, Levey was no longer regularly consulted: until the end of 1978, we find that the Gallery's letters to

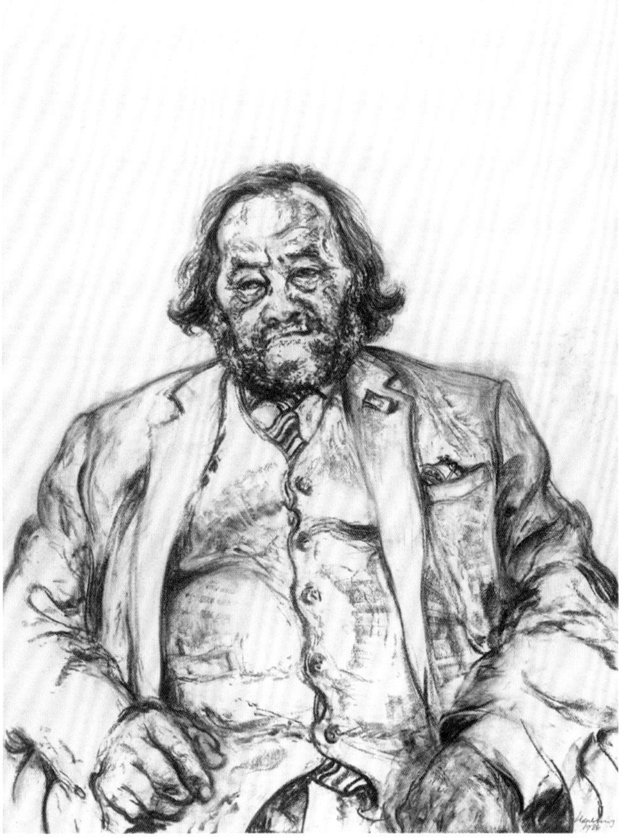

Levey continue to ask for his 'permission to use the Chipperfield Bequest Fund' or to ask his 'advice and guidance on proposed purchases for the Gallery',[14] but thereafter such requests cease.

Southampton's new art adviser: Dr David Brown at the Tate Gallery

The external advisory role for purchases in contemporary art passed, informally at first, to the Tate Gallery (the Tate relationship was ratified officially in 2012).[15] The two institutions had already been in touch over the purchase of works using the Smith Bequest Fund, whose purchasing committee had always included, as noted, the director of the Tate Gallery or his nominated representative. David Brown (fig. 68) became Southampton's external specialist for matters modern and contemporary, and he did much to encourage the growth of in-house expertise in these areas. He had gained his first curatorial post in 1973 at the Scottish National Gallery of Modern Art, Edinburgh, where in just over a year in post he had mounted exhibitions of the work of Duncan Grant, Roger Hilton and Richard Long. Brown's association with the Tate Gallery started the following year, in 1974, when he was appointed assistant curator for its modern collection. There, he continued to organise important exhibitions in the field, including one on the St Ives School in 1985, the year he retired.

Brown's earliest involvement with Southampton began when, as a private collector, he approached Maurice Palmer for advice. He blossomed under the mentorship, with Palmer advising him to focus on acquiring British contemporary art.[16] His later involvement as adviser to Southampton Art Gallery was initiated when, at Palmer's request, he started to visit London dealers on the gallery's behalf, but this activity ceased in 1970. Liz Goodall contacted him afresh in 1975 to renew his advisory role in the light of her decision to concentrate on contemporary acquisitions. Brown advised on purchases of works by Adrian Heath, Anthony Hill and Terry Frost in 1976, and then on further purchases of work by Kim Lim, Stephen Willats, Hamish Fulton and Tony Cragg in 1977. The new arrangement with the Tate Gallery was recognised more widely after the purchase of the McKenna in 1978 when Levey agreed, 'since his knowledge of contemporary art was limited' to let Brown take the lead as Southampton's art adviser.[17] Apparently Brown 'gave his advice for the love of the Gallery' – having been born a few miles away in Romsey, he always regarded Southampton as his home town and retained a loyalty to its local gallery.[18] Brown was keen to assist, his determination borne out of what he saw as a failure of national and regional galleries to engage with up-to-date artistic developments.

In a feisty review in the *Art Monthly* in February 1977, Brown pointed out that public institutions were 'neglecting opportunities to acquire works of the real avant garde [sic] of today'. In a call to arms, he stated: 'Art in new idioms which have lasting qualities often seems "difficult", tough, abrasive and almost anti-art when it first appears. This is the kind of work regional galleries should collect.'[19] One such pioneering museum director was Michael Compton, director at the Ferens Art Gallery, Hull from 1960 to 1965. Brown, acting for Southampton, soon became another. The first work bought on his advice was in 1976 – *Central Park, New York* by Maxwell Armfield (fig. 69, cat. 45) – a Southampton artist born near Ringwood. Brown clearly thought it a very good picture because he put it on record that '[he] and Richard Morphet had wanted the Tate to buy it'[20] (Morphet joined the Tate in 1966, becoming keeper of the Modern Collection in 1986).

With Brown's help from the mid-1970s to his death in 2002, Southampton's post-1900 acquisitions 'were built up in three key areas, two concerned modern British art – Surrealist art and the St Ives School – while the third was new British art – not only painting, then undergoing a quiet renaissance, but also sculpture and, importantly, broadly conceptual work.'[21] In these fields, Southampton competed with very few other regional galleries. Its most serious rival was probably Swindon Museum and Art Gallery, which amassed an impressive collection with help from Morphet.

Modern and contemporary British art: purchases, bequests and gifts

Together, Brown and Goodall scoured London to find up-and-coming talent; at the time, few dealer galleries other than the Lisson were promoting new art. As a second approach, they attended artists' postgraduate degree shows 'to talent spot and catch artists on the way up'.[22] It was in this way that

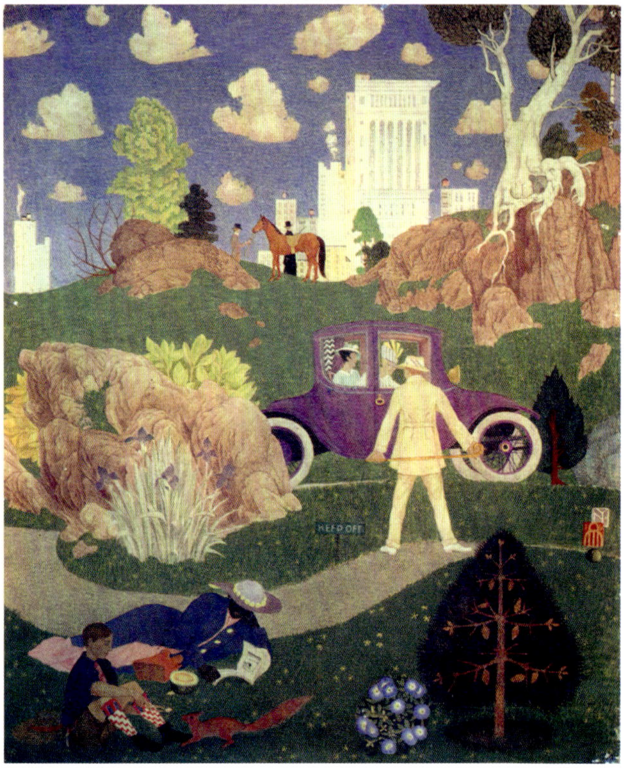

FIG. 69
Maxwell Armfield (1881–1972)
Central Park, New York, 1916
Tempera on canvas, 64.2 × 39 cm
Southampton City Art Gallery, SOTAG 42/1976

FIG. 70
Bryan Wynter (1915–1975)
Monumental, 1956
Oil on canvas, 202 × 101.5 cm
Southampton City Art Gallery, SOTAG 15/2006

Southampton acquired its first work by the sculptor Tony Cragg, *One Stone in Four*. Purchased in 1977 for £250 from the Royal Academy Diploma Show,[23] it was the first of the sculptor's works to enter the collection of any public museum. Previously, two notable and distinctive bronze sculptures by Michael Ayrton had been acquired in 1973, *Reflective Heads II* (cat. 46) and *Minotaur Waking.* Other bronzes purchased during this period include *Bye Bye the Elephant* by Barry Flanagan in 1981, followed by several of his popular 'signature' sculptures including *Boxing Hare on Anvil* bought in 2002 (cat. 47) and Antony Gormley's *The Diver* in 1984. Maggi Hambling's small multi-media *First Dragon* was purchased in 1996 (cat. 48). The purchase of major British sculpture over the last

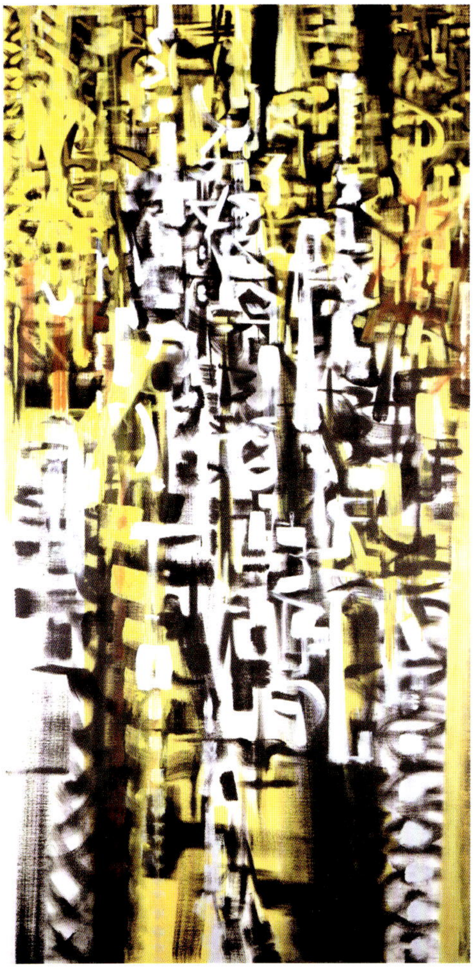

half-century has significantly enhanced the core of work by French nineteenth-century sculptors acquired during the 1950s as discussed in Chapter 4.

Such purchases were enabled because Southampton's acquisition strategy and track-record received strong support from artists and dealers, often in terms of reductions on the final sale price. Southampton staff also became adept at submitting persuasive applications to funding bodies, spending increasing time and effort applying to the Contemporary Art Society (mentioned earlier) and the Arts Council England/V&A Purchase Grant Fund, and for grants from the NACF and their own Friends of Southampton's Museums, Archives and Galleries (FoSMAG).

The collection also expanded through the generosity of David Brown himself, who in 2002 bequeathed 220 modern British paintings to Southampton (in a similar act of generosity, Brown left his works on paper to the British Museum). Given that a great love was the St Ives School, unsurprisingly Brown's bequest included prime examples by its major exponents, including Terry Frost's *Silver and Grey*, Wilhelmina Barns-Graham's *Glacier Vortex* (cat. 49) and 15 paintings by his close friend Roger Hilton, including *Figure 1961*.

Additionally, Southampton and the Tate shared the proceeds from the sale of David Brown's house, which resulted in each institution receiving £200,000–250,000 to purchase further works of art. This new funding stream allowed Southampton to focus on acquiring in five areas of British art that reflected Brown's interests, namely 'British surrealists, St Ives School, established contemporaries, rising star contemporaries and a major 1960s artist.'[24] For instance, Bryan Wynter's *Monumental* (fig. 70) was purchased in 2006 (with a discount from the artist's estate) as the 'last available classic vertical format painting of his key 1950s period' and as 'a major museum quality work which would feature in regular displays of the St Ives School, alongside work by Ben Nicholson, Patrick Heron, Peter Lanyon, Roger Hilton, Terry Frost and Wilhelmina Barns-Graham'.[25]

The exhibition *Boom Boom Cluster: David Brown Bequest* was mounted at Southampton in 2004 to tell the story of Brown's abiding relationship with the Art Gallery. When Tim Craven (then acting director of Southampton City Art Gallery) sent a copy of the catalogue to the National Gallery, he explained to its then director, Charles Saumarez Smith, the 'momentous' nature of Brown's generosity: 'It has, and through his NACF administered bequest fund, will continue to make an outstanding difference to the Permanent Collection and its ability to exemplify all aspects of British modern art for future Gallery visitors and scholars.'[26] Southampton's collaboration with Bridget Riley was a case in point.

Sean Rainbird, Tate adviser at the time, suggested that Southampton should try to acquire one major painting with its new windfall funding. Rainbird 'proposed a discussion with Bridget Riley' for various reasons: although one of the UK's most distinguished painters and still producing strong and innovative work, she was represented in Southampton's collection by only one minor work on paper (a mass-produced print), and it was thought that having a major work by her could help contextualise and underpin the Gallery's post-1976 abstract painting collection. Although Riley's *Around* (1963) had been bought by the Ferens Gallery, Hull in 1965 and the Fitzwilliam Museum, Cambridge had acquired a Riley as part of its subscription to CAS in 1996, none of her work had been accessioned into any UK regional collection for a couple of decades.

Realising they would not be able to afford one of Riley's paintings produced in the 1960s, Rainbird, together with Craven, met with the artist to discuss a way forward. She readily agreed to produce a new work for Southampton and *Red Movement* was the result (fig. 76). Being expensive, it was secured through a mixture of funding streams – the NACF and the MLA/V&A Purchase Grant Fund – to supplement money from the Dr David and Liza Brown Bequest Fund, while the painter herself sold the work with a considerable discount and also donated supporting sketches and preparatory works (cat. 51). Rainbird recalls: 'I was fortunate to visit her in Royal Crescent one morning to view it – a thirteen-foot major format painting. Before going upstairs, we chatted over extremely strong coffee and an excellent croissant. The painting was fantastic and a great addition to the Southampton collection.'[27] Craven heralded it as 'one of the most important acquisitions in the Gallery's history (comparable with Monet's *The Church at Vétheuil* in 1975, fig. 64, cat. 41) – an entirely fitting employment of Dr Brown's outstanding legacy.'[28] Not everyone agreed; certain city councillors opposed the expense involved and Southampton's *Daily Echo* vilified the acquisition when it was first shown in public. Notwithstanding, the fruitful relationship between the painter and the Gallery continued when the Arts Council's show *Bridget Riley: Flashback* (2009–10) included Southampton City Art Gallery as one of the venues.

Since the Millennium, Southampton City Art Gallery has continued to expand its impressive holdings of earlier twentieth-century British art. One growth area worth drawing attention to is that of English Surrealist art, which had been of constant interest from the time that Conran had borrowed works by Ithell Colquhoun for the 1939 opening of Southampton Art Gallery to the purchase in 1977 of Eileen Agar's important relief in mixed media, *The Object Lesson*, bought 'to make a more coherent grouping around [Southampton's] Paul Nash *Archer*'.[29] In 2002, the National Association of Decorative and Fine Arts Societies funded Southampton's acquisition of *The Hermit Discovered* (fig. 71) by Desmond Morris, who, although best known for his work in human and animal behaviour (he was the author of the landmark study, *The Naked Ape*, of 1967), was also a Surrealist painter. This work is characteristic for its brightly coloured, rounded entities that Morris called 'biomorphs'. It was also in 2002 that John Banting's *Time for Tea (Foliage Fantasy)* was paid for by FoSMAG. Banting was one of the first British artists to engage with Surrealism, its influence detectable in his work from 1930 onwards. FoSMAG, together with money from the Orris Bequest Fund, also helped pay in 2009 for Conroy Maddox's *Les Champs Magnetiques*, the title derived from a classic Surrealist text by André Breton and Philippe Soupault. It was from the NACF that funding came in 2005 to buy Selby Bigg's *Composition* in which a strange

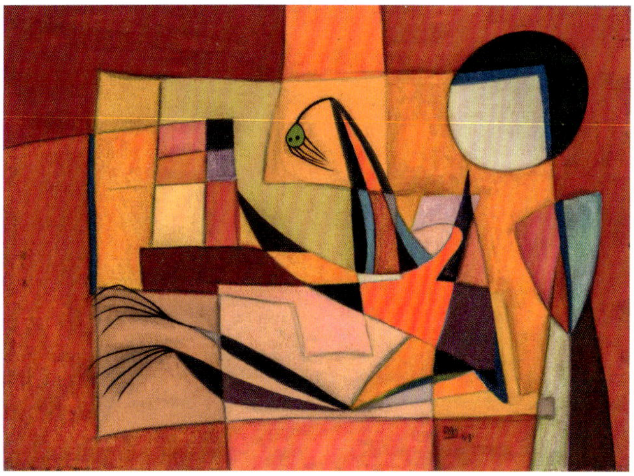

FIG. 71
Desmond Morris (b. 1928)
The Hermit Discovered, 1948
Oil on canvas, 40.8 × 56 cm
Southampton City Art Gallery, SOTAG 4/2002

object, inspired by ships and machinery, floats by a quayside. Once more, this work manifests Surrealist ideas, even though the painter never formally joined the movement.

Southampton has been able to increase its holdings of early twentieth-century British art in recent years through two particularly generous bequests. In 2012, Southampton City Art Gallery received the second largest collection in its history: the Philip Schlee Collection comprised drawings, prints and paintings by 44 artists working between 1920 and 2004, including Gillian Ayres, David Bomberg, Christopher Le Brun, Roger Hilton, David Hockney, Peter Lanyon, Henry Moore and Paul Nash. The collection was assembled by Philip Schlee (1924–2001), with the assistance of his brother Nick Schlee, between 1992 and 2004. To reflect the collection's broad range and eclectic approaches to drawing contained within it, Southampton mounted an exhibition the year after it received the bequest called *Drawn together, Drawn apart* (2013), which displayed a selection of works from the Philip Schlee Collection, including landscapes, compositional sketches and observational life model drawings, including Henry Moore's pen, ink and wash drawing, *Seated Nude*.

The second important bequest came in 2015, from the abstract artist George Dannatt and his wife Ann. The couple donated a substantial group of paintings, drawings, sculptures and prints by key figures associated with the St Ives School, all produced in the 1950s, 60s and 70s (Pallant House, Chichester received works of art on paper and sculptures in addition to paintings and materials for their library). In order to share this important gift with the public, Southampton mounted an exhibition called *Air Water Stone* (2015), which included a choice selection of works from it, including some by Terry Frost and Wilhelmina Barns-Graham, old friends of the Dannatts. Displayed alongside were works from Southampton's permanent collection, including items from the Dr David and Liza Brown Bequest, to remind visitors of the Gallery's longstanding engagement with this kind of art.[30] The George Dannatt Trust also funded a three-year project to conserve 14 of Southampton's modern and contemporary sculptures. The exhibition, *In Trust: Caring for Sculpture* (2018–19), showcased the results of this project.

An important initiative through which Southampton was able to demonstrate its continued commitment to contemporary British art was the CAS's 'Special Collection Scheme' of 1998–2005, funded by the National Lottery. Ultimately, 15 regional museums benefited through the acquisition of '610 works of fine art and craft by 313 different artists and makers with a total purchase price of almost £3 million'.[31] Gill Hedley, Director of CAS at the time (she moved there after her time at Southampton), worked with Margot Heller, Director of Southampton City Art Gallery, to persuade senior management of their responsibility at Southampton to build on the lead it had over other regional collections and to buy some very challenging works of art. Each of the participating museums accepted gifts of different kinds of contemporary artistic production; Hedley recalls that for Southampton she and Heller 'settled on wall painting and moving image work'.[32] Douglas Gordon's wall drawing *Silence in the Museum* was acquired, for instance, under the Special Collection Scheme in 1995. Earlier in the year, CAS had given Southampton another of Gordon's works, a two-screen projection film titled *Hysterical*, which few other regional venues would have accepted at the time. Gordon went on to win the 1996 Turner Prize – the most high-profile award for artists working in Britain.

As artists experiment with new media, Southampton City Art Gallery has made sure to acquire certain prime examples. *Robots in Distress* (2017) is a digital piece that current curator Clare Mitchell acquired soon after it was made. Created by boredomresearch, a collaboration between British visual artists Vicky Isley and Paul Smith, the pair use technology to inspire animations as poetic expressions of scientific data or mathematical formulae. *Robots in Distress* focuses on an underwater fleet of robots created to monitor – and respond with synthetic emotions to – the heavily polluted environment of the Venetian lagoon.[33]

Southampton's collection now boasts works by numerous Turner Prize winners including Chris Ofili and Martin Creed, both of whom won this prestigious award largely as a result of exhibitions of their work at Southampton (both curated by Godfrey Worsdale, then Art Gallery Manager), in addition to other winners such as Jeremy Deller, Gilbert & George, Antony Gormley, Mark Wallinger and Rachel Whiteread, as well as of Turner Prize nominees such as Ian Hamilton Finlay, Lucian Freud and George Shaw. Shaw's *Scenes from the Passion: The Unicorn* (cat. 50), for instance, was purchased by Southampton in 2004, using the Smith Bequest Fund, with assistance from the NACF. Shaw was subsequently nominated for the Turner Prize in 2011 and in 2014 began his time as a National Gallery associate artist. The series of works he produced during the London residency became a touring exhibition, with Southampton as the final venue in 2016.

A number of contemporary female artists active in the UK are likewise represented in the collections of both Southampton and London. Maggi Hambling became the first postholder of the National Gallery's Artist in Residence Scheme (supported by the Arts Council), which enabled practising artists to interact both with the whole collection and with the public. During her residency of 1980–81, she painted a series of portraits of Archie MacDonald, one of the Gallery's warders. In the space of a year, Southampton and London had both acquired one of these likenesses (cats 52–53). A related scheme for associate artists began at the National Gallery in 1989. Paula Rego was the inaugural postholder, and George Shaw the last, in 2014–16.[34] During her association with the National Gallery, Rego created a mural inspired by the work of Carlo Crivelli (about 1430/5–about 1494) entitled *Crivelli's Garden* for the Sainsbury Wing's Dining Rooms, while a second reponse to paintings in the Gallery's collection was her etching influenced by Salvator Rosa's *Witches at their Incantations* (cats 55–56). In 1993, Southampton acquired (as a gift) another of Rego's etchings, her *Sing a Song of Sixpence II*, which formed part of the artist's *Nursery Rhyme* series (cat. 54).

One of Southampton City Art Gallery's most recent acquisitions is Rosalind Nashashibi's *South of France* (cat. 57). This work was presented in 2019 by CAS, at the very same time that the National Gallery announced that Nashashibi was to be its first artist in residence in a newly reinstated scheme – part of the Gallery's new Modern and Contemporary Programme. For the current exhibition, *South of France* has been paired with Nashashibi's *Rio* (cat. 58), the latter a work that Nashashibi created in 2020 as part of her London residency.

Important redisplays, loan exhibitions and touring exhibitions for Southampton

Much exciting work has been done from the mid-1980s to show the new modern and contemporary acquisitions alongside older works in the art gallery's refurbished Main Hall, to encourage fresh ways for visitors to engage with art. Gilbert & George's monumental picture, *Four Knights* (fig. 72), was displayed, for instance, within sight of Reynolds's *Cornet Nehemiah Winter* (fig. 54) to make visual links between two very different yet equally striking youthful male portraits. Arranging works of art in interesting juxtapositions against off-white interiors was, as Gill Hedley (the curator responsible for many of the pairings) has recalled, 'an unusual kind of hang at that time when the new fashion was for a revival of imitations of country house interiors for academy galleries, a style led by Timothy Clifford in Manchester. Southampton was a weird hybrid – not Victorian/Edwardian and not a white cube.'[35]

The inspiration to be drawn from such juxtapositions was underscored by Liz Goodall, who explained that 'in Southampton it is seen as an advantage to show contemporary art in the same building as a collection of earlier works.'[36] This statement came in the catalogue co-authored by Goodall, Luckett and Ronald Alley, Keeper of the Modern Collection, Tate Gallery, with catalogue notes by Hedley. It accompanied an important touring exhibition of 1985, *One City A Patron: British Art of the 20th Century from the Collections of Southampton Art Gallery*. Organised by the Scottish Arts Council, and curated by Goodall, 45 important works of art from Southampton's permanent collection were sent to venues in Scotland (Glasgow, Dundee, Perth, Ayr and Edinburgh). Among the exhibits were Allen Jones's *Pathway*, McKenna's *Fourment*, Ben Nicholson's *Two Forms*, Walter Sickert's *The Juvenile Lead* and Stanley Spencer's *Patricia Preece*. There was also Christopher

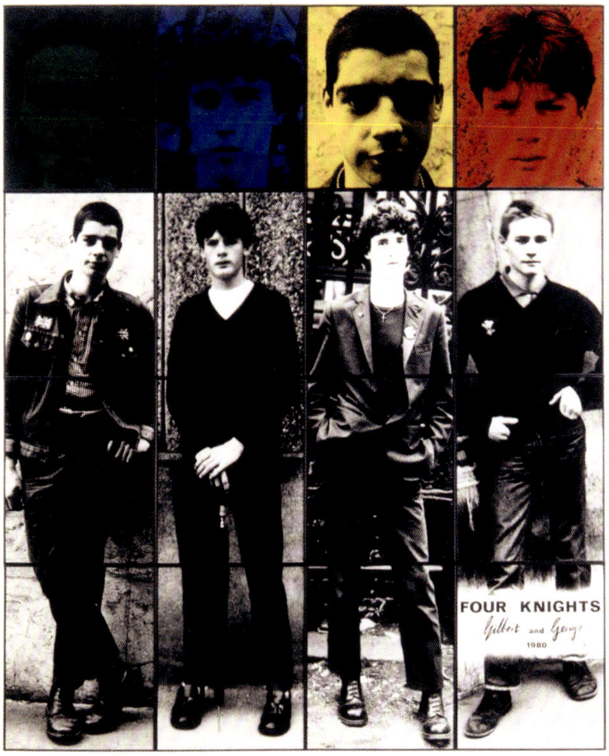

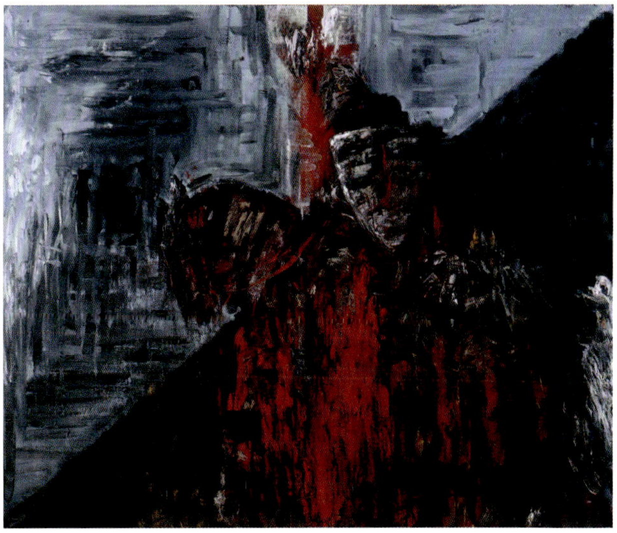

FIG. 72
Gilbert & George (b. 1943, b. 1942)
Four Knights, 1980
60.5 × 50.5 cm
Photograph
Southampton City Art Gallery, SOTAG 17/1981

FIG. 73
Christopher Le Brun (b. 1951)
Sir Tristram, 1984
Oil on canvas, 25.4 × 29.2 cm
Southampton City Art Gallery, SOTAG 10/1984

Le Brun's *Sir Tristram* (fig. 73), a work which resonates with the youthful male portraits by Gilbert & George discussed earlier, which were likewise included in the 1985 touring exhibition.

In the catalogue, Goodall took the chance to record the fact that despite some negative press coverage, Southampton's post-1975 purchasing policy had been generally well received. She noted that visitor levels had 'more than doubled since the early 1970's' and '[g]enerous gifts and loans towards the purchase of modern works of art [had] been received from private sources, as well as the donation of individual pieces.'[37] She also robustly defended the rationale behind Southampton's increasing emphasis on collecting contemporary art: 'Showing recent work and encouraging enquiry about it is one means of paving the way for the art of tomorrow, as well as providing future generations with a firmer basis for appreciating new artistic ideas.'[38]

Even with this focus on contemporary art, exhibitions of paintings of the past have not been overlooked. The most ambitious collaborative exhibition project in Southampton's history took place in 1997 when Stephen Snoddy, Southampton's then director, co-organised a two-way international exhibition exchange between Hampshire and Bizkaia (Vizcaya) in northern Spain. On this occasion, Southampton sent 61 historical British paintings to Bilbao for a show entitled *Modern British Painting from Reynolds to Nicholson* at the Museo de Bellas Artes de Bilbao (Museum of Fine Arts of Bilbao).[39]

Since the Millennium, one of the most ambitious exhibitions has been *Ancient Landscapes, Pastoral Visions: Samuel Palmer to the Ruralists*, organised in 2008, in association with the Arts Council, with other venues at Falmouth Art Gallery and Victoria Art Gallery, Bath. Beginning with etchings by Samuel Palmer, the show explored the development of landscape painting in the post-First World War era, when painters including the Nash brothers, John Piper and David Inshaw produced artistic responses to romanticised sites in the British countryside such as Stonehenge and the White Horse, Uffington.

An exciting recent development has been the increasing number of historical paintings loaned from Southampton's collection to regional, national and international venues. For instance, a local partnership has flourished in the last few years with the Russell-Cotes Art Gallery & Museum in nearby Bournemouth, which has resulted in two popular exhibitions. The most recent of these is *Beyond the Brotherhood: The Pre-Raphaelite Legacy* (2019–20), which traced the influence of Pre-Raphaelite art on later artistic movements including in contemporary art, book illustration and film. At the time of writing, Sofonisba Anguissola's *Portrait of the Artist's Sister in the Garb of a Nun* (cat. 13) has just returned from Madrid, where it was a prized loan in the Prado's exhibition, *A Tale of Two Women Painters: Sofonisba Anguissola and Lavinia Fontana* (22 October 2019–2 February 2020), which showcased the work of two of the greatest women painters of all time. It is arguably one of the most-travelled paintings in Southampton's permanent collection, having been lent to exhibitions at Cremona's Centro Centrale in 1994, and to Vienna's Kunsthalle and Washington's National Museum of Women in the Arts in 1995. The other painting that has recently been feted internationally is J.M.W. Turner's *Fishermen Upon a Lee-Shore in Squally Weather* (cat. 31), which went to Japan in 2018 as part of a three-leg touring exhibition of Turner's work.[40]

Thinking more specifically about loans from Southampton to the National Gallery since the Millennium, the most recent is Monet's *The Church at Vétheuil* (fig. 64, cat. 41), another star item from Southampton's permanent collection, which was shown at London's blockbuster exhibition, *Monet & Architecture* (Sainsbury Wing, April–July 2018; see Appendix). This was the latest of a handful of important individual loans to Trafalgar Square over the years, starting with van Everdingen's *Allegory of Winter* (cat. 15) lent to the National Gallery's 1976 exhibition, *Art in 17th Century Holland*. In reverse direction, the tradition of National Gallery loans and touring exhibitions to Southampton City Art Gallery has continued; for instance, Henri Rousseau's much-loved painting *Surprised!* went on tour to Southampton in 1993, with stops also at Leicester and Leeds.

Southampton and London collaboration: 1976 to the present

At the same time that the expert adviser role transferred to the Tate in 1976, the National Gallery was starting to work with many more regional galleries. Neil MacGregor, Levey's successor as director in London from 1987 (MacGregor served until 2002) has recalled that from the start of his directorship 'there were fewer close connections with specific institutions than there had been. ... In the 1990s, the focus was much more on relationships across the whole of the UK, as acquisitions became less important (funding effectively stopped for many municipal collections) and exhibitions and loans moved central stage.'[41] Seeing the need for more collaborative partnerships with mutual sharing of experiences and expertise, the National Gallery developed a 'National Programme' scheme, which complemented its increasing number of international collaborations, many of the latter necessitated by the trend for blockbuster exhibitions. Yet it is of crucial importance to note that the 'special relationship'[42] between Southampton Art Gallery and the National Gallery did not completely fade away. Since the mid-1970s, it has flourished, firstly in terms of public engagement, and more recently in terms of conservation and scientific analysis of works of art (see the two 'In Focus' sections at the end of the chapter). There have been several projects over the last 50 years that have generated particularly close and fruitful collaboration.

The first of these took place in February 1978. Howarth wrote to the National Gallery with a wish-list of long loans from the National Gallery that could bolster Southampton's permanent collection in certain areas. This followed a tradition of such activity between the institutions – and between the National Gallery and countless other regional galleries – but this episode was particularly carefully planned by Southampton and was of long duration. Of the initial list provided, Howarth explained that his 'overall preference' was for the '"Early Italian and Netherlandish" selection' because Southampton Art Gallery was 'a little weak on the 15th and 16th Centuries'.[43] In accompanying notes, well-argued reasons for individual loans were given; for example, *The Rest on the Flight into Egypt* by the workshop of Joachim Patinir (fig. 74) was requested from London to fill a gap next to Southampton's triptych by Goswijn van der Weyden (cat. 22), another 'Antwerp [painter]' and to 'complement it by showing further the Northern use of a landscape setting'. Similarly, Howarth made a case for juxtaposing Southampton's Sofonisba Anguissola (cat. 13) with London's *Portrait of a Lady* by a follower of Bronzino (fig. 75), given that the latter was 'a contemporary artist, and a contrasting one'. The outcome was that seven long term loans arrived at Southampton Art Gallery in September 1978, where they remained for about eight years, although the Patinir stayed even longer, returning to the National Gallery only in July 1992 (see Appendix).[44]

Two decades later, in 1999, Southampton City Art Gallery celebrated its 60th anniversary. The high point of a year of celebrations was a 'travelling companions display', *Great Dutch Paintings on Tour from the National Gallery*, which saw a consignment of 18 works go to Southampton from the National Gallery (16 April–13 June 1999).[45] Portraits, still lifes,

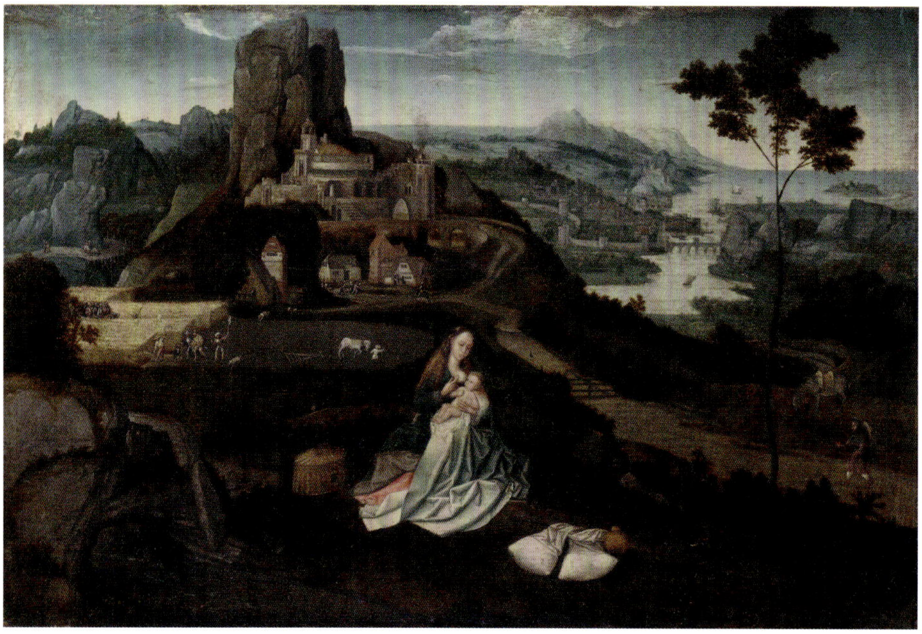

FIG. 74
Workshop of Joachim Patinir (active 1515; died not later than 1524)
Landscape with the Rest on the Flight into Egypt, about 1518–20
Oil on oak, 33 × 49.7 cm
The National Gallery, London, NG3115

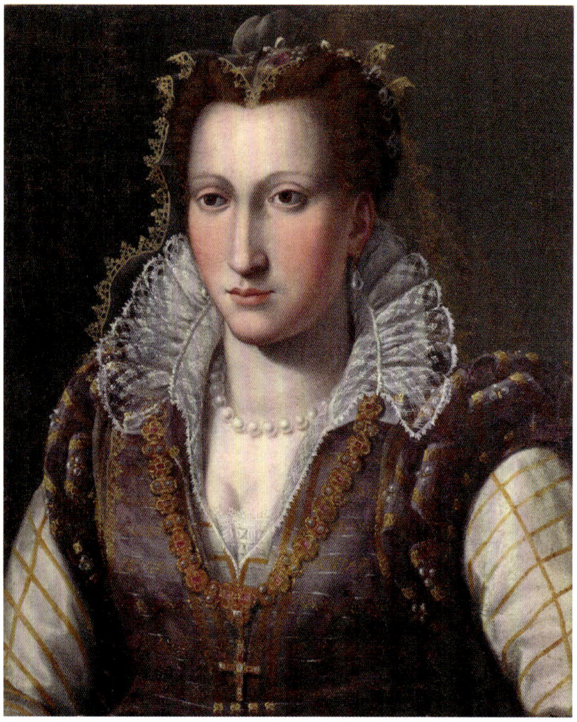

FIG. 75
Follower of Bronzino (1503–1572)
Portrait of a Lady, probably 1575–85
Oil on wood, 58.7 × 48.6 cm
The National Gallery, London, NG2085

landscapes, townscapes and marine paintings by Rembrandt, Vermeer, de Hooch, Hals, Ruisdael and Hobbema were loaned from London; remarkably, there were no repeats from an earlier, even larger exhibition, *The National Gallery Lends: Dutch Genre Painting* (17 June–23 July 1978) when 28 paintings had come to Southampton (see Appendix). Once again the loans from London were hung amongst representative paintings like the Koninck from Southampton's Dutch seventeenth-century collection.

Among the evening lectures and special events that accompanied the 1999 exhibition was a talk by Alexander Sturgis, the National Gallery's curator of the show, and another by David Bomford, by now a long-standing conservator at Trafalgar Square. The official report which Worsdale submitted to the Heritage Lottery Fund at the end of the project spoke warmly of Southampton's relationship with the National Gallery, noting that there were 'no problems or even gaps for improvement and collaborations at all levels were smooth running, effective and informative'. He concluded: 'The resounding message which this collaboration sends out is a great ratification of this new policy of access to collections. It seems clear that this success is one that we should all strive to build upon.'[46] His opinion was backed up by the attendance figures; it was reported that there had been 22,100 visitors – an increase of 44% on the previous year.[47] Rebecca Moisan, Southampton's conservator, who was responsible for condition checking the loans under Bomford's supervision, recalls: 'It was very well advertised. I remember seeing paintings of tulips sailing by on the sides of buses and feeling a great sense of pride. I think that it was one of the most significant exhibitions that Southampton has been involved in over the last 25 years.'[48]

In 2019 Southampton City Art Gallery turned 80. To mark this new milestone in its history, it organised an in-house exhibition, *From Generous Beginnings to Lasting Legacies*. Furthermore, it successfully applied to the National Gallery and Art Fund Curatorial Traineeship Programme assisted by the Vivmar Foundation. Aimed at nurturing the next generation of curators, these traineeships offer young museum professionals a 22-month training programme, with six months in London, before working on a specific curatorial project at a chosen regional museum partner, with continued mentoring from London. Southampton's project bid was to undertake sustained new research into its longstanding, unique and important, if under-studied, relationship with the National Gallery. The trainee selected for the project was Jemma Craig, an ideal appointment given her previous experience undertaking research and helping with exhibitions at Southampton City Art Gallery including *George Shaw: My Back to Nature* – an exhibition, as noted, which originated at the National Gallery.[49] Craig's working relationship with her National Gallery mentor, Susanna Avery-Quash, was described in the Art Fund's *Art Quarterly* magazine (Winter 2020) as a 'perfect partnership'.[50]

Their preliminary research findings were shared during a panel discussion at the London Art Fair in February 2020, an event which came about after Southampton had been chosen as museum partner for the Art Fair. This prestigious partnership also provided the City Art Gallery with an opportunity to showcase the collection's remarkable history and some of its riches through a display at the fair. A powerful selection of modern and contemporary British paintings and sculpture – including works by Sickert, Lowry, Spencer, Nicholson, Ayrton, Hambling and Le Brun – made clear to contemporary, international audiences why Southampton City Art Gallery's art collection is regarded as one of the finest in the UK. Research into the historic relationship between Southampton and London generated by the curatorial traineeship has continued throughout 2020 and into 2021. Its culmination is the current publication and the exhibition it accompanies, *Creating a National Collection: The Partnership between Southampton City Art Gallery and the National Gallery*.

Chipperfield's 'fervent desire' to 'substantially benefit the town of [his] adoption' by providing for the visual arts has been met, and his foresight that the best means of making his vision a reality was through a partnership between Southampton and the National Gallery has proven correct. One commentator has praised the collection as 'representing in microcosm the breadth and depth of Western European painting'.[51] This exhibition and publication have demonstrated just how much Southampton City Art Gallery has benefited from the determination and ambitious vision of a handful of dedicated and capable people involved with its management and development over the years, including colleagues from two of London's national galleries. Even if at the beginning, its relationship with the National Gallery was necessarily one-sided, it is clear how it evolved into a partnership between equals, thereby providing a model for collaboration that continues to be valid. If its past is anything to go by, we should be confident that Southampton's historic partnership with London will continue to evolve in distinctive and beneficial ways.

41 (LEFT)

Claude Monet (1840–1926)

The Church at Vétheuil, 1880

Oil on canvas, 50.5 × 61 cm
Purchased with the assistance of the Victoria and Albert Museum/MGC Purchase Grant Fund, 1975
Southampton City Art Gallery, SOTAG 183/1975

42 (RIGHT)

Claude Monet (1840–1926)

The Petit Bras of the Seine at Argenteuil, 1872

Oil on canvas, 52.6 × 71.8 cm
Bequeathed by Sir Robert Hart Bt, 1971
The National Gallery, London, NG6395

Claude Monet was a central figure in the French Impressionist movement, adhering to its principles throughout his life. From the 1860s, Monet and other Paris-based artists began exploring a shared interest in open-air painting and subjects drawn from contemporary life. It would be after their first exhibition in Paris in 1874 that they became known as the Impressionists. Their pioneering paintings had been facilitated particularly by the developments of the collapsible metal paint tube, which allowed paint to be stored ready for use outside as well as in the studio.

In 1871, after a year spent in England and Holland during the Franco-Prussian War and the Paris Commune, Monet returned to France and until 1878 settled in Argenteuil, a Parisian suburb on the River Seine. Already partially industrialised, Argenteuil was also a centre for pleasure boating, an activity Monet much enjoyed. The National Gallery's picture, however, does not focus on modern life but rather on the timeless tranquillity of nature. It depicts the Petit Bras, a small tributary of the river with its island that had been a retreat for Parisians since the eighteenth century. The diagonal of the poplar trees on the riverbank leads the eye back into the distance, while the empty foreground and sense of light and air contribute to the overall effect of peace. The muted tones of grey and mauve evoke an overcast sky, which, together with the

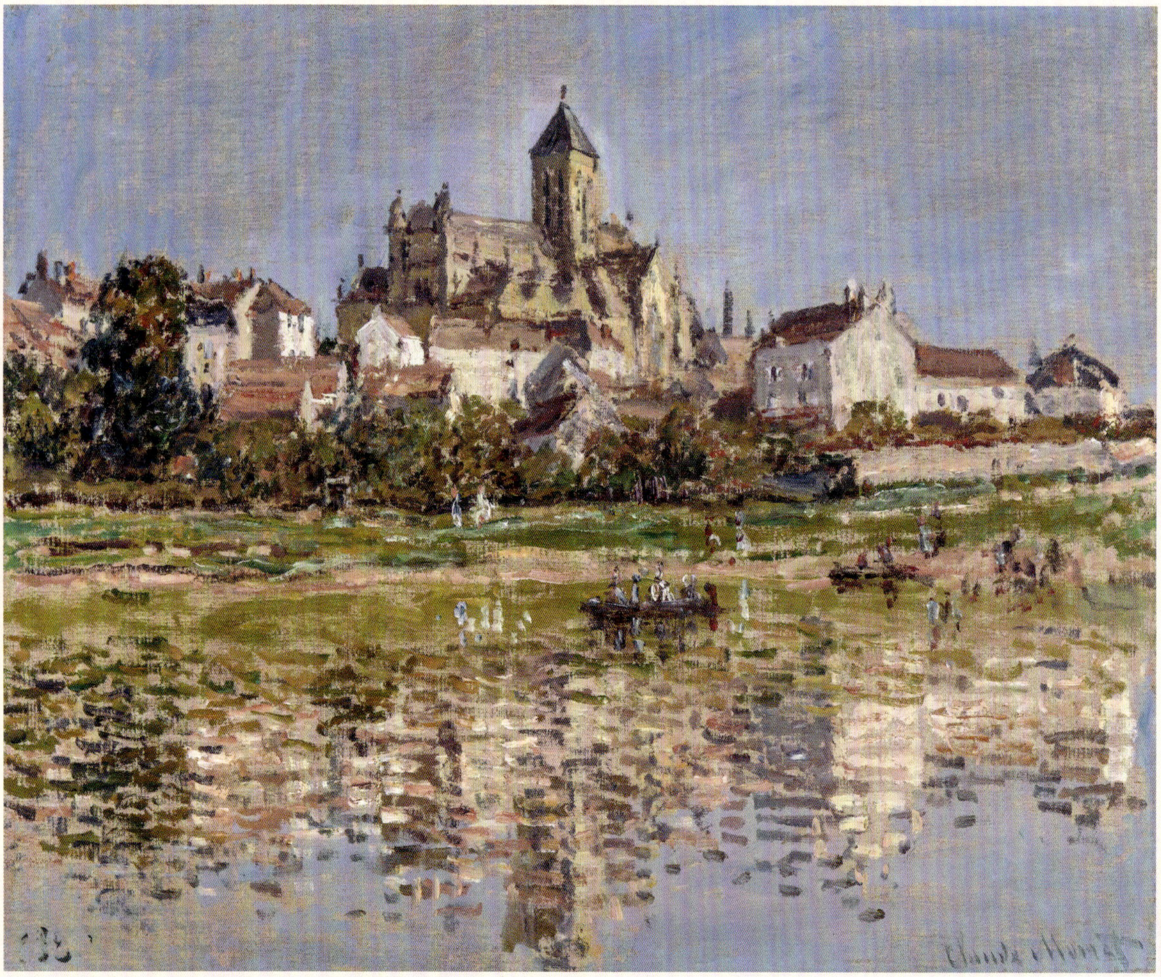

misty atmosphere, suggest a winter's day. Monet used a variety of brushstrokes, ranging from light feathery touches for the trees to bold horizontal strokes in the foreground and water. His fascination with the reflective qualities of water was a constant theme in his art.

The water's effects are likewise captured in the Southampton picture. Monet moved with his family to Vétheuil in 1878. Despite his wife's death the following year, and the break-up of the Impressionist group in the 1880s, this proved to be an important period of artistic development. He started to paint series of different subjects under changing light and atmospheric conditions. While some were natural subjects like poplar trees and waterlilies, others depicted architecture, such as Rouen Cathedral. The church at Vétheuil also became the subject of a series, this version painted in summer from a boat on the Seine. To capture constantly changing effects of light and colour, Monet had to work quickly using rapid dabs of the brush, a technique which is particularly noticeable in the shimmering reflections on the water.

Whereas the National Gallery Monet was bequeathed by Sir Robert Hart in 1971, Southampton had to pay £56,284 for theirs just four years later. This was the most significant sum it had ever paid for any work of art, and it depleted the Chipperfield Bequest Fund, but all the parties concerned were thrilled that such an important painting had been secured by this ambitious regional gallery. However, as a result of the acquisition, Southampton decided to concentrate on purchasing modern British and contemporary art that was comparatively more affordable than works by historical European painters, especially those as popular as the French Impressionists. This decision meant that *The Church at Vétheuil* was the last pre-1900 painting that Southampton City Art Gallery ever purchased.

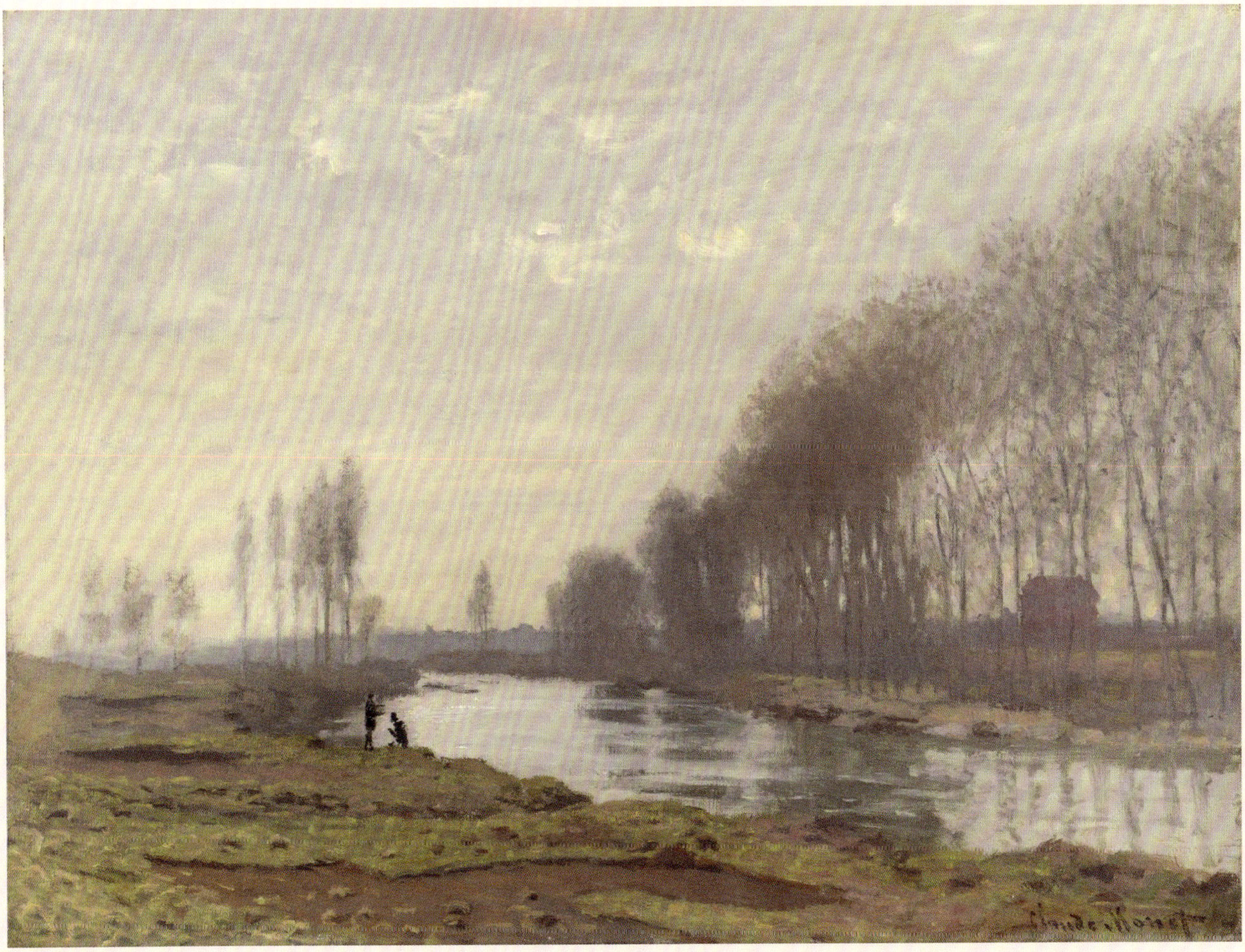

43

Stephen McKenna (1939–2017)

Fourment, 1977

Oil on canvas, 12.2 × 8 cm
Purchased with the assistance of the Victoria and Albert Museum/ MGC Purchase Grant Fund, 1978
Southampton City Art Gallery, SOTAG 24/1978

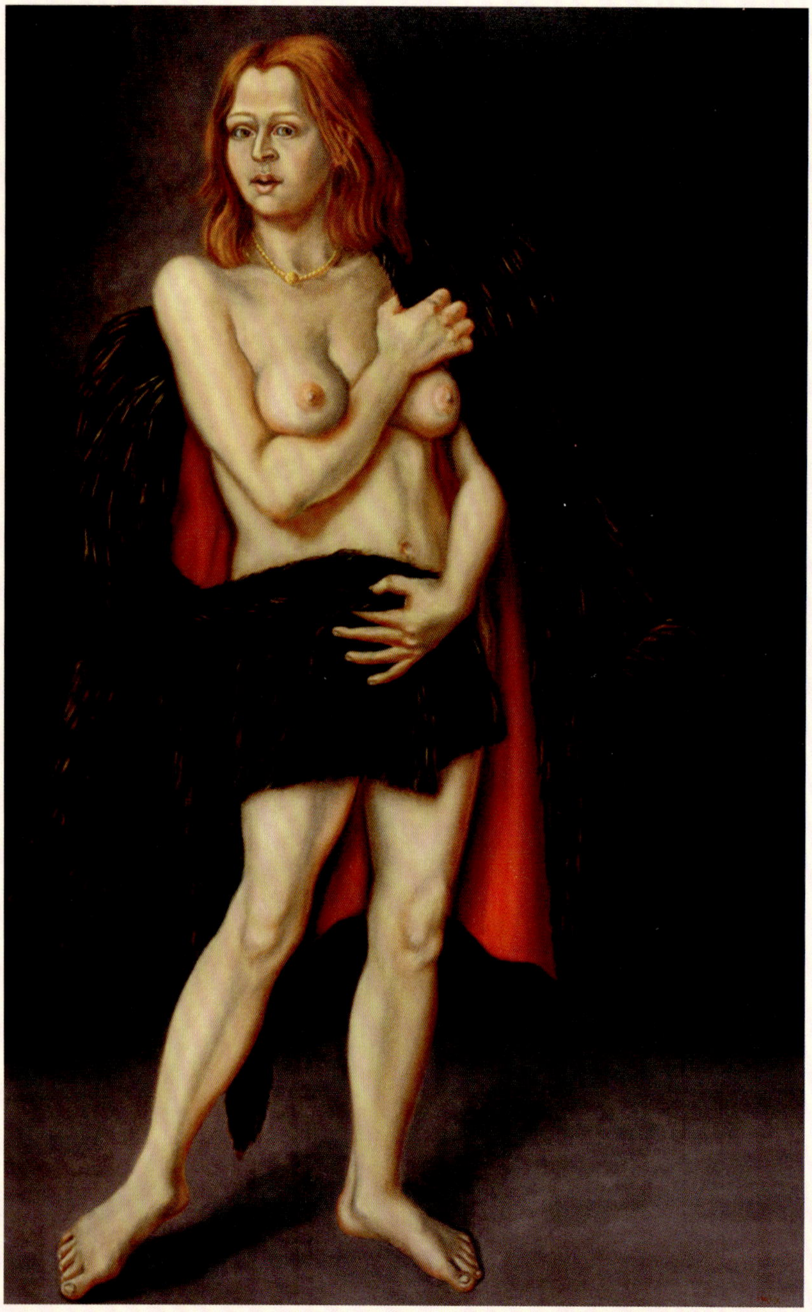

Stephen McKenna was a British artist known for his postmodern figurative painting; examples of his work can be found in the collections of Tate, the British Council and the Imperial War Museum, London, as well as in Southampton. McKenna studied at London's Slade School of Fine Art between 1959 and 1964 under Harold Cohen, developing a type of figurative painting which critiqued the tradition exemplified by the teaching of two earlier influential Slade professors, Henry Tonks (cat. 9) and William Coldstream.

Fourment caused a moment of crisis between curators in Southampton and the National Gallery's director at the time, Michael Levey. In July 1978, Levey recorded his 'considerable hesitation' over *Fourment*, noting it seemed 'quite expensive', and wondering what it would bring to the collection in terms of aesthetic value.[1] Not long after, he wrote back to say he had been in touch with Dr David Brown of the Tate Gallery. Brown had supplied 'most useful information about McKenna' which had helpfully contextualised McKenna's work within 'the continuing tradition of painting from the 16th and 17th centuries'.[2] Indeed, the work is a direct response to Rubens's celebrated portrait of his second wife, Helen Fourment, in the Kunsthistorisches Museum, Vienna (fig. 67). However, the English twentieth-century painter brings the subject up to date and transforms it into a more provocative image verging on soft porn. After corresponding with Brown, Hendy expressed his warm support for the purchase and praised Southampton Art Gallery's enlightened policy of buying modern work, which its staff were then just starting to pursue in earnest.

44

David Redfern (b. 1947)

Work, 1977

Oil on canvas, 87.2 × 121.8 cm
Purchased with the assistance of the Victoria and Albert Museum/MGC Purchase Grant Fund, 1979
Southampton City Art Gallery, SOTAG 16/1979

David Redfern has had a diverse artistic career. Having enrolled at London's Slade School of Fine Art in 1969, he worked as a gallery assistant at the newly opened Serpentine Gallery between 1971 and 1984, after which he taught art and design at Croydon College until 2011. In 2000, he was elected to the London Group – an artist-run group established to foster talent outside the Royal Academy – and later became its archivist, publishing *The London Group: A History, 1913–2013* in 2013, the group's centennial year. Southampton City Art Gallery has built up the largest collection of works by the London Group in the UK, and in 2014 Redfern and fellow member Victoria Rance curated *From David Bomberg to Paula Rego: The London Group in Southampton*, an exhibition which included numerous examples of the group's work alongside other contemporary art from Southampton's collection.

Redfern is best known for creating sculptural 'assemblages' and 'constructions', but in the 1970s and 80s painting was his preferred medium. This picture evokes an iconic nineteenth-century painting of the same title by Ford Madox Brown (1865), which depicted people going about their daily business on a street in Hampstead, London. A century later, Redfern's *Work* was painted in almost the same spot. The earlier image's influence is clear, in the arched-top structure, and its overall composition and subject matter, which attempts to portray all kinds of people including labourers in the centre, passers-by to the left, and the intellectual to the right. However, Redfern has deliberately updated the image by including contemporary cultural references such as the Labour Party poster, the 'People at Work' sign and cars.

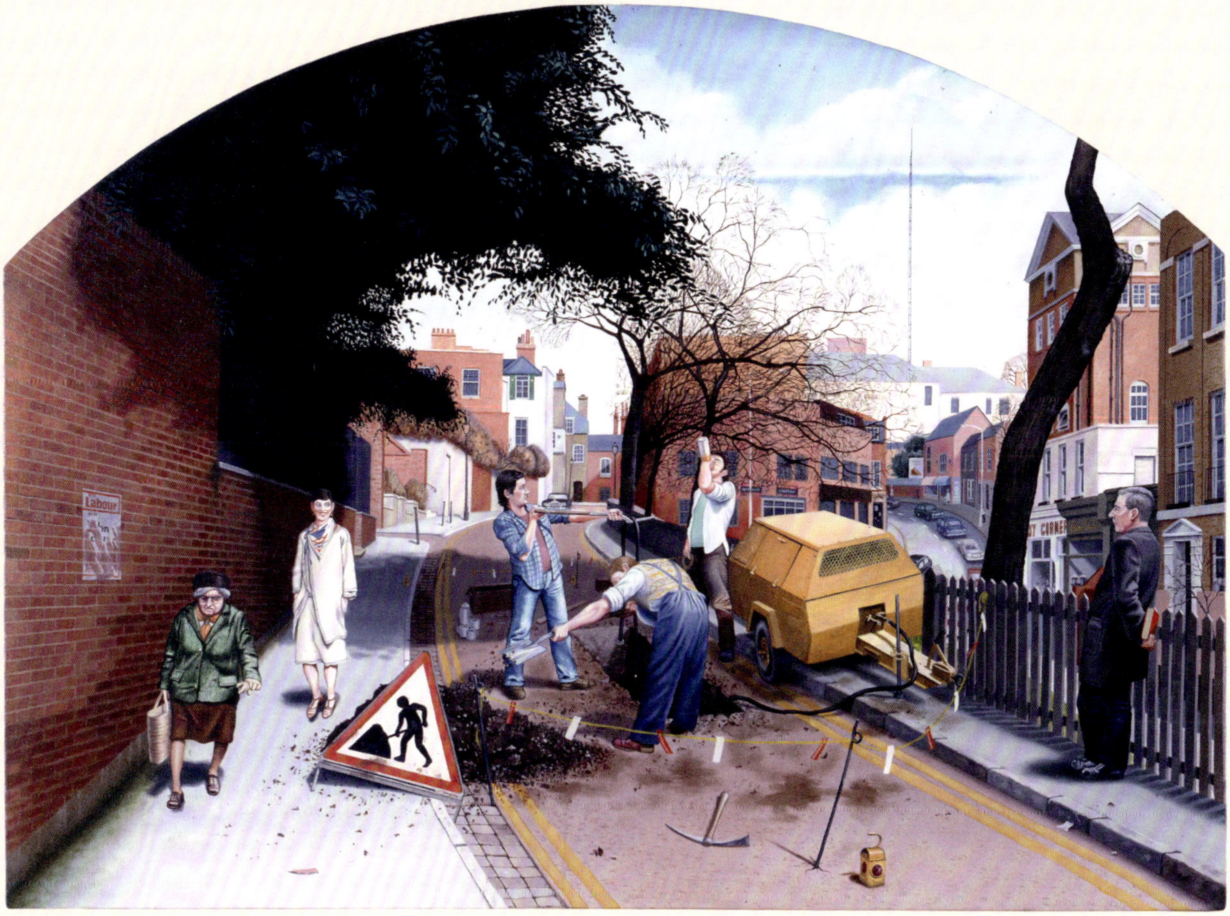

45

Maxwell Armfield (1881–1972)
Central Park, New York, 1916

Tempera on canvas, 64.2 × 39 cm
Purchased with the assistance of the Victoria and Albert Museum Purchase Grant Fund, 1976
Southampton City Art Gallery, SOTAG 42/1976

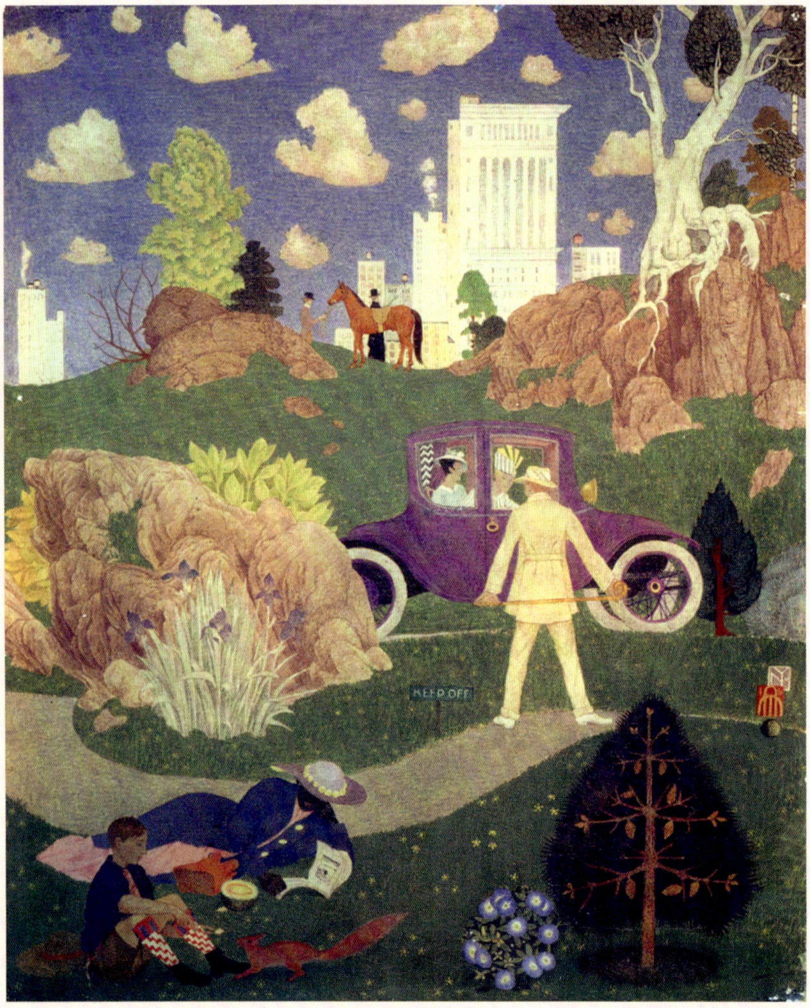

After Southampton Art Gallery started to focus on acquiring modern art, it relied on advice from the Tate Gallery rather than the National Gallery. David Brown was instrumental in building up Southampton's collection of twentieth-century British works, his first purchase being this painting, although contemporary art increasingly became his focus.

In 1908, *The Times* hailed Armfield in his first significant solo exhibition at the Carfax Gallery, London as 'a man of originality and promise ... his gifts are undoubted.'[3] His work spanned book illustration, poetry, music, and theatre. He taught across America with his wife, playwright Constance Smedley, and painted this abstracted landscape during their seven-year stay in New York (1915–1922). The painting's modern treatment flattens the pictorial space and its employment of vibrant colours evokes the 'ubiquitous and unexpected' colours of Central Park that thrilled the artist.[4]

Overlooked after the Second World War, Armfield saw a revival of interest in his work, culminating in an exhibition *Homage to Maxwell Armfield* at London's Fine Art Society in 1970. *Central Park, New York* was acquired six years later, and three more Armfields reached Southampton through Brown's bequest of 2002: *The Tower* (*Trees, Lucca*), *Bunch of White* and *'Pacific Patterns', the Artist's House at Berkeley, California*.

Three of the four, including this one, are tempera paintings, a technique about which Armfield wrote two important books – *A Manual of Tempera Painting* (1930) and *Tempera Painting Today* (1946) – as part of the early twentieth-century revival of interest in this medium. Armfield was a local painter, having been born in Ringwood, Hampshire.

46

Michael Ayrton (1921–1975)
Reflective Heads II, 1971–73

Bronze, 40 × 26 × 18 cm
Purchased through the Chipperfield Bequest Fund, 1973
Southampton City Art Gallery, SOTAG 10/1973

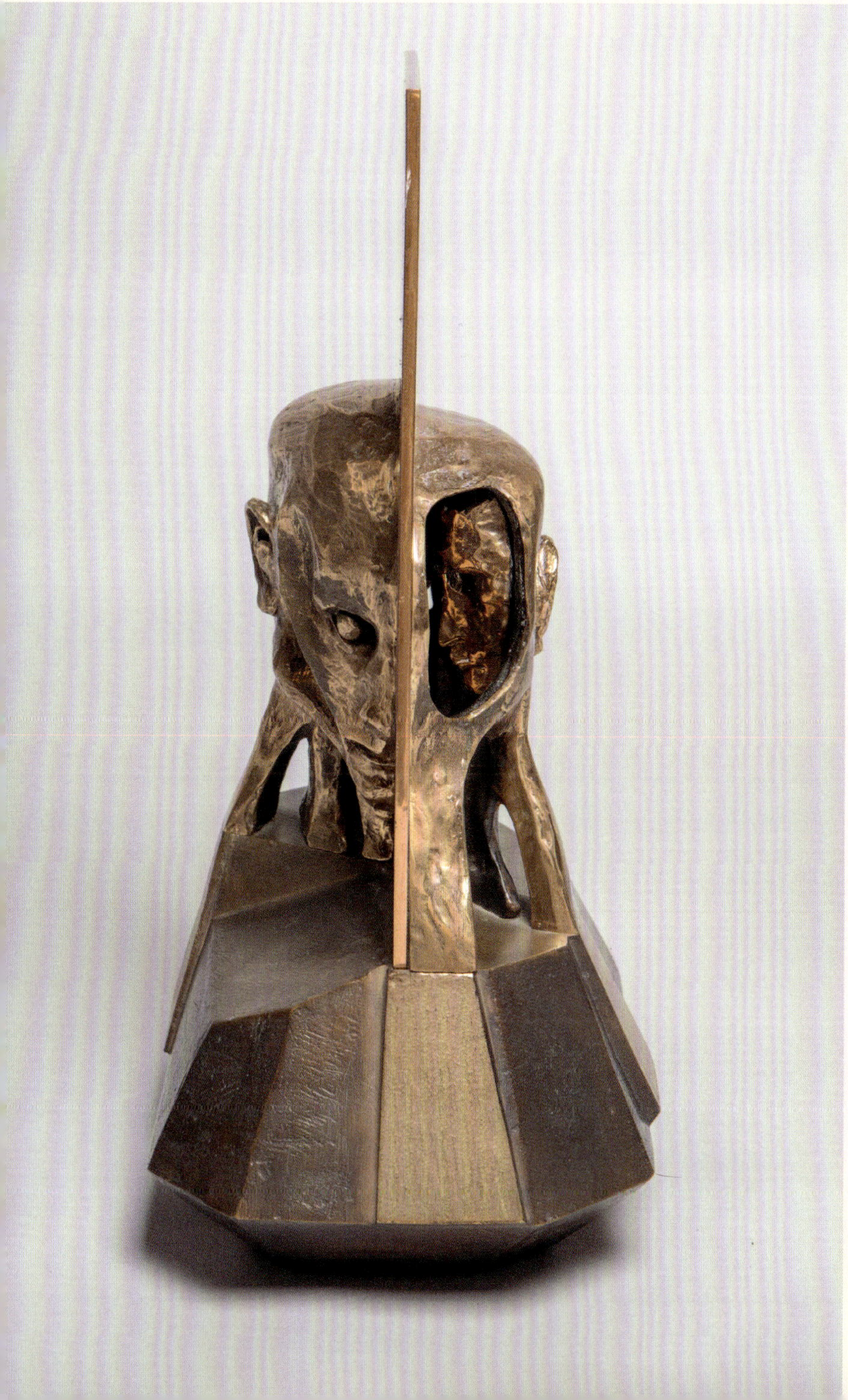

Michael Ayrton was a British artist who began as a Neo-Romantic painter alongside Graham Sutherland, John Piper and Keith Vaughan. In the late 1940s, encouraged by the internationally famous sculptors Alberto Giacometti and Henry Moore, Ayrton turned to sculpture. A versatile artist, he also produced designs for theatre sets and costumes and practised as a book illustrator, filmmaker, broadcaster and writer.

Much of Ayrton's distinctive work is associated with flight, mirrors and mazes, including his novel *The Maze Maker* (1967), which won the Heinemann Award for Literature. Whatever medium he used to express himself, Ayrton was also constantly drawn to themes from classical mythology. Subjects that proved particularly inspirational were the tale of Daedalus and Icarus, and the figure of the Minotaur. Southampton acquired his bronze *Minotaur Waking* in 1973.

Reflective Heads II is a second piece by Ayrton purchased by Southampton City Art Gallery. It is the later and smaller of two preliminary models for a huge 6.7-metre sculpture now in Troy, Michigan, USA. It deals with the idea of identity: on each side of the polished bronze screen, there is a head facing in opposite directions while a smaller face is found nestled inside each one.

Since 2013–14, as part of its 'Art on Wheels' outreach scheme, Southampton City Art Gallery began to visit schools. In addition to taking prints and paintings from its permanent collection into classrooms to engage schoolchildren with real works of art, it now also brings along a few sculptures, including *Reflective Heads II*.

47

Barry Flanagan (1941–2009)
Boxing Hare on Anvil, 1984

Bronze, 103 × 58 × 22.5 cm
Bequeathed by Dr David and Liza Brown, 2002
Southampton City Art Gallery, SOTAG 207/2002
Bridgeman Images

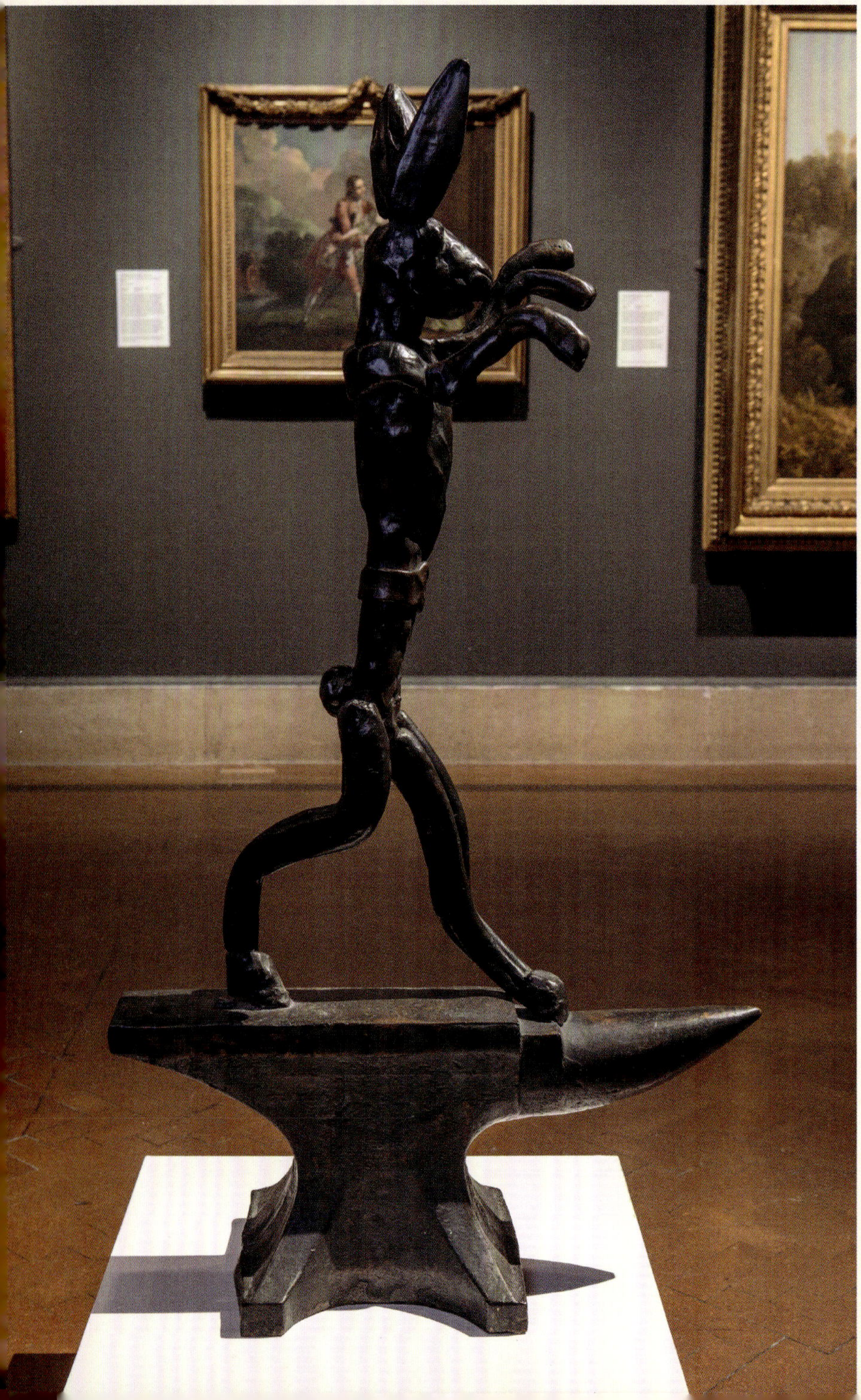

Flanagan was a daring conceptual artist as revealed in Tate's retrospective of his early works (1965–1982) in 2011. Although he made prints and drawings, and produced *A Hole in the Sea*, a film for a Land Art TV exhibition in 1969, Flanagan is best known for his bronze statues made in the 1980s of hares and other animals perched or leaping in motion, of which there are two examples in Southampton's collection.

Inspired by George Ewart Evans's *The Leaping Hare* (1976), a literary exploration of the life and legend of the hare, as well as memories of hares bounding through the British countryside, Flanagan began depicting hares in the late 1970s. The athletic animal quickly became a defining feature of his oeuvre. The dynamic image of hares was, for the artist, a way of speaking about human existence and of humankind's relationship to the animal world in particular. For the ancient Egyptians, hares represented life and were worshipped for their swiftness and energy; in Chinese mythology, the hare is a symbol of immortality and is the sole inhabitant of the moon. In Southampton's *Boxing Hare on Anvil*, the hare stands in profile (reminiscent of ancient Egyptian art) on an anvil – another well-known motif of Flanagan's. The artist used it from the early 1980s until his death in 2009 as an alternative symbol of strength and bravery.

Maggi Hambling OBE, CBE (b. 1945)
First Dragon, 1992

Ceramic, paint and Perspex,
23.5 × 44.5 × 33 cm
Donated by the Contemporary Art Society, 1996
Southampton City Art Gallery, SOTAG 6/1996

Maggi Hambling has established her reputation as one of Britain's foremost painters and sculptors over the last four decades; she was awarded an OBE for her services to painting in 1995, followed by a CBE in 2010. She trained at Camberwell School of Art and the Slade in the 1960s. Although principally a painter, Hambling is also known for her work as a sculptor.

Some of her outdoor sculpture in London has attracted controversy, including *A Conversation with Oscar Wilde* and her recent *Sculpture for Mary Wollstonecraft*. Her steel *Scallop* on Aldeburgh beach in Suffolk, which sits at four metres high, is another public memorial, in this instance to the celebrated English composer, conductor and pianist Benjamin Britten.

Maggi Hambling's *First Dragon* forms part of a small but significant collection of contemporary sculptures which Southampton City Art Gallery has built up from the 1970s onwards. It was acquired in 1996, the same year that saw Hambling's exhibition, *Sculptures in Bronze 1993–95*, at Marlborough Fine Art, London. Hambling had only started using bronze in 1993, hand-modelling sculptures in wax which were then converted into durable bronze using traditional techniques, such as sand-casting. Tate owns one bronze from Hambling's early series: *War Coffin*, a small, rough sand-cast piece intended to be shown on a plinth with suspended objects that chime when in motion.

In contrast, Southampton's *First Dragon* is made from fired clay and Perspex, an unusual combination of a traditional and an innovative sculptural material. Created in 1992, this striking, abstracted representation of a dragon is as freely modelled as it is painted, the dynamic qualities of its pose – raised back leg, arched back, twisted head – emphasised by the rapidly applied paint.

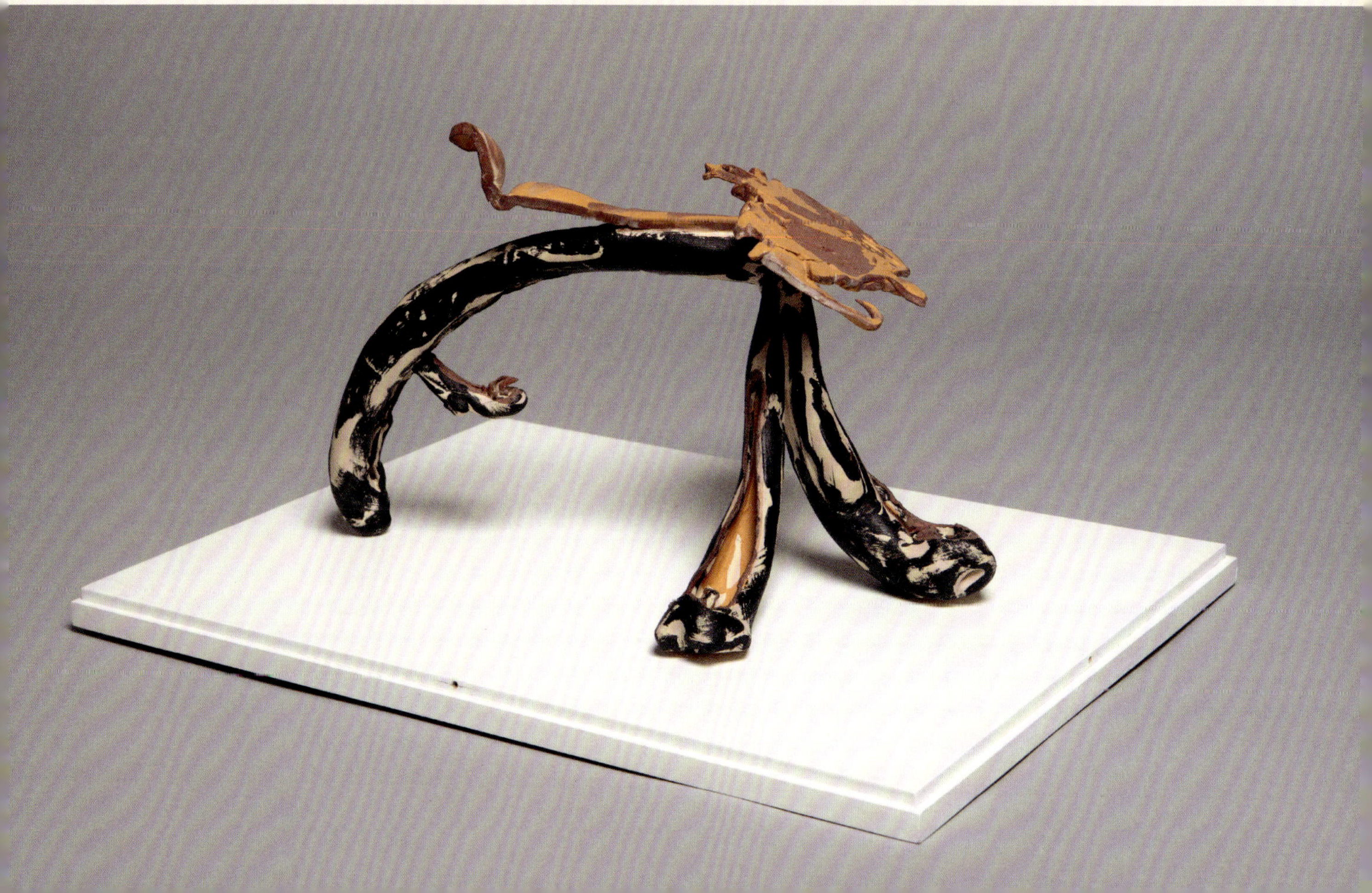

49

Wilhelmina Barns-Graham (1912–2004)
Glacier Vortex, 1951

Oil on canvas, 60 × 71.5 cm
Bequeathed by Dr David and Liza Brown, 2002
Southampton City Art Gallery, SOTAG 208/2002

Glacier Vortex is one of 220 works of modern British art given to Southampton City Art Gallery in 2002 through the Dr David and Liza Brown Bequest. After the purchase of Monet's *The Church at Vétheuil* in 1975 (cat. 41) had depleted the Chipperfield Bequest Fund, curators decided to shift their acquisition policy towards collecting primarily modern British art. Specialist advice was sought from Brown, who helped secure many important works, and further augmented the collection through his generous bequest. One of his great loves was the St Ives School, which explains why his collection contained numerous examples by significant artists in the group, including 15 paintings by his great friend Roger Hilton.

Having studied in Edinburgh, Barns-Graham moved to St Ives in 1940, where she met and set up a studio next to Ben Nicholson's, and also worked alongside sculptors Naum Gabo and Barbara Hepworth. She became a leading member of the St Ives School with a focus on abstraction (a direction fostered by international trends) and the Penwith Society, a local group which in 1949 broke away from the more conservative St Ives artists. Barns-Graham first exhibited in London in a group exhibition of six artists at the Redfern Gallery in 1948, going on to have her first London solo show – *Recent Paintings and Glacier Constructions* – there too, in 1952.

A sculptural quality emanates from *Glacier Vortex*, a work Barns-Graham produced after visiting Switzerland's Grindelwald Glacier in 1949. The subject fascinated the artist, and united her interest in form, light and space. She explained: 'This likeness to glass and transparency, combined with solid rough ridges made me wish to combine in a work all angles at once, from above, through, and all round, as a bird flies, a total experience.'[5]

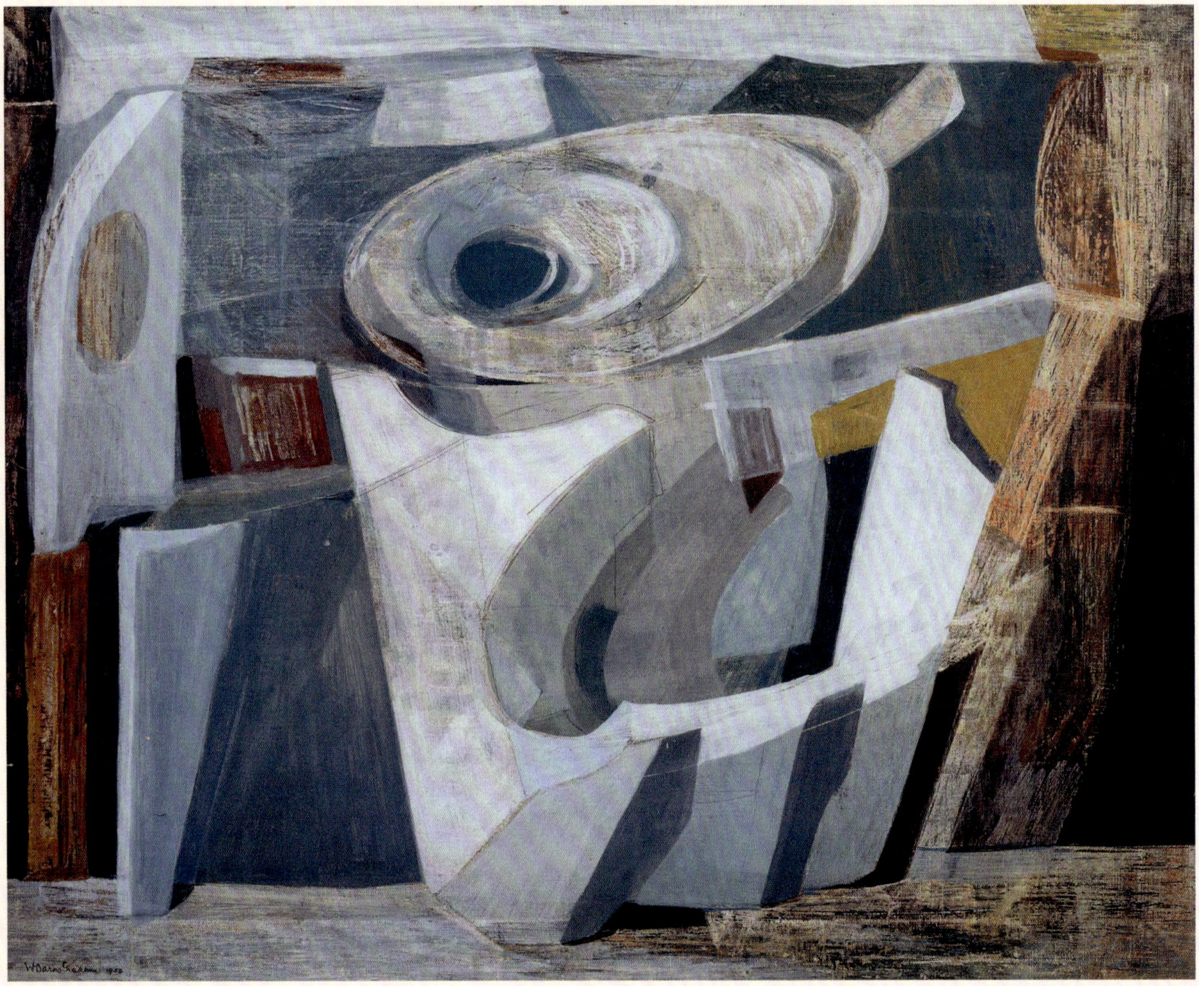

50

George Shaw (b. 1966)

Scenes from the Passion: The Unicorn, 2003

Humbrol enamel on board,
91.6 × 121.2 × 5.2 cm
Purchased through the Smith Bequest Fund with assistance from the National Art Collections Fund, 2004
Southampton City Art Gallery,
SOTAG 5/2004

George Shaw is an English artist noted for his depictions of suburban subject matter and contemporary urban life. This work is a figurative painting of a deserted pub and is from a series inspired by the Tile Hill housing estate on the outskirts of Coventry, where the artist grew up. Shaw photographed the area and began working on the series, after completing a master's degree at London's Royal College of Art.

A distinctive element of Shaw's work is his use of Humbrol enamel paint, traditionally associated with generations of children painting Airfix models. He uses restrained colours subtly to convey light and shadow, which he painstakingly builds up, layer upon layer, to produce paintings of photographic quality.

In 2014, Shaw began a two-year position as associate artist at the National Gallery. During his association, Shaw produced a series of more than fifty paintings and drawings, including woodland landscapes, which were responses to depictions of different scenes found in the National Gallery's pre-1900 collection. When the touring show *George Shaw: My Back to Nature* was subsequently organised in 2016, Southampton City Art Gallery was chosen as the final venue.

Scenes from the Passion is a modern interpretation of the mythological woodlands found in historical paintings and the natural world. The complete absence of people evokes an eerie intensity and sense of desolation. This is a characteristic element of much of Shaw's work and is also present in his sketch of a tangled wood at the edge of suburban Coventry, *Almost Lost (I)*, which was acquired for Southampton City Art Gallery's collection in 2008.

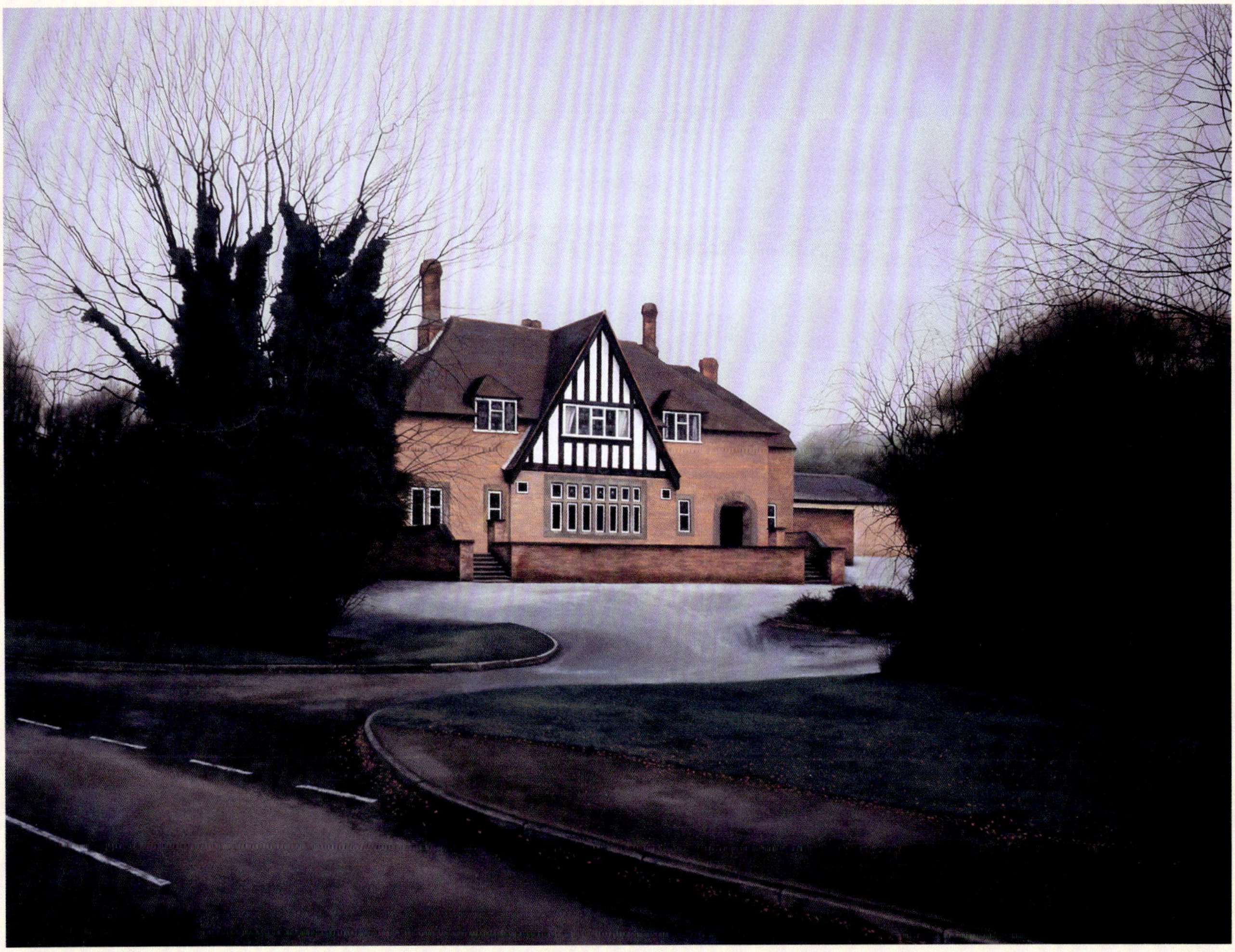

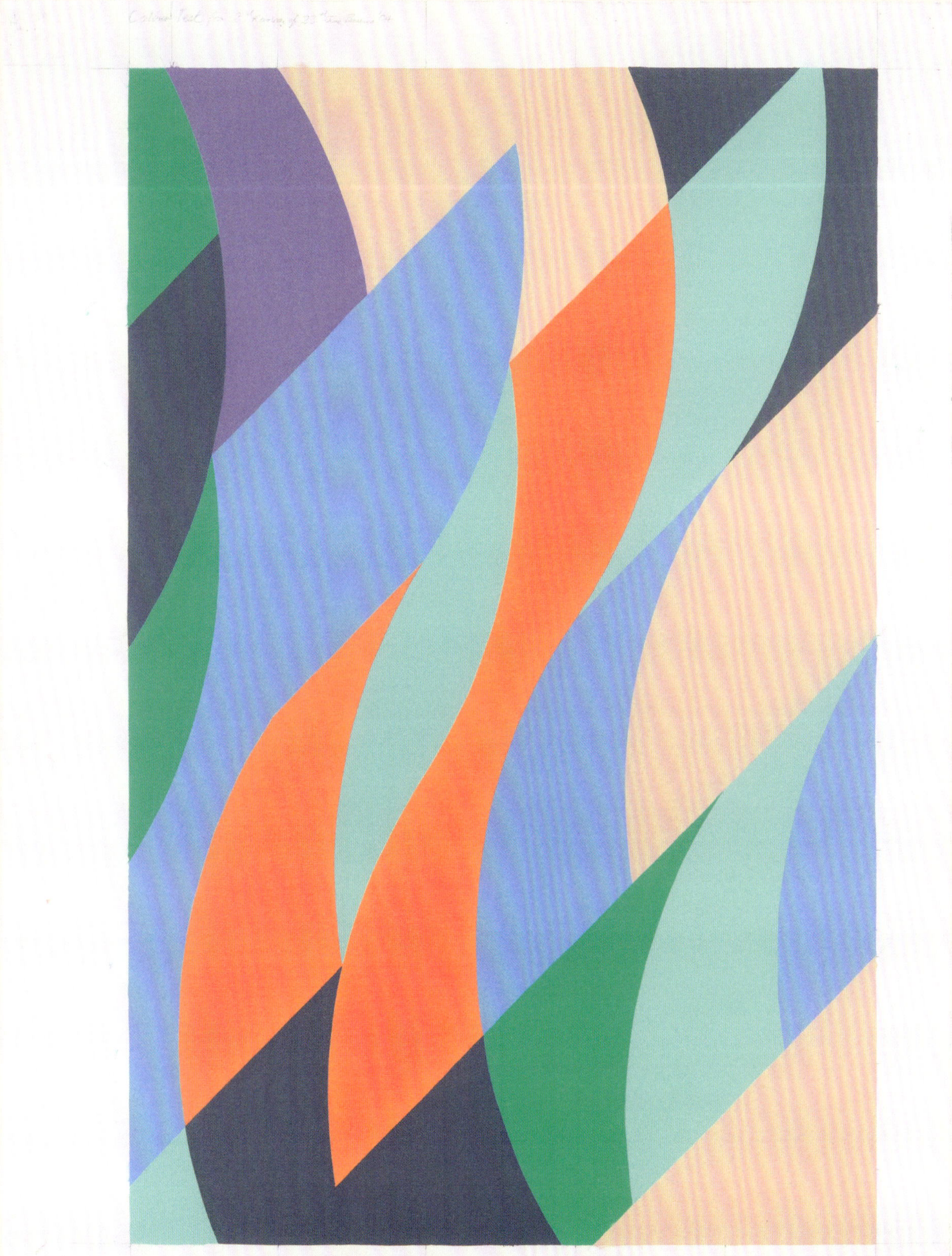

51

Bridget Riley (b. 1931)

Oil Test for Red Movement, 2004

Oil on acrylic undercoat on linen, 152 × 113.5 cm
Acquired with *Red Movement* (2005) through the Dr David and Liza Brown Bequest Fund, with the assistance of the Victoria and Albert Museum Purchase Grant Fund, the Museums, Libraries and Archives Council and the National Art Collections Fund, 2006
Southampton City Art Gallery, SOTAG 12/2007b

In 1992, Southampton received from David Brown, its former contemporary art adviser, a generous bequest of 220 modern British paintings and money to purchase further works. Current staff and the then external adviser, Sean Rainbird, were keen to use the windfall to purchase one truly significant piece. Rainbird proposed a discussion with Bridget Riley, given that by then she was one of the UK's most distinguished painters and he felt her work could 'contextualise and underpin the Gallery's post-1976 abstract painting collection'.[6] As a result, Riley was commissioned to paint *Red Movement* (fig. 76). Its acquisition was heralded as a milestone in the gallery's collecting history, described in a funding application as an acquisition of comparable importance to Monet's *The Church at Vétheuil* (cat. 41).

Oil Test for Red Movement, 2004 is a preparatory study for *Red Movement*, and like the final work, includes a sequence of curving elements set within diagonal parallel boundaries to create a wave-like abstraction. Riley's use of pattern and colour on an epic scale celebrates and challenges our perception as the viewer.

Riley sold the work to Southampton with a large discount and also donated supporting sketches and preparatory works, including this one, in 2007. Southampton City Art Gallery was the first regional collection to acquire a work by Riley in a couple of decades, and her monumental painting proved a valuable addition to the collection. Fittingly, in 2009–10, Southampton City Art Gallery was chosen as a venue for the Arts Council's retrospective exhibition, *Bridget Riley: Flashback*. Riley was delighted to learn of this decision.

FIG. 76
Bridget Riley (b. 1931)
Red Movement, 2005
Oil on linen, 135.3 × 322.3 cm
Southampton City Art Gallery, SOTAG 12/2007

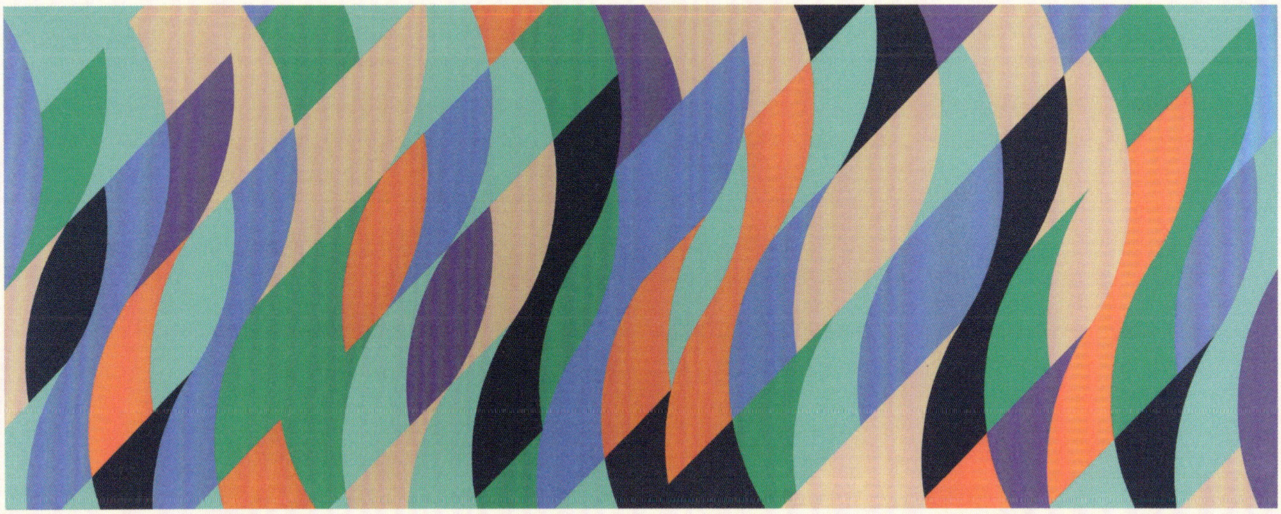

52 (LEFT)

Maggi Hambling, OBE, CBE (b. 1945)

Mac with Shadows, 1981

Oil on canvas, 66.9 × 66.5 cm
Purchased from Maggi Hambling, 1982
Southampton City Art Gallery, SOTAG 13/1982

53 (RIGHT)

Maggi Hambling, OBE, CBE (b. 1945)

Portrait of Archie MacDonald, 1980–81

Oil on canvas, 105 × 100 × 3.5 cm (framed)
Presented by Maggi Hambling, 1981
The National Gallery, London, H11

Maggi Hambling was appointed as the National Gallery's first artist in residence in 1980–81. At the end of her residency, she presented her *Portrait of Archie MacDonald* to the Gallery. The sitter was a Canadian who came over to England during the Second World War and stayed. Hambling met him during her residency because he was employed at the time as a gallery attendant, as the stitching on his pocket spelling out 'Security' makes clear. Hambling produced other paintings of the same sitter, including

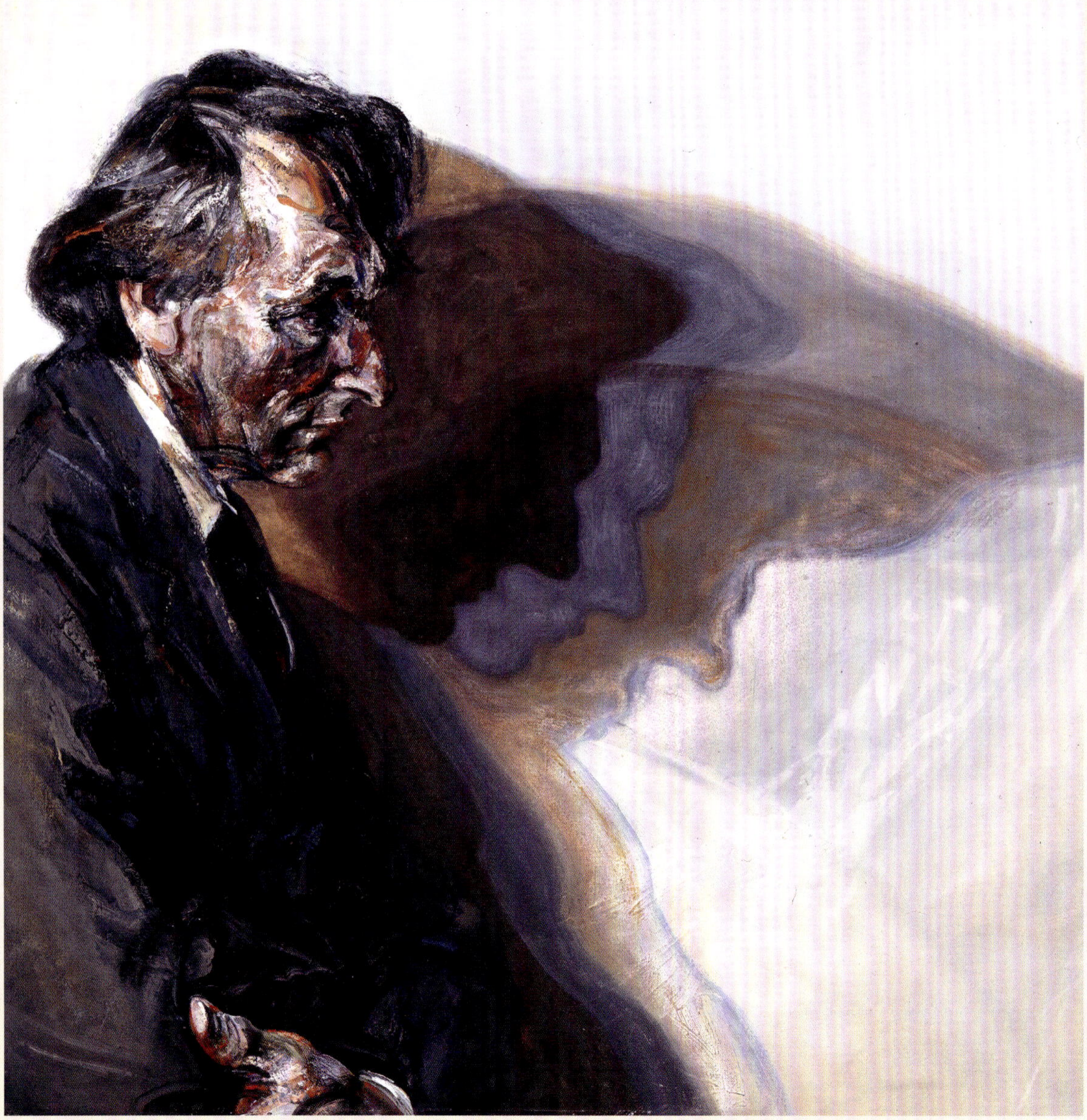

Mac with Shadows, which Southampton Art Gallery purchased in 1982. Several differently coloured shadows stretch and fill the canvas, as though a light has been shone on Mac from several directions at once. The expressive use of paint helps to produce a portrait of psychological intensity, fulfilling Hambling's aim to paint what goes on inside each person.

Other works by Hambling have been acquired for Southampton's collection, including a sculpture, *First Dragon* (cat. 48), and two more portraits, both bequeathed by David Brown in 2002 – *Catherine Parkinson*, and the other, *Untitled*, which is a likeness of fellow artist Roger Ackling with a parrot. Ackling has his own links with Southampton City Art Gallery: as a friend and collaborator of Richard Long, he used sunlight to burn forms into pieces of found wood. The Gallery holds a work on paper by Ackling produced this way: *And They Cast Their Shadows*, made in 1977.

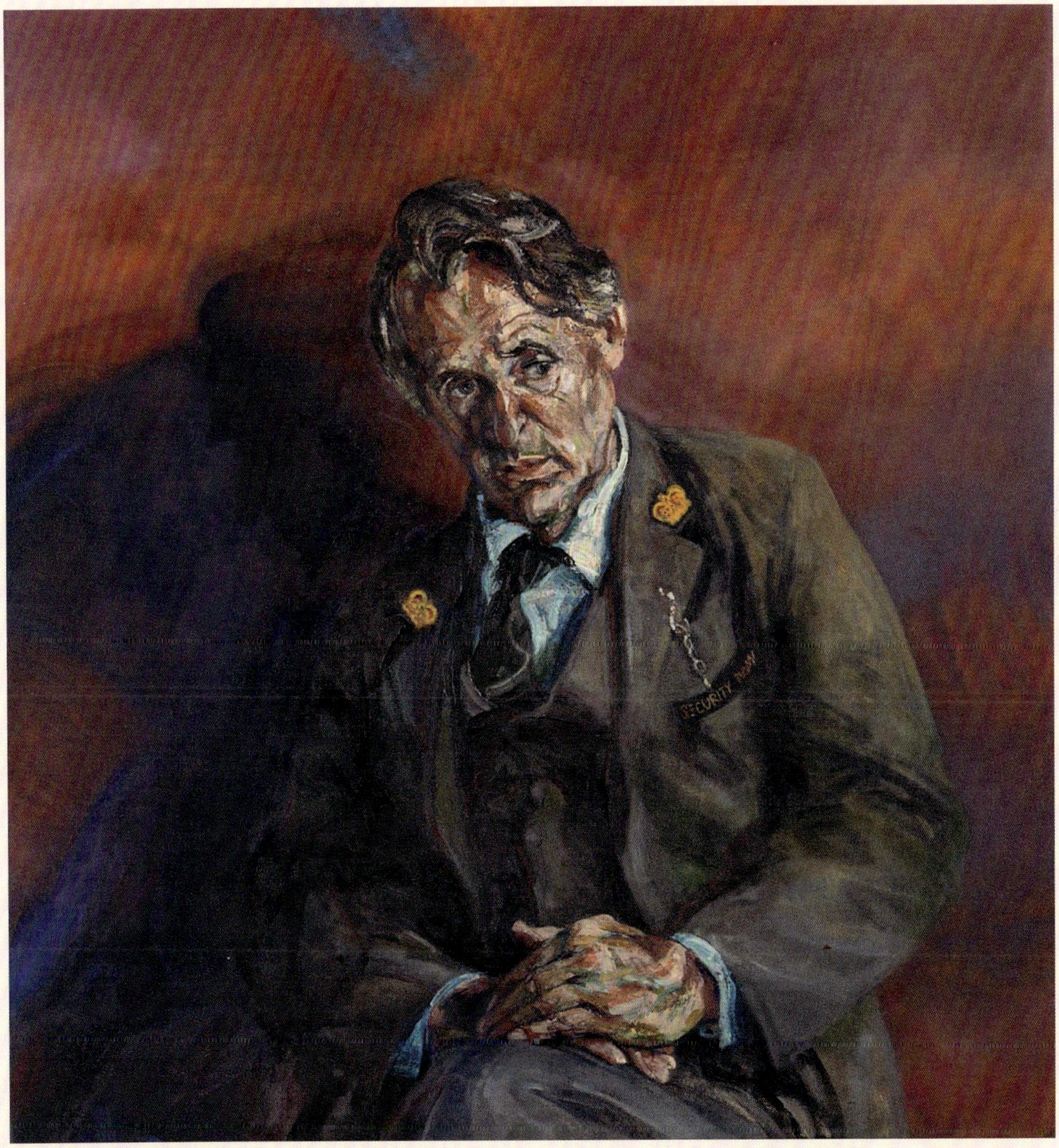

54 (BELOW)

Paula Rego (b. 1935)
Sing a Song of Sixpence II, 1989

Etching with aquatint, 52 × 38 cm
Southampton's Museums, Archives and Galleries, 1993
Southampton City Art Gallery, SOTAG 12/1993

55 (OPPOSITE, TOP)

Paula Rego (b. 1935)
Witches at their Incantations after Salvator Rosa, 1991

Etching with aquatint, 66.5 × 81.5 × 2 cm (framed)
NG commission, 1990
The National Gallery, London, H21

56 (OPPOSITE, BOTTOM)

Salvator Rosa (1615–1673)
Witches at their Incantations, about 1646

Oil on canvas, 72 × 132 cm
Bought, 1984
The National Gallery, London, NG6491

Salvator Rosa was one of the most unconventional artists in seventeenth-century Italy. The National Gallery's painting, a macabre display of witchcraft, depicts witches casting a number of bizarre spells under a pitch-dark night sky. Rosa, who trained in Naples, developed an interest in the supernatural while working in Florence in the 1640s. Scenes of witchcraft and the occult were rare in art, and Rosa's decision to paint such imagery attests to his curiosity for the less usual intellectual preoccupations of his age. This interest informed the subject matter of his etchings as well as some of the satires he wrote.

Paula Rego responded to Rosa's work with an etching of her own in 1991, which she produced as a commission for the National Gallery. She was the Gallery's first associate artist (1989–90) and, during her residency, painted the mural entitled *Crivelli's Garden* for the National Gallery Dining Rooms. According to Rego, the mural was inspired by Carlo Crivelli's altarpiece, *The Madonna of the Swallow* in the National Gallery's collection, while the figures of saints were modelled on members of staff who worked at the Gallery at that time.

Rego had created *Sing a Song of Sixpence*, another etching with aquatint, a few years earlier. Southampton acquired the work in 1993. It developed from several drawings depicting traditional nursery rhymes. To produce her *Nursery Rhyme* portfolio, made for her granddaughter, Rego worked directly onto the etching plates. It is a tribute to her skilled draughtsmanship that most of her etchings were immediately successful and needed no reworking. The solid and rather menacing silhouettes of some of the 'four and twenty' blackbirds from the rhyme fill the foreground, while other birds burst from the pie to the surprise, and perhaps dismay, of the onlookers.

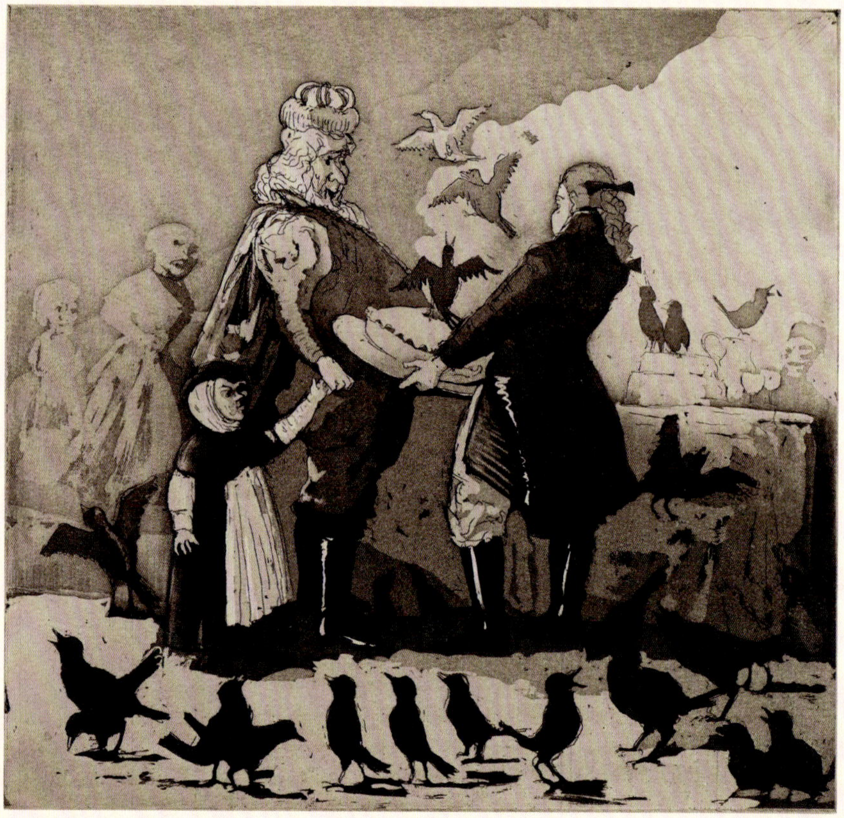

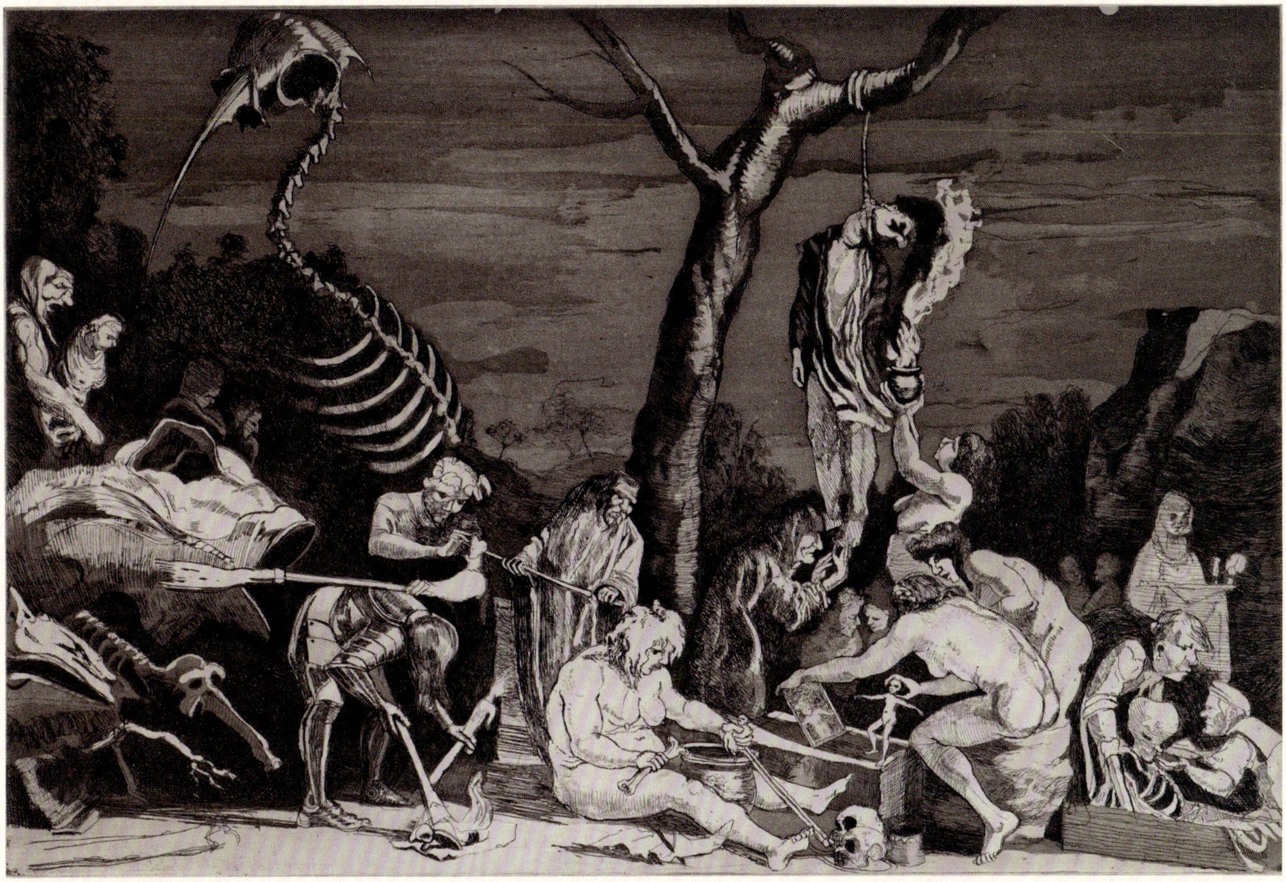

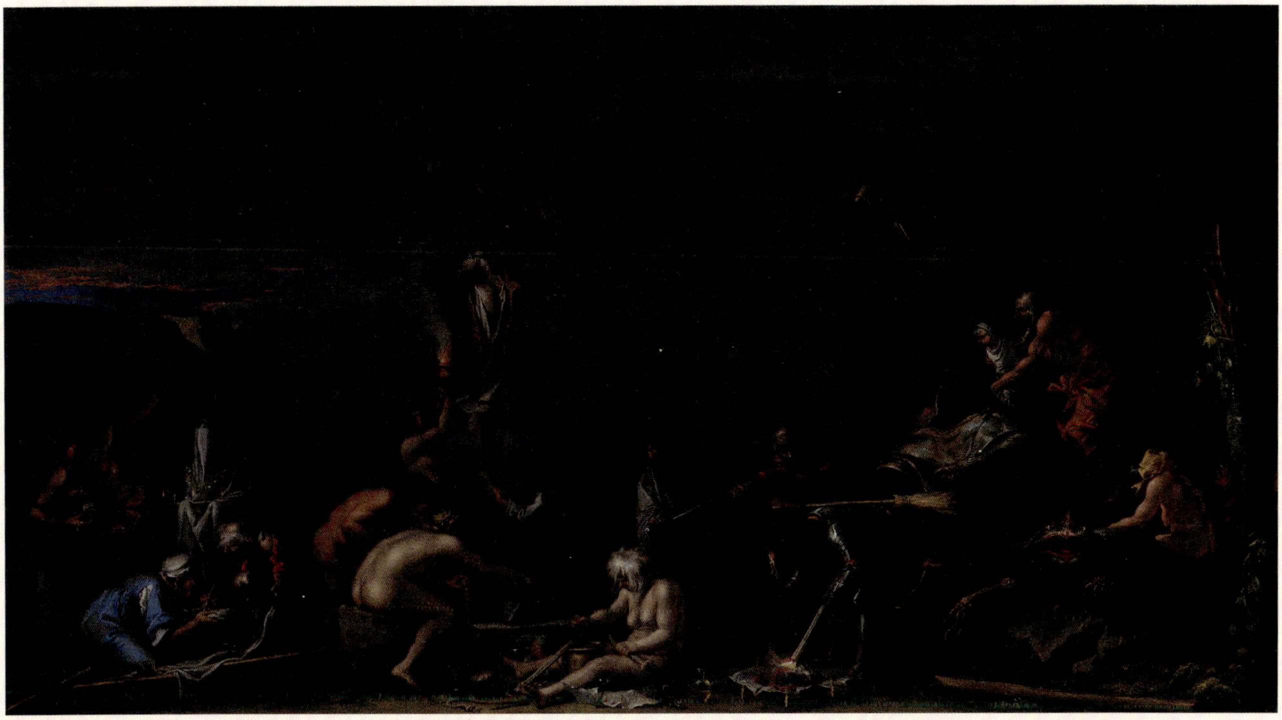

57

Rosalind Nashashibi (b. 1973)

South of France, 2018

Oil and nylon tights on canvas
Presented by the Contemporary Art Society, 2019–20
Southampton City Art Gallery, SOTAG 15/2019

58

Rosalind Nashashibi (b. 1973)

Rio, 2019

Oil on canvas, 150 × 120 cm
Collection T. Buck Marshall, New York
Courtesy of the artist and GRIMM Amsterdam | New York

Rosalind Nashashibi is a London-based artist and 2017 Turner Prize nominee, known for her paintings, prints and films. She was appointed as the most recent National Gallery artist in residence for 2019–20 in its new Modern and Contemporary Programme. Over the course of a year, Nashashibi has worked closely with staff at the National Gallery, keeping abreast with its ongoing research to fuel her own artistic dialogue with its historical art collection.

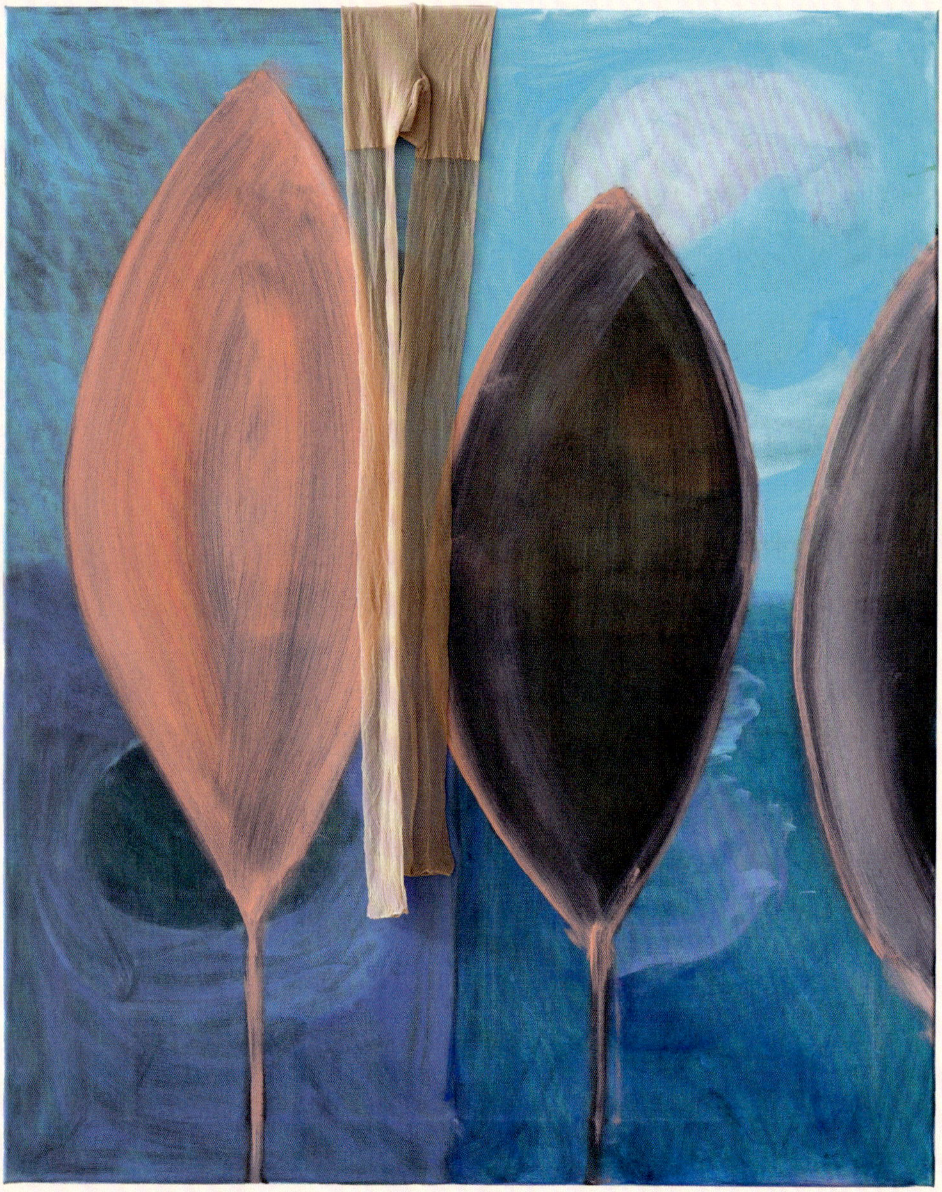

The recent exhibition, *An Overflow of Passion and Sentiment* (2 December 2020–21 June 2021), presented a group of Nashashibi's paintings in one of the Gallery's major Spanish rooms, alongside seventeenth-century paintings by Diego Velázquez, Jusepe de Ribera and Francisco de Zurbarán. Her new paintings explore how motifs taken from those old masters take on new meanings when placed in a different context within and alongside her own work.

Nashashibi's paintings, like her films, move between concrete depictions and more impressionistic forms and figures. Her work aims to illuminate how individuals balance the different aspects of their lives including work, family and community. She also investigates how the known environment can quickly transform into unexpected abstraction. The Southampton work, *South of France*, is a recent acquisition of 2019–20, which characteristically takes as its starting point an everyday object – in this case, a pair of nylon tights, which sits on the surface of the picture and becomes abstracted by what is seen around and through it. It speaks in interesting ways to *Rio*, a work that Nashashibi created during her London residency, its forms and colours echoing those of the French poplar trees depicted in the background of Southampton's picture.

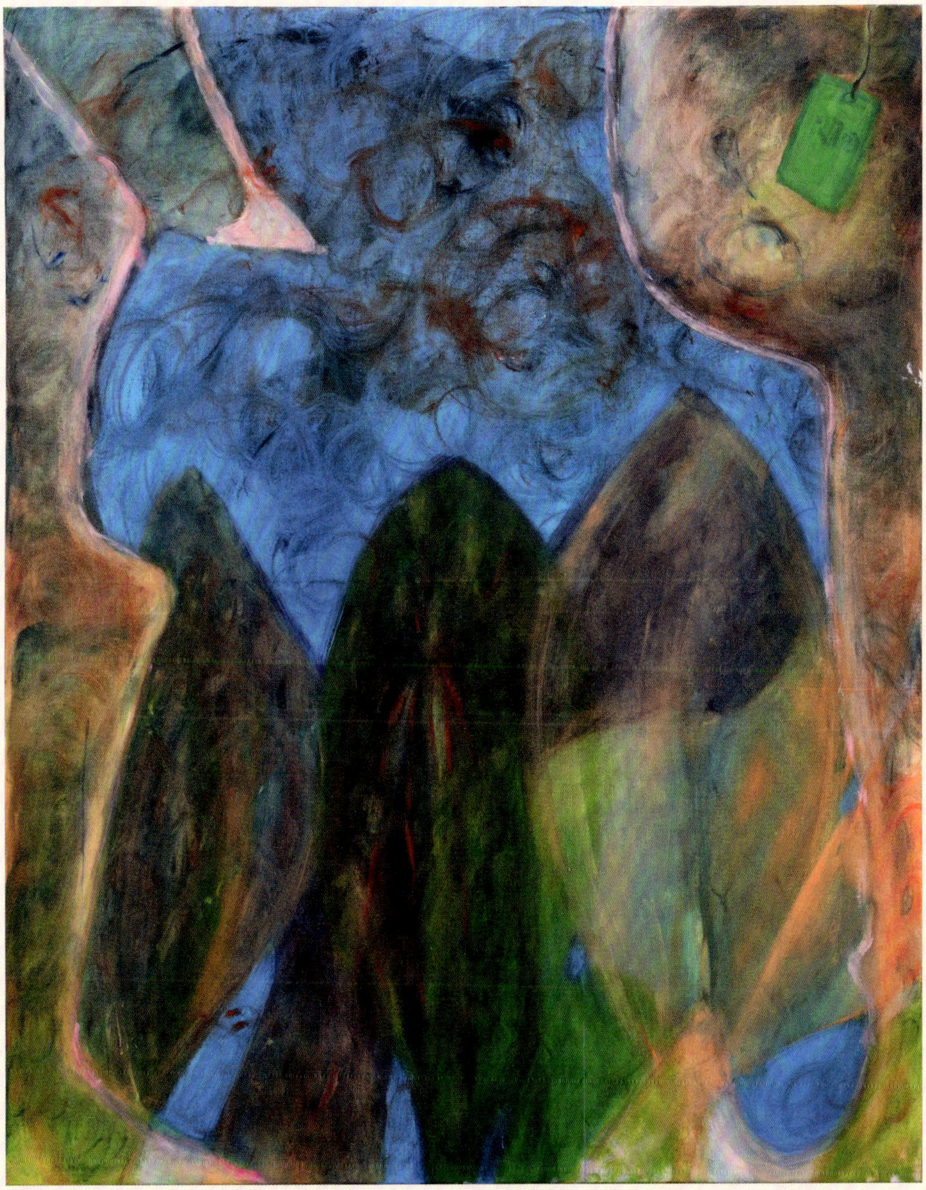

In Focus

Links between Southampton City Art Gallery and the National Gallery

From the 1970s, exciting conversations flourished between the then newly established learning teams in Southampton and London. Importantly, Helen Luckett, who worked at Southampton Art Gallery from 1974, forged links with Alistair Smith, who was responsible for establishing the National Gallery's education department.

Les Buckingham, who began working as an education officer at Southampton in 1975, recalled the effect of some pioneering National Gallery initiatives on Southampton's thinking: for example, London's *Painting in Focus* was adapted to become Southampton's *Painting of the Month*.[1] In both venues the series concentrated on one painting, sharing some new aspect of research into its making or meaning. Again, in 1983, the National Gallery's director Michael Levey mounted a ground-breaking exhibition in which pictures were displayed without labels to encourage audiences to take an extended look at the paintings. Given that labels had become a firm fixture of museum education, this was a thought-provoking initiative. Former Southampton colleagues have recalled how this influenced a more creative approach to labels in their own subsequent displays.

Southampton led the way on numerous occasions, especially when thinking about provision for schools. Although the theme of educating children into visual literacy had been a recurrent one in the *Museums Journal* since its foundation in 1901, progress was slow. Before dedicated departments were established, gallery education was largely dependent on the commitment of individual curators. Luckett published several forward-thinking articles about pedagogical practice in art galleries, based on her first-hand experience at Southampton. For instance, 'Education Through Art', which appeared in the *Oxford Art Journal* in 1979, recorded some of the innovative early practices she helped to introduce at Southampton. After the Arts Council published its policy on education in 1983, Luckett published a response, 'Ten Years of Gallery Education,' in *The Journal of Aesthetic Education* in 1985, which brought the record of work undertaken at Southampton Art Gallery up to date.

Particularly innovative was Luckett's extended engagement with one Southampton primary school – Wildground Junior School in Dibden Purlieu – over three interrelated projects. The first experiment challenged a group of eight-year-olds to curate an exhibition, the result of which, *Why, Why, Wildground?*, opened at Southampton Art Gallery in 1977–78. The children mostly selected early twentieth-century paintings, including works by Charles Ginner, Henri Gaudier-Brzeska and John Piper, which they discussed through labels, hung lower than usual for the benefit of their child-height peers, and in a 'picture book' – their take on a traditional exhibition catalogue. It is worth noting that, in the introduction to their picture book, one of the two 'very special' books credited as sources of inspiration was the National Gallery's *Looking, Drawing and Sitting-Still Book*, written by Alistair Smith (1974, fig. 77). Significantly, this initiative inspired similar projects by local galleries in Yorkshire.

Through Children's Eyes (fig. 78), a second exhibition which was organised in 1982, focused on 14 contemporary works: four from Southampton's collection and eight from the Arts Council's collection, supported by a couple of other loans from artists. This project involved a different set of children but the same dedicated staff. Luckett explained that the aim was to see whether, in relation to selecting a group of modern paintings, the children's 'lack of inhibitions, [and their] curiosity and imagination' would enable them to 'come to enjoy them thoroughly themselves and introduce them to more incredulous adults.'[2] The resulting exhibition confirmed this was the case.

The final initiative, an exhibition called *Changing Minds*, took place in 1988, and again focused on a group of paintings from Southampton's collection, supplemented by a few works from the Arts Council's collection. Proposed as a sequel to *Through Children's Eyes*, it involved many of the same children from the second project who were now teenagers attending a number of different secondary schools. As had been the case with the second exhibition, the Arts Council toured the end result. The children whose lives were changed (twice over) by this deep engagement with art were well aware of how distinctive things were at Southampton. According to Luckett, at the end of a preliminary brainstorming session for the third collaboration, the teenagers 'practically demanded to do some more work with the Gallery "because you don't work like this anywhere else with pictures."'[3]

Despite the cultural conservatism of the 1980s, Southampton Art Gallery was key in shaping expectations of what a regional gallery education programme could achieve, along with other enterprising arts organisations such as the Hayward Gallery, London; Whitechapel Art Gallery, London; Tate Liverpool and Cornerhouse, Manchester.[4] In 1988, Southampton's efforts were acknowledged when the Art Gallery was chosen to host the Arts Council conference, which proposed the National Association for Gallery Education as a national body.

Today, Southampton's learning programme reaches a greater range of people than ever before.

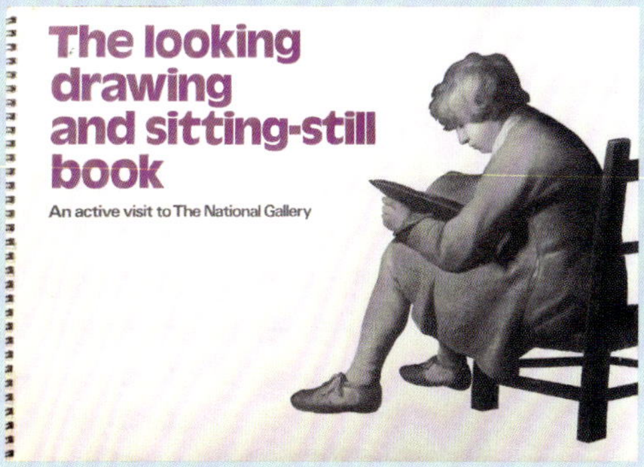

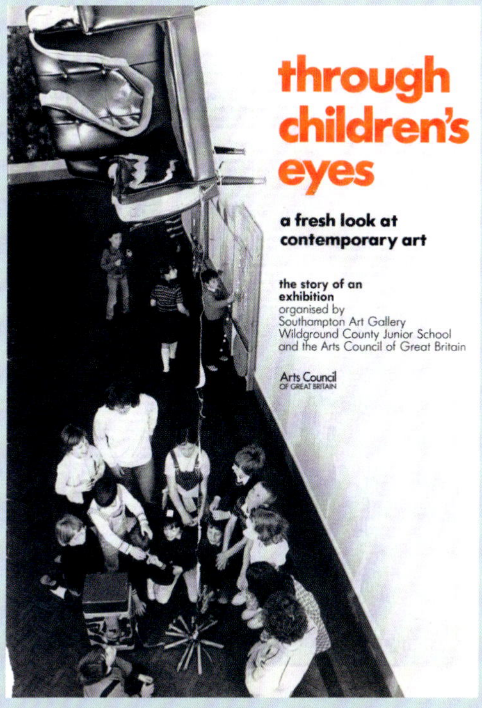

FIG. 77
The looking, drawing and sitting-still book (1974) by Alistair Smith

FIG. 78
Through Children's Eyes, 1982, front cover of the exhibition catalogue. Arts Council of Great Britain

Innovative approaches continue to be promoted. For instance, a regular feature is now its 'Gallery Touch Tours' for people with visual impairment and a 'Please-Do-Touch' trail encouraging participation from the under-5 age group. Another initiative is Southampton's 'Art on Wheels' scheme, which enables school children to experience works of art, often sculptures, first-hand and in the comfort of their own classrooms.

In Focus
Links between Southampton City Art Gallery and the National Gallery

Southampton Art Gallery's first official conservation officer, W.J. (Bill) Shanly, was appointed in 1963, the year the institution published its first conservation report. Shanly had been employed as the gallery's technician since 1949.

In March 1961, Palmer made enquiries about a low-power microscope,[1] and, in October, casually commented to Hendy: 'By the way, we now have our own ultra-violet apparatus ... and can find out more about the surface condition of pictures',[2] which confirms that by this date Southampton had a fledgling in-house conservation studio. Archival documentation reveals that this equipment had been bought on the advice of Stephen Rees Jones, then head of the Courtauld Institute's technology department, with responsibility for training a generation of painting conservators. Owning such up-to-date equipment was fairly unusual for a regional gallery and proves just how rich Southampton's collection was in terms of the number of old masters it included, and the staff's ability to take proper care of such a collection.

Rees Jones also assisted Palmer with undertaking technical examinations, including X-radiographs of Southampton's paintings by Cesare da Sesto and Goswijn van der Weyden (cats 24 and 22). These investigations revealed that both sixteenth-century works were in excellent physical condition. Earlier on, Palmer had got into the habit of seeking advice from the National Gallery, as and when the need arose. The first such interaction took place when Arthur Lucas conserved Allegretto Nuzi's *Coronation of the Virgin* (fig. 50; cat. 21) in 1960.[3] Lucas was contacted again,

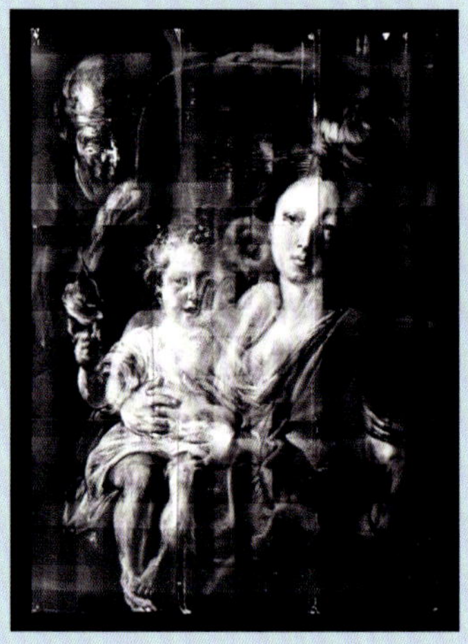

FIG. 79
X-radiograph of Jordaens's *The Holy Family* from Southampton, made at the National Gallery. The National Gallery, London/ Southampton Cultural Services

in 1963, about the treatment of Cesare da Sesto's *Saint Jerome* – work which he carried out the following year.[4]

Ambrose Scott-Moncrieff began as Southampton's second conservator in the 1970s, having trained with Helmut Ruhemann, who also taught both David Bomford and Martin Wyld, the leading figures within the National Gallery's own conservation department during the 1980s and 90s. Scott-Moncrieff collaborated with National Gallery colleagues over producing X-radiograph images of Southampton's *Holy Family* by Jacob Jordaens in 1976 (fig. 79). The resulting photograph proved valuable to Southampton during restoration work on the painting, when a thick layer of discoloured varnish was removed. The X-radiograph also confirmed several changes and further links between Southampton's painting and the National Gallery's two works by Jordaens, especially the repeated motif of a wicker chair.

Southampton's 'ArtLease' scheme, which began in 1970, had its origins in an 'office loans scheme' of the 1950s – a response to local businesses asking to borrow paintings. The scheme, which still runs today, started to fund conservation work during the 1970s and continued to do so into the next decade, thanks to the efforts of Tim Craven, who became the lead conservator at Southampton. The income generated by the scheme allowed for scientific equipment to be upgraded while 'visits to colleagues in the National Gallery kept Southampton at the forefront of new thinking about restoration and scientific research'.[5] For instance, Craven enjoyed a three-month secondment in 1983, when he gained invaluable experience working alongside Bomford and Wyld.[6] Bomford recalls that Craven 'became a valued colleague' and that Scott-Moncrieff 'was regularly in the National Gallery paintings' workshop downstairs, learning about relining canvases from craftsman Louis Howard.'[7] In addition, several fixed-term posts – ideal for graduates in the field – were created. Indeed, the first role of Southampton's current conservator, Rebecca Moisan, was as an ArtLease conservation officer.

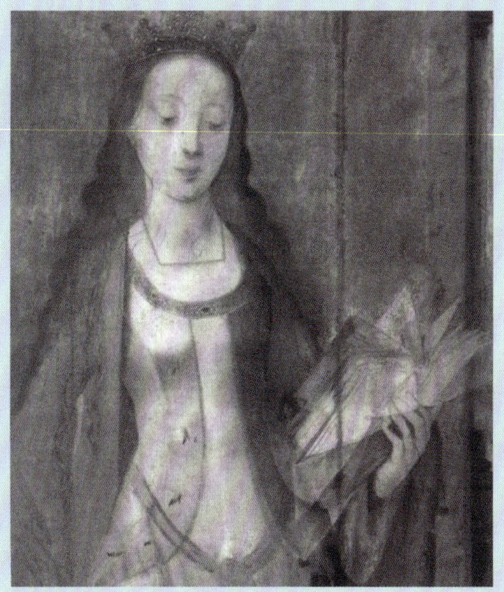

FIG. 80
Infrared reflectogram of Goswijn van der Weyden's *Saint Catherine and the Philosophers*, from *National Gallery Technical Bulletin* (2003): detail of the central panel. The National Gallery, London

In the last two decades, collaborations between Moisan and Rachel Billinge, Research Associate at the National Gallery, have produced X-radiographs and infrared reflectograms of some of Southampton's key old master paintings. In 2000, X-radiographs of Philips Koninck's *An Extensive Landscape* (cat. 28) were made by the National Gallery, and cross-sections of its paint layers taken by Kilian Anheuser (then Lecturer in Conservation Science, Cardiff University). The processes and results were explained in an exhibition at Southampton called *Take a Closer Look*. Another collaboration took place in 2001 over Nuzi's altarpiece. The work's size and fragile state made it unfit to travel, so imaging equipment was taken from London to Southampton to investigate the painting in situ. At the same time, van der Weyden's triptych (fig. 80) was examined, the preliminary results arousing so much interest that the painting was sent to London in Summer 2001 for more extensive technical imaging. Particular attention was paid to the coat of arms on its reverse side. The results were published in *The National Gallery Technical Bulletin* (2003). Sofonisba Anguissola's portrait (cat. 13) was examined in the most recent collaboration in 2019.

During the investigations of the van der Weyden triptych, Billinge drew attention to the fact that the painting was constrained by its frame and so, in 2005, Moisan raised funds for a new one to be made. This turned into another collaboration with the National Gallery because the frame was constructed by Isabella Kocum, a long-standing member of its framing department. Kocum had written in 2003, referencing a frame round Hans Memling's *Le Marriage Mystique de Saint Catherine* of 1479 in the Musée Memling in Bruges as a possible prototype.[8] Her new frame for Southampton's triptych was subsequently constructed on that model.

APPENDIX

Summary of Loan History between the National Gallery and Southampton City Art Gallery

I. Loans from the National Gallery to Southampton City Art Gallery

For Temporary Exhibitions

1946: 7–28 September 1946 *Spanish Paintings* (Arts Council touring exhibition)
Diego Velázquez, *Kitchen Scene with Christ in the House of Martha and Mary*, probably 1618 (NG1375)
Studio of El Greco, *The Agony in the Garden of Gethsemane*, 1590s (NG3476)
Francisco de Zurbarán, *Saint Francis in Meditation*, 1639 (NG5655)
Francisco de Goya, *A Picnic*, 1785–90 (NG1471)
Francisco de Goya, *A Scene from El Hechizado por Fuerza ('The Forcibly Bewitched')*, 1798 (NG1472)

1965: 27 November–18 December 1965 *Marine Paintings* (Arts Council touring exhibition)
Ludolf Bakhuizen, *An English Vessel and a Man-of-war in a Rough Sea*, probably 1680s (NG819)
Jan van de Cappelle, *A Small Dutch Vessel before a Light Breeze*, probably about 1645–55 (NG2588)

1978: 17 June–23 July 1978 *The National Gallery Lends: Dutch Genre Painting*
Jacob van Velsen, *A Musical Party*, 1631 (NG2575)
Pieter de Hooch, *A Musical Party in a Courtyard*, 1677 (NG3047)
Judith Leyster, *A Boy and a Girl with a Cat and an Eel*, about 1635 (NG5417)
Nicolaes Maes, *Interior with a Sleeping Maid and her Mistress ('The Idle Servant')*, 1655 (NG207)
Nicolaes Maes, *A Woman scraping Parsnips, with a Child standing by her*, 1655 (NG159)
Gabriel Metsu, *A Man and a Woman seated by a Virginal*, about 1665 (NG839)
Caspar Netscher, *Two Boys blowing Bubbles*, about 1670 (NG843)
Caspar Netscher, *A Lady teaching a Child to read, and a Child playing with a Dog ('La Maîtresse d'école')*, probably 1670s (NG844)
Adriaen van Ostade, *An Alchemist*, 1661 (NG846)
Jan Miense Molenaer, *A Young Man playing a Theorbo and a Young Woman playing a Cittern*, probably 1630–32 (NG1293)
Jan Victors, *A Village Scene with a Cobbler*, about 1650 (NG1312)
Hendrick Pot, *A Merry Company at Table*, 1630 (NG1278)
Cornelis Bega, *An Astrologer*, 1663 (NG1481)
Willem Duyster, *Two Men playing Tric-trac, with a Woman scoring*, about 1625–30 (NG1387)
Willem Duyster, *Soldiers fighting over Booty in a Barn*, about 1623–24 (NG1386)
Hendrick Sorgh, *Two Lovers at Table*, 1644 (NG1056)
Hendrick Sorgh, *A Woman playing Cards with Two Peasants*, 1644 (NG1055)
Jan Steen, *An Interior with a Man offering an Oyster to a Woman*, probably 1660–65 (NG2559)
Dirck Hals, *A Party at Table*, 1626 (NG1074)
Gabriel Metsu, *The Interior of a Smithy*, about 1657 (NG2591)
Olivier van Deuren, *A Young Astronomer*, about 1685 (NG2589)
Quiringh van Brekelenkam, *Interior of a Tailor's Shop*, about 1655–61 (NG2549)
Pieter Codde, *A Woman holding a Mirror*, 1625 (NG2584)
Jacob Ochtervelt, *A Woman standing at a Harpsichord, a Man seated by her*, probably 1675–80 (NG2143)
Arent (?) Diepraem, *A Peasant seated smoking*, about 1650 (NG3534)
Arent Arentsz., *Fishermen near Muiden Castle*, about 1630 (NG3533)
Pieter Quast, *A Man and a Woman in a Stableyard*, probably 1630s (NG2856)
Adriaen van der Werff, *A Boy with a Mousetrap*, about 1678–79 (NG3049)

1993: 30 September–14 November 1993 National Gallery Touring Exhibition: *Henri Rousseau, Surprised!*
Henri Rousseau, *Surprised!*, 1891 (NG6421)

1996: 13 June–4 August 1996 *Painters of Le Havre: Boudin, Monet, Dufy and their Contemporaries*
Claude Monet, *The Museum at Le Havre*, 1873 (NG6527)

1999: 16 April–13 June 1999 *Great Dutch Paintings on Tour from the National Gallery*
Hendrick ter Brugghen, *Jacob reproaching Laban for giving him Leah in place of Rachel*, 1627 (NG4164)
Jan Jansz. Treck, *Still Life with a Pewter Flagon and Two Ming Bowls*, 1651 (NG4562)
Johannes Vermeer, *A Young Woman standing at a Virginal*, about 1670–72 (NG1383)
Pieter de Hooch, *A Woman and her Maid in a Courtyard*, about 1660/61 (NG794)
Probably by Rembrandt, *Portrait of Margaretha de Geer, Wife of Jacob Trip*, 1661 (NG5282)
Gerard ter Borch, *An Officer dictating a Letter*, about 1655–58 (NG5847)
Jan Steen, *The Interior of an Inn ('The Broken Eggs')*, about 1665–70 (NG5637)
Emanuel de Witte, *The Interior of the Oude Kerk, Amsterdam, during a Sermon*, about 1660 (NG6402)
Aelbert Cuyp, *A Hilly River Landscape with a Horseman talking to a Shepherdess*, about 1655–60 (NG53)
Gabriel Metsu, *A Woman seated at a Table and a Man tuning a Violin*, about 1658 (NG838)
Jan van de Cappelle, *A River Scene with a Large Ferry and Numerous Dutch Vessels at Anchor*, about 1665 (NG967)
Jan van Huysum, *Flowers in a Terracotta Vase*, 1736–37 (NG796)
Nicolaes Maes, *Christ blessing the Children*, 1652–53 (NG757)
Gerbrand van den Eeckhout, *Four Officers of the Amsterdam Coopers' and Wine-rackers' Guild*, 1657 (NG1459)
Gerrit Berckheyde, *The Market Place and the Grote Kerk at Haarlem*, 1674 (NG1420)
Meindert Hobbema, *A Woody Landscape with a Cottage*, about 1665 (NG995)
Jacob van Ruisdael, *Two Watermills and an Open Sluice at Singraven*, about 1650–52 (NG986)
Frans Hals, *Portrait of a Woman with a Fan*, about 1640 (NG2529)

2001: 12 October–30 December 2001 *The Stuart Portrait: Status and Legacy*
Anthony van Dyck, *Portrait of George Gage with Two Attendants*, probably 1622–23 (NG49)
Style of Anthony van Dyck, *Portraits of Two Young Englishmen*, about 1635–40 (NG3605)

2018: 4 May–1 September 2018 *George Shaw: My Back to Nature*
Hendrick van Balen the Elder and Follower of Jan Brueghel the Elder, *Pan pursuing Syrinx*, possibly after 1615 (NG659)
Sebastiano Ricci, *Bacchus and Ariadne*, probably 1700–10 (NG851)

2021: 28 May–4 Sept 2021 *Creating a National Collection: The Partnership between Southampton City Art Gallery and the National Gallery*
Workshop of Goswijn (Goossen) van der Weyden, *The Visitation of the Virgin to Saint Elizabeth*, about 1516 (NG1082), cat. 23
Cesare da Sesto, *Salome*, probably about 1510–20 (NG2485), cat. 25
Salvator Rosa, *Witches at their Incantations*, about 1646 (NG6491), cat. 56
Gaspard Dughet, *View of the Roman Countryside, possibly Tivoli*, about 1670 (NG161), cat. 27

Philips Koninck, *An Extensive Landscape with a Hawking Party*, probably about 1670 (NG836), cat. 29
Claude Monet, *The Petit Bras of the Seine at Argenteuil*, 1872 (NG6395), cat. 42
Thomas Gainsborough, *Dr Ralph Schomberg*, about 1770 (NG684), cat. 34
Maggi Hambling, *Portrait of Archie MacDonald*, 1980–81 (H11), cat. 53
Paula Rego, *Witches at their Incantations after Salvator Rosa*, 1991 (H21), cat. 55

On Long Loan from the National Gallery to Southampton City Art Gallery

1951–4: 7 January 1951–3 December 1954
Aelbert Cuyp, *Peasants and Cattle by the River Merwede*, about 1658–60 (NG1289)

1951–63: 7 January 1951–1 March 1963
Hendrick van Steenwyck the Younger and Jan Brueghel the Elder, *The Interior of a Gothic Church looking East*, 1615 (NG2204)

1952–63: 9 October 1952–1 March 1963
Harmen Steenwyck, *Still Life: An Allegory of the Vanities of Human Life*, about 1640 (NG1256)

1953–58: 7 December–30 July 1958
Cornelis Bega, *An Astrologer*, 1663 (NG1481)
Imitator of Rembrandt, *A Study of an Elderly Man in a Cap*, 17th century (NG2539)
Dutch, *Portrait of a Dutch Commander(?)*, probably 1651 (NG3315)
Jan Cornelis Haccou, *A Road by a Cottage*, 1819 (NG3683)

1953–63: 7 December 1953–1 March 1963
Jan Davidsz. de Heem, *Still Life*, about 1664–65 (NG2582)
Jacob van Ruisdael, *A Cottage and a Hayrick by a River*, about 1646–50 (NG2565)

1954–63: 12 January 1954–1 March 1963
Simon de Vlieger, *A Dutch Man-of-war and Various Vessels in a Breeze*, about 1638–45 (NG3025)

1954–63: 13 January 1954–1 March 1963
Adriaen van der Werff, *Portrait of a Man in a Quilted Gown*, 1685 (NG1660)
Eglon Hendrik van der Neer, *Judith*, about 1678 (NG2535)
Philips Wouwerman, *Two Horsemen at a Gipsy Encampment, One having his Fortune told*, 1650–68 (NG2282)
Willem van de Velde, *Calm: A Dutch Ship coming to Anchor and Another under Sail*, 1657 (NG870)

1958–63: 28 April 1958–1 March 1963
David Teniers the Younger, *A Cottage by a River with a Distant View of a Castle*, about 1650 (NG861)
Jacob Ochtervelt, *A Young Lady trimming her Fingernails, attended by a Maidservant*, probably 1670–75 (NG2553)
Meindert Hobbema, *Cottages in a Wood*, about 1660 (NG2570)
Francesco Guardi, *Venice: The Arsenal*, 1755–60 (NG3538)

1960–63: 28 November 1960–1 March 1963
Probably by Francesco Zugno, *The Finding of Moses*, after 1740 (NG3542)

1966–75: 5 September 1966–22 September 1975
Jan Wijnants, *A Landscape with Two Dead Trees, and Two Sportsmen with Dogs on a Sandy Road*, probably 1665–75 (NG972)
Lorenzo di Credi, *The Virgin adoring the Child*, 1490–1500 (NG648)
Meindert Hobbema, *A Woody Landscape*, about 1665 (NG685)
Aert van der Neer, *A River Landscape with a Village*, probably about 1645 (NG2534)
Jan van der Heyden, *The Huis ten Bosch at The Hague*, 1665–75 (NG1914)
Alvise Vivarini, *Portrait of a Man*, 1497 (NG2672)

1970–5: 9 February 1970–22 September 1975
Jacob Ochtervelt, *A Woman standing at a Harpsichord, a Man seated by her*, probably 1675–80 (NG2143)

1978–79: 21 July 1978–20 September 1979
Follower of Bronzino, *Portrait of a Lady*, probably 1575–85 (NG2085) fig. 75

1978–86: 21 July 1978–5 February 1986
Johan Barthold Jongkind, *River Scene*, 1860–80 (NG4583)
Andries Vermeulen, *A Scene on the Ice*, about 1800 (NG1850)
Nicolas de Largillierre and Studio, *Mme de Souscarrière (?) and her Page*, probably 1729 (NG3883)
Workshop of Giovanni Bellini, *The Virgin and Child*, about 1490–1500 (NG3078)

1978–92: 21 July 1978–17 July 1992
Workshop of Joachim Patinir, *Landscape with the Rest on the Flight into Egypt*, about 1518–20 (NG3115), fig. 74

1979–86: 8 May 1979–5 February 1986
Workshop of Sandro Botticelli, *The Virgin and Child with Saint John and Two Angels*, probably about 1490–1500 (NG226)

30 October 1980–5 February 1986
Follower of Bronzino, *Portrait of a Lady*, probably 1575–85 (NG2085), fig. 75

II. Loans from Southampton City Art Gallery to the National Gallery

1976: 30 September–12 December
Art in 17th century Holland
Ceasar Boetius van Everdingen, *Allegory of Winter*, 1650 (SOTAG 188), fig. 34, cat. 15

1986: 3 September–23 November
Dutch Landscape
Jacob van Ruisdael, *The Dunes near Haarlem*, late 1640s (SOTAG 1/1964), cat. 30

2002: 18 July–6 October *Light*
Paul Delvaux, *A Siren in Full Moonlight*, 1940 (SOTAG 87/1963)

2008: 21 November 2007–10 February
Discoveries: New Research into British Collections
Christopher Nevinson, *Loading Timber at Southampton Docks*, 1917 (SOTAG 4/1962)

2012/13: 31 October 2012–20 January 2013
Seduced by Art: Photography Past and Present
Richard Billingham, *Hedgerow (New Forest)*, 2003 (SOTAG: 2004/11)

2018: 9 April–29 July The Credit Suisse Exhibition: *Monet & Architecture*
Monet, *The Church at Vétheuil*, 1880 (SOTAG 183/1975), cat. 41

Temporary Deposits (pictures from Southampton which came to London for technical examination)

1999: returned 17 December
Philips Koninck, *An Extensive Landscape*, 1650s (SOTAG 2/1963), cat. 28

2001: 2 July–30 September
Goswijn (Goossen) van der Weyden, *Saint Catherine and the Philosophers*, early 16th century (SOTAG 1/1958) cat. 22

2019: June 2019
Sofonisba Anguissola, *The Artist's Sister in the Garb of a Nun*, 1551 (SOTAG 3), cat. 13

LIST OF EXHIBITED WORKS

Creating a National Collection: The Partnership between Southampton City Art Gallery and the National Gallery (28 May–4 September 2021)

Gallery 0

Frederick Golden Short
(1863–1936)
New Forest, 1900
(SOTAG 507); cat. 2
Southampton City Art Gallery

Mary Hayllar (1862–about 1950)
The Lawn Tennis Season, 1881
(SOTAG 241); cat. 4
Southampton City Art Gallery

Franz Meerts (1836–1896)
The Old Attorney, mid-nineteenth century
(SOTAG 401); cat. 6
Southampton City Art Gallery

Leonard Frank Skeats (1874–1943)
Robert Chipperfield, JP, before 1911
(SOTAG 526); cat. 1
Southampton City Art Gallery

Frederick Lee Bridell (1830–1863)
The Fisherman's House, 1854
(SOTAG 57); cat. 3
Southampton City Art Gallery

Gallery 1

Eugène Louis Boudin (1824–1898)
Moonlight Village Scene, Le Faou, Brittany (Marine effet de lune), perhaps 1867
(SOTAG 45); cat. 7
Southampton City Art Gallery

Sir Henry Tonks (1862–1937)
The Torn Gown, 1897
(SOTAG 584); cat. 9
Southampton City Art Gallery

Lucy Elizabeth Kemp-Welch
(1869–1958)
Timber Run in the Welsh Hills
(SOTAG 317); cat. 5
Southampton City Art Gallery

Walter Richard Sickert
(1860–1942)
The Mantelpiece, 1907
(SOTAG 517); cat. 10
Southampton City Art Gallery

Joaquín Sorolla y Bastida
(1863–1923)
Estuary of the Nalón, Asturias, 1883
(SOTAG 542); cat. 8
Southampton City Art Gallery

Nicolaes Maes (1634–1693)
Portrait of A Man, 1670s or 1680s
(SOTAG 385); cat. 11
Southampton City Art Gallery

Jacob Jordaens (1593–1678)
The Holy Family, before 1628
(SOTAG 315); cat. 12
Southampton City Art Gallery

Sofonisba Anguissola
(about 1532–1625)
The Artist's Sister in the Garb of a Nun, 1551
(SOTAG 3); cat. 13
Southampton City Art Gallery

Johannes Moreelse (after 1602–1634)
The Young Poet, about 1630
(SOTAG 110); cat. 14
Southampton City Art Gallery

Camille Pissarro (1830–1903)
View from the Versailles Road, Louveciennes, 1870
(SOTAG 461); cat. 16
Southampton City Art Gallery

Caesar Boëtius van Everdingen
(about 1616–1678)
Allegory of Winter, 1650
(SOTAG 188); cat. 15
Southampton City Art Gallery

Spencer Gore (1878–1914)
View from a Window, 1909
(SOTAG 221); cat. 17
Southampton City Art Gallery

Henry Lamb (1883–1960)
Edie McNeill, 1911
(SOTAG 330); cat. 18
Southampton City Art Gallery

Gallery 2

Allegretto Nuzi (active 1354; died 1373/74)
The Coronation of the Virgin, 1360
(SOTAG 1403); cat. 21
Southampton City Art Gallery

Goswijn (Goossen) van der Weyden (active 1492; died after 1538)
Saint Catherine and the Philosophers, 1510
(SOTAG 1/1958); cat. 22
Southampton City Art Gallery

Workshop of Goswijn (Goossen) van der Weyden
The Visitation of the Virgin to Saint Elizabeth, about 1516
(NG1082); cat. 23
The National Gallery, London

Cesare da Sesto (about 1477–1523)
Saint Jerome as a Hermit in the Desert of Chalcis, 1520
(SOTAG 2/1958); cat. 24
Southampton City Art Gallery

Cesare da Sesto (about 1477–1523)
Salome, probably about 1510–20
(NG2485); cat. 25
The National Gallery, London

Salvator Rosa (1615–1673)
A Mountain Landscape, 17th century
(SOTAG 1/1961); cat. 26
Southampton City Art Gallery

Gaspard Dughet (1615–1675)
View of the Roman Countryside, possibly Tivoli, about 1670
(NG161); cat. 27
The National Gallery, London

Philips Koninck (1619–1688)
An Extensive Landscape, 1650s
(SOTAG 2/1963); cat. 28
Southampton City Art Gallery

Philips Koninck (1619–1688)
Extensive Landscape with a Hawking Party, probably about 1670
(NG836); cat. 29
The National Gallery, London

Jacob van Ruisdael
(1628/29–1682)
The Dunes near Haarlem, late 1640s
(SOTAG 1/1964); cat. 30
Southampton City Art Gallery

Thomas Gainsborough
(1727–1788)
George, Lord Vernon, 1767
(SOTAG 1494); cat. 33
Southampton City Art Gallery

Thomas Gainsborough
(1727–1788)
Dr Ralph Schomberg, about 1770
Bought, 1862
(NG684); cat. 34
The National Gallery, London

Joseph Wright of Derby
(1734–1797)
Landscape, 1780
(SOTAG 1416); cat. 32
Southampton City Art Gallery

J.M.W. Turner (1775–1851)
Fishermen Upon a Lee-Shore in Squally Weather, 1802
(SOTAG 1396); cat. 31
Southampton City Art Gallery

Claude Monet (1840–1926)
The Church at Vétheuil, 1880
(SOTAG 183/1975); cat. 41
Southampton City Art Gallery

Claude Monet (1840–1926)
The Petit Bras of the Seine at Argenteuil, 1872
(NG6395); cat. 42
The National Gallery, London

Edgar Degas (1834–1917)
Danseuse mettant son bas (Dancer putting on her Stocking), statue modelled between the 1890s and 1911; cast between 1921 and about 1936
(SOTAG 1418); cat. 38
Southampton City Art Gallery

Auguste Rodin (1840–1917)
Femme accroupie (Squatting Woman), clay model, 1881–82; cast about mid-1950s
(SOTAG 1422); cat. 39
Southampton City Art Gallery

Aristide Maillol (1861–1944)
Femme au crabe (Woman with Crab)
Original terracotta model by Maillol 1930; cast about early 1950s
(SOTAG 1464); cat. 40
Southampton City Art Gallery

Gallery 3

Graham Sutherland (1903–1980)
Red Landscape, 1942
(SOTAG 1369); cat. 19
Southampton City Art Gallery

Mark Gertler (1891–1939)
The Rabbi and his Grandchild, 1913
(SOTAG 6/1968); cat. 37
Southampton City Art Gallery

John Craxton (1922–2009)
Dark Landscape, 1943
(SOTAG 1378); cat. 20
Southampton City Art Gallery

Gwen John (1876–1939)
Mère Poussepin, 1920
(SOTAG 1456); cat. 36
Southampton City Art Gallery

Charles Ginner (1878–1952)
Early Morning, 1917
(SOTAG 12/1969); cat. 35
Southampton City Art Gallery

Stephen McKenna (1939–2017)
Fourment, 1977
(SOTAG 24/1978); cat. 43
Southampton City Art Gallery

Maxwell Armfield (1881–1972)
Central Park, New York, 1916
(SOTAG 42/1976); cat. 45
Southampton City Art Gallery

David Redfern (b. 1947)
Work, 1977
(SOTAG 16/1979); cat. 44
Southampton City Art Gallery

Maggi Hambling OBE, CBE (b. 1945)
Mac with Shadows, 1981
(SOTAG 13/1982); cat. 52
Southampton City Art Gallery

Maggi Hambling OBE, CBE (b. 1945)
Portrait of Archie MacDonald, 1980–81
(H11); cat. 53
The National Gallery, London

Paula Rego (b. 1935)
Sing a Song of Sixpence II, 1989
Donated by the Friends of
(SOTAG 12/1993); cat. 54
Southampton City Art Gallery

Paula Rego (b. 1935)
Witches at their Incantations after Salvator Rosa, 1991
(H21); cat. 55
The National Gallery, London

Salvator Rosa (1615–1673)
Witches at their Incantations, about 1646
Bought, 1984
(NG6491); cat. 56
The National Gallery, London

Wilhelmina Barns-Graham (1912–2004)
Glacier Vortex, 1951
(SOTAG 208/2002), cat. 49
Southampton City Art Gallery

George Shaw (b. 1966)
Scenes from the Passion: The Unicorn, 2003
(SOTAG 5/2004); cat. 50
Southampton City Art Gallery

Michael Ayrton (1921–1975)
Reflective Heads II, 1971–73
(SOTAG 10/1973); cat. 46
Southampton City Art Gallery

Maggi Hambling OBE, CBE (b. 1945)
First Dragon, 1992
(SOTAG 6/1996); cat. 48
Southampton City Art Gallery

Barry Flanagan (1941–2009)
Boxing Hare on Anvil, 1984
(SOTAG 207/2002); cat. 47
Southampton City Art Gallery

Gallery 4

Bridget Riley (b. 1931)
Oil Test for Red Movement, 2004
(preparatory work), 2004
(SOTAG 12/2007b; cat. 51
Southampton City Art Gallery

Rosalind Nashashibi (b. 1973)
South of France, 2018
(SOTAG 15/2019); cat. 57
Southampton City Art Gallery

Rosalind Nashashibi, (b. 1973)
Rio, 2019
cat. 58
GRIMM Gallery

SOURCES AND SELECT BIBLIOGRAPHY

National Gallery Archive (NGA)

NG16/201/1
Registry files: Southampton: Chipperfield Bequest, 1930–34: catalogue of 1927 annual exhibition, copy of court order, correspondence with Southampton town clerk, Gleadowe, press cutting re: building

NG16/201/2
Registry files: Southampton: Chipperfield Bequest, 1935–36: loan of Burne-Jones pictures, correspondence with town clerk, advice on building, copies of offers

NG16/201/3
Registry files: Southampton: Chipperfield Bequest, 1937–38: correspondence with curator and town clerk, list of Chipperfield Bequest acquisitions, offers, correspondence with dealers

NG16/201/4
Registry files: Southampton: Chipperfield Bequest, 1939–50: curatorial correspondence (loans, etc.), copy of scheme, copy of catalogue, correspondence regarding appointment of new curator, sculpture competition

NG16/201/5
Registry files: Southampton: Chipperfield Bequest, 1951–58: sculpture competition, acquisitions, opening of new hall

NG16/201/6
Registry files: Southampton: Chipperfield Bequest, 1959–67: acquisitions

NG16/201/7
Registry files: Southampton: Chipperfield Bequest, 1968–79: acquisitions

Southampton City Archives (SCA): records of the Southampton Art Gallery 1930–68

SC/ART/1–24: General correspondence files, 1937–70. In particular:
SC/ART/1/1/2
Art Exhibitions Bureau c/o Royal Academy 1937–44

SC/ART/1/2/1–20
General correspondence files, 1937–67. In particular:
SC/ART/1/2/7 British Institute of Adult Education, London, 1937–46
SC/ART/1/2/15–17 Barber Institute and Birmingham Art Gallery correspondence

SC/ART/1/8/1–10
General correspondence files, 1937–66. In particular:
SC/ART/1/8/5 William Burrough Hill correspondence

SC/ART/1/13/1–9
General correspondence files, 1939–64. In particular:
SC/ART/1/13/9 Museums Association 1938–1957

SC/ART/1/22/1–12
General correspondence files, 1937–66. In particular:
SC/ART/1/22/2 War Artists Advisory Committee, 1946–50
SC/ART/1/22/3 War damage repairs, 1941

SC/ART/2
Miscellaneous correspondence files

SC/ART/3/
Bequests, in particular:
SC/ART/3/1/1–27 Chipperfield Bequest files, 1930–38
SC/ART/3/2/1–10 Frederick William Smith Bequest files
SC/ART/3/4/1–3 National Gallery correspondence

Board Meeting Minutes, 1938–68

Southampton City Art Gallery Conservation and History Files

Chipperfield Art Bequest Files; Smith Art Bequest files

Artist files; gallery exhibition files archive 1939–present, including catalogues, leaflets, books, correspondence

Art Gallery maps and other images, including scans and X-radiographs of works in the collection

Copies of corporation and other funds' records and relevant council minutes

Conservation history records including correspondence files

Secondary sources

BOSMAN 2008
S. Bosman, *The National Gallery in Wartime*, London 2008

BROWN 1977
D. Brown, 'Works lent by Van Abbemuseum, Eindhoven', *Art Monthly*, 4, no. 1 (February 1977), pp. 21–22

CRACK 2019
P. Crack, 'Justifying the 'Italian Primitives': Public Acquisitions in Twentieth-Century Britain', unpublished PhD thesis, Courtauld Institute, University of London, 2019

DUNCAN AND CRAVEN 2005
R. Duncan and T. Craven, *Boom Boom Cluster: The David and Liza Brown Bequest*, exh. cat., Southampton City Art Gallery, Southampton 2005

ELLIS AND ROE 2007
A. Ellis and S. Roe (eds), *Oil Paintings in Public Ownership in Hampshire: Southampton and the Isle of Wight*, London 2007

FORD 1931
P. Ford (ed.), *Southampton: A Civic Survey*, Southampton 1931

FOSS 2007
B. Foss, *War Paint: Art, War, State and Identity in Britain, 1939–1945*, New Haven and London 2007

GAUNT 1969
W. Gaunt, 'Southampton – a gallery that started from scratch', *The Times*, 7 October 1969, p. 12

GOODALL 1985
E. Goodall, *One City a Patron: British Art of the 20th Century from the Collection of Southampton Art Gallery*, exh. cat., Glasgow, Dundee, Perth, Ayr and Edinburgh, Southampton 1985

HEANEY 2000
G.P. Heaney, 'The Development of Labour Politics in Southampton 1890–1945', unpublished PhD dissertation, University of Southampton 2000

HEDLEY 2020
G. Hedley, *Arthur Jeffress: A Life in Art*, London 2020

HUTCHISON 1986
S.C. Hutchison, *History of the Royal Academy, 1768–1986*, London 1986 (2nd edn)

KEMPSKI ET AL. 2020
M. Kempski, J. Kirby, V. Leanse and K. Mandy (eds), *'Tales of the Unexpected' in Paintings Conservation*, London 2020

LAVELL 2006
B. Lavell, 'William Lacy: Soldier and Artist (1809–1892)', *FoSMAG Magazine*, 58 (Spring 2006), pp. 8–9

LEMON 1911
J. Lemon, rev. F.J.C. Hearnshaw, *Reminiscences of Public Life in Southampton*, 2 vols, Southampton 1911

LEONARD 2012
A.G.K. Leonard, 'Stag Gates and all that', *Southampton Local History Forum Journal*, 19 (Spring 2012), pp. 3–9

LONDON 1988
Changing Minds: Looking at Art Through Older Children's Eyes, exh. cat., South Bank Centre, London 1988

LUCKETT 1979
H. Luckett, 'Education Through Art: Eleven Years After', *Oxford Art Journal*, 2, no. 3 (October 1979), pp. 50–53; https://doi.org/10.1093/oxartj/2.3.50 (accessed 21 January 2020)

LUCKETT 1982
H. Luckett, *Through Children's Eyes: A fresh look at contemporary art: the story of an exhibition organised by Southampton Art Gallery, Wildground County Junior School and the Arts Council of Great Britain*, Arts Council of Great Britain, 1982

LUCKETT 1985
H. Luckett, 'Ten Years of Gallery Education', *Journal of Aesthetic Education*, 19, no. 2 (1985), pp. 125–24; doi:10.2307/3332469

MANN 1989
J.F. Mann, *Southampton People: Eminent Sotonians and Assorted Characters*, Southampton 1989

MCCLELLAN 2003
A. McClellan (ed.), *Art and its Publics, Museum Studies at the Millennium*, Oxford 2003

MCEWAN 2005
J. McEwan, 'Finding Salvation', *Spectator*, 1 January 2005; https://www.spectator.co.uk/article/finding-salvation (accessed 8 February 2021)

MCNAY 2017
A. McNay, 'Meet the Collectors: Robert Chipperfield', *Art Quarterly* (Autumn 2017), pp. 47–50

MCNAY 2020
A. McNay, 'Shaping futures: A perfect partnership', *Art Quarterly* (Winter 2020), pp. 82–83

NASH AND SHERWOOD 2002
S. Nash & M. Sherwood, *The University of Southampton: An Illustrated History*, London 2002

NEAL 2014
P. Neal, *The Story of Southampton*, Gloucestershire 2014

PEARSON AND KEENE 2017
C. Pearson and S. Keene (eds), *Museums in the Second World War: Curators, Culture and Change*, London and New York 2017

PRESTON 2008
R. Preston, '"Pursuit of Knowledge under Difficulties": The Audit House Library, Southampton, 1831–63 and Winchester Library & Museum, 1851–63', *Journal of the Southampton Local History Forum* (2008), p. 14

STOURTON 2016
J. Stourton, *Kenneth Clark: Life, Art and Civilisation*, New York 2016

SUMMERFIELD 2007
A. Summerfield, 'Interventions: Twentieth-Century Art Collection Schemes and their Impact on Local Authority Art Gallery and Museum Collections of Twentieth-Century British Art in Britain', unpublished PhD dissertation, City University, London 2007

TAYLOR 1999
B. Taylor, *Art for the Nation: Exhibitions and the London Public, 1747–2001*, Manchester 1999

WATERFIELD 2015
G. Waterfield, *The People's Galleries: Art Museums and Exhibitions in Britain, 1800–1914*, New Haven and London 2015

WRIGHT 1998
C. Wright, *Renaissance to Impressionism: Masterpieces from Southampton City Art Gallery*, London 1998

Online sources

'The Borough of Southampton: General Historical Account' in W. Page (ed.), *The Victoria History of Hampshire and the Isle of Wight, vol. 3 (The Victoria History of the Counties of England)*, London 1908, pp. 490–524; see https://www.british-history.ac.uk/vch/hants/vol3/pp490-524 (accessed 30 March 2020)

Southampton Daily Echo, 'HERITAGE: The History of Southampton's Civic Centre', 8 August 2018; https://www.dailyecho.co.uk/news/16406241.heritage-the-history-of-southamptons-civic-centre/ (accessed 26 May 2020)

University of Southampton Special Collections Blog, 'Celebrating the contribution of women: Lady Swaythling', 8 March 2017; https://specialcollectionsuniversityofsouthampton.wordpress.com/2017/03/08/celebrating-the-contribution-of-women-lady-swaythling/ (accessed 14 April 2020)

University of Southampton Special Collections Blog, J.C. Ruthven, 'Southampton in the 1920s', 7 February 2020; https://specialcollectionsuniversityofsouthampton.wordpress.com/2020/02/07/southampton-in-the-1920s/ (accessed 21 May 2020)

NOTES

Chapter 1: Origins

1. Southampton City Art Gallery was 'designated' by the Government's Museums, Libraries and Archives Council in 1998 as possessing pre-eminent national significance.
2. See National Gallery Archive (hereafter NGA), NG6/4/68, letter to T.W. Shore, 23 June 1874.
3. NGA, NG6/4/95, letter to T.W. Shore, 27 January 1875.
4. NGA, NG6/5/300, letter to T.W. Shore, 3 July 1878.
5. NGA, NG6/6/545, letter from the Secretary of the Hartley Institution to F. Burton, 7 May 1880.
6. Wright 1998, p. 5.
7. http://sotonopedia.wikidot.com/page-browse:lacy-william (accessed 21 January 2021); B. Lavell, 'William Lacy: Soldier and Artist (1809–1892)', *FoSMAG Magazine*, 58 (Spring 2006), pp. 8–9.
8. http://sotonopedia.wikidot.com/page-browse:hartley-henry-robinson-and-hartley-institution (accessed 21 January 2021).
9. Preston 2008, p. 9.
10. Preston 2008, p. 14.
11. 'History of Southampton Art Society', https://www.facebook.com/seesouthampton/posts/the-history-of-southampton-art-society-established-in-1885-at-the-time-there-wer/1270951446402836/ (accessed 21 January 2021).
12. Waterfield 2015, p. 166.
13. See https://www.dailyecho.co.uk/news/18167417.man-whose-good-work-changed-southampton-better/ (accessed 21 January 2021).
14. McNay 2017, p. 50.
15. 'Mr. R. Chipperfield, JP' obituary in *Southampton Times Broadsheet* (5 August 1911). See also http://sotonopedia.wikidot.com/page-browse:chipperfield-robert (accessed 21 January 2021).
16. The history of the Titanic is explored in Southampton's SeaCity Museum, which opened in 2012. Its exhibits include a 1:25 scale interactive model of the Titanic; see https://seacitymuseum.co.uk/titanic-story (accessed 21 January 2021).
17. Wright 1998, p. 6.
18. Goodall 1985, p. 4.
19. Southampton City Council, Council Minutes 'General Purposes Sub-Committee meeting – with Public Libraries Committee', 26 February 1926, p. 418.
20. SCA, SC/ART/3/2/2, 'Re: Frederick William Smith, deceased: Memorandum relating to the bequest of income of the Testator's residuary estate for the purchase of pictures to become the property of the Corporation of Southampton, 1 January 1932', pp. 2, 3.
21. Smith Art Bequest folder, Southampton City Art Gallery history files, Conservation Studio, letter from Page, Gulliford & Gregory Solicitors to town clerk, 27 May 1931.
22. Nash and Sherwood 2002, p. 14.
23. http://sotonopedia.wikidot.com/page-browse:lemon-sir-james (accessed 21 January 2021).
24. See https://www.dailyecho.co.uk/news/18167417.man-whose-good-work-changed-southampton-better/ (accessed 21 January 2021).
25. Once National Gallery directors became art advisers to Southampton Art Gallery they advised against such purchases. For instance, Kenneth Clark noted: 'I am not much in favour of buying portraits of celebrated men unless they are good pictures: I would prefer a photograph.' See NGA, NG16/201/2, letter from K. Clark to G.A. Waller, 16 May 1936.
26. http://sotonopedia.wikidot.com/page-browse:foster-welch-lucia (accessed 21 January 2021).
27. University of Southampton Archive, MS 383.
28. University of Southampton Archive, MS 244.
29. Leonard 2012, pp. 3–9.
30. It was purchased with the blessing of National Gallery director Augustus Daniel; see NGA, NG16/201/1, letter from A. Daniel to town clerk, 24 June 1932.
31. Waterfield 2015, p. 199.
32. Waterfield 2015, p. 117.

Catalogue

1. [Sir Theodore Martin], obituary, *Art Journal* (January 1864), p. 12.

In Focus: Building

1. Email from Liz Goodall to the authors, 12 February 2021.
2. Email from Liz Goodall to the authors, 12 February 2021.

Chapter 2: Ambitions

1. https://www.thefreelibrary.com/Kenwood%27s+lost+chapter%3A+Julius+Bryant+reveals+the+forgotten+story+of...-a0114477248 (accessed 21 January 2021).
2. NGA, Minutes of Board Meetings, vol. 10, p. 103: 12 November 1929.
3. NGA, Minutes of Board Meetings, vol. 10, p. 107: 12 November 1929.
4. NGA, Order of the Chancery Division of the High Court of Justice, 23 January 1930, pp. 3–4.
5. Points 9 and 10(ii), respectively, of the schedule for the 'Scheme for the Establishment, Administration and Management of the Charity to be known as the Chipperfield Art Gallery and School of Art at Southampton'.
6. Stourton 2016, p. 88.
7. NGA, NG16/201/1, undated sheet titled 'Chipperfield Bequest Southampton City Council' filed at the start of this first correspondence file.
8. NGA, NG16/201/1, letter from A. Daniel to R. Gleadowe, 16 May 1931.
9. NGA, NG16/201/1, letter from A. Daniel to R. Gleadowe, 16 May 1931.
10. NGA, NG16/201/1, letter from A. Daniel to R. Gleadowe, 16 May 1931
11. NGA, NG16/201/1, letter from town clerk to A. Daniel, 9 May 1931.
12. Quoted in Waterfield 2015, p. 199.
13. Quoted in Waterfield 2015, p. 199.
14. NGA, NG16/201/1, letter from A. Daniel to town clerk, 17 May 1933.
15. NGA, NG16/201/1, letter from town clerk to A. Daniel, 15 July 1930.
16. NGA, NG16/201/1, letter from A. Daniel to town clerk, 20 May 1931.
17. NGA, NG16/201/1, letter from A. Daniel to R. Gleadowe, 16 May 1931.
18. NGA, NGA, NG16/201/1, letter from A. Daniel to town clerk, 20 May 1931.
19. NGA, NG16/201/1, letter from A. Daniel to R. Gleadowe, 16 May 1931.

20. NGA, NG16/201/1, letter from A. Daniel to town clerk, 20 May 1931.
21. NGA, NG16/201/1, letter from A. Daniel to R. Gleadowe, 20 January 1933.
22. NGA, NG16/201/1, letter from town clerk to A. Daniel, 10 February 1933.
23. NGA, NG16/201/1, letter from A. Daniel to R. Gleadowe, 26 January 1933.
24. See http://sotonopedia.wikidot.com/page-browse:shayer-william-and-family (accessed 21 January 2021).
25. NGA, NG16/201/1, letter from A. Daniel to town clerk, 10 March 1933.
26. NGA, NG16/201/1, letter from town clerk to A. Daniel, 5 May 1933.
27. NGA, NG16/201/1, letter from A. Daniel to town clerk, 24 June 1932.
28. NGA, NG16/201/1, letter from A. Daniel to town clerk, 24 June 1932.
29. NGA, NG16/201/1, letter from A. Daniel to town clerk, 5 July 1932.
30. NGA, NG16/201/1, letter from A. Daniel to town clerk, 24 June 1932.

Catalogue

1. NGA, NG16/201/1, letter from A. Daniel to town clerk, 24 June 1932.
2. https://www.musee-orsay.fr/en/collections/works-in-focus/painting/commentaire_id/the-beach-at-trouville-7185.html?S=&tx_commentaire_pi1%5BpidLi%5D=509&tx_commentaire_pi1%5Bfrom%5D=841&cHash=ef16d98c4d&print=1&no_cache=1& (accessed 21 January 2021).
3. NGA, NG16/201/5, letter from M. Palmer to P. Hendy, 11 July 1951.

Chapter 3: Solid Foundations

1. Stourton 2016, pp. 95, 97.
2. Quoted in Stourton 2016, p. 135.
3. NGA, NG16/201/1, letter from town clerk to K. Clark, 8 May 1834.
4. NGA, NG16/201/1, letter from R. Gleadowe to K. Clark, July 1934.
5. NGA, NG16/201/1, letter from K. Clark to town clerk, 7 July 1934.
6. NGA, NG16/201/1, letter from Mr Enness to K. Clark, regarding the Rothwell picture, July 1934. See https://www.artuk.org/discover/artworks/portrait-of-a-lady-17955. (Accessed 21 January 2020).
7. NGA, NG16/201/1, letter from K. Clark to town clerk, 5 July 1934.
8. NGA, NG16/201/2, letter from town clerk to K. Clark, 21 June 1935.
9. NGA, NG16/201/2, letter from K. Clark to town clerk, 10 May 1935.
10. See, for instance NGA, NG16/201/2, letter from K. Clark to G.A. Waller, 9 May 1936.
11. NGA, NG16/201/1, letter from town clerk to K. Clark, 3 October 1934.
12. See also NGA, NG16/201/1, letter from S.G. Kimber to K. Clark, 5 December 1934.
13. NGA, NG16/201/1, letter from K. Clark to town clerk, 4 October 1934, and letter of thanks from S.G. Kimber to K. Clark, 5 December 1934, confirming the purchase price of £3,500. See also SCA, SC/ART 3/1/2, letter from Violet Henderson accepting £3,500 for the *Perseus Series*, 28 November 1934.
14. NGA, NG16/201/1, letter from K. Clark to town clerk, 4 October 1934.
15. NGA, NG16/201/2, letter from town clerk to K. Clark, 7 March 1935.
16. NGA, NG16/201/2, letter from K. Clark to town clerk, 8 March 1935.
17. NGA, NG16/201/2, letter from K. Clark to town clerk, 8 March 1935.
18. Waterfield 2015, pp. 212–13.
19. Waterfield 2015, p. 208.
20. NGA, NG16/201/1, letter from town clerk to K. Clark, 29 June 1934.
21. NGA, NG16/201/2, letter from K. Clark to town clerk, 24 June 1935.
22. NGA, NG16/201/2, letter from town clerk to K. Clark, 26 June 1935.
23. NGA, NG16/201/2, letter from K. Clark to G. A. Waller, 14 March 1936. The Sub-Committee comprised the Mayor (Alderman Saunders), Sir Sidney Kimber, and Councillors Matthews and Waller.
24. NGA, NG16/201/2, Minutes of the Chipperfield Bequest Sub-Committee, 2 April 1936, reporting on a meeting with K. Clark on 26 February 1936.
25. NGA, NG16/201/2, letter from K. Clark to G.A. Waller, 1 April 1936.
26. NGA, NG16/201/2, notice of the Chipperfield Bequest Sub-Committee, enclosed with letter from G.A. Waller to K. Clark, 3 April 1936.
27. NGA, NG16/201/2, Minutes of the Chipperfield Bequest Sub-Committee, 2 April 1936.
28. For example, Clark wrote to inform the sub-committee of the Chipperfield Bequest about 'a very fine early ... Sisley' which he had 'seen for sale in Paris'; see NGA, NG16/201/3, letter from K. Clark to G.A. Waller, 25 March 1936. Again, Clark wrote to the town clerk on 25 February 1938, recommending 'two or three pictures' that he had found on a recent trip to Paris, promising to send details.
29. NGA, NG16/201/3, letter from K. Clark to town clerk, 11 October 1937. His reasoning, given in the letter, was that: 'A collector in Sheffield would not attempt to sell his belongings to the Southampton Gallery unless he had exhausted all other possible means of sale.'
30. For example, Clark bid for a Raeburn at Christie's on 12 May 1934; see NGA, NG16/201/3, letter from K. Clark to secretary of the Chipperfield Bequest Sub-Committee, 11 May 1934. Clark also got Horace Buttery, the National Gallery's picture restorer to bid on a group of portraits by Joseph Wright of Derby at Christie's in May 1936; see NGA, NG16/201/2, letter from H. Buttery to K. Clark, 15 May 1936.
31. NGA, NG16/201/3, letter from K. Clark to town clerk, 13 May 1937.
32. NGA, NG16/201/3, letter from K. Clark to town clerk, 26 July 1937. The quotation comes from Clark's letter to the town clerk of 17 September 1937.
33. NGA, NG16/201/3, letter from town clerk to K. Clark, 13 September 1937.
34. See NGA, NG16/201/2, letter from K. Clark to town clerk, 3 July 1935 (Alma Tadema) and K. Clark to G.A. Waller, 6 July 1936 (Ensor).
35. It became known that Southampton Art Gallery was seeking old pictures; several letters survive from London dealers and local Southampton residents, dated May and June 1936, offering works of art in response to notices about the Chipperfield Bequest, published in *The Times* and Southampton's *Echo*.
36. See NGA, NG16/201/2, letters from G.A. Waller to K. Clark, 15 May and 10 June 1936.
37. Wright 1998, p. 81.
38. NGA, NG16/201/2, letter from town clerk to K. Clark, 15 May 1936: the original sale price had been £120.
39. NGA, NG16/201/2, letter from K. Clark to town clerk, 26 June 1936.
40. NGA, NG16/201/2, letter from K. Clark to town clerk, 17 September 1936.
41. NGA, NG16/201/2, letter from K. Clark to town clerk, 2 December 1936. On Clark's recommendation of 29 January 1937, the price of £280 was agreed by the sub-committee (see letter from them of 20 February), and accepted by the dealer, Vitale Bloch.
42. Clark sold it for the same price (18 gns) that he had paid for it at Christie's eight months earlier. See NGA, NG16/201/2, letter from K. Clark to town clerk, 4 September 1936.
43. NGA, NG16/201/3, letter from K. Clark to town clerk, 15 December 1937.
44. NGA, NG16/201/3, letter from K. Clark to Sir Alec Martin of Christie's, 14 December 1937.

45. NGA, NG16/201/2, letter from K. Clark to G.A. Waller, 1 April 1936. See also letter from town clerk to K. Clark, 10 June 1936.
46. NGA, NG16/201/3, letter from K. Clark to town clerk, 8 November 1937.
47. NGA, NG16/201/3, letter from K. Clark to town clerk, 15 December 1937.
48. NGA, NG16/201/3, letter from K. Clark to town clerk, 25 February 1938.
49. NGA, NG16/201/1, letter from K. Clark to S.G. Kimber, 3 December 1934.
50. See NGA, NG16/201/3, letter from K. Clark to town clerk, 7 February 1938.
51. See NGA, NG16/201/3, letter from S.G. Kimber to K. Clark, 22 June 1938, asking for his opinion about the candidates. See Clark's response of 25 June, in which he suggests that of the five applicants, G.L. Conran and A.C. Sewter were the best. See also letter from S.G. Kimber to K. Clark, 4 July 1938, informing him that Conran had been appointed. In Clark's response of 5 July, he said that Conran was 'an excellent appointment'.
52. NGA, NG16/201/3, letter from K. Clark to G.L. Conran, 2 December 1938.
53. NGA, NG16/201/3, letter from G.L. Conran to K. Clark, 30 November 1938.
54. NGA, NG16/201/4, letter from K. Clark to G.L. Conran, 7 March 1939.
55. Southampton's archives preserve some of the reports that Conran made of these trips, submitted to Sir Sidney Kimber, chair of the Civic Centre Committee.
56. In fact, Clark's opinion had been sought a few years earlier about the 'artistic merit' of the pictures in the original Chipperfield Collection and whether he had 'any objection' to the sub-committee 'distributing the pictures among the Schools or elsewhere'; see NGA, NG16/201/2, letter from G.A. Waller to K. Clark, 28 April 1936. In his response of 29 April 1936, Clark declined getting involved, stating: 'I have no doubt that you and the other members of the Chipperfield Bequest Sub-Committee who take a special interest in the arts will know if there is anything in Mr. Chipperfield's collection which it would be desirable to retain for the new gallery.'
57. See NGA, NG16/201/4, letter from G.L. Conran to K. Clark, 16 June 1939.
58. NGA, NG16/201/4, letter from K. Clark to G.L. Conran, 16 March 1939.
59. NGA, NG16/201/4, letter from G.L. Conran to K. Clark, 20 March 1939.
60. Originally the Chipperfield Bequest Sub-Committee purchased John's *A Canadian Soldier*, but the painter visited Conran to say that he would rather that they took 'Brigit'; see SCA, SC/ART 3/4/1, letter from G.L. Conran to K. Clark, 9 May 1939 (regarding substitution); letter from A. John, accepting an offer of 400 guineas for *Brigit*, 13 May 1939; and letter from K. Clark, giving his guarded approval, 31 May 1939.
61. *Patricia Preece* was purchased by Maurice Palmer using the Frederick William Smith Bequest Fund as was Spencer's *Resurrection*, bought in 1950. Earlier, Conran mentioned to Clark that he had 'recently bought a Spencer' using his 'other [Smith Bequest] fund' – presumably this is a reference to Spencer's *Pound Field, Cookham*, acquired in 1936; see NGA, NG16/201/3, letter from G.L. Conran to K. Clark, 30 November 1938.
62. G.L. Conran, 'Introduction to the pictures', for pamphlet titled *Corporation of Southampton Art Gallery: Opening of the New Art Gallery and Exhibition of Paintings by their Royal Highnesses the Duke and Duchess of Gloucester, 26 April 1939*, p. 5, copy in Art Gallery history files, Conservation Studio, Southampton City Art Gallery.
63. NGA, NG16/201/4, letter from G.L. Conran to K. Clark, 16 June 1939.
64. NGA, NG16/201/3, letter from G.L. Conran to K. Clark, 20 December 1938.
65. NGA, NG16/201/3, letter from K. Clark to G.L. Conran, 22 December 1938.
66. See NGA, NG16/201/3, letter from G.L. Conran to K. Clark, 7 January 1939. The document referred to as providing the guidelines was enclosed: 'Scheme for the Establishment Administration and Management of the Charity to be known as the Chipperfield Art Gallery and School of Art at Southampton (Framed pursuant to Order dated 26 July 1916)'.
67. NGA, NG16/201/4, letter from G.L. Conran to K. Clark, 1 February 1939. The follow-up letter from Conran to Clark of 8 March 1939, included the following list of loan requests: loan requests (here with updated attributions): Fantin Latour (now Tate N01952); Corot (NG2625); Largillière and studio (NG3883); de Grilleau (NG3964); Dughet (NG98); Chardin (NG1664); Coques (NG821); van der Aack (NG1397); Ruisdael (NG989); and Follower of Ruisdael (NG2566).
68. NGA, NG16/201/4, letter from G.L. Conran to K. Clark, 21 June 1939.
69. For the formation and dispersal of the Cook Collection, see E. Danziger, 'The Cook Collection, its Founder and its Inheritors,' *The Burlington Magazine* 146 (2004), pp. 444–48.
70. NGA, NG16/201/4, letter from G.L. Conran to K. Clark, 12 July 1939. See also their related correspondence of 1 July and 9 August 1939.
71. Waterfield 2015, p. 210.
72. Quoted from Clark's letter to Sir Alec Martin of Christie's, 14 December 1937 (NGA, NG16/201/3), where he was explaining why he had not purchased any other painting except for Etty's *The World before the Flood*, despite 'lik[ing] the nudity in the other pictures'.
73. See Stourton 2016, pp. 106–07.
74. NGA, NG16/201/4, letter from K. Clark to G.L. Conran, 4 July 1939.
75. NGA, NG16/201/4, letter from G.L. Conran to K. Clark, 7 October 1939. In a letter of 25 June 1938 Clark mentioned "the Saloon boss of Southampton" with whom I am on good terms' being Sir Francis Kimber but this must be a slip of the pen: it was Sir Sidney Kimber who was chair of the Civic Centre Committee.
76. NGA, NG16/201/4, letter from G.L. Conran to K. Clark, 7 November 1939.
77. NGA, NG16/201/4, letter from K. Clark to G.L. Conran, 13 November 1939.
78. NGA, NG16/201/4, letter from K. Clark to G.L. Conran, 24 November 1939.
79. NGA, NG16/201/4, letter from H. Jackson Seed to K. Clark, 25 November 1939.
80. Bosman 2008, pp. 17–32, 73–88.
81. 'Southampton Blitz: City Remembers on 75th Anniversary', *Daily Echo*, 30 November 2015, https://www.dailyecho.co.uk/news/14112339.photos-southampton-blitz-city-remembers-on-75th-anniversary/ (accessed 21 January 2020).
82. NGA, NG16/201/4, letter from G.L. Conran to K. Clark, 7October 1939. Clark's response of 10 October proves that he was fully supportive.
83. NGA, NG16/201/4, letter from G.L. Conran to K. Clark, 7 October 1939.
84. NGA, NG16/201/4, letter from G.L. Conran to K. Clark, 7 November 1939.
85. SCA, letter from G.L. Conran to K. Chick, 17 August 1939.
86. SCA, letter from K. Chick to G.L. Conran, 17 May 1939.
87. SCA, letter from the British Institute of Adult Education, 3 July 1939. Conran would write (in vain) to Clark on 7 November 1939 to ask if any of the 'your lecturers might be free to undertake such a series'.
88. SCA, SC/ART/3/4/2, letter from L. Browse to Southampton Art Gallery, 14 August 1942.

Catalogue

1. NGA, NG16/201/2, minutes of the Chipperfield Bequest Sub-Committee, 2 April 1936.
2. NGA, NG16/201/3, letter from K. Clark to town clerk, 25 February 1938.
3. NGA, NG16/201/7, letter from A. Howarth to M. Davies, 16 April 1973.

In Focus: People

1. NGA, NG16/201/3, letter from K. Clark to S. Kimber, 25 June 1938.
2. NGA, NG16/201/3, letter from R. Byron to K. Clark, June 1938.
3. NGA, NG16/201/3, letter from K. Clark to G.L. Conran, 2 December 1938.
4. NGA, NG16/201/3, letter from K. Clark to G.L. Conran, 17 November 1938.
5. NGA, NG16/201/4, letter from G.L. Conran to P. Hendy, 19 March 1946.
6. NGA, NG16/201/4, letter from town clerk to P. Hendy, 17 January 1950.
7. Interview with Liz Goodall, conducted by the authors, 19 October 2020.
8. Email from Les Buckingham to the authors, 6 October 2020.
9. Email from Les Buckingham to the authors, 6 October 2020.
10. Email from Les Buckingham to the authors, 6 October 2020.
11. Email from Les Buckingham to the authors, 6 October 2020.
12. NGA, NG18/201/7, letter from A. Howarth to M. Levey, 28 August 1978.
13. Email from Britta New to the authors, 10 March 2021.

Chapter 4: Reputation

1. NGA, NG16/201/4, letter from G.L. Conran to P. Hendy, 19 March 1946.
2. NGA, NG16/201/4, letter from G.L. Conran to P. Hendy, 19 March 1946.
3. NGA, NG16/201/4, letter from G.L. Conran to P. Hendy, 8 July 1946.
4. Summerfield 2007, p. 166.
5. On CAS, see Hedley 2020, pp. 162–66. Conran became Honorary Secretary to CAS in the 1950s and 60s.
6. Hedley 2020, p. 161.
7. Hedley 2020, p. 163.
8. Wright 1998, p. 11.
9. Wright 1998, p. 13; Hedley 2020, p. 190.
10. 'Hampshire artists "hung" at So'ton', *Southern Daily Echo*, 5 July 1947.
11. Arts Council Review, 1946–47.
12. See file stored in the V&A's archive at Blythe House: ACGB/75/148: K. Clark Loan Collection (1951–60).
13. 'Soton Art Gallery's new hall said to be "inspiring"', *Southern Daily Echo*, 14 April 1953.
14. NGA, NG16/201/4, letter from town clerk to P. Hendy, 15 December 1949.
15. See, for instance, NGA, NG16/201/5, letters from M. Palmer to P. Hendy, 21 and 28 November 1951.
16. See, for instance, NGA, NG16/201/5, correspondence between M. Palmer and P. Hendy, 28 November, 1 and 17 December 1951.
17. 'Images: Information: Museum & Art Gallery Education Services', No. 8, Summer Term 1977.
18. NGA, NG16/201/5, letter from P. Hendy to A.J. McDonnell, 26 April 1951.
19. NGA, NG16/201/5, Hendy's reference-letter for Palmer, 14 February 1953.
20. See, for instance, NGA, NG16/201/5, letter from P. Hendy to M. Palmer, 24 November 1958.
21. NGA, NG16/201/5, letter from P. Hendy to M. Palmer, 11 February 1958.
22. 'Soton Art Gallery's new hall said to be "inspiring"', *Southern Daily Echo*, 14 April 1953.
23. See R. Wenley (ed.), *The Barber Institute of Fine Arts: Foundations of a Collection*, London, 2012, p. 10.
24. NGA, NG16/201/5, letter from M. Palmer to P. Hendy, 2 November 1957.
25. NGA, NG16/201/5, letter from M. Palmer to P. Hendy, 13 December 1957.
26. Crack 2019, pp. 158–60.
27. SCA, SC/ART 3/2/4, solicitors' letter concerning the Smith Bequest, 17 September 1951.
28. SCA, SC/ART 3/2/4, letter from M. Palmer to the Art Gallery Committee, 5 September 1951.
29. NGA, NG16/201/5, letter from M. Palmer to P. Hendy, 16 December 1952.
30. NGA, NG16/201/5, letter from P. Hendy to M. Palmer, 23 December 1952.
31. SCA, SC/ART 3/2/4, letter from Page, Gulliford and Gregory, Solicitors, to town clerk, 8 August 1951.
32. Crack 2019, p. 162 includes as 'recent purchases [of early Italian art] from the regions': 'Simone Martini's *A Saint holding a Book* from the BMAG, Lorenzo Monaco's *John the Baptist entering the Wilderness* from Leicester, and Taddeo Gaddi's *Crucifixion and Lamentation* from Bristol.' Crack also notes (p. 154) that Bristol Museum & Art Gallery received several Italian fifteenth- and sixteenth-century paintings with the Ferdinand Schiller Bequest of 1946, and purchased a Bicci di Lorenzo in 1954.
33. NGA, NG16/201/5, letter from P. Hendy to M. Palmer, 17 December 1957.
34. Wright 1998, p. 12.
35. NGA, NG16/201/5, letter from M. Palmer to P. Hendy, 22 September 1953.
36. NGA, NG16/201/5, letter from P. Hendy to M. Palmer, 2 October 1953.
37. NGA, NG16/201/5, letter from P. Hendy to M. Palmer, 16 January 1957.
38. NGA, NG16/201/5, letter from M. Palmer to P. Hendy, 21 January 1957.
39. NGA, NG16/201/6, letter from M. Palmer to P. Hendy, 15 May 1959.
40. NGA, NG16/201/6, letter from M. Palmer to P. Hendy, 17 May 1961.
41. NGA, NG16/201/6, letter from P. Hendy to M. Palmer, 8 April 1964.
42. NGA, NG16/201/6, letter from M. Palmer to P. Hendy, 12 June 1964.
43. NGA, NG16/201/6, letter from M. Palmer to P. Hendy, 26 June 1967.
44. See NGA, NG16/201/5, letter from P. Hendy to M. Palmer, 5 August 1952.
45. NGA, NG16/201/6, letter from P. Hendy to M. Palmer, 1 April 1965.
46. A point made by Homan Potterton, an assistant keeper at the National Gallery (1974–80), in a talk he gave at Southampton in 1977; email from H. Luckett to the authors, 24 September 2020.
47. NGA, NG16/201/5, letter from P. Hendy to M. Palmer, 26 March 1956.
48. See NGA, NG16/201/5, letter from M. Palmer to P. Hendy, 27 March 1956.
49. NGA, NG16/201/5, letter from P. Hendy to M. Palmer, 8 April 1957. Hendy was keener on Romney's portrait of Lord Ducie, also at Leggatt's. Palmer secured both portraits at this time.
50. NGA, NG16/201/5, letter from M. Palmer to P. Hendy, 17 May 1957.
51. NGA, NG16/201/5, letters from M. Palmer to P. Hendy, 27 March 1956 and 3 and 30 April 1956.
52. NGA, NG16/201/5, letter from M. Palmer to P. Hendy, 11 July 1951 (first quotation) and letter from Palmer to Hendy, 17 July 1951 (second quotation).
53. NGA, NG16/201/5, letter from M. Palmer to P. Hendy, 6 August 1952.
54. NGA, NG16/201/7, letter from M. Palmer to M. Davies, 22 March 1969.
55. Oral interview with Tim Craven, conducted by the authors in October 2020.
56. NGA, NG16/201/7, letter from A. Howarth to M. Davies, 17 July 1974.
57. Obituary: 'Mr. Mark Gertler, Jewish Painter', *The Times*, 26 June 1939, p. 9.
58. NGA, NG16/201/5, letter from P. Hendy to M. Palmer, 19 October 1954.
59. NGA, NG16/201/7, letter from M. Palmer to M. Davies, 25 June 1968.

60. NGA, NG16/201/7, letter from M. Davies to M. Palmer, 2 July 1968.
61. NGA, NG16/201/5, letter from P. Hendy to M. Palmer, 1 November 1954.
62. NGA, NG16/201/5, letter from P. Hendy to M. Palmer, 5 August 1952.
63. NGA, NG16/201/5, letter from P. Hendy to M. Palmer, 1 August 1952.
64. NGA, NG16/201/6, letter from M. Palmer to P. Hendy, 26 June 1967.
65. Summerfield 2007, p. 169.
66. Waterfield 2015, pp. 222–23.
67. NGA, NG16/201/5, letter from M. Palmer to P. Hendy, 2 September 1952.
68. NGA, NG16/201/5, letter from M. Palmer to P. Hendy, 2 March 1953.
69. NGA, NG16/201/5, letter from M. Palmer to P. Hendy, 9 May 1952 and Hendy's response of 13 May.
70. See NGA, NG16/201/6, letter from M. Palmer to P. Hendy, 19 March 1959, and Hendy's supportive response of 23 March.
71. There are numerous letters concerning this ill-fated project, starting with NGA, NG16/201/4, letter from G.L. Conran to P. Hendy, 10 September 1947, requesting he sit on the judging panel.
72. See NGA, NG16/201/4, letter from P. Hendy to M. Palmer, 14 November 1958; see also SCA Council Minutes, 8 March, 24 May and 11 June 1957.
73. See NGA, NG16/201/5, letter from M. Palmer to P. Hendy, 12 January 1955.
74. Q. Bell in *The Listener*, quoted in E. Goodall, 'One City a Patron', in Goodall 1985, p. 4.
75. See Hedley 2020; http://www.artwarefineart.com/gallery/arthur-tilden-jeffress-1905-1961 (accessed 21 January 2021).
76. NGA, NG16/201/7, letter from A. Howarth to M. Levey, 5 May 1975.
77. See Hedley 2020, pp. 202, 231.
78. NGA, NG16/201/4, letter from M. Palmer to P. Hendy, 2 June 1950, and Hendy's reply of 9 June.
79. Summerfield 2007, p. 169.
80. See Notes 'Southampton/Exeter' by Graham Binns to J. Wood Palmer' in file on the Southampton Loan Exhibition, preserved as part of the Arts Council archive at V&A Blythe House, ref: ACGB/121/969.
81. V&A Blythe House, ACGB/121/969, letter from J. Wood Palmer to M. Palmer, 22 February 1955.
82. V&A Blythe House, ACGB/121/969, see foreword to the printed List of Works by Philip James, Art Director of the Arts Council.
83. Letter from M. Palmer to P. Hendy, 21 December 1967.
84. Gaunt 1969, p. 12.
85. Email from Liz Goodall to the authors, 30 September 2020.

Catalogue

1. Letter from A. Jeffress to B. Martindale, 20 June 1955, cited in Hedley 2020, p. 207.
2. SCA, SC/ART 3/2/4, letter concerning the Smith Bequest, 8 August 1951.
3. F. Zeri, 'Un'ipotesi sui rapporti tra Allegretto Nuzi e Francescuccio Ghissi', *Antichità viva*, 14, no. 5 (1975), pp. 3–7.
4. Quoted in Wright 1998, p. 85.
5. NGA, NG16/201/6, letter from M. Palmer to P. Hendy, 15 May 1959.
6. NGA, NG16/201/6, letter from M. Palmer to P. Hendy, 12 June 1964.
7. NGA, NG16/201/6, letter from P. Hendy to M. Palmer, 8 April 1964.
8. NGA, NG16/201/5, letter from M. Palmer to P. Hendy, 15 February 1959.
9. NGA, NG16/201/5, letter from M. Palmer to P. Hendy, 13 December 1957.
10. NGA, NG16/201/6, letter from M. Palmer to P. Hendy, 21 December 1967.
11. NGA, NG16/201/5, letter from P. Hendy to M. Palmer, 8 April 1957.
12. NGA, NG16/201/5, letter from M. Palmer to P. Hendy, 17 May 1957.
13. Cited in https://www.southamptoncityartgallery.com/object/sotag-196912/ (accessed 21 January 2021).
14. Augustus John is often quoted as saying: 'In fifty years' time, I will be known as the brother of Gwen John'; see, for instance, post by Catherine Jamieson, 'Quiet Intensity: the life and art of Gwen John', https://artuk.org/discover/stories/quiet-intensity-the-life-and-art-of-gwen-john (accessed 21 January 2021).
15. 'Mr. Mark Gertler, Jewish Painter', in *The Times*, 26 June 1939, p. 9.
16. This catalogue entry is based on research carried out by Sarah MacDougall and Prof. Aviva Burnstock.
17. NGA, NG16/201/5, letter from P. Hendy to M. Palmer, 17 January 1955.
18. NGA, NG16/201/5, letter from M. Palmer to P. Hendy, 12 January 1955.

Chapter 5: Pastures New

1. Interview with Liz Goodall, conducted by the authors in October 2020.
2. NGA, NG16/201/7, letter from A. Howarth to M. Levey, 5 May 1975.
3. NGA, NG16/201/7, letter from A. Howarth to M. Levey, 5 May 1975. See other important letters on the purchase, 30 May 1975 and 1 September 1975.
4. NGA, NG16/201/7, letter from A. Howarth to M. Levey, 29 June 1979.
5. See Council's Leisure Committee Minute of 6 June 1979, copy in director's file on Southampton City Art Gallery, currently kept in the director's office at the National Gallery (hereafter NG SC file).
6. Bristol Art Gallery's F.P.M. Schiller Bequest of 1946 included some old masters; Manchester City Art Gallery's Assherton Bennet Bequest of 1979 comprised seventeenth-century Dutch and Flemish pictures.
7. Albrecht Dürer's master print of 1513 depicting *Knight, Death and the Devil* was bequeathed in 1983. In 1990, Lady Bonham-Carter bequeathed to Southampton City Art Gallery 'a modest sketch optimistically attributed to Carlo Maratta'; see Wright 1998, p. 15.
8. The sculpture was dismissed as a pile of bricks (see, for instance, Colin Simpson, 'The Tate Drops a Costly Brick', *Sunday Times*, 15 February 1976, p. 53) and was also defaced.
9. NGA, NG16/201/7, letter from A. Howarth to M. Levey, 3 February 1976.
10. NGA, NG16/201/7, letter from M. Levey to A. Howarth, 24 August 1976.
11. NGA, NG16/201/7, letter M. Levey to A. Howarth, 21 December 1977.
12. NGA, NG16/201/7, letter from M. Levey to E. Goodall, 18 July 1978, in response to a letter he had received on 13 June 1978.
13. NGA, NG16/201/7, letter from M. Levey to E. Goodall, 24 August 1978.
14. NGA, NG16/201/7, letters from A. Howarth to M. Levey, 13 June 1978 and 15 November 1978.
15. See NG SC file, email from N. Penny to V. de Wit, 19 December 2011. The Gallery's board of trustees endorsed the director's decision regarding the formal transfer of responsibility to Tate on 26 January 2012; see letter from N. Penny to L. Shepherd, 9 February 2012.
16. See Tim Craven's introduction in Duncan and Craven 2005; and J. McEwan, 'Finding Salvation', *The Spectator*, 1 January 2005; https://www.spectator.co.uk/article/finding-salvation (accessed 8 February 2021).
17. See letter from T. Craven to E. Goodall, 7 June 2010, and Goodall's written response to Craven, 17 June 2010; photocopies of both documents in NG SC file.
18. See Duncan and Craven 2005.
19. Brown 1977, p. 22.
20. Extract from a photocopy from an unsourced publication, attached to email from T. Craven to S. Woolgar,

1 September 2011, a copy of which is in NG SC file.

21. Liz Goodall, email to the authors, 15 February 2021.
22. Correspondence between Goodall and the authors, 19 October 2020.
23. See NGA, NG16/201/7, letter from A. Howarth to M. Levey, 12 December 1977.
24. 'Supporting Statement' from Art Fund Grant Application for Riley's *Red Movement*, submitted by Tim Craven, 4 August 2008, copy in NG SC file.
25. Undated extract from the 'Supporting Statement' from Art Fund Grant Application for Wynter's *Monumental*, submitted by Tim Craven, copy in NG SC file.
26. NG SC file, letter from T. Craven to C. Saumarez Smith, 29 November 2004.
27. Email from Sean Rainbird to the authors, 2 November 2020.
28. 'Supporting Statement' from Art Fund Grant Application for Riley's *Red Movement*, submitted by Tim Craven, 4 August 2008, copy in NG SC file.
29. NGA, NG16/201/7, letter from E. Goodall to M. Levey, 11 July 1977.
30. See *Air Water Stone*, Southampton City Art Gallery (25 July 2015–28 November 2015); https://www.southamptoncityartgallery.com/whats-on/air-water-stone/ (accessed 21 January 2021).
31. See https://www.contemporaryartsociety.org/special-projects/the-special-collection-scheme-1998-2005/ (accessed 21 January 2020).
32. Email from Gill Hedley to the authors, 20 September 2020.
33. See: http://www.featart.eu/index.php?id=30 (accessed 21 January 2021).
34. The associate artist scheme has now been replaced by the National Gallery's new Artist in Residence Programme (a one-year on-site residency for mid-career artists) and the National Gallery Contemporary Fellowship (a two-year research fellowship with subsequent exhibition for an artist who has made a significant contribution to the art of the twentieth and twenty-first century).
35. Email from Gill Hedley, 20 September 2020.
36. E. Goodall, 'One City a Patron', in Goodall 1985, pp. 5–6.
37. E. Goodall, 'One City a Patron', in Goodall 1985, p. 6.
38. E. Goodall, 'One City a Patron', in Goodall 1985, p. 5.
39. In exchange, Southampton hosted the loan exhibition *Tradition and Modernity in Basque Paintings, 1880–1939*. The National Gallery's current director, Gabriele Finaldi, then its Curator of Later Spanish and Italian Painting, was on the advisory council of the Bilbao Museum and recalls that he 'strongly encouraged the collaboration'; email from G. Finaldi to the authors, 11 September 2020.
40. 'Turner returns to Southampton City Art Gallery', at: https://www.southamptoncityartgallery.com/2018/09/turner-returns-southampton-city-art-gallery/ (accessed 21 January 2021).
41. Email from Neil MacGregor to the authors, 11 September 2020.'
42. NGA, NG16/201/7, letter from A. Howarth to M. Levey, 12 December 1978, where Howarth spoke of 'the special relationship we feel we have with you, your staff and your Gallery'.
43. NGA, NG16/201/7, letter from A. Howarth to M. Stewart, 10 February 1978.
44. See SCA, SC/TC files 118, finalised list of loans recorded in minutes of the Southampton Leisure Sub-Committee, 21 September 1978.
45. NGA, NG16/201/7, letter from M. Hersov to G. Worsdale, 12 February 1999. All 18 loans went on to a second and final venue: Leeds Art Gallery Leeds (23 June 1999–29 August 1999).
46. NGA, NG16/201/7, report by G. Worsdale to the Heritage Lottery Fund.
47. NGA, NG16/201/7, note from E. Jones to M. Hersov, 18 June 1999.
48. Email from R. Moisan to the authors, 8 February 2021.
49. See https://www.nationalgallery.org.uk/about-us/press-and-media/press-releases/the-national-gallery-and-art-fund-foster-new-museum-talent (accessed 21 January 2021).
50. McNay 2020, p. 82.
51. Wright 1998, p. 16.

Catalogue

1. NGA, NG16/201/7, letter from M. Levey to E. Goodall, 18 July 1978.
2. NGA, NG16/201/7, letters from D. Brown to M. Levey, 23 August 1978, and from M. Levey to E. Goodall, 24 August 1978.
3. See essay in Christie's auction catalogue for sale no. 18760, *300 Years of British Drawings*, Lot 57; https://onlineonly.christies.com/s/300-years-british-drawings/maxwell-ashby-armfield-r-w-s-ringwood-1881-1972-dorset-57/109462 (accessed 21 January 2020).
4. N.G. Bowe, 'Constance and Maxwell Armfield: An American Interlude 1915–1922', *The Journal of Decorative and Propaganda Arts*, 14 (Autumn 1989), p. 16.
5. https://www.southamptoncityartgallery.com/object/sotag-2002208/ (accessed 21 January 2021).
6. Email from S. Rainbird to the authors, 2 November 2020.

In Focus: Learning

1. Email exchange between Les Buckingham and the authors, September 2020.
2. Luckett 1982.
3. See London 1988.
4. See F. Allen, 'Situating gallery education' in Tate Encounters, Edition 2 (2008), pp. 1–12; http://www2.tate.org.uk/tate-encounters/edition-2/tateencounters2_felicity_allen.pdf (accessed 21 January 2020).

In Focus: Conservation

1. See SCA SC/ART/2/2/3, letter from M. Palmer to R.& J. Beck Ltd, 29 March 1961, requesting details on a low-power microscope, similar to that recently acquired by the Courtauld Institute.
2. NGA, NG16/201/5, letter from M. Palmer to P. Hendy, 17 October 1961.
3. See invoice from A. Lucas to M. Palmer, listing conservation work undertaken on the Nuzi, 2 March 1960, in artist file in conservation studio, Southampton City Art Gallery. It seems that Lucas was first approached in December 1957; the altarpiece was delivered on 17 April 1958; he returned it in February 1960.
4. See report from A. Lucas to Southampton Art Gallery, 30 November 1964, outlining the treatment he had undertaken on the Cesare da Sesto. The panel had been returned on 3 November.
5. *Friends of Southampton's Museums, Archives & Galleries (FoSMAG) Newsletter* 82 (2017).
6. Email from Tim Craven to the authors, 26 September 2020.
7. Email from David Bomford to the authors, 3 November 2020.
8. Letter from I. Kocum to R. Moisan, 17 June 2003.

PHOTOGRAPHIC CREDITS

© The Estate of Maxwell Armfield/Bridgeman Images © Southampton Cultural Services: fig. 69, cat. 45

© Estate of Michael Ayrton © Southampton Cultural Services: cat. 46

© Wilhelmina Barns-Graham Trust © Southampton Cultural Services: cat. 49

© Estate of Stephen Bone. All Rights Reserved, DACS 2021 © Southampton Cultural Services: fig. 42

Jean Boswell Farquharson © the copyright holder © Southampton Cultural Services: fig. 21

Daniel Buren © DB – ADAGP Paris and DACS, London 2020. Photograph © Joe Low © Southampton Cultural Services: fig. 18

Thomas Cantrell Dugdale © The artist's estate © The Courtauld, UK/Bridgeman Images: fig. 5

© Jemma Craig/The National Gallery, London: fig. 77

Photograph © Paul Carter © Southampton Cultural Services: figs 4, 26, 47, 64, 65, 78; cats 6, 10, 41

Photograph © Paul Carter © the copyright holder © Southampton Cultural Services: fig. 13

© Elizabeth Conran: fig. 38

© Estate of John Craxton. All rights reserved, DACS 2020 © Southampton Cultural Services: cat. 20

© The Estate of Barry Flanagan/Bridgeman Images © Southampton Cultural Services: cat. 47

© Gilbert & George © Southampton Cultural Services: fig. 72

© Liz Goodall: fig. 49

© Charlie Hackett, artist & lecturer, Grays School of Art, Scotland: fig. 43

© Maggi Hambling © The National Gallery, London: cat. 53

© Maggi Hambling © Southampton Cultural Services: cats 48, 52

© Maggi Hambling © Tate: fig. 68

© Allen Jones. Photograph © Paul Carter © Southampton Cultural Services: fig. 59

Photograph W.R. Kay © Southampton Cultural Services: inside front and back cover

© Kunsthistorisches Museum Wien, Gemäldegalerie, fig. 67

© Courtesy of the Estate of Henry Lamb/ Bridgeman Images, © Southampton Cultural Services: cat. 18

© Christopher Le Brun © Southampton Cultural Services: fig. 73

Edith M. Leeson Everett © the copyright holder © Southampton Cultural Services: fig. 10

© Richard Long. All Rights Reserved, DACS 2020 © Southampton Cultural Services: fig. 17

Photograph © Joe Low © Southampton Cultural Services: fig. 27

© The Estate of L.S. Lowry. All Rights Reserved, DACS 2020. © Southampton Cultural Services: fig. 56

© Estate of William MacQuitty © National Portrait Gallery, London: fig. 24

© Courtesy of the Estate of Stephen McKenna and Kerlin Gallery, Dublin © Southampton Cultural Services: fig. 66, cat. 43

© Image copyright granted by David Messum Fine Art Ltd. © Southampton Cultural Services: cat. 5

© Courtesy of Desmond Morris. Photograph © Paul Carter © Southampton Cultural Services: fig. 71

Rosalind Nashashibi © Courtesy of the artist © Southampton Cultural Services: cat. 57

Rosalind Nashashibi: Private collection. Photograph © Dirk Pauwels © Courtesy of the artist and GRIMM Amsterdam/New York: cat. 58

© Courtesy National Gallery of Art, Washington. Samuel H. Kress Collection: fig. 41

© The National Gallery, London: figs 14, 20, 29, 31, 33, 44, 51, 55, 62, 63, 74, 75; cats 23, 25, 27, 29, 34, 42, 56

© The National Gallery, London © Southampton Cultural Services: figs 79, 80

© National Portrait Gallery, London: figs 19

© Sydney W. Newbery © Southampton Cultural Services: fig. 15

© David Redfern © Southampton Cultural Services: cat. 44

Paula Rego © the artist © Southampton Cultural Services: cat. 54

Paula Rego © the artist © The National Gallery, London: cat. 55

© Rijksmuseum, Amsterdam: fig. 35

© Bridget Riley 2020. All rights reserved. Photograph © Paul Carter © Southampton Cultural Services: fig. 76; cat. 51

© Claude Rogers Estate © Southampton Cultural Services: fig. 37

George Shaw © the artist. Courtesy of Anthony Wilkinson Gallery, London © Southampton Cultural Services: cat. 50

© Southampton Cultural Services: figs 1, 2, 3, 6, 7, 8, 9, 10, 11, 12, 16, 22, 23, 25, 28, 30, 32, 34, 36, 39, 40, 42, 45, 48, 50, 52, 53, 54, 57, 61, 64; cats 1, 2, 3, 4, 5, 7, 8, 9, 11, 12, 13, 14, 15, 16, 17, 21, 22, 24, 26, 28, 30, 31, 32, 33, 35, 36, 37, 38, 39, 40

© Estate of Graham Sutherland © Southampton Cultural Services: figs 46, 60; cat. 19

© Angela Verren Taunt. All rights reserved, DACS 2020. © Southampton Cultural Services: fig. 58

© Wynter Estate © Southampton Cultural Services: fig. 70

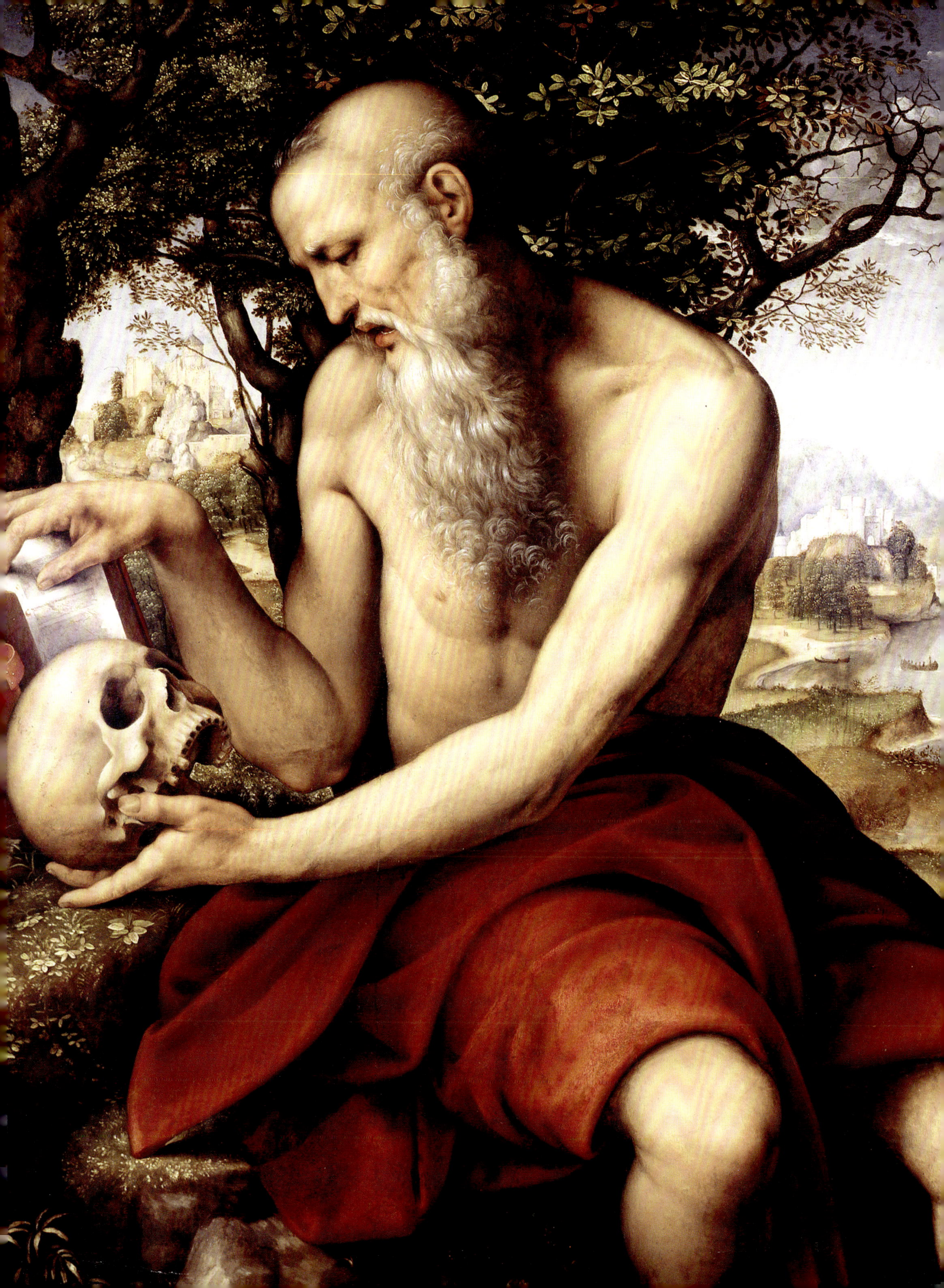

INDEX

ACKNOWLEDGEMENTS

This book and accompanying exhibition are part of the Art Fund and National Gallery Curatorial Traineeship Programme assisted by the Vivmar Foundation. Southampton City Art Gallery and the National Gallery would like to thank the following for their generous support of this publication: Art Fund with the assistance of the Vivmar Foundation; Friends of Southampton's Museums, Archives and Galleries (FoSMAG), and The Audley Group.

We, the authors, Susanna Avery-Quash and Jemma Craig, would like to acknowledge what a collaborative and happy project this has been from the start and how many colleagues from Southampton, London and elsewhere have played key roles to ensure its success, despite the Covid-19 pandemic.

We would like to thank the following people for their support and encouragement of the project at the National Gallery: Gabriele Finaldi, Director; Caroline Campbell, Director of Collections and Research; Christine Riding, Head of Curatorial Department; and Karen Eslea, Head of Learning and National Programmes. At Southampton City Council Cultural Services: Carolyn Abel, Head of Culture and Tourism; Dan Matthews, Collections and Exhibitions Manager; and Clare Mitchell, Curator, Southampton City Art Gallery.

We would like to express our gratitude to the following current National Gallery colleagues for their assistance with our research: Alan Crookham, Research Centre Manager; Nicholas Smith, Archivist; Laura Noble, Library and Archive Assistant; Mariko Takata, Library, Information and Archive Services Assistant as well as Anne Fay, Public Programmes Manager; Claire Hallinan and Samantha Saward in the registrars' department; Isobel Muir, AHRC Collaborative PhD student; and Eleanor Richards, PA to the Director. We are grateful to Zoryana Mishchiy, Licensing Executive, and Rebecca Thornton in the Gallery's picture library with help in securing images. Current colleagues in the curatorial, conservation and learning departments have commented on sections in earlier drafts and we remain immensely grateful to them for generously sharing their expert knowledge: Rachel Billinge, Caroline Campbell, Bart Cornelis, Karen Eslea, Susan Foister, Daniel Herrmann, Britta New, Chris Riopelle, Letizia Treves and Matthias Wivel. Particular heartfelt thanks go to Christine Riding for help with all aspects of the publication and exhibition.

Sincere thanks go as well to former National Gallery colleagues: to previous directors, Neil MacGregor, Charles Saumarez Smith and Nicholas Penny for answering our questions and sharing their insights about Southampton; and to David Bomford, former Senior Restorer; Mary Hersov, former Head of Exhibitions; and Colin Wiggins, long-standing member of the education department and latterly Special Projects Curator, again for sharing their memories.

We are grateful to current Southampton colleagues for their help and encouragement with our research: especially Dan Matthews and Clare Mitchell; Andy Ball, Exhibition Officer; Tom Laver, Assistant Curator; Rebecca Moisan, Conservator, as well as Richard Arthur, Southampton Central Library Assistant Supervisor; Jo Smith, Joe Baldwin and Jo Wren of Southampton City Archives. In relation to the associated exhibition, we would like to thank Exhibition Officers Andy Ball, Stu Rodda and especially Jess Whitfield; learning team members Kate Mitchell and Liza Morgan; as well as Ben Hall, Freelance Paintings Conservator, Tom Proctor, Freelance Frame Conservator and Rebecca Moisan, for helping us present the works at their best; and Josef Hill, Freelance Technician, for installing the exhibition in conjunction with Southampton City Art Gallery's exhibitions team. We are grateful to all the front of house team who will be the face of the associated exhibition.

Numerous former Southampton colleagues have been friends of the project from the start. We are deeply grateful to the following individuals for their joyful involvement, generous sharing of memories and ongoing guidance and encouragement, including feedback on drafts of the book: Liz Goodall, Gill Hedley and Helen Luckett. Profound thanks also go to others who shared reflections, memories and lively stories, particularly Les Buckingham, Tim Craven, John Hoole, Ambrose Scott-Moncrieff and Stephen Snoddy. We are also grateful to Sean Rainbird, Director of the National Gallery of Ireland for sharing reminiscences and insights about his time as Tate adviser to Southampton.

Outside our institutions, we would like to thank Christopher Marsden, Senior Archivist of the Victoria and Albert Museum and Peter Crack for help with research queries. We are very much indebted to Giulia Calvi, who assisted with editing the texts for the catalogue and exhibition during her work placement with Susanna in 2021 as part of the Courtauld's MA, 'Curating the Art Museum'. Susanna would like to thank family members Charles and Charlotte Avery for reading an earlier draft of the book and Victoria Avery for help with the sculpture entries. Jemma is grateful for ongoing support from her mother Jackie Stafford, partner, Aaron Laishley, and great friend and supportive colleague throughout the traineeship, Corinna Henderson, for instilling Jemma with confidence when she needed it the most. Her thanks go to all former and existing Cultural Services team members for encouragement and love, particularly Richie Gooding, Lucy Loader, Alan Findlay and Emily Pierce-Goldberg.

We would like to thank most sincerely our expert editor, Rachel Giles, for her continual, good-humoured help with sorting out countless editorial matters and to our inspirational designer Adrian Hunt for turning our manuscript into such a fine-looking book.

Thank you to all readers of this publication and visitors to the exhibition. We hope that the story we tell will demonstrate what a significant art collection Southampton City Art Gallery has and what collaboration at its best can achieve.